EFFECTIVE INTERVENTIONS FOR CHILD ABUSE AND NEGLECT

EFFECTIVE INTERVENTIONS FOR CHILD ABUSE AND NEGLECT

An Evidence-based Approach to Planning and Evaluating Interventions

Geraldine Macdonald

University of Bristol

JOHN WILEY & SONS, LTD

Chichester · New York · Weinheim · Brisbane · Singapore · Toronto

Other Wiley Editorial Offices

John Wiley & Sons, Inc., 605 Third Avenue,
New York, NY 10158-0012, USA

Wiley-VCH Verlag GmbH, Pappelallee 3,
D-69469 Weinheim, Germany

Jacaranda Wiley Ltd, 33 Park Road, Milton,
Queensland 4064, Australia

John Wiley & Sons (Asia) Pte Ltd, 2 Clementi Loop #02-01,
Jin Xing Distripark, Singapore 129809

John Wiley & Sons (Canada) Ltd, 22 Worcester Road,
Rexdale, Ontario M9W 1L1, Canada

Library of Congress Cataloging in Publication Data

Macdonald, Geraldine M.
Effective interventions for child abuse and neglect : an evidence-based approach to planning and evaluating interventions / Geraldine Macdonald.
p. cm.
Includes bibliographical references and index.
ISBN 0 471 49146 2 (cloth : alk. paper)—ISBN 0 471 49147 0 (pbk. : alk. paper)
1. Child welfare—Evaluation.   2. Child Abuse—Prevention—Evaluation.   3. Abused children—Services for—Evaluation.   4. Evaluation research (Social action programs)   I. Title.

HV713 .M25 2000   362.76'8—dc21   00–043550

British Library Cataloguing in Publication Data

A catalogue record for this book is available from the British Library

ISBN 0 471 49146 2 (cloth)
ISBN 0 471 49147 0 (pbk)

Typeset in Palatino by Footnote Graphics, Warminster, Wiltshire
Printed and bound in Great Britain by Biddles Ltd, Guildford, Surrey
This book is printed on acid-free paper responsibly manufactured from sustainable forestation, for which at least two trees are planted for each one used for paper production.

Nothing in this volume provides a remedy for an absence of parental love and positive regard. I was fortunate enough to have parents who supplied plenty of both.

This book is dedicated to my mother, Beryl Joyce Williams, whom I still greatly miss.

CONTENTS

Part B Child Maltreatment

Part D Assessment and Evidence-based Practice

ACKNOWLEDGEMENTS

Completing this book leaves me with a debt of gratitude to many people. Barnardo's initially approached me to undertake a review of interventions in child protection, and provided some financial support to assist with that. I received help in that enterprise from Alice Winkley. That work triggered the idea of a more comprehensive volume, addressing what we know about the causes and consequences of abuse and neglect, and how best to approach the business of assessment, decision-making, intervention and evaluation. Barnado's was generous enough to give the project its blessing. The editorial staff at John Wiley's have been invaluable in easing the transition to completed book, and I particularly appreciate the patience and forbearance of Comfort Jegede and Helen Ilter.

Child protection research is a complex area, to which many have contributed. Without their work, no such volume would be possible. Therefore, at the broadest level, it is essential to acknowledge those primary researchers and writers on whose work this volume draws so heavily, and those who have the foresight to support such research. Responsibility for how their work has been interpreted in this volume lies with me.

On a more personal level, a number of people have been generous of their time and wisdom. Listing such people is always a hostage to fortune, but the following deserve to be mentioned: Jane Dennis, Jane Gibbons, Kenneth Iain Macdonald, Tony Newman, Helen Roberts and Brian Sheldon. Jane Dennis provided expert help in searching for relevant material and spent many hours helping to identify numerous records that went missing (after *my* tracking system fell short of the efficient model one routinely advocates to research students). Jane Gibbons and Tony Newman provided useful feedback on an early draft of some of the central chapters. Helen Roberts is a force to be reckoned with. Together with Barnardo's she has helped to place the issue of evidence-based child care firmly on the national agenda. She continues to ask questions that others fear to ask, and is not averse to pointing out that the Emperor is rather poorly clad. As she is aware, promoting evidence-based policy and practice has been something of a battle, assuming it means what this book wishes to argue it should. It is a battle that others have been fighting for a long time. Brian Sheldon is one such veteran, and I am particularly grateful to him for being a long-standing friend, mentor and critic. His willingness to proof-read material for a colleague who doesn't much care for the task is deeply appreciated. The combination of feedback on one's prose and on its content is precious. Kenneth Iain Macdonald also kindly brought his critical eye to bear on the final page proofs. Despite my aversion to the proof-reading enterprise, I do bring myself to do the deed and so any remaining errors are mine alone.

Barbara Hudson merits especial thanks. I first met Barbara in Oxford in 1977 when I became one of her graduate social work students. She is a remarkable woman, clever, extremely knowledgeable across a range of issues (both inside and outside social work) and kind. She is uncompromising in her approach to social work, which is more fundamentally user-centred than that of many who make claim to such. Barbara introduced me to behaviour therapy, which she promoted because, and only because, of its promising record in the helping professions. In discussion about the basis on which one makes decisions about how to set about intervening in people's lives, she introduced me to the principles of evidence-based decision-making, although at that time the phrase had not been coined. She also went out of her way to help me develop as a practitioner and later as a writer and an academic. I am deeply grateful to her.

Finally, but by no means least, I would like to thank my husband (Kenneth Iain) and children (Ezra and Rachael) who have put up with so much. The irony of being a somewhat absent mother whilst writing a book on child protection was lost on none of us. They treated me gently and I thank them.

ABOUT THE AUTHOR

Geraldine Macdonald is Professor of Social Work at the University of Bristol. She is also Visiting Professor at the Centre for Evidence-Based Social Services at the University of Exeter. She qualified as a social worker in 1979 and worked as a social worker and senior social worker for Oxfordshire Social Services, specialising in work with children and families. Her research interests include the evaluation of the effects of social interventions, particularly social work, decision-making in child protection and ethical issues in social work research and practice. She has recent publications in each of these areas.

She is actively involved in promoting the development, availability and use of systematic reviews of interventions relevant to health and social care. Between 1995 and 1999 she was Archie Cochrane Research Fellow at Green College, University of Oxford. Professor Macdonald is Co-ordinating Editor of the Cochrane *Developmental, Psychosocial and Learning Problems* Review Group. The Cochrane Collaboration seeks to prepare, maintain and make accessible systematic reviews of health care interventions. She is also co-convenor, with Haluk Soydun, of the Social Work and Social Welfare Group within the Campbell Collaboration. The Campbell Collaboration is a sibling collaboration to Cochrane which aims to prepare, maintain and make accessible systematic reviews of interventions in education, social welfare and criminology.

INTRODUCTION

Child protection is a complex social endeavour. It is one of the few areas where the state seeks to intervene in an otherwise private arena, that of family life, and where a range of professional groups and organisations, as well as the general public, are expected to play a part. It is a problematic endeavour too. Child physical abuse, child neglect, psychological maltreatment and child sexual abuse are all socially constructed in ways which make definition, discussion and decision-making technically challenging (see Hendrick 1997). Whilst few would be concerned about parents sometimes shouting at their children, and few would disagree that beating a child with a stick or raping a nine year old were unacceptable, there is often less consensus between the shoulders of the curve as to what comprises child maltreatment or 'child abuse'. Differences in perception exist across class, across culture, and between genders and generations.

These differences are carried into the professional role and are often exacerbated, rather than minimised, by professional affiliation, as the history of child abuse inquiries and research studies only too graphically testifies (see Giovanonni and Beccera 1979). Failures in child protection regularly cost the lives of some fifty children a year and blight many more. Investigations which subsequently exonerate those under scrutiny can nonetheless cause great pain to parents and children alike, with devastating effects for some families. A concern to protect children from serious injury or death, coupled with a concern not to intervene unless necessary has resulted in a primary focus of resources and endeavour on those families where the risks appear serious and immediate. Preventive work easily becomes a poor relation in child care and protection services, particularly when resources are limited, even though this might prove an effective and efficient strategy in the longer term. This is the socio-political context in which the development of an evidence-based approach to practice must be considered.

EVIDENCE-BASED PRACTICE

As in other areas of social intervention, things that 'work' in child protection may be far from desirable. Children may be protected from significant physical harm by removal or by different forms of parental surveillance, but if poverty or poor housing are the central issues, or if parents who lack certain skills are not being offered appropriate help, then such strategies may be organisationally expedient but ethically dubious. They may leave children physically safe but developmentally, emotionally and socially vulnerable.

Decision-making in child protection is not about protection from *all* risk, but usually only from those that are immediate and/or apparent. Rarely can we guarantee that when we intervene to remove children from imminent risk that the alternatives we provide (substitute care) will themselves not constitute a source of harm to a child's growth and development, not to mention his or her future life chances and happiness. When children are removed from parental care, such protection from an identified source of harm typically entails separation from a range of positive influences on a child's development, such as continuity of care and living with an adult with whom there is an emotional bond and who may well care for that child, albeit inadequately. Many decisions are, therefore, a judgement of relative risks. Further, decisions to remove children from their carers constitute only one kind of decision within child protection. Many decisions concern whether, and how, to assist families in 'the middle ground', where children are less well cared for than they should be, or where children may be being mis-treated, but where the risk is less extreme or less immediate (see Gracia 1995).

Whether assistance is afforded to children and families depends on a range of factors. Professional perceptions and assessments of risk, profes-sional knowledge of the range of adverse effects on children, awareness of the meaning of events, behaviours and circumstances in the lives of children toward whom we have a duty of care, parental and professional receptivity to suggested interventions, as well as resources and professional competence all play a part. What is offered is even more precarious. Staff generally decide early on in their professional careers what kind of theoretical or therapeutic approach they prefer, and undertake assessment and care plan-ning on the basis of such prior influences. Some teams or agencies offer a particular set of services but not others. In other words, in child protection and child care, we have some way to go towards an evidence-based approach to assessment and intervention.

Evidence-based practice indicates an approach to decision-making which is transparent, accountable, and based on a careful consideration of the most compelling evidence we have about the effects of particular interventions on the welfare of individuals, groups and communities. It is the essentially interventionist nature of social work and other helping professions that places an ethical responsibility on managers and practitioners to intervene on the basis of the best available evidence about the effects of their actions on children's lives. The history of social welfare research testifies to the fact that good intentions are not enough; the helping professions have an immense capacity to do harm as well as good, and there is ample evidence that we tend to overestimate the latter and underestimate the former. Therefore, as well as an appropriate recognition of the importance of the law, policy, professional and social values and practice wisdom, the essence of the movement towards an evidence-based approach to practice is that our decisions about whether, when and how to intervene in the lives of children and families should be informed by current best evidence of the effects of those interventions available to us.

THE FOCUS OF THIS BOOK

This book is primarily concerned to provide practitioners, managers and policy makers working in the field of child protection with a critical overview of what research evidence suggests are effective strategies. As this literature is dauntingly wide and complex, there is only limited scope to engage in crucial debates such as those referred to in the previous passages. Throughout the book, however, the position taken on these important issues is stated as clearly as possible. This transparency should enable readers critically to evaluate the validity, relevance and acceptability of the conclusions drawn.

The focus is primarily on those interventions aimed at individuals, groups, and communities. Not included, therefore, are a number of important socioeconomic interventions that would, if there was sufficient political will, be more likely to impact positively on the lives of the thousands of children who come within the remit of the child protection system, than the sum total of effort currently expended by health and social care professionals in this field (see Roberts 1999). However, in the absence of such political will (and some might argue, economic resources), it is important to enable practitioners to choose the most effective responses they can, within the systems in which they operate.

The premise of this volume is therefore that there are some problems that are justifiably addressed at this 'micro' level. Some of these arise from predominantly personal, psychological and interpersonal factors, and are appropriately addressed at that level. Others may not be wholly precipitated by personal or interpersonal problems, but this may be the only sphere of influence open to social workers and other service providers. Whilst some problems may be predominantly or wholly attributable to socio-economic

XX   INTRODUCTION

factors far beyond the influence of health or social services, it may nonetheless be appropriate to offer forms of help, such as social support or certain
kinds of therapeutic work. Although these do not address causal factors,
there may be important strategies whereby families are enabled to cope with
stresses, and the damage to children's health, development and well-being
minimised. Put another way, neither headache nor a thrombosis-prone
bloodstream are due to lack of aspirin, but it may still make sense in some
circumstances to take some.

LIMITATIONS

In addition to macro-level socio-economic interventions, there are other
areas of research that are excluded from this volume. In the past two
decades, the U.K. government has invested vast resources in reviewing and
reordering the legislative framework in which child protection takes place.
The problems associated with the policies, procedures and practices of child
protection have been given high priority on international and national
research agendas, and this has been complemented by (and has often been
responsive to) the findings of public and other inquiries into untoward
incidents and fatalities.

Research into the effectiveness of procedural change, whilst important in
considering the effectiveness of child protection, is not included for two
reasons. First, this research is generally more widely known than other forms
of evaluative research. In the U.K., much of this work is sponsored by the
Department of Health, and tends to be implemented into policy and practice.
Secondly, relatively little of this research incorporates a focus on what
constitutes effective interventions that are designed to address the particular
problems associated with abuse. A key element in making informed
decisions in child protection is knowledge about *what* sorts of problems are
amenable to *what* sorts of interventions, in *what* circumstances, and with *what*
degrees of certainty. Unless more attention is paid to these questions, and to
helping families change when this is appropriate, then children will be poorly
served, regardless of how effective the overall system of child protection
appears to be. These are the questions with which this book is concerned and
it is therefore designed to complement reports such as *Messages from Research*
(DoH 1995).

FINALLY

This volume builds on other attempts already made to bridge this gap
between research and practice (e.g., Gough 1993; Fink and McCloskey 1990;

Oates and Bross 1995; Becker *et al.* 1995; Finkelhor and Berliner 1995). It endeavours to provide a cautious interpretation of the best available evidence concerning effective practice in child protection and to provide a basis upon which readers can develop and maintain an evidence-based approach to their practice. In order to achieve this, the book begins with an introduction to some key issues in evaluating effectiveness (both conceptual and methodological) and in critically appraising research studies. This is important because of the worryingly high 'chaff to wheat ratio' that exists in research into the effectiveness of planned interventions. The position taken is that the 'best evidence' is that which is available from methodologically rigorous and relevant studies, and it is important that users of research are aware that not all studies carry equal evidential status. This is followed by a summary of research which makes an empirically-based contribution to our understanding of child abuse and neglect. The third section of the book presents what evidence currently exists about 'what works' in key areas of child protection. Partly because of the diverse nature of the literature (different definitions, different samples and so on) it has been rather difficult to organise. Studies have been grouped according to whether or not they are concerned to prevent abuse, or whether they aim to stop abuse from recurring. Of course, on one level all work is preventive in that it aims to stop future occurrences of abuse, and the following categorisation of research studies, often used in the research literature, reflects this, *viz.*:

Primary prevention: interventions aimed at whole communities or populations irrespective of any known particular risk. These interventions are typically educational in nature, and aimed at helping parents acquire general parenting skills or raising awareness of issues such as child sexual abuse. These programmes are variously targeted at professionals, parents, children, and communities.
Secondary prevention: interventions aimed at individuals who are identified as being at high risk of abuse.*
Tertiary prevention: interventions aimed to ensure that abuse which has already occurred does not occur again. It includes the provision of help to children who have been abused and, for example, to parents whose children have been abused by others, as well as studies examining the effectiveness of work with sex offenders.

This does not make for a neat division of studies, but it is difficult to contemplate an organisational principle that would serve better, given the overlap of research in terms of interventions used, participants, and service contexts. The basis for attempting it is that interventions designed to prevent abuse from happening and those which are designed to prevent *further* abuse

---

* Rather confusingly, in some literatures these are referred to as 'primary prevention'.

typically emphasise different contributory factors, and often operate at different ecological levels. Thus, interventions aimed at *primary* or *secondary prevention* often operate at community level, and feature interventions aimed to raise awareness of abuse, to strengthen informal support networks for families, and to enhance the economic and social well-being of parents by helping them acquire further education or work skills, seek employment and assist in arranging, or providing, child care. Those aimed at *tertiary prevention* (responsive interventions) are often primarily concerned with the individual competence and skills of parents, for example in managing their children's behaviour without resort to excessive physical punishment, or providing adequate care and supervision. These programmes are more likely to contain interventions particularly designed to tackle factors associated with abuse at the individual and family level, and to include direct measures of abusive incidents or of parental and child behaviours thought to be directly related to the probability of future abuse.

Of course, this is a matter of emphasis, rather than a strict categorisation, and studies aimed at secondary prevention often embrace a range of assumptions regarding causation as well as a range of interventions. However, grouping studies according to their expressed aims provides a means of comparing relative effectiveness of programmes and interventions, and highlights relevant methodological issues; for example, do primary prevention studies provide data from sufficiently long follow-up periods, and use relevant measures? Each chapter in Part C examines studies concerned with child physical abuse, child physical neglect, emotional abuse and neglect, and child sexual abuse. In many areas it has not been possible to separate out interventions aimed at specific aspects of physical, emotional or psychological maltreatment and the significance of this is discussed at various points. The final section considers the implications of an evidence-based approach to assessment. The first chapter in this section considers a range of factors which threaten assessment quality. This is followed by a chapter concerned with strategies to support an evidence-based approach to assessment, monitoring and evaluation. The final chapter considers similar issues in relation to risk assessment and suggests some strategies for improving practice in this area. The age range of children with whom the book is concerned is 0 to 17 years.

PART A
Evidence-based Policy and Practice

1

EVALUATING EFFECTIVENESS

Evaluating the effectiveness of social interventions of any kind is not easy, and the complexities of the child protection field accentuate many of the methodological challenges social scientists encounter whenever they try to make sense out of the messy, reactive world of human behaviour and human relationships. It also presents some that are particular to working with vulnerable people, including children and some of these problems are discussed later (see Chapter 2). However, in order to make sense of these challenges, it is important to know something about the range of evaluative tools available, and to see how they can be used in determining our effectiveness at preventing child abuse and neglect, and helping those who have been subject to maltreatment.

This is not an introduction to research methods, nor does it provide an inclusive overview of good research. There are many good research studies looking at child protection using qualitative or so-called 'mixed' methodologies (e.g., Thoburn *et al.* 1995; Brown 1984). Qualitative studies shed light on how those with whom we work understand their social milieu. Without this understanding we cannot begin to conceptualise interventions which will be acceptable, let alone be effective. There is still a dearth of qualitative studies of children's own experiences of interventions, but even here there are some admirable examples of work in this field (Little and Kelly 1995; Butler and Williamson 1994) and a growing number of researchers addressing the challenges of this approach, and the skills needed (see Garbarino and Stott 1992; Alderson 1990). However, the development of effective services requires other kinds of evidence. The research designs described below are those which attempt to estimate the relationship between what we do and any changes experienced by those whom we seek to help. The confidence we can have that a particular set of outcomes is attributable to our actions, and not to other collateral influences, depends in large part on the research design used, and its careful execution.

THE CHALLENGES OF EVALUATION

A number of problems face the worker who wishes to assess his or her effectiveness, or that of their service or team, or who may be trying to judge the reliability of a research report. The following hypothetical situation highlights some of the key issues.

Suppose a particular family centre wishes to evaluate a discussion group aimed at improving the parenting skills of a group of parents whose children have been placed on the Child Protection Register because of evidence of neglect. Suppose the programme runs for eight weekly sessions, each session lasting two hours. Suppose further that at the end it is considered by the workers and parents to have been a success for those who did not drop out. Suppose that these judgements are based on the self-reports of the parents, upon the workers' observations of parents' increasing self-esteem, and upon improvements in the apparent well-being of the children (who have been cared for in a crèche during the parents' group). Before asserting that 'discussion groups work' we need to ascertain not only that these improvements have indeed taken place but that they are, in fact, attributable to the effects of the group. It is very difficult to do this if we do not have mechanisms for ruling out competing explanations such as those listed below:

(i)   These parents might have improved simply with the passage of time, and developed more confidence in their parenting ability. Alternatively, problems that may have been preventing them caring adequately for their children may simply have 'remitted', as many do (cf. Rachman and Wilson 1980).

(ii) The children might have become more manageable and interesting as a result of weekly exposure to skilled crèche supervisors.

(iii) Other external factors might be responsible for changes, such as improved income support, additional help from social services, due to the children's registration, such as extra day care.

(iv) The perceived improvement in the parents might be due to the fact that in the course of the intervention they had learned the 'right things to say', having been asked the same kind of questions at the beginning and end of the programme, and become familiar with the expectations of the workers.

(v)   Workers' familiarity with the parents may have led them selectively to perceive or emphasise those aspects of their behaviour with which they are most concerned, and about which they had limited information at the start of the programme.

(vi) Those who stayed might have been highly motivated parents who would have improved anyway. Alternatively, those parents who dropped out might have done just as well as those in the programme. We simply do not know.

These alternatives constitute reasonable 'Ah, but . . . ' responses to claims that a particular programme is responsible for change. What they highlight are what researchers call 'threats to internal validity', or reasons why something other than the intervention being examined might be responsible for the results of a study, whether good or bad. Emotional predispositions and prior learning come in here. It is not unusual for students and practitioners to be methodologically meticulous when appraising a study whose results are unpopular, whilst methodologically more forgiving when results support a preferred way of working. In essence, one of the challenges we have is to conduct evaluations in such a way that we minimise the likelihood of competing explanations, irrespective of the results. In research terms, we need study designs that have optimum 'internal validity' (see Campbell and Stanley 1973) or 'attributive confidence' (see Macdonald and Sheldon 1992).

Evidence-based decision-making in child protection entails that those on the receiving end of social interventions should expect these to be selected on the basis of the best available evidence. It is problematic for those in the helping professions that the best source of evidence comes from a research strategy that it is not always possible to use in child protection research (or indeed in other areas of social welfare), but at the same time is less frequently deployed than it might be—the randomised controlled trial (RCT).

STUDIES WITH EXPERIMENTAL DESIGNS (RANDOMISED CONTROLLED TRIALS)

What gives RCTs the edge over other designs is the random allocation of research participants into two groups, with the intervention under investigation then applied to one and not to the other. With large enough samples this procedure allows us to control for two sources of bias:

(i)   we control for selection bias i.e., we don't pick those we think are most likely to respond well (about which we may, in any case, be wrong);
(ii) we control for bias arising from the influence of extraneous variables i.e., if other factors are exerting an influence they will be doing so in *both* groups, therefore any differences in the groups receiving the intervention we are interested in—the experimental group—can be more confidently attributed to the intervention.

In other words, well conducted RCTs score best on 'internal validity'. The RCT structure does not dissolve all our problems—for example, we may well worry about what our 'intervention' actually is, for example if a group is 'effective' is its effectiveness due to the discussions, the worker's directions, or the companionship of others? We need to ensure that the measures we use are meaningful and that changes they record are not due to bias on the part of those gathering the information. These are problems we have to address whatever our research design. RCTs simply ensure that, once we solve them, we can have confidence in the result.

Randomised controlled trials enjoy an unrivalled claim to attributive confidence. That is to say, they are best able to rule out competing explanations. It is this research design that can settle disputes—at any one point in time—about the relative efficacy of two forms of intervention, or of intervention versus non-intervention. Given the theoretical affiliations of workers, and the political investment in favour of certain programmes (just suppose Safari holidays could be shown to turn delinquents into upright citizens . . .), randomised controlled trials comprise essential cornerstones to an evidence-based approach.

People worry about the ethics of randomisation, particularly to a 'no-treatment' condition, and there are interesting stories to be told from medical research about the lengths to which people will go to subvert the randomisation process, because of concerns about patient welfare (Silverman 1980). The starting point for randomisation is, however, that often we simply do not *know* what works, or works best and such side-stepping represents the misguided confidence that we, as practitioners, can have in our working methods. It also highlights a practical requirement of RCTs, namely that those involved understand them and are in agreement with the need for such a step in this area. Service users are often more readily persuaded of the utility of RCTs than are many professionals (see Oakley 1989).

Example I—The Alameda Project
(Stein and Gambrill 1974; 1976)

This research project aimed to tackle the problem of 'decisional drift' of children languishing—in an unplanned way—in foster care. The children had been accommodated for protective purposes, two-thirds of them for reasons of neglect. The researchers wanted to assess whether an intensive, natural parent focused service could enhance placement outcomes for children. 482 children were randomly assigned to two groups. Families of children in the *experimental* condition received intensive help from three full-time post-graduate, qualified social workers, directed at problems that were identified as preventing rehabilitation. The starting point for workers in the experimental conditions was to focus some attention on the natural parents and involve them actively in deciding what outcomes they wanted for their children and for themselves. Families of children in the *control* condition received regular services from workers in the Child Welfare Department. Four outcomes were possible for children in either group:

1. Return of child to natural parents.
2. Child placed for adoption (with parents voluntarily, or by court order, relinquishing their rights).
3. Appointment of a legal guardian.
4. Positive identification of children who would need to remain in long-term foster care—with subsequent planning for this.

Though the RCT framework controls for systematic bias, it nevertheless makes sense to examine the distribution of known pertinent variables. When researchers checked that the groups were comparable on key variables (such as age, problems identified) they found few significant differences apart from (i) a significantly higher incidence of drug abuse amongst experimental parents; (ii) children in the experimental group were somewhat younger; and (iii) children in the control group were more likely to have been in care due to poor supervision. In analysing their data the researchers were careful to check for any effect of age, controlling particularly for length of time in care, and using statistical techniques were able to rule out either as responsible for the results they obtained.

Caseloads in the experimental condition were smaller (35 cases per worker in the experimental group compared with 49 in the control group) but more active. In order to involve parents, workers in the experimental group took a firm stance on parents visiting their children i.e., they required contact and facilitated it. Centrally, they made heavy use of detailed contracts, agreed with parents, and characterised by clear, specific goals, and precise identification of interim objectives needed to meet these goals. In order to help parents meet their goals appropriate help was offered or arranged. This project, and other studies, demonstrates the importance of contracts or working agree ments as sources of information and clarifying expectations—an empowering tool which provides a reference point for parents who wish to hold workers accountable. Further, contracts can motivate parents (parents who signed contracts in this project were much more likely to follow through with plans and have their children restored as a consequence). Finally, if all is not well, they provide strong evidence upon which to base decisions about alternative permanent plans for children's futures. In the Alameda project, the clarity of worker expectations, and the level of support and assistance provided, made it easier for parents to understand and accept decisions *not* to return children home where goals had not been met.

1. Overall, almost half (48%) of the children in the experimental group were returned home, or 'headed out' of foster care compared with just 11% of the control group.
2. Significantly fewer children in the experimental group were left in long-term foster care at the end of the project (only 21% compared with 60% in the control group).

3. Out of ten problem areas identified, there was a significant difference between the groups in respect to three areas, all in favour of the experimental condition, namely measures of parent-child interaction; personal parental problems, and marital difficulties. Problems unaffected were legal difficulties, maintaining court-directed appointments with community counselling services, and visiting children.

4. Although a child's chances of restoration were extremely good in *either* group *when identified problems were resolved* (91% and 83% in the experimental and control group respectively), more problems were resolved in the experimental group. Further, children in the control group were more likely to be restored *despite* unresolved problems (43% of families were reunited with unresolved problems) which would have reduced their chances of a successful restoration.

5. Although the study did not report on the consequences of this, other research suggests that attempts at reunification in families where the precipatating problems remain unresolved are unlikely to succeed (see for example, Hess *et al.* 1992). This last point illustrates the importance of identifying all pertinent outcome measures, having long-term follow-ups whenever possible (atypically, this project followed families for up to two years), and understanding RCTs in the context of other research findings, such as relevant longitudinal studies (Rowe and Lambert 1973; Gibbons *et al.* 1995).

The large sample size, the detailed description of the interventions undertaken (including samples of contracts agreed with parents), the careful checks made on the comparability of the two groups, the use of 'hard' outcome measures, and appropriate statistical analysis, give this study considerable weight. That is to say, we can be reasonably sure that it is the pattern and content of help offered families in the experimental group that accounts for their improved outcomes. Of course, it is still open to criticism. For example, the 'project' nature of the experimental condition might have attracted more skilled and better motivated workers who performed better under the scrutiny of the researchers. Nonetheless the size and design of the study make it hard to argue that these factors alone, regardless of *what* these workers did, would account for these results.

This study highlights two important issues for those concerned with evidence-based practice. Firstly, it signals the need to carefully attend to the *content* of practice, even in an area of child care that is generally well-understood, with clear (albeit sometimes contested) policies and procedures. Knowledge of the adverse effects of 'decisional-drift' and agreement about the desirability of permanency planning are not sufficient. The problems that cause and maintain family breakdown, or trigger state concern, need to be specifically addressed if we are to stop the 'revolving door' syndrome whereby children are rehabilitated only to be accommodated again at a later date. Secondly, the Alameda study was published in 1974 and yet, despite its sound methodology and significant results, it is little known and has had only limited influence on practice, not just in the U.K. but also in the United States where it was conducted. One of the most pressing issues facing the welfare agencies is the dissemination of research findings to those who need them most, in a form that is easy to access and understand.

STUDIES WITH QUASI-EXPERIMENTAL DESIGNS

The realities of child protection mean it is not always possible to allocate clients to different services or wait-list control groups. Reasons for this encompass ethical as well as practical concerns, though the intransigence of both sets of difficulties may be exaggerated (Macdonald and Macdonald 1995). The likely cost of randomised controlled trials, the desirability of large samples, and the fairly loose relationship that often exists between our under-standing of social problems such as child abuse and the responses we make to them, means it is neither possible nor sensible to place all our evaluative eggs in this methodological basket. What is essential is that alternative approaches to evaluation are designed, analysed and interpreted in ways that address the concerns which can make it difficult to be sure that any improvements we see, in those we are trying to help, are in fact due to our efforts. A more commonly used method is to design studies that benefit from one of more control groups, but to which participants are not randomly allocated—the quasi-experimental design.

These studies are similar insofar as some clients receive a service whilst others do not or receive another service, but instead of random allocation, researchers take clients occurring 'naturally', and establish a control group matched on characteristics thought to be important, for example, socio-economic facts, severity of problem, duration of problem, and so on.

Example 2—Addressing the Developmental Delays Associated with Child Abuse and Neglect

Child abuse and neglect carry developmental consequences for affected chil-dren. Culp and his colleagues (1987a,b; 1991) assessed the impact of a thera-peutic day care programme on the developmental scores of 35 children who had been mistreated by their parents, by comparing them before and after the programme with the scores of a matched group who had not yet been enrolled in such a programme.

All children were under six years of age. The researchers selected a control group matched for age, sex, race, and diagnostic category (abuse, neglect, abuse and neglect, sibling abused). In other words, they endeavoured to make sure the groups were equivalent on those aspects they thought might affect their developmental trajectory, in order to rule them out as competing explanations. The success of this strategy is dependent upon our specifying those factors which are most likely to exert an influence on outcomes. For example, in this study, researchers did not consider it appropriate to control for family size, or the health of children or parents. If evidence from other sources suggested that these were important factors on developmental delay, the study would be considerably weakened.

Children were enrolled in the programme for an average of 7.6 months with a range from 4.4–15.9 months. Discharge was determined by programme staff on a variety of clinical indicators including assessment of overall family functioning, the provision of needed social services, and the child's classroom performance and behaviour.

In the treatment condition, children participated in group activities for six hours a day, five days a week. There was a high adult to child ratio (1:2) with the major focus on the development of strong teacher–child relationships. The environment was designed to facilitate the development of self-esteem, caring peer relationships, and to help children to recognise and deal with their own feelings. The programme included typical pre-school learning activities. In addition, individual child treatment, parental counselling and education services were integrated with the group programme. Parent services included group counselling, parent education classes, individual therapy, if warranted, and a 24 hour crisis telephone line.

Children were assessed before (pre-test) and after (post-test) the programme. Post-test scores for the experimental children were significantly higher in skill attainment than their matched controls in five areas: fine motor, cognitive, gross motor, social/emotional, and language. Comparisons between the experimental and control group at post-test showed significant differences between the two in all five areas, all in favour of the experimental group. A later analysis of changes in self-concept showed that children in the experimental group also showed improvements in self-concept compared with children in the control group (Culp et al. 1991). The authors observed that because of the composite nature of the treatment programme, it is not possible for the effects of the classroom intervention to be separated from the family intervention provided by the programme. They might also have pointed out that the classroom intervention was also composite (was it, for example, important to the outcome that the 'environment was designed to facilitate the development of self-esteem'?) This is a serious problem which is not uncommon in this literature—and to which RCTs are not immune. It is understandable that the drive to find something that works should result in the bundling together of diverse 'good practices', but if, as was the case here, the package appears to 'work', we are left uncertain which bit(s) of the package is/are the 'active ingredients'. This is not an infrequent problem in child protection research.

STUDIES WITH NON-EXPERIMENTAL DESIGNS

Research designs within this category are evaluated interventions but with no random allocation and no pre-intervention matching of groups, if indeed a comparison group is used at all. Taken singly, results based on studies using these designs are, at best, suggestive.

However, attributive confidence can be enhanced in two ways. Firstly, if a number of such studies featuring a range of clients in different circumstances produce similar results, then one can feel more confident that the intervention is influencing the changes. Such a pattern would indicate that it might be worth investing the time and resources involved in experimental and quasi-experimental research to place these results further beyond doubt. Secondly, if experimental studies featuring similar procedures and approaches already exist, in the absence of glaring 'additional' methodological inadequacies, we can have more confidence in interpreting the results of pre-experimental studies. Here are two examples of a non-experimental study, each highlighting different problems, but with sufficient strengths to build upon.

Examples: Non-experimental Designs

Improving Child–Parent Relationships

Cautley (1980) evaluated a project in which workers aimed to reverse negative relationships between parents and children, by means of a short-term intervention. These were based on careful assessments which included three systematic observations in the clients homes. Goals were agreed with the family (as in many of these studies, in fact) and the intervention comprised: parent training (all families), family therapy (two families), and counselling and marital counselling (eight families)

Work with 14 of the 33 families was judged to have been effective, defined as 'significant positive changes judged likely to last'. Work was thought 'partially effective' for 10 families, that is, some positive changes had occurred but staff had little or no confidence that they would be maintained. For eight families, all but one of which withdrew from treatment, work was judged ineffective. The family which remained made so little progress that the team sought termination of parental rights.

Therapy for Sexually Abused Pre-adolescent Children

This is an example of a post-test only study (Corder *et al.* 1990), in which the absence of pre-test measures requires that we treat an otherwise exceptionally well-documented study with due caution. The title is apposite 'A Pilot Study for a Structured Time-limited Therapy Group for Sexually Abused Pre-Adolescent Children'. In this work a range of techniques were used to improve:

- cognitive and emotional mastery (group discussion, games and art activity);
- self-esteem (cognitive re-labelling using role-play, 'chants and cheers', and interaction with other abused children);
- problem solving and self-protection skills (structured learning experiences—board games, role play);
- ability to seek help and support;
- an understanding of the abuse between mother and child.

The absence of pre-post measures is a great pity given the good rationale of the programme and the promising anecdotal evidence from participants and parents. Funding for a more rigorous evaluation was being sought when this article was published. Feedback from parents and children was positive indicating reduced anxiety levels, increase in children's willingness to talk about their experience with their mothers, increase in understanding of abuse and the development of some mastery skills for avoiding future abuse of themselves and others (one child was reported as helping a classmate to report the classmate's abuse to the school counsellor). Children also said they felt the group had reduced feelings of guilt and made them feel more safe.

Both studies benefit from a detailed description of *what* was done, and the Cautley study is exemplary in the thought given to appropriate outcome measures, that is to measures which are directly associated with the nature of the problem. Both suffer from testing the effectiveness of 'composite' interventions (see above) and the Corder *et al.* study—admittedly only reported as a pilot study—is much weaker than it might otherwise be due to the absence of pre-intervention measures. In other words, we do not know the extent and precise nature of the problem prior to the intervention, and are not in a position to assess whether or not the 'outcomes' are reliable and valid indicators of changes brought about by the intervention.

OTHER RESEARCH METHODS

Client Opinion Studies

Client opinion or 'service-user' studies give us valuable insights into how clients understand what service providers in welfare, health and education are trying to achieve; what it feels like to be on the receiving end of someone else's professional good intent; what side effects are produced; and why and how clients attribute patterns of change, no difference, or deterioration to the actions of staff.

For purposes of quality audit, this approach to evaluation is an important source of data, and one in which the British have a good track record. Unfortunately the correlation between satisfaction (or dissatisfaction) and the achievement of pre-intervention goals is loose, to say the least (McCord 1978), and time and time again the message comes that clients usually like their social workers and other caring professionals, like the *way* they interact with them; appreciate their endeavours, value their support, but rarely understand *what* they are endeavouring to achieve and *how* they expect to do it. In understanding the relationship between process and outcome, these data are best collected as important qualitative data within the framework of other research methods.

In spite of these reservations, data from client opinion studies can be useful in understanding elements of the 'helping' process. There is a long tradition of such studies within the U.K. and they are easily carried out at the level of an individual project or service, and can be used to refine and reconsider particular services, and provide feedback to partner agencies (Gribbens 1992; Fraenkel *et al.* 1998). Audits of client opinion are not infrequently commissioned by local authority social services departments, and social work students regularly undertake small exploratory studies of this kind whilst on practice placements. Even when of exceptional quality, few of these internal studies reach the public forum.

Example: Client Opinion Study—Magura and Moses (1984)

Views of Parents of Children at Risk

This study elicited the views of 250 parents of children at risk who had been supervised for a period of between 5–6 months by three social work agencies with at least one child receiving home services. These 250 represent one third of eligible parents but the problem of bias was carefully managed in the study design.

- Clients repeatedly testified to the pervasive, deleterious influence of material deprivation on their children, both with regard to physical child care and indirectly in the area of parental stress, anxiety and depression.
- Caseworkers however, demonstrated little interest in, or influence over, this area (an old problem, see Mayer and Timms 1970). About one third of all clients who had coping problems of some kind at follow-up attributed the cause to insufficient income or financial difficulties— 'the continual inability to afford the necessities of daily life.'

- Despite the openness with which parents discussed their disciplinary problems, the changes reported seemed, to the researchers, tenuous. Few parents considered their disciplinary problems solved. They questioned the appropriateness of caseworker reliance on counselling in preference to interventions such as Parent Effectiveness Training.
- Only 25% of clients reported any fundamental disagreement with the agency over the facts of the referral, but 60% volunteered one important criticism of the agency. The authors suggest that clients should have access to any mechanisms set up to deal with complaints, which, even if not valid, result in 'sincere disaffection and resentment' if not aired and debated.

The authors recommend the routine inclusion of clients' views in this area, not least of all to provide corrective feedback to staff on their views of the key issues in families at risk.

Single-case Experimental Designs

The use of so-called 'single-case experimental designs' is one way of intro-ducing rigour into the evaluation of individual pieces of work, whether this is with groups, families, or individual users. Essentially, the researcher, or practitioner, makes a careful assessment of a problem or situation before intervention, which is quantitative rather than purely qualitative, and which provides a picture of the problem over a short period of time. In other words, even when the problems are qualitative in nature e.g., depression, or anxiety, or anger, it is possible—and desirable from the point of view of evaluation—to measure this, simply by asking users to estimate the intensity or per-vasiveness of their feelings on a simple Likert-type scale (e.g., a scale from 1 [no problem]–5 [a permanent problem]). Optimally, one uses scales which have been validated (tested to ensure that they measure what they purport to measure), and which are reliable (tested to ensure they give accurate and replicable measures). The result is a *baseline* of the problem: a picture of the frequency, intensity and duration of particular difficulties (such as the use of physical punishment, temper tantrums, binges, arguments, mood swings) or strengths (which you may wish to build upon, e.g. initiating play with a child, going out, cooking a meal, talking to a neighbour). This will provide a yardstick by which to measure progress. Essentially, one then intervenes in the situation, and either continues to use the measures which provided the baseline (which may well comprise a parent keeping a record of his or her own behaviour, or that of a child) or, minimally, repeats the measures at the end of the programme. Again, quantitative records based on standardised instruments, or the use of data collected by others, provide a check against 'wishful thinking'. Experience with users suggest that, whilst every attempt must be made to minimise the extra demands placed on parents who are already up against it, when 'pitched right' the approach to monitoring the progress of work in this way can be empowering for parents, who can question a lack of progress in the event that they are doing what they agreed but the hoped-for improvements have not come about.

Needless to say, the above account is over-simplified. It does not address the range of factors that can prejudice the accuracy of baseline measures, and strictly speaking it is not 'experimental'. That is to say, it can only provide evidence that change took place, rather than that any identified change was attributable to the intervention itself, for all the reasons set out in the section on randomised controlled trials. It is possible, within single case methodology, to introduce experimental rigour by moving beyond a simple 'pre-post' measurement (called an AB design) to more elaborate designs which do enable one to develop confidence in the links between intervention and outcome (typically, multiple-baseline designs). These are not discussed here, but interested readers are referred to work by Bloom and Fischer (1982), Kazi and Wilson (1996), Barlow and Hersen (1984) and Sheldon (1988).

SURVEYS

Surveys do not themselves provide a means of evaluating practice, but they are important tools in establishing effective service provision. In general terms, surveys provide useful information about the prevalence of particular characteristics. They afford a helpful corrective element to the associations we can erroneously be tempted to make when working in settings which serve groups experiencing or presenting particular problems. For example, many of our assumptions concerning risk factors in child abuse are based on clinical experience, or research based on clinical samples. We do not know how prevalent those factors which *appear* to be significant in the histories of our clients are in the general population. We rarely encounter those families and individuals who, *despite* certain life experiences, do *not* abuse their children, do *not* become delinquent, and do *not* develop low self-esteem; or have low self-esteem but do *not* damage their children. Surveys can help us more accurately to 'weight' these factors in relation to others. Of course, poor surveys can exacerbate this problem, as in the case of surveys of the incidence (number of new cases reported over a certain period) and prevalence (the number of people who report having been abused) of sexual abuse which use vague definitions (e.g. Baker and Duncan 1985). A useful discussion of these problems in relation to child sexual abuse can be found in Pilkington and Kremer (1995a,b).

In recent years it has been surprisingly rare for managers and service providers to have, at their fingertips, a clear idea of the extent and nature of need in the area or field for which they are responsible. This rather worrying state of affairs is currently being addressed by a range of initiatives within the U.K., ranging from community-based surveys commissioned by local authorities and voluntary agencies (Imrie and Coombes 1995; Gordon and Loughran 1997) to the requirement that local authorities develop Children's Services Plans which inevitably draw on relevant survey data (Quinton 1996).

In Britain a great deal of evaluative research has been of this kind, exploring the impact of policy shifts and changes in legislation on the lives of children in care, or at risk of care. Surveys can also shed light on the gaps than can exist between the good intentions of organisational and policy changes and the working reality, and pinpoint reasons why things might not be working according to plan e.g., a survey of care management in the personal social services might conclude that it is a useful analytic approach, with a sound philosophy, being pursued by enthusiastic staff who find themselves unable to achieve their aspirations because of resource shortage, lack of co-operation from other agencies, or poor quality control strategies, and so on.

COHORT STUDIES

Cohort studies interview or otherwise follow-up a number of people at more than one point in time. Data are collected from the same people over a period of months or years, so that information on a child at, say, one, five or nine years old, can be related to the same child (now adult) say at 19, or 29 years. Data from cohort studies can be subjected to particular forms of statistical analysis which allow researchers to examine the interaction of variables at various levels e.g. individual, community, societal. They enable one to identify how certain factors mediate the relationship of others, or moderate their strength or direction (Baron and Kenny 1986; Ferri 1993).

Cohort studies relevant to child protection fall into two main categories, birth cohorts and cohorts selected for particular reasons e.g., having been identified as abused or neglected.

Birth cohort studies are those in which a large sample of children born between a certain period (a day, a month, a year) are followed up to adulthood. They are particularly useful because they provide researchers with sufficient data to explore not just the impact of particular variables (poverty, family size, infant ill-health, maternal ill-health, physical abuse and so on), but the inter-relationship between these, and the ways in which other, protective factors (IQ, good schooling, a caring grandparent) mitigate their adverse effects. Unfortunately, for the purposes of understanding child maltreatment (both causes and consequences) good birth cohort studies are expensive, and require the collaboration of researchers from a range of disciplines—a rare occurrence. Blaxter (1986) provides a useful summary of pertinent cohort studies, to which one should now add the Avon Longitudinal Survey of Parents and Children (see Golding 1990). Such studies are currently producing a wealth of data which should further our understanding of what factors and interactions of factors conspire to produce poor outcomes for children generally, and how neglect and abuse develop and with what consequences. Most important, they may shed some light on what factors, including the availability of formal and informal networks of help, exert protective influences on children's health and welfare. We give a key reference from each:

- The National Survey of Health and Development (Wadsworth 1991)
- Second Generation Study (first born children of the above cohort) (Wadsworth 1985)
- The National Child Development Study (Ferri 1993)
- Newcastle Thousand Families Study (Kolvin *et al.* 1983)
- Aberdeen Child Development Study (Illsley 1967)
- Child Health and Education Study (Osborn and Milbank 1985)
- Children of the Nineties (Golding 1990)
- Minnesota Mother–Child Project (Pianta *et al.* 1989)
- Western Australia Child Health Survey (Zubrich 1997)
- The Cambridge Delinquency Study (Farrington 1996).

Other studies follow-up particular groups in the population such as:

- Mothers at risk (Kruk and Wolkind 1983)
- Temperament (Chess and Thomas 1990)
- Children of young mothers (Phoenix 1990)
- Childhood experiences and parenting behaviour: children in care (Rutter and Quinton 1984)
- Maltreated children (Egeland and Sroufe 1981; Lynch and Roberts 1982).

All of these studies collect both health and social data, and the sorts of questions which well-designed research of this type can help us to answer are: What are the social consequences of the way in which health events are dealt with by services? What are the effects of social policy changes or changes over time in the social environment? Which is more important, family of origin or later environment?

Cohort studies can give some indication of the effects of changing social and family policies, as well as the effects of particular ways of living family life. As Ferri (1993) points out:

'the moves towards ameliorating economic and social inequality, which took place during the childhoods of the National Child Development Study sample have been reversed in recent years . . . What have all these changes meant for the lives and experiences for those in their thirties?' (Ferri 1993, pp 3–4.)

It would be misleading to suggest that cohort studies can give a complete answer to the question of what works in family and social policies, but they can give helpful pointers. In particular they can help us to identify the characteristics of children from disadvantaged backgrounds who do well, offering us an opportunity to build on people's strengths (see Rutter 1985).

Although, over a period of time, some people become lost to follow-up, data from these studies remain a remarkable repository of information on the growth and development of children and young people, and as children and young people in these samples progress into adulthood, allow researchers to explore associations between early development and experiences, and later outcomes.

2

PARTICULAR CHALLENGES IN CHILD PROTECTION RESEARCH

A number of problems render the task of summarising trends in the field of child protection particularly challenging. These include:

- a paucity of evaluations meeting minimum criteria of rigour, such as the inclusion of a control or comparison group, adequate sample size, acceptable rates of attrition (Fink and McCloskey 1990; Oates and Bross 1995);
- variations in the definitions of abuse and neglect used by child care professionals and researchers, and an absence of information in some studies (see Giovannoni 1989, Aber and Zigler 1981). This can make it difficult to group studies in ways to compare like with like. For example, the question 'does family therapy do better than parent education for cases of physical neglect?' is difficult to answer if relevant studies are using different definitions (e.g., 'neglect' can mean a failure to provide adequate physical care in one study, and a range of things, including inadequate supervision, in another). A number of reviewers have identified this problem, but researchers have yet to take this problem seriously. This does not make the task impossible, but it means that it is made more complex, and the conclusions we draw must typically be more cautious than they might otherwise be;
- variations in the conceptualisation of the causes of abuse used in studies. Some organise interventions based on the perception of abuse as a function primarily of poverty and related social stresses, whereas others might develop strategies based on the view that personal characteristics are the main contributory factor (see Part C);
- variations in the range, relevance and reliability of outcome measures used, and a reliance of self-report data (see Fantuzzo and Twentyman 1986). Much needed are reliable, valid and meaningful methods of

operationalising definitions of abuse and neglect which will facilitate the measurement of change;

- a failure to specify precisely what the intervention is, or to say why and how it is expected to bring about the changes desired (see Fink and McCloskey 1990);
- a tendency to use composite interventions i.e., social support *plus* child management *plus* advocacy. Coupled with an absence of experimental design and good outcome measures it is generally difficult to identify those ingredients of programmes which account for any success reported;
- different studies recruit samples from different populations, making comparison difficult, and casting doubt on the generalisability of study results, particularly when samples are recruited from clinical populations (see Widom 1988);
- populations are rarely large (e.g., the caseload of an agency caseload) and samples are rarely selected randomly (see Widom 1988). Both factors result in skewed and unrepresentative samples and again limit the generalisability of results;
- the variety and combinations of interventions used make it difficult to isolate 'effective' components or identify trends (see Oates and Bross 1995);
- a range of methodological weaknesses within studies, such as attrition (see Macdonald 1998);
- a preponderance of studies (particularly from the United States of America) with clients whose difficulties are markedly less serious than those with whom child care professionals typically work, and where work is undertaken in more controlled settings than those available to most helping professionals.

Many of these problems arise because of the complexity of this area of work, and genuine ethical and technical problems inherent in child protection research. Restriction to only those studies which avoided or minimised these problems would be ideal, but as will become clear, this would probably be premature given the paucity of rigorous research currently available to us. Certainly, the best must not be made the enemy of the good, but equally we cannot afford to disattend to the issues, and be all-forgiving and all-inclusive. Warm glows can be had from such an all-inclusive stance, but this will not result in improved services.

VALUES AND PROCESSES IN OUTCOME RESEARCH

This book is primarily concerned with outcome studies, rather than studies which examine the processes of intervention. Of course, these are not mutually exclusive categories, as will become clear from subsequent chapters, but some aspects of work merit particular consideration, because of their fundamental role in social work practice.

Those employed in welfare agencies are, in my experience, typically principled individuals who take seriously the need for careful scrutiny of the assumptions and values they bring to the helping process. Particularly important features of contemporary practice are issues of empowerment, client participation, and anti-oppressive practice. These concepts increasingly appear in the aims and evaluations of child protection research. Important though they are as principles of good practice, they require us to be clear in *what* we mean when we use these terms, *how* they relate to effectiveness, and *how* they should be evaluated, whether as an end in themselves (as might well be the case if one is endeavouring to develop a culturally-appropriate and anti-oppressive form of service provision) or as a means to an end (as might be the case if we were to hypothesise that user participation will increase attendance and behavioural change in a parents' group). In evaluative research it is particularly important that behavioural evidence of 'values' is made explicit and potentially measurable. This can be illustrated with a brief discussion of two tenets of practice which appear particularly common in the literature, user participation and empowerment, and which frequently appear both as important 'ends in themselves' and as strategies for ensuring relevance of, and participation in, programmes of intervention, thereby enhancing chances of effectiveness.

User Participation

For the most part, the participation of users in decisions and plans that affect their lives is an issue of good practice. Undertaken on a community level, such participation can enable people fundamentally to alter the perception of problems often held by professional staff (Beresford and Croft 1993; Striefal *et al.* 1998). The involvement of user groups has also shifted research agendas in definitive ways. Specificity and clarity are what we should be striving for in research terms, followed perhaps by research which endeavours to assess the relative efficacy of interventions which give more or less weight to these aspects, and consumer surveys of the usefulness of interventions aimed at empowerment and participation.

The Alameda Project (see page 6) provides an example of the importance of participation in goal attainment. As we have seen, this large-scale randomised controlled trial sought to ascertain the effectiveness of intensive, highly structured forms of intervention in facilitating permanency plans for children drifting in foster care. One of the most significant interventions made by the project workers was to spend time with the parents of children in care, helping them decide which outcomes they wished to pursue (adoption, return home, etc.) and then doing their best to address the problems that needed to be overcome in order to realise these well-debated objectives. At the end of the project, one of the findings was that those parents who had wanted their children returned but had failed to realise their aspirations (goals not attained, court refused recommendations) felt that they had been treated well. That is, the typical view was that social workers and others had done all they could, and so clients felt they had been given a fair chance. This effect also facilitated alternative plans for the children involved.

Empowerment

Empowerment is a particularly slippery concept when it comes to evaluation (Macdonald and Macdonald, 1999a). What successful empowerment looks like will depend upon a number of things, including how the concept is operationalised, the context in which the work is undertaken, and so on. One very concrete definition of empowerment is one which ensures that users are provided with services which workers can justify in terms of their evidence base, which have a clear rationale, and in relation to which workers can state clearly how it is anticipated that these services will achieve the desired outcomes. This kind of information maximises user choice, and gives service-users a means by which to hold workers accountable for their involvement in their lives.

Empowerment, partnership, and self-esteem are just three of a number of important concepts in practice which have something of a Rorschach quality, meaning different things in different contexts. They are often emphasised by researchers, but few provide direct evidence of change in problems or issues of concern, and this needs to be treated with caution by consumers of research.

ORIGINS OF STUDIES

It will quickly become apparent that by far the largest number of outcome studies conducted in the area of child protection are from the United States, and this raises the issue of comparability and relevance of study findings to the U.K. and other countries.

This apparent bias reflects the state of play with regards to evaluative research in child protection and highlights two major differences between the U.K. and the U.S.A. In the latter, the government has formally recognised the extent and significance of the problem of child abuse and neglect (National Research Council, Panel of Research on Child Abuse and Neglect 1993) and the impact of poverty on children's health and welfare (Comprehensive Child Development Program, authorised by Congress in 1988), and taken steps to address both, at federal and state level. Secondly, although more money is spent on development than evaluative research in the United States, they nonetheless enjoy a stronger tradition of *rigorous* evaluation (see Striefal *et al.* 1998).

In drawing on material from the United States, especial attention has been paid to the question of transferability to the other contexts, with particular reference to the legislative, organisational and professional context of the U.K. The argument that is often made is that the origins of studies limits the transferability of results to other policy contexts. For some social interventions this may be true: for example, in relation to interventions aimed to increase clients' access to work and income support, where the aims of social policy may have important implications for the relevance or replicability of certain strategies to the U.K., or elsewhere. This is least likely to be the case where inter- or intra-personal interventions are concerned, particularly where these are based on empirically validated theories of human behaviour, such as social learning theory. The principles of social learning theory, for example, which make a central contribution to our understanding of child abuse and neglect, are universal in their application. They are about how human beings acquire (or fail to acquire) certain skills, attitudes and patterns of behaviour, in which cultural expectations form one important environmental factor to be taken into account. The interpretation of research findings and their application need to be culture-, gender- and class-specific, but their validity is not intrinsically threatened by changes of government, or geographical borders. Similar arguments are tenable with regard to therapeutic interventions.

The identification of specific problems, differences or difficulties, generally highlights a need to tailor approaches, rather than constituting a reason, either for ignoring them or 'writing them off' as inapplicable. Such issues may underline the need for policy context-specific evaluation and development, but that would be appropriate wherever an approach was originally tried and tested. This is particularly important when one is looking to generalise from a 'demonstration' project, with the particular motivational properties (for workers and users alike) of something new, scarce, and (therefore) special. Having given this issue particular thought it seems likely that there is more in the reporting of interventions that 'grates' than in the studies themselves. So, for example, if it was a choice between a U.K. body of research, and a U.S.A. body of research, then U.K. practitioners *might* be able to make a case for the primacy of the former (in the U.K.) all things being methodologically equal. However, this is not the case. Most research studies reported in English language journals are American. In these circumstances, we have an ethical obligation to be critical consumers of what evidence there is, to take from it what we can, and to adjust what we need to in order to tailor messages from this research to our own circumstances, and then evaluate the results—as rigorously as possible.

It is probably easiest to take this course in areas of secondary and tertiary prevention, insofar as the majority of these interventions are of the kind described above. It is more problematic at the level of primary prevention, as the social and service contexts are very different, and may impact more directly. But even here we do draw on this material because there *are* points of comparability, and the American literature provides examples of preventive efforts that we should consider, or at least bear in mind when reflecting on our own endeavours.

3

EVIDENCE-BASED PRACTICE

The possibility of evidence-based practice rests on a number of things. First, investment in good quality research. Secondly, access to reliable summaries of the available evidence. Thirdly, the ability of practitioners to make use of that evidence in their assessments and intervention plans. Fourthly, the ability to implement or commission the skills and services indicated by such summaries; and finally, the ability to carefully monitor and review the progress of individual cases. The previous chapters considered the relative merits of different kinds of research and the particular challenges facing researchers working in this particular area. This chapter considers the remaining elements, focusing particularly on the preparation, maintenance and accessibility of reliable summaries, or *systematic reviews*.

LITERATURE REVIEWS

It is not only when considering single studies that we need to consider things like 'bias' or 'error'. Error and bias can also bedevil attempts to identify the overall trends across several studies. Bias can invalidate attempts to summarise research studies in a number of ways:

- Firstly, it can influence the ways in which studies are identified in the literature, for example, by limiting searches and the inclusion of studies to English language sources.
- Secondly, a reliance on a single method of searching, e.g., electronic searching, can result in the non-identification of large numbers of relevant studies (Dickersin *et al.* 1995).
- Thirdly, bias can enter into and influence decisions regarding which studies to include and which to exclude. Having decided to accept only a particular form of study (for example, randomised controlled trials or

quasi-experimental studies) it is easy to lower one's evidential threshold when faced with a dearth of such studies in the literature—a particular problem in child protection research. Further, there is a natural human tendency to be more methodologically forgiving of studies which support a preferred or favoured view than with those which do not. Relying on experts in a particular area is not necessarily the answer to such problems. Experts may be less objective than non-experts and may, for example, give undue weight to research they themselves have undertaken relative to research done by others. Similarly, experts often have strong opinions about the focus of their work, which can lead them to judge evidence differently according to whether it supports their beliefs. We are often more susceptible to these pushes and pulls because few professionals are trained in the kinds of critical thinking skills which can help to minimise their impact, either as a reviewer or as a consumer of reviews (see Macdonald and Sheldon 1998). They are also hard to identify (or even, perhaps, to be aware of) because in the traditional literature review one is not expected, nor indeed required, to spell out how one approached the task; what search strategy one used; what studies were included and excluded and for what reasons, and so on.

Such sources of bias can combine with simple human error seriously to undermine the confidence that can be placed in many of the literature reviews currently available in this field. The result is that what at first sight appear to be useful summaries can in fact be flawed and misleading representations of the 'state of play'. Some examples of these 'worthy but could do better' reports are provided later, together with exceptions. The latter represent a different approach to summarising research findings.

SYSTEMATIC REVIEWS AND META-ANALYSES

These issues of bias and error are not unique to our field, or that of health care (where considerable efforts are now being made to limit its influence— the Cochrane Handbook 1999). J.E. Powell, writing about problems in a field a thousand miles from our own (classical Greek) but identifying an identical problem, and in the footsteps of his mentor, A.E. Housman, denouncing 'in savage footnotes' sloppy scholarship (Auden 1967—Collected Shorter Poems).

'The way in which Lockwood, the previous year, had addressed the manuscripts of Aristophanes in the British Museum, would be futile, even if treated intelligently; for it assumes that six manuscripts out of 240 are likely to have individual importance or to be closely related among themselves from the simple circumstance of their being conveniently accessible together in the British Museum.' (Heffer 1998, p. 45)

Although a relatively recent development, methods are now available which enable reviewers to apply scientific principles to the synthesis of research (whatever their field). Reviews produced in this way are generically referred to as systematic reviews. When augmented with statistical analyses, they are typically referred to as meta-analyses.

Transparency has already been emphasised as an important component of evidence-based practice. Such a 'pinning to the mast' of decisions regarding such matters as a search strategy, or what studies to include, is one means of minimising reviewer bias. Systematic reviews require reviewers to state clearly their decision-making rules for each stage of the process at the outset (transparency). Therefore, readers are provided with information about (i) the ways in which the reviewers identified potential studies (the search strategy); (ii) the criteria they used to determine whether or not a study met their inclusion criteria, (iii) the details of excluded studies; (iv) the criteria used to judge methodological quality (study validity); (v) how studies were subsequently weighted; (vi) the ways in which data were extracted, and (vii) how these were combined and analysed. Readers are therefore in a position to make some judgement about the faith they can place in the conclusions of the review, to make a judgement about its relevance to their clients and/ or work setting, and indeed to take issue with the reviewers if this seems appropriate. Should they wish, they can 're-run' the review and check its reliability.

The problems identified earlier that are associated with more traditional narrative reviews are highlighted in one overview of treatments in child sexual abuse (Simpson 1994) and another, more extensive overview of interventions in child maltreatment (Becker *et al.* 1995). Simpson's literature review (1994) of 'selected sources' in the area of child sexual abuse (Simpson 1994) was intended 'to inform the development of a comprehensive and co-ordinated strategy on the treatment of child sexual abuse—addressing the needs of child and adult survivors, adult perpetrators and children and adolescents who abuse'. The review is essentially a summary and critique of studies illustrative of different kinds of approaches to work with child survivors and adult survivors. Simpson described her literature search as follows: an extensive literature review of established texts, recent new texts, and selection of articles from contemporary journals (1990 onwards). The rationale was that in reviewing such a cross section

'the established texts will allow evaluation of the major, perhaps more tradi-tional treatment approaches, the new texts will allow evaluation of the more contemporary approaches, and the journals will reveal innovative and experi-mental approaches. The journal articles in particular reflect an international rather than British perspective, which is important given the generally accepted notion that some countries, *e.g.* the U.S.A., are more advanced in terms of treat-ment approaches.' (Simpson 1994, p. 3)

This is a rather extreme example of a constellation of potential sources of bias that systematic reviews are designed to minimise. Simpson, aware of the importance of scientific methods, is concerned about how few attempts there have been to apply these to the outcome of therapy in this field (Dempster and Roberts 1991). However, rather than start from the premise of what would count as acceptable evidence (or—ideally—the best available evidence), she argues that we must 'begin to make sense of the existing work in order to build on it'. Simpson concludes that few studies showed promise and some (notably psychoanalytically derived therapies) suggested deterioration effects. She is appropriately critical of the studies she summarises, but the way in which the review was undertaken makes it difficult to know what prescriptive value to place on her conclusions. We do not know, for example, how the picture might change if the review were comprehensive rather than illustrative, or if it covered developments on record in non-English language sources.

An example of an apparently more rigorous review, which yet fails to make explicit the premises on which it draws its conclusions, is that of Becker *et al.* (1995). This review—the work of a Child Abuse and Neglect Working Group of the American Psychological Association—purports (i) to map extant research on both the short- and long-term effects of child physical abuse, neglect, psychological maltreatment and sexual abuse, and (ii) to review outcome research of interventions aimed at child victims and adults who were abused in childhood. Although the authors rightly comment upon the methodological limitations of research in the field, they fail to demonstrate any adherence to rigour in their overview, except to highlight evidence from experimental studies—where these exist. Even here, however, no information is given as to how these studies were identified, how they were assessed for methodological quality, or how the data from various studies were managed. Indeed, the general sense is that this review was not at all systematic. Therefore, although Becker *et al.* conclude that there is evidence for effectiveness of interventions in a number of areas, their conclusions do not command the confidence that an enterprise of this kind needs in order to be secure and worthwhile. The time-consuming task of preparing research overviews, together with their potential importance in informing busy practitioners, make it essential that we rethink the basis on which these are produced. The consequences of misinformation make the technical quality of reviews, as well as single studies, an ethical issue.

There are, as yet, few systematic reviews in the field of child protection, but this situation is changing. Where they exist, this volume draws heavily upon them. Elsewhere, it seeks to provide an overview of studies relevant to a particular aspect of prevention, drawing primarily on studies which are at the most rigorous end of the methodological spectrum, taking care to highlight any problems which should signal the need for a degree of caution regarding the confidence that we can place in the results. Where there appears to be a noteworthy and promising trend, as defined in a number of high quality studies of interventions which suggest a consistent pattern of findings, these are also signalled. As indicated earlier, some studies are discussed which have not yet been so rigorously evaluated (including some which have no comparison group) but where their rationale is logically consistent at a theoretical level, backed by a empirical findings in related areas, and where preliminary evaluative data are promising. Such non-experimental studies are often a first port of call in exploring the effectiveness of particular interventions, and are important as indications of promising approaches.

The search strategy for this review was to use search terms such as: abuse, emotional abuse, neglect, maltreatment and sexual abuse. Such a broad approach was used (i.e., sensitive rather than specific) because it was designed to identify high quality studies relevant to our understanding of child abuse and neglect, from all the fields with a potential contribution to make, as well as those evaluating the effects of particular kinds of intervention. The several thousand 'hits' this produced in databases such as Medline and PsychLit were then screened for relevance, and full articles, books or chapters were secured. References that appeared in articles or books were then followed up. Therefore, although the field is replete with studies which are relatively weak in their design and implementation, it is hoped that little of the rigorous studies which were being primarily targeted were missed. Throughout studies were favoured which have the following features:

- researchers make explicit their understanding of the issues with which they are concerned;
- report provides detailed information about the intervention (either by reference to an available text or within the study) that would permit replication;
- authors say clearly why and how the intervention is expected to impact upon the problem(s) of concern;
- authors provide an adequate description of the methodology used;
- authors provide a detailed account of their sampling procedures;
- authors make explicit the rationale for their choice of control group, where randomisation was not used;
- report demonstrates that the control group (if used) was matched on relevant variables (as far as these can be known);
- researchers use standardised measures of relevance to the issue (including real-life indicators);
- reports reveals an appreciation of the limitations of the research design, including sample size, attrition, data analysis and so on;

- studies which are of close or passing relevance to the U.K. and to the problems with which staff are most concerned.

Some of the studies (and reviews) have relevance to more than one issue. There are some areas of practice where it has not been possible to identify any rigorous evaluative research, but where there are studies whose rationale appears sound and preliminary data, or data from studies using non-experimental research designs, look promising. Sometimes, particularly with examples from the United States, evaluations are in progress. Examples of these are included when preliminary data from staff and users suggest there is something worth developing—and therefore evaluating rigorously.

EVIDENCE-BASED DECISIONS

On one level it is a truism to say that the quality of a decision made in child protection can only be as sound as the rationale underpinning it. But it is here that one of the major challenges to evidence-based practice lies. On first acquaintance the research base pertaining to the understanding of child abuse (of all kinds) is of bewildering complexity. Theories abound. Research is conducted within a range of disciplinary contexts, with contributions by psychologists, geneticists, sociologists, social policy analysts and economists (amongst others), each emphasising the role played by factors within their field of study. One temptation is to see these strands as sources to choose between, and it is not unusual to encounter colleagues who view child abuse through one particular theoretical or disciplinary filter. Another is to assume that all are compatible and complementary, and simply 'pick and mix' as appears fit. The view taken here is that neither approach is compatible with an evidence-based approach to assessment and intervention (see Macdonald 1998).

THEORIES OF CHILD ABUSE AND NEGLECT

Despite the emphasis placed in practice on the use and integration of research and theory, surprisingly little attention has been paid to the fact that the way we are led to see the world, or choose to see it, fundamentally influences our responses to it. For example, if we think that early childhood experiences of abuse increase risk, we may take a different view of the likely outcome of case in which both parents were abused as children, than if they were not. The lives and well-being of thousands of children were influenced by the significance attached by the helping professions to Bowlby's theories of maternal deprivation. It was a very long time before Rutter's critique of this work persuaded many that the issues were—at the very least—more complex (Rutter 1972). How we conceptualise abuse and neglect, our beliefs about what accounts for the development and maintenance of patterns of maltreatment, and what consequences we think will follow, will all impact significantly on the assessments we make and the decisions which follow from them. Therefore, the 'choices' we make in terms of our understanding of the causes of child abuse and neglect will have a significant effect on the decisions we make and the interventions we choose.

Examples are available from any area of welfare intervention, whether it is child protection, mental health or criminal justice. Policies towards young offenders have shifted considerably as the perceived causes of such behaviour have changed from lying with lax parenting, family breakdown, criminogenic tendencies, or poverty and diminished life-chances. Such views are, of course, not unrelated to dominant ideologies and political preferences, and when professionals act out of step with these they risk the displeasure of politicians, as is evident in the British public's response to the news that persistent offenders had been sent 'on Safari' (on the 'diminished life chances' model of offending). Even if effective in eliminating further offending, the idea that this might be achieved by anything remotely pleasurable is unlikely to meet with public approval.

In child protection we are similarly replete with theories and perspectives. The choices we make are just as likely to be influenced by chance factors as by the quality of the underpinning evidence. For example our views of the causes of parental ill-treatment may be influenced by who and what we are exposed to during training, as well as our personal experience and beliefs. The nature of the problem is encapsulated in the following list which appears in an introductory volume on child abuse and neglect:

- Ethnological and sociobiological perspectives
- The psychodynamic perspective
- Behaviourism and learning theory
- Family dysfunction theory
- Sociological perspectives
- The feminist perspective
- Children's rights.

These alternatives appear in a chapter entitled *Alternative Theory Bases in Child Abuse*. The author is not alone in taking such an approach (which in this instance may reflect the editorial brief), and will remain anonymous. The underlying assumption is that theories provide equally valid alternative ways of viewing the world. However, two things suggest otherwise. First, and simplest, whilst some perspectives are complementary, some of these theories are inherently contradictory and cannot be espoused at the same time, at least not by anyone who wishes to make even a modest claim to clear thinking. To believe one is to regard the other as invalid. This is not to say that, for example, psychodynamic theories and learning theories are not grappling to understand and explain the same phenomena, but that their formulations are not compatible. The rationale often presented for a multiplicity of theories (even those that appear to contradict one another) is the fact that because human behaviour is complex we surely need lots of different explanations to capture the reality of its different parts (distinctions between theories, perspectives, and empirical data are often glossed over). There is a different view, which Dingwall succinctly presents as follows:

> 'Child-abuse research . . . has many of the characteristics of a pseudo-science, "a kind of wish-fulfilment, enabling people to discover what they would like to believe" (Blum 1978). Feminists discover that it is all an expression of patriarchy; utopian socialists that it is a perversion of capitalism; conservatives that it is a symptom of moral decay.' (Dingwall 1989, p. 49)

At times one has to make a choice. We must aspire to something better if we are not to be stuck with what one author has referred to as a *knowledge-pile* rather than a *knowledge base* (Sheldon 1978). The question is, on what basis should one opt for one theoretical approach rather than another? This takes us to the second reason why we should regard some theories as having stronger claims on our attention than others, *viz.*, their empirical status.

EVIDENCE-BASED CHOICES

As yet there is no consensus as to how competing theories should be evaluated, both within disciplines and in terms of their respective contributions to understanding. This is true both of theories and research which purport to *explain* human behaviour and social problems, and those which make claims in respect of securing desired changes—*effectiveness*. In the absence of agreed ground rules as to how one *should* make choices, such a 'laissez faire' approach to knowledge leaves workers with rather more professional freedom than is probably justified by our current knowledge base. This situation is made more serious by the predominant location of child protection within bureaucratic structures in which management—even when concerned with quality audit and assurance—is preoccupied with process, rather than content. *What* one chooses to do, *how* one chooses to formulate a problem, are rarely challenged.

The argument made here is that, as with outcome research, the *method* and *methodological quality* of research underpinning theories should be a determining factor in evaluating their relative merits. Now it is of course not unusual for theories to predate empirical support, and therapeutic theories and methods often develop from clinical practice before their empirical base is established (see Teasdale 1993). Similarly, we are sometimes confident about the efficacy of an intervention long before we understand the mechanisms of its effects (see Elwood 1997). However, empirical testing plays an important part in both the development of theories and of evidence-based interventions. Medawar puts it as follows:

> 'Scientific theories begin . . . as stories, and the purpose of the critical and rectifying episode in scientific reasoning is precisely to find out whether or not these stories are about real life.' (Medawar 1982)

Some theories, e.g., psychoanalytic theories, have never been submitted to such a process, and yet continue to exercise a major 'pull' on professional practice. Medawar again:

> 'We are still so deeply steeped in the tradition of which [William] Blake was one of the founders, that we find it difficult to realise that the intensity of the conviction with which we believe a theory to be true has no bearing upon its validity, except insofar as it produces a proportionately strong inducement to find out whether it is true or not. Some theories have enjoyed an unduly long lease of life because of a certain, dark visceral appeal.' (Medawar 1982, p. 17)

So evidence-based practice requires not just the minimisation of bias in the evaluation of the effects of interventions, but in research which aims to make sense of the development of social problems such as those which contribute to child abuse and neglect. This requires a rigorous attention to methodological detail and research design. Here is how one experienced researcher put it some years into a successful career in this field:

> '. . . as I re-read the early essays on child abuse, and even some of the current essays which purport to document numerous psychological traits associated with child abuse, I find profiles of my students, my neighbours, my wife, myself and my son. It would almost seem that some of these researchers are right when they conclude that child abusers are a random cross-section of the population. However, their research does not tell us anything. Because control groups were not used, there is absolutely no basis upon which to draw any conclusions whatsoever.' (Gelles 1987, p. 203)

Prospective studies, with control groups where appropriate, are as important in laying the foundations of evidence-based practice, as are rigorous outcome studies (see Chapter 1). The two should, in an ideal world, have a reciprocal relationship, and clearly do in some areas. Part B of this volume endeavours to present an overview of research relating to our understanding of child abuse and neglect, with regard to such methodological considerations, and discusses these particular issues in more detail.

IMPLICATIONS FOR TRAINING

Clearing the methodological undergrowth is only a first step towards improving the evidential base on which we intervene in the lives of vulnerable people. We need other things too. We need to engage professional educators and validating bodies in a debate about the content of professional curricula. It is often possible to predict the theoretical preferences of qualifying workers from information about where they have trained (see Marsh and Triseliotis 1996 for an example from social work). At present, many courses socialise students into ways of working and seeing the world, rather than into strategies for critically analysing the quality of evidence that comes their way, and which they use (or not) as the basis for decision-making. Once these alignments have taken place, they are difficult to change. One of the things which differentiates occupations such as clinical psychology and social work is that there is a very intimate relationship between what we do and how we do it. That is to say, whatever therapeutic approach we use, we implement it in the context of a relationship which itself is an important mechanism of influence and change. Often we make a considerable investment in developing skills within a particular framework which then becomes a 'second skin'. It is much more difficult (both emotionally and practically) to move away from one mode of practice to another, particularly if this entails a completely different way of viewing the world. This is in contrast to some health interventions where it is relatively simply to change one prescribing pattern to another, or where programmes are more detached from the people delivering them. Here, much of our professional identity is invested in what we do, and the methods *we choose*. Consider the advice of the editor of a Training Pack for Child Protection Advisors, produced by the National Society for the Prevention of Cruelty to Children in 1990, which had commissioned a narrative overview of research in the field at that time:

> 'Suppose, for example, we adopt a very strict criterion and consider only those methods which have been tested using the protocols of experimental research. We will quickly discover that they are very few in number and restricted almost entirely to behavioural techniques which train parents to use less abusive forms of discipline (or, more generally, make available a wider range of parenting skills).' (Paley 1990, p. M-3-1)

The particular antipathy that has existed about cognitive–behavioural approaches is addressed at a later point. A combination of professional socialisation, personal investment and a scepticism (to put it mildly) about the status that should be accorded experimental methodology can place considerable obstacles in the path of developing an evidence-based approach to policy and practice, particularly when the trends do not set easily to received wisdom.

CRITICAL THINKING SKILLS

One way forward might be ensure that all qualifying courses equip their students with the skills of critical thinking (see Gibbs and Gambrill 1996) and the ability to evaluate their own practice (see discussion of single case designs in Chapter 1). Systematic attempts have been made to do this with regard to social work training in the U.S.A. (see Reid 1994; Gambrill 1997), although the impact on practice has yet to be rigorously evaluated. Such developments are rare within the U.K. Local authorities in the South and South West of England have been engaged in a training programme to introduce their qualified staff to the skills necessary to critically appraise research studies, and early signs are that this has been well-received by staff (Critical Appraisal Skills Project Report 1999).

THE ORGANISATIONAL CONTEXT

Child protection agencies and academics responsible for training professional staff need to think seriously and strategically about the bases on which they wish their policies and practices to rest, and the contribution that good evidence should make to these. They need to consider what degree of professional freedom is or is not appropriate in particular circumstances. It is not that one wishes unduly to curtail either academic freedom or professional autonomy, but there is some evidence that not all service users currently receive the best help that they might because of the decisions of individual practitioners or the approach of particular agencies ('the answer is family therapy, now what's the problem?') and this presents important ethical questions which any accountable profession must take seriously and address appropriately.

KNOWING HOW TO

Knowing 'what works' is not sufficient to do what works, particularly for those whose training did not equip them with the skills necessary to implement particular approaches. This is again something that those responsible for curriculum design and for continuing professional education policies should address with some urgency. As will become clear from this volume and as is apparent in the wider literature, some of the most promising interventions require knowledge and skills that are least often found on the curricula of qualifying courses, particularly in social work. As well as making changes here, one must also address the 'remedial' training needs of large numbers of already qualified staff.

FINALLY

This chapter demonstrates that there are a number of difficulties to overcome in developing an evidence-based approach to policy and practice in child protection, besides the availability of good quality evidence of what might constitute an effective response to any of the range of problems associated with child protection. Good quality evidence, such as that produced in systematic reviews, is unlikely to be sufficient in itself to guarantee appropriate changes in practice—even if we could ensure that those who needed it had easy access to it. But it is a necessary place to begin. This then is the starting place for the following summary of research trends in our understanding of child abuse and neglect, and the identification of what appear to be effective approaches to intervention. Hopefully, it will provide a stimulus to the preparation of many systematic reviews which focus attention on particular interventions or problem areas.

PART B
Child Maltreatment

4

FACTORS ASSOCIATED WITH CHILD MALTREATMENT

In endeavouring to determine the relative contribution of different factors thought to be implicated in abuse and neglect, some researchers have designed studies in which they strive to hold certain factors constant in order to assess the relative impact of others. Twin studies provide a good example of rigorous attempts to disinter the relative contributions of genetic factors from environmental influences in conditions such as mental illness or aggression. Such studies make an important contribution, and form the basis of a good deal of our current knowledge about the range of factors that appear to be implicated in child maltreatment (see Table 4.1 further on). However, the problem with a simple correlational approach to interpersonal behaviour is that it sheds little light on important dynamic factors. Put simply, despite the strength of the correlation between some factors and abuse or neglect, we still do not know which families are at risk. For example, why is it that despite a strong correlation between poverty and neglect, this does not hold for most families? What factors protect in dire circumstances? How do we begin to assess whether a particular family with whom we are working is more likely to fall in to one category (neglectful) rather than another (non-neglectful)? What makes some parents and children apparently resilient to environmental stresses that have deleterious effects on others? Are there, as yet, the beginnings of confident answers to any of these questions? This book provides some answers to these, and other questions.

INTEGRATIVE APPROACHES

In response to the limitations of research which concentrates on single factors associated with maltreatment, and in order better to understand the interplay between various factors—often operating at different levels (personal, interpersonal, cultural etc.)—a number of writers have proposed frameworks for developing appropriate research questions and research strategies, organising research findings, and using these to develop appropriate responses (e.g., Bronfenbrenner 1979; Sameroff and Chandler 1975; Cicchetti and Rizley 1981). They emphasise four things:

(i)   the dynamic contribution of genetic, biological, psychological, environmental and sociological influences, and their cumulative impact over time;
(ii) the fact that some factors increase the risk of abuse, whilst others exert a protective, or insulating effect;
(iii) that some factors can have an enduring impact, whilst others can be different from time to time or transient;
(iv) that an understanding of abuse requires that we examine the interplay of factors at different levels of analysis: the individual level (e.g., parents and children); the family; the community, and the society whose cultural values and beliefs serve to perpetuate maltreatment (see Belsky 1993). They therefore afford a means of integrating research findings from a range of disciplines, with due regard to their empirical status. This is generally referred to as the human ecological framework.

This framework helps us to understand why it is that families who are apparently similar in many key aspects can differ in their responses to stress, or in their general ability to provide adequate parenting. For example, a parent who has him- or herself received good parenting, and is therefore able to understand and empathise with his or her child, may well be able to exert more self-control in the face of extremely difficult behaviour than someone who is less able to place themselves in their child's shoes, *or* who may be inclined to make negative attributions ('she's doing it deliberately to annoy me. . .'), *or* who themselves have had very poor experiences of parenting leaving them ill-equipped to handle conflict, *or* who is under financial stress.
Such frameworks help us to do four important things.

- First, they emphasise that in order to understand how some adults come to abuse children one needs to look beyond neat singleton factors to the range of influences which research suggests shape and trigger abusive behaviour. Minimally this requires scepticism of 'grand theories' which purport to explain everything (e.g., psychodynamic theories), and a cautious consideration and use of perspectives which in some incarnations endeavour to interpret all data through one particular filter e.g., feminist perspectives.
- Secondly, they highlight the importance of *process*, that is, how factors interact, and why single studies might sometimes suggest that, for

example, poverty is a factor associated with neglect, whilst others draw different conclusions. Checklists of so-called risk factors do not lend themselves to summative interpretation (i.e., the more factors, the more risk). Risk factors, particularly those from different 'categories' (e.g., environmental, interpersonal) interact in a range of ways, with some factors acquiring force over time, and others having more the characteristics of straws breaking the backs of already over-burdened camels.

- Thirdly, they direct our attention to the strengths and strategies which appear to protect some individuals from engaging in abusive behaviour despite sharing many of the circumstantial and personal characteristics (or 'risks') that seem to precipitate it in others, and protect some individuals who are mistreated from the deleterious consequences which beset many others. These factors are only rarely the focus of research, usually via the analysis of longitudinal data sets (see the previous chapter) and are more often the focus of community-based interventions than more 'clinic-based' ones.
- Fourthly, it emphasises the centrality of assessment to effective work in child protection. The principles of a good assessment are presented in Chapter 11. The guiding principle should be that assessors consider the range of factors which research suggests may be implicated, and how these interact in a particular family. This should facilitate an hypothesis (a problem-formulation) describing how certain factors are thought to have interacted to produce abuse *in this family*, and—almost by implication— where the focus of intervention should be.

In short it seems that (i) a range of factors can play a causal role in child physical abuse, (ii) some factors are 'proximal' i.e., operate in the 'here and now' or are of recent origin, whilst others are 'distal' and/or have a more cumulative effect e.g., early childhood separation; (iii) some factors may exert a protective influence and act as 'buffers' against the deleterious effects of adverse events e.g., a supportive adult partnership or social network, and (iv) the dynamic interplay of all factors means that the significance of one set of variables depends, to some extent, on the presence or absence of others.

Table 4.1 provides a résumé of factors that have been implicated in child physical abuse and neglect. The majority are included either because they enjoy some empirical support from longitudinal studies or from controlled studies (in which abusive or 'high risk' parents are compared with 'matched controls'). Some are based on studies which are less secure (e.g., retrospective studies based on samples which may not be representative). An important point to emphasise is that this is *not* a list of factors, each of which is known to exert a causal effect, or directly to elicit abuse. The folly of such an approach is evident from even a brief consideration of its implications. Rather, they are factors which, in various dynamic relations, at times

Table 4.1:   Factors implicated in potentiating abuse

Levels of influence	Significant factors	Relevant studies
Sociological	Cultural and social values, particularly views of the family, marriage, and the status of children	Garbarino 1996
	Racism	Tulkin 1972
	Social and educational resources e.g., day care	Pransky 1991
	Legislation	
	Social systems for identifying and managing abuse.	
Environmental 1	Poverty	Drake and Pandey 1996; Elder 1974
(Social)	Housing	Quinton and Rutter 1984a
	Employment/unemployment	Steinmitz and Strauss 1974
	Parental status	Pelton 1981; Zuravin and DiBlasio 1996
	(age, single/couple/step-parent)	
	Family size	Young 1964
	Social isolation	Seagull 1987; Bishop and Leadbeater 1999; Kotch *et al.* 1999
	Stress	Thompson 1994
Environmental 2	Parent-child interactions	Biringen and Robinson
(Familial)	(number, valence, kind)	1991
	Discord between carers	Strauss 1983
	Child Behaviour	Azar and Bobar 1997
	Aversive management style	Oldershaw *et al.* 1986
	Family history	Patterson 1982
	Stress	Simons *et al.* 1992
	Aggression (parent or child)	Patterson 1982
	Domestic violence	Edleson 1999
Genetic	Gender	Elder 1980
	Temperament (child)	Thomas, Chess and Birch 1968
	Disability/chronic illness (child or parent)	Belsky and Vondra 1989
Biological	Prematurity/low birthweight (child)	Klein and Stern 1971
(bio/genetic)	Developmental delay (child)	Zigler 1980
	Learning disabilities (parent or child)	Feldman 1998
	Physical disabilities (child)	Ammerman *et al.* 1988
	Mental illness (particularly maternal depression)	Radke-Yarrow & Klimes Dougan 1997; Weinber & Tronick 1998
	Substance misuse (parent)	Luthar *et al.* 1997
Psychological	Developmental history (prior abuse; early separation)	Chichetti and Toth, 1995

Table 4.1: *(continued)*

Levels of influence	Significant factors	Relevant studies
Psychological *(continued)*	Attachment (adults to children)	Crittenden and Ainsworth 1989; Azar 1997
	Parental perceptions/expectations of children	Azar and Rohrbeck 1986; Newberger and Cook 1983
	Parental attributions of children's' behaviour	Sameroff and Feil 1985
	Negative affect (parent)	Crittenden 1993
	Parental empathy	Bugental *et al.* 1989
	Parental self-esteem	Crittenden 1992
	Parental self-efficacy	Cohler *et al.* 1970
	Locus of control/impulse control	Bandura 1977
	Child management skills	Olds 1997
	Conflict resolution skills	Campbell 1995; Azar *et al.* 1984

(perhaps over time), conspire to increase the chances of abuse or neglect occurring. Some, such as a parent's own experience of parenting, may exert a long-term or 'distal' influence, whilst others, such as a child's behaviour, may exert a more immediate or 'proximal' and 'transient' effect (see Maccoby and Martin 1983). The impact of any factor will depend on the presence of others, and the interaction between them. Where applicable, the final column of the table provides examples of relevant studies, and more comprehensive reviews or overviews which address these issues include Belsky 1984, Milner and Dopke 1997; Belsky and Vondra 1989; Campbell 1995; Kaufmann and Zigler 1989; Rutter 1989; Wolfe 1985. Many of these factors are discussed in more detail when the rationale behind particular approaches is reviewed in following chapters. The next section reviews one research study which has endeavoured to map these dynamic effects in a longitudinal, prospective study—The Minnesota Mother–Child Interaction Study (see Pianta *et al.* 1989).

THE MINNESOTA MOTHER–CHILD INTERACTION RESEARCH PROJECT

Prospective, longitudinal studies enable us to begin to understand how and in what circumstances these factors interact to potentiate abuse. Their strength lies in their ability (i) to examine the antecedents of maltreatment in a predictive fashion, (ii) to identify those factors associated with the development and maintenance of less than adequate parenting and (iii) to identify those factors which appear to discriminate at-risk groups who do not go on to abuse or neglect their children, thereby giving us some insight into protective factors or factors associated with resilience (see Heller *et al.* 1999). Most importantly, these studies allow researchers to identify the social and psychological processes which might explain why it is that some factors act in a protective way, or how a particular constellation of factors lead to particular kinds of maltreatment. The study presented in this section, and referred to at several points throughout this book, is a rare example of such an approach. Although it focuses solely on the parenting of mothers (a common problem in this area) it nonetheless affords an example of the kind of research we should be investing in, and provides useful information about mothers who are often primary carers, and the intergenerational transmission of abuse.

Egeland and his colleagues (see Pianta *et al.* 1989) conducted a prospective, longitudinal study of 267 first-time mothers in the U.S.A. At the time of enrolment on the study their children were considered at risk for maltreatment due to economic disadvantage (these mothers were reliant on public assistance clinics for their antenatal care). Comprehensive multiple assessments of child and parental competence were conducted at birth and at regular, scheduled intervals throughout the children's early school years. The researchers conceptualised maltreatment with reference to the parameters of care-taking that enhance the optimal development of children:

> 'It has been a consistent finding in the parenting literature that predictable, available, sensitive, and responsive caretaking within a structured and organized home environment enhances the development of children.' (Maccoby and Martin 1983) (Pianta *et al.* 1989, p. 224)

Maltreatment was therefore defined as the extent to which parents deviated from this pattern, both quantitatively and qualitatively. The researchers identified a range of maltreatment patterns, ranging from a global identification of inadequate care (used at year one to identify inadequate mothers), to more specific subtypes of abuse, including physical neglect (used at two years and six years). By the time the children were twelve months old, thirty-two mothers were identified as seriously maltreating their infants, eleven of whom had been referred to child protection agencies. Examples of signs leading to such a classification included: untreated wounds, no place for the child to sleep, leaving the child unsupervised and exposed to hazards. Their progress over time was compared with that of 33 other mothers, drawn from the same 'high risk' sample, but who were considered to be providing adequate care (determined on the basis of direct observation in the home). These two groups were compared on a range of variables and the researchers conclude that the data justify the attention given to maternal characteristics in maltreatment;

> 'In general, mothers in the abusive group were younger, less educated, and less prepared for pregnancy and they differed on a wide variety of personality and

attitude measures (Egeland and Brunnquell 1979). However, a particularly salient variable that discriminated the good from maltreating caretaker was a measure of 'psychological complexity' (Cohler, Weiss, and Greenbaum 1970) that tapped the mother's understanding of and relationship with the infant.' (Pianta *et al.* 1989, p. 225)

By 'psychological complexity' the researchers mean the mother's understanding of her infant's needs and of her relationship with the child. This confirms other work which suggests that a parent's understanding of parenting, their feelings about it, together with their own level of emotional development, are important mediators in determining the impact of environmental and other stressors (Newberger and Cook 1983, Sameroff and Feil 1984).

The study suggested that maltreating mothers did not differ from the comparison group with regard to overall levels of stressful life events, but appeared to cope with these in an angry and ineffective fashion:

'maltreating mothers were characterised prenatally by their relatively high levels of anxiety, aggression, dependence, and defensiveness a well as being less well aware of the difficulties and demands of parenting. These high stressed mothers who maltreated their children appeared to cope with stress in an angry and ineffective fashion. The stressful life events appeared to permeate every aspect of their lives and were not isolated to specific situations.' (Pianta 1989, p. 225)

Continuity of Abuse and Neglect

The experience of abuse and/or neglect in childhood is commonly considered to increase the risk of a person becoming an abusive or neglectful parent themselves. Further, one of the challenges in decision-making in child protection is assessing the longer-term implication of a particular constellation of events and behaviour patterns at one point in time for a child's safety and well-being. This particular project, because of its longitudinal nature, affords us some insight into the nature of continuities within childhood and the relationships between early childhood experiences and later ones. The researchers tracked the quality of relationships across a six year period. The following is a summary of some of their findings.

At Two Years

By the time the children were two years old the number of mothers classified as maltreating their children had increased to forty-four. This included twenty-three of the original thirty-two mothers identified as providing inadequate parenting when their children were twelve months old—an overlap of 85%. Five of the original thirty two families—whom the researchers describe as 'characterised by extremely chaotic households and parental psychopathology'—had dropped out of the study. The four families who were not classified as maltreating their children at age two were accounted for by the fact that two had been placed out-of-home (one adopted and one placed with a grandmother) and two were still being maltreated, but by their father rather than the mother. At this stage the researchers were using four categories of maltreatment:

- *physically abusive.* In this group mothers ranged from those who engaged in frequent and intensive physical punishment (e.g., severe spanking) to unprovoked outbursts leading to serious injuries e.g., cigarette burns.
- *hostile/verbally abusive.* Mothers in this group found continual fault with their children and were harshly critical of them. The authors describe these mothers as constantly berating and harassing their children.
- *psychologically unavailable.* Some mothers appeared only to interact with their children when absolutely necessary, were generally unresponsive and often passively rejectful. They gave no indication of enjoying their relationship with their child.
- *neglectful.* Mothers who appeared irresponsible or who appeared unable to manage the day-to-day tasks of parenting were categorised as neglectful. Children whose mothers fell into this group were often not adequately cared for or protected.

Mothers were categorised on the basis of direct observation in the home, during laboratory-based tasks or by self-report. All of the mothers were known to child protection services and cross checks were made with the relevant files. These forty-four mothers were compared to another group of mothers identified as good caretakers ($n = 85$), generally described as providing responsive, sensitive caretaking. The distribution of maltreatment across kinds of abuse was as follows: physically abusive ($n = 24$) hostile/verbally abusive ($n = 19$), psychologically unavailable ($n = 24$) and neglectful ($n = 24$). The numbers in each category exceed forty-four because most mothers clearly fitted more than one category. One clear implication is that for most children, experience of more than one subtype of abuse will be the rule rather than the exception. The relatively high prevalence of maltreatment in this group (some 16%) is thought by the researchers to be attributable to the fact that maltreatment was defined more broadly in relation to the parameters of good parenting (rather than the criteria for referral to child protection services), to the fact that the sample was chosen for its 'high riskness' and to the fact that the researchers got to know the families so well over the period of the study, and therefore obtained information on the quality of care that would not normally be available. The implication of this is that the problem of maltreatment is probably much more prevalent than available data suggest (Garbarino 1992).

At Six Years

At six years the authors identified forty-seven mothers who were mal-treating their children by the time they were six years old. Twenty-four of these mothers had been identified as providing inadequate parenting when their children were age one year. Of these twenty four, seventeen were deemed to fall within at least one of the maltreatment groups at the six year point (71%). Three of the remaining seven who were not classed as mal-treating are accounted for as follows; one was living with a grandmother, one was in paternal custody, one had been adopted. A further three had been dropped from the maltreatment group because they were no longer technic-ally maltreated due to the fact that in two cases the mothers were seriously mentally ill, and in a third the mother had moved state and was refusing continued participation having been charged with killing her second child (the study focused on first-borns). The authors conclude that because the reasons for these children no longer living with their mothers were partly attributable to their mother's inability to care for them that a figure of 71% probably represents an underestimate of the degree of continuity of maltreatment. This study also reminds us that child abuse and neglect can, and does, result in the death of large numbers of children each year (see Reder and Duncan 1999; Sanders *et al.* 1999).

At this time the researchers identified the children again as subject to *four* categories of abuse. Physical abuse, psychological unavailability and neglect-ful remained, but at this point they dropped the category of 'verbally abusive and hostile'. This decision was taken because (i) this category had proved to be the most subjective and had the highest degree of overlap with other categories, particularly physical abuse, (ii) the researchers did not have the opportunity to conduct standardised observation sessions as they had when the children were 12 months old. This meant they could not collect com-parable data on 'verbal interactions' and these conceptual and methodological problems persuaded them to drop this as a separate form of maltreatment. At this stage they added the category *sexual abuse*. Using these categories, the distribution was as follows: physical abuse ($n = 16$), psychologically unavail-ability ($n = 16$), neglect ($n = 17$) and sexual abuse ($n = 11$). At this stage maternal behaviour within these categories was epitomised as follows:

- *physically abusive*. In this group mothers continued to use excessive physical punishments and to engage in unprovoked violent outbursts. These mothers were so categorised on the basis of self-report, direct observation and cross checking of child protection records.

- *psychologically unavailable*. Similar patterns of interaction (or non-interaction) were noted at this stage as at year two. By age six, women often reported that they did not like their children and would rather not have to care for them. The researchers noted an appearance of depression and listlessness.
- *neglectful*. Lack of supervision marked this group of mothers whose children were frequently left alone for long periods of time or in dangerous situations—essentially being left to fend for themselves at an age when they did not have the necessary skills e.g., making their way in the city, feeding themselves. Homes were typically unsanitary and children were physically neglected.
- *sexual abuse*. This group was identified via maternal reports and liaison with child protection services. The researchers summarise the range and extent of abuse as follows:

'Two of the children in this group were abused sexually by their mothers, five children had experienced direct physical (genital) sexual contact with an assortment of older (male) family members, and four had experienced sexual contact with older (male) children. In each case the perpetrator . . . was at least in the teenage years.' (Pianta *et al.* 1989, p. 230)

These mothers were compared with a control group of sixty-five carers drawn from the original eighty-five identified at year two, having excluded from the original group any mothers where there was any question of maltreatment. Although there was marked continuity in the number of mothers maltreating their children at age six who had been identified as so doing during the first year of their child's life, the overlap between maltreatment categories was less marked and the pattern of maltreatment had shifted. Whilst roughly one third of mothers who were neglectful and/or psychologically unavailable to their children at year two, remained so at year six, this held for only 21% ($n = 5$) of physically abusive mothers. The authors conclude that the former categories may represent more chronic conditions than physical abuse, but note that the small sample size, and the overlap of categories make this far from certain.

In general terms, the majority of women identified as maltreating their children at age two years continued to maltreat their infants at age six. Nothing predicts behaviour like behaviour in this and virtually all other client groups. Of those who were no longer identified as maltreating, the majority were excluded for reasons that were associated with maltreatment e.g., their children were no longer in their care because of inadequate parenting, abuse and neglect. Those that remained in the study (and classed as non-maltreating) were described by the authors as 'at best marginal caretakers' (Pianta *et al.* 1989). Those whose parenting improved, attributed the improvement to the quality of their relationships with partners, and this perception was confirmed by those interviewers who had known the mothers throughout the study. Changes in the quality of these relationships was seen to have a direct bearing on mothers' caretaking abilities.

Antecedents to Abuse and Neglect

On the basis of the data collected on all participants (control groups and maltreating groups) throughout the six years, the authors identified the following antecedents to abuse and neglect:

General Observations

1. Maltreating mothers consistently differed from their control groups with regard to the emotional support they experienced from significant others in their lives e.g., husband, boyfriend, family members, friends.
2. Lack of social support and insularity characterised all types of maltreatment.
3. Between years two and six, households in which physical abuse, neglect and psychological unavailability were identified were characterised by greater life stress at several assessment points.
4. Homes in which sexual abuse occurred were marked by extreme forms of stress. The researchers noted extreme disorganisation and chaos, frequent moves, physical abuse of the mothers by husbands and boyfriends coupled with extreme dependence of mothers on them, and maternal substance misuse. The researchers are not sure in which direction these factors interacted. That is to say, it may be that general life stress left mothers unable to protect their children from sexual advances by older males, or that their personal histories and lack of interpersonal competence led them into relationships with men in which they, and their children were victimised.

At Six Months

1. Women in the physically abusive group were assessed as more tense, depressed, angry and confused than the control group.
2. Mothers in the neglect group were more tense, and anxious, and less intelligent than the control group.
3. Women in the 'psychologically unavailable' group were more tense, depressed, angry, and confused than the controls.
4. Mothers of children who had been sexually abused were also more tense, depressed, angry and confused than controls.

At Thirty Months

1. Maltreating mothers showed less interest in, and knowledge about, their child's development, as indicated by responsiveness, involvement, and provision of appropriate play materials.
2. Physically abusive, neglectful and psychologically unavailable mothers engaged in more restrictive care-taking practices.
3. All groups, but particularly those in which neglect and sexual abuse occurred, had lower scores on a scale measuring the global quality of the home environment (HOME).

At Six Years

1. At six years, *physically abusive mothers* were more tense, depressed, angry and confused than the control group mothers, according to their scores on the Profile of Moods Scale (POMS—Caldwell *et al.* 1966). Other measures indicated they were more depressed, less intelligent, more anxious and more likely to act impulsively and in an extreme fashion.
2. *Neglectful mothers* were more tense (POMS) and appeared less intelligent than control group mothers, thinking more concretely than control group mothers. Compared with control group mothers they were generally more sceptical of relationships and more emotionally unstable.
3. *'Psychologically unavailable' mothers* were more tense, angry, depressed and confused (POMS).
4. *Mothers of children who had been sexually abused* were similar to 'psychologically unavailable' mothers in that they were also more tense, angry, depressed and confused (POMS) than control group mothers. However, these mothers were also deemed to be more calculating and more restless when compared with control group mothers.

Pianta *et al.* (1989) conclude:

> 'The pattern of differences between the control and maltreatment groups on personality and mood variables indicates that, collectively, these are experiencing marked emotional turmoil. The measures on which they differed from the control group suggest that these mothers felt threatened by interpersonal demands placed upon them and perhaps were unable to establish any type of intimate relationship in which mutual interdependency and trust are crucial to adaptive functioning' (Pianta 1989, p. 238)

The size of the final sample, at six years, meant the researchers were not able to use statistical techniques to assess the extent to which particular combinations of the factors listed above might be predictive of particular forms of maltreatment. Instead they could only look at their relationship to maltreatment overall. They found that maternal emotional instability was the best predictive factor, followed by home environment (which, as the authors point out, is by definition 'highly deviant'), support and stress levels, maternal IQ and negative mood state. Using another statistical technique (discriminant function weighting) the authors say that these factors accurately predicted 83% of the total number of cases, with 87% of control group mothers and 75% of maltreatment group cases accurately classified. This means that 25% of the actual maltreating mothers were wrongly classified as non-maltreating ($n = 5$). Similarly, 13% of non-maltreating mothers were wrongly classified as maltreating ($n = 5$). The authors rightly warn that in order for these results to be applied in any screening procedure the results would need to be validated in a further, much larger sample.

Those who Change

The authors were interested to see if it was possible to distinguish between those groups of mothers whose maltreatment continued, and those who moved out of a pattern of maltreatment to adequate parenting. Again, because of the small sample sizes it was not possible to examine such continuities and discontinuities with maltreatment types, but they were able to undertake some preliminary analysis based on the combined data from all maltreatment groups and the control groups. They also warn that, because of the difficulties inherent in identifying maltreatment and the risks of misclassification, this is a very tentative exercise. That said, their analyses suggested that those mothers who were maltreating at two years, but not at six years, differed in the extent to which they had become more outgoing and personable, more mature and less reactive to their feelings, and were more realistic and better at problem-solving. Somewhat surprisingly, both those mothers who were classed as non-maltreating at the six year assessment point and control group mothers evidenced more stress and less emotional support than those mothers who continued to maltreat their children over the period of the study. The authors interpret this as evidence of the importance of maternal psychological characteristics as a mediator and differentiating factor between those mothers who continue to maltreat from those who do not. Interview data revealed that several of the women who had ceased to maltreat their children had participated in interventions directed at their parenting styles, which they had found supportive and nurturing. Other data testified to the importance of providing information about children's needs and giving clear guidance on how to meet these.

One of the measures used in the study, the 16PF (a personality inventory) suggested that those mothers who continued to maltreat their children differed from those who did not in two important areas: cognitive (they were less able to problem-solve) and social (they were less out-going, were more reactive to emotional stimuli). Insofar as these relate to perceptions and feelings about close relationships the authors hypothesise that this is further evidence that there is a link between a parent's internal working model of relationships and their ability to adequately provide for a child's developmental, psychological and emotional needs. This is a subject which is discussed further on pages 62–65. Insofar as these models may be developed in the course of early childhood experience, the authors then consider the relationship between a mother's own experience of parenting and the adequacy of her own.

Intergenerational Transmission of Abuse

Analyses of the data revealed that a mother's own childhood experience of maltreatment substantially increased her risk of maltreating her own children, although this did not match on to 'type' of abuse i.e., neglected mothers who maltreated their children did not necessarily neglect them; physically abused mothers who maltreated their children might neglect their own, and so on. The authors are careful to point out that although this pattern was true for a substantial number of mothers, there were also significant numbers of mothers who had experienced maltreatment in their childhood but who gone on to provide adequate care, raising the interesting question about the processes which intervene to moderate or exacerbate the impact of early childhood experiences. They discuss their findings in relation to attachment theory, which they see as providing an important means of integrating a range of research findings from research into abuse and neglect. Importantly, it suggests the processes whereby parents who have themselves been abused or poorly cared for, come to be at heightened risk of maltreating their own children. The contribution of attachment theory is discussed in some detail later.

OTHER STUDIES

Pianta et al.'s findings concerning intergenerational continuities and discontinuities are reinforced by Rutter's overview of this and other relevant studies (Rutter 1989). Rutter's own follow-up study of ninety-four girls admitted to one of two Children's Homes (run on group cottage lines) in 1964 because their parents could not cope, provided evidence of similar patterns of continuities and discontinuities, which appear to implicate other factors and mechanisms. Rutter and his colleagues compared these girls with a comparison group of 51 young people, randomly selected from the general area population who had never been admitted to care and who were living with their parents. Rutter's summary and discussion are well worth careful attention, and highlight the complexity of this area. The study suggests the following:

(i) Experiences of minor parenting problems that are *not* associated with generally poor psychosocial functioning (in parents) are not associated with intergenerational transmission of parenting problems.

(ii) Experiences of bad parenting may be a necessary antecedent for the development of severe parenting difficulties, but they are not a sufficient condition. Current social circumstances and current experiences of support from partners are also influential.

(iii) The more substantial the experience of poor parenting the greater the risk of poor parenting being passed to the next generation. This effect appears to represent a 'knock-on' effect in which one experience of adversity exposes children to others. Rutter provides the example of parental deviance (defined as 'a criminal record in adult life, psychiatric treatment, alcoholism or dependency on "hard drugs"') which carries a genetic risk factor and also results in a 'hostile, discordant environment leading to disrupted parenting and then admission to an institution' (Rutter 1989) which carries its own 'risk load'. Thus, no single life experience is decisive. Rather, each one influences the likelihood and the impact of others. As Rutter puts it:

> 'developmental continuity lies as much in social connections between different forms of adverse environments as in any internal effects on the child's own personality development.' (Rutter 1989, p. 340)

This may account for the fact that early behaviour problems were highly correlated with poor parenting.

(iv) Those in poor social circumstances were more likely to evidence poor parenting (whether in the control group or in the group *looked after*). Poor social circumstances (e.g., lack of basic facilities, overcrowding) were more prevalent amongst those mothers who had been *looked after* than controls (suggesting that some childhood experiences of adversity placed one at risk of poor social circumstances). When social circumstances were held constant, those *looked after* were more likely to evidence poor parenting. Rutter concludes that poor parenting is associated with parenting adequacy independently of social circumstances, but that the latter (whether in the control group or in the group *looked after*) amplifies its effect.

(v) The role of marriage (or partnership) was similar, and stronger in its effect. In brief, a good stable partnership with a non-deviant man exerted a strong protective effect. In exploring the meaning of this association Rutter notes that 'planfulness' ('choosing' a partner as part of a longer-term life-plan) was a significant variable which generalised to other areas of activity. It seems that women in the *looked after* group were much less likely to have planned their marriage than those in the control group (defined as having known their partner for at least six months before co-habitation and making a positive decision to marry— compared with marrying for 'negative' reasons such as an unplanned pregnancy). However, this did not explain away the association as it appears that women who had not 'planned' their relationship, but who 'struck lucky' with their partner or spouse, benefited equally as much as those who had been more 'intentional' in their actions. Similarly, those who had planned but not found themselves living with someone who was supportive were as vulnerable as those who had drifted into a long-term relationship for less than positive reasons.

(vi)   In endeavouring to answer the question: 'why did some women plan their lives, whereas others seemed just to drift from adversity to adversity without any attempt to alter their life situations?' (Rutter 1989), Rutter highlights the protective role of positive school experiences. It seems that participants in this study could be divided according to their experiences at school. Those in the *looked after* group who had had a positive experience were more likely to have a good outcome but this did not differentiate between those in the control group. This, Rutter suggests, is evidence that positive experiences often act as a buffer *only* in the face of adversity.

(vii) Studies can only examine the impact of factors about which they have collected data. Recognising that this study (as indeed any study) may be ignoring other important protective factors, Rutter reflects on the mechanisms whereby these protective factors may exert their influence. He draws attention to research which stresses the importance of feelings of self-esteem and self-efficacy in determining people's willingness and ability to deal with the day-to-day challenges of life. He speculates that for some girls with a history of adverse experiences, some experience of success (for example, indicated by positive memories of school, or significant relationships established whilst in care—an altogether rare occurrence, it must be emphasised) may not only dilute the impact of aversive experiences, but may also instil or develop a sense of competence and an ability to influence one's life.

Although Rutter is exploring a rather different set of mediators than those considered by Pianta *et al.* there is considerable overlap in terms of the constructs used to operationalise attachment theory, and this is discussed in the following section. Both attachment theory and research into the continuities and discontinuities of maltreatment, emphasise the importance of regarding parents, as well as children, within a developmental framework. Before proceeding to consider these aspects in more detail it is important to consider one of the weaknesses of the general literature, *viz.* the absence of data on fathers, and the implication of this for that research which is available, such as that conducted by Pianta, Rutter and their colleagues.

CODA: MOTHER-BLAMING?

It is important to end with one or two points on a matter of particular importance. Both Rutter's study, and that of Pianta *et al.* focus on mothers rather than parents. Pianta *et al.* are at pains to stress that they are not making a case for blaming mothers for maltreatment. Rather, they have focused on mothers as primary caretakers whose parenting is influenced by a range of factors, not least of all their own childhood experiences of parenting and their enthusiasm for attachment theory is partly due to its potential ability to account for a wider range of more immediate influences on behaviour in the current environment. They clearly encountered abusive fathers in the course of their study, and their focus on mothers was primarily because it was a study in which they were endeavouring to unpick a complex area, and test a particular integrative model of maltreatment. There is, in principle, no reason why their findings should not apply to fathers as well as to mothers, or at least be tested with a male sample. However, it is also the case that—as far as one can ascertain—similar work has not been replicated with a sample of male carers and the wider literature remains biased towards mothers. This is also true in outcome research. It would be a serious error, however, to dismiss the findings of such studies on the grounds that they have not included fathers, unless there are sound reasons for thinking that their exclusion (or lack of presence) invalidates the results and the conclusions drawn. Further, whatever we would like to believe about the changing roles of men, women currently continue to be the major providers of care to children. As Pianta and his colleagues point out, few if any of the mothers in their study would actively or purposefully maltreat their children, and many aspired towards more adequate parenting. A sound knowledge of the impact of a range of influences on the parenting capacities of mothers, and an understanding of the processes which mediate those experiences, are essential to an adequate assessment of family functioning, and to the development of strategies most likely to provide routes out of maltreatment towards 'good-enough' parenting. We may need more studies, and perhaps better studies, which involve fathers or partners, and we certainly need to develop a clearer focus on the role that fathers or male carers play in abuse and neglect, if only in their abandonment of mothers and children. However, the neglect of this area does not invalidate the findings of studies of the kind described here, which make an important contribution to a difficult area.

ATTACHMENT THEORY

Attachment theory originated in the work of John Bowlby, but has since been developed, empirically investigated, and reformulated by others (see Crittenden 1992; George 1997). It emphasises development in the context of relationships, and in particular considers the earliest relationship, that between a child and his or her primary carer, as crucial to future relationships. In its original form it was a marriage of concepts from psychoanalytic theory and ethology (see Suomi *et al.* 1976). It is the latter concepts that appear to have particular relevance to an understanding of maltreatment (see George 1997), particularly the principles of *protection* and *internal working models*.

The principle of *protection* is that the primary function of the child–parent relationship is safeguarding development and survival, and it is this which prompts such behaviour as proximity-seeking—a desire for the child to be near and under the eye of the parent and *vice versa*. Whilst the behavioural manifestations may shift, the overall goal of protecting the child, and being protected, remain unchanged. Thus, an infant may well crawl towards his or her mother if frightened, whereas at six years the establishment of eye contact reassurance is sufficient. Both devices, however, serve the same purpose, and are similarly prompted.

Internal working models are hypothetical constructs. They are thought to be the representations of the child–parent relationship that the child constructs on the basis of his or her experience with the parent(s), possibly from as early as 12 months (Bowlby 1969, 1973). It is this which is thought to inform an individual's expectations about him/herself and others. Relationships which fail adequately to protect or reassure, or are unpredictable, can lead to insecure or anxious, or disorganised attachments (see Howe 1989). These, in turn, will compromise the expectations that children have of themselves and others in later years. So, for example, women who have experienced maltreatment or rejection in their early relationships with primary carers may be more likely to enter adult relationships which elicit experiences which validate their perceptions of themselves and others (Sroufe and Fleeson 1986). Because early relationships shape what we understand and know about relationships, later ones are likely to replicate early ones. Poor attachment relationships may also account for some of the psychological characteristics which appear to differentiate maltreating from nonmaltreating parents. For example, insecure or disorganised attachments may be responsible for, or contribute to, emotional reactivity, mistrust, anxiety over competence, and depressed affect (Pianta *et al.* 1989). Of particular importance in child protection is the extent to which the child sees himself or herself as worthy or unworthy of care and protection, and the extent to which s/he sees others as available or unavailable to provide care and protection—essential building blocks of trust in others and a sense of self-worth. Within the model used by Pianta *et al.* it would appear that the internal working models or relationships that these children develop result in a set of expectations about themselves and others which place them at risk.

This conceptualisation gains credence from research which focuses on those women who, whilst maltreated as children, do *not go on* to abuse or neglect their own children. Two sets of findings are of interest. First, there is some evidence that the adverse consequences of mild maltreatment can be offset by the presence in a child's life of a loving, nurturing and supportive parent or parent surrogate (Egeland *et al.* 1984). In this study, these women also established good relationships with spouses and adult peers. Secondly, the evidence that women who received supportive help directed at parenting skills and which took into account their own childhood experiences achieved greater emotional stability and maturity (Pianta *et al.* 1989; Main and Goldwyn 1984; Ricks 1985; Zeahnah and Zeanah 1989).

There is therefore, growing evidence to support the hypothesis that the poor quality and content of the attachment relationship between maltreated children and their parents increases the risk of them becoming inadequate or maltreating parents. However, the mechanisms whereby these experiences exert their influence are still a matter of debate, and different researchers put forward different views. Measures of attachment are very much oriented towards young children, and it is increasingly difficult to judge what behaviours or ways of relating amongst older children or young people might be symptomatic of poor attachments. Traditionally, ideas have been informed by psychodynamic theory, suggesting, for example, that the entirety of a relationship resides within each individual, who then learns not only what it is to be a victim (for example, the recipient of abusive parenting) but also learns the role of the victimiser via observation. Researchers like Sroufe and Fleeson have suggested that because early relationships shape one's understanding and knowledge of relationships, they replicate early experiences in later ones. Thus,

> 'Both sides of these early relationships become validated when they later remain as victims in peer relationships and become victimisers of their own children as caretakers.' (Pianta *et al.* 1989, p. 248)

The prescriptive consequences of such formulations point to the need to alter the internal working models of parents, but afford minimal suggestions as to how this might be done. Such relearning may occur when women find themselves in relationships where they are valued and have an opportunity to relearn ways of relating in close relationships, but the implications for formalised intervention are less clear. At best they suggest the need for a relatively long-term therapeutic relationship in which the therapist endeavours to use the relationship to help a parent reconstruct their internal working models and integrate thoughts and feelings which may have become 'split off' in an attempt to cope with the demands of every day life (see Bowlby 1969 and 1980). However, there is limited support for such a formulation or for the effectiveness of such interventions. More importantly, children's lives run on a time-scale which requires that decisions and interventions be taken in a time-scale in keeping with their developmental needs. In the next Chapter we consider a model put forward by Sandra Azar which appears to have particular promise as a basis for designing effective strategies for intervening.

5

TYPES OF MALTREATMENT

This chapter considers those factors which appear to have some particular salience for specific kinds of maltreatment, but it does so rather tentatively. As should be clear from the previous chapter it is difficult to say with any confidence that particular factors will place an individual at risk of a particular form of maltreatment. A majority of factors appear to be associated with maltreatment *per se* and research is presently concerned with developing theoretical and conceptual frameworks which afford the most helpful explanations of their interaction and their effects. The use of attachment theory as an explanation for intergenerational transmission of abuse is one such development and is discussed below. However, in the following sections, particular types of maltreatment are discussed and consideration is given to those factors and relationships thought most important with regard to each, and their consequences for children. The chapter also addresses problems of definition and identification and the implications of these for practice and effective intervention.

THE PHYSICAL ABUSE OF CHILDREN

Definitions of Child Physical Abuse

The dilemmas in respect of defining and developing models to account for abusive behaviour towards children are immediately apparent when one considers debates about the acceptability of physical punishment (see Pediatrics 1996) and the relationships between physical punishment and abusive violence. Gelles (1991) has argued for a distinction to be made between the two (which does not imply that he condones the former), but some see violent abuse as one end of a continuum of violence, with actions like a 'slap' lying at the other. Some see physical abuse positioned at one extreme end of a continuum of disciplinary styles associated with normal parenting (see Azar 1989a; 1997), or as something qualitatively distinct, and attributable to factors such as disturbed attachments, which have fractured the parent–child relationship, resulting in 'abnormal' parenting (see Carlson *et al.* 1989). The choices one makes—and choose we must in the absence of compelling evidence in favour of one or the other—has major ramifications for policy and practice. The decisions we make determine the data we collect (whether as practitioners or researchers) and how we interpret them (Wolfkind and Gelles 1993); they determine the conceptual and theoretical models we develop to better understand and predict abuse, and the directions we look to find optimal strategies of prevention and intervention (Azar *et al.* 1998).

Factors Associated with Child Physical Abuse

It is well-recognised that a range of factors, operating at different ecological levels, interact to precipitate physically abusive behaviour in parents. However, the most useful models, from a practitioner's point of view, are those which suggest mechanisms whereby such factors interact to produce the inter-personal problems between parents and children which are the more immediate precursors to physical abuse.

Transactional or ecological approaches have already been discussed. These are approaches which place parent–child interactions in a wider familial and social context, which take into account both distal and proximal 'triggers' and 'protective factors' and which view parental behaviour in terms of a development framework (Belsky 1993). It is relatively easy to understand how poverty, poor housing, or conflict between adults can increase the risk of physical abuse to children within the family, and it is not difficult to understand how drug or alcohol misuse might do likewise. The more personal (i.e. a particular individual's history) and interpersonal mechanisms which set the scene for abuse, perhaps exacerbated by these other factors, have been less well understood, and this section explores some of these. This is not to suggest that other factors are less important, and indeed their special significance in primary prevention is discussed later (see Chapter 7). However, it may be that one can exercise influence at this transactional level, and that one may need to if one is successfully to prevent a recurrence of physical abuse. This section draws particularly on the work of psychologist Sandra Azar.

A Social Cognitive Framework for Understanding Child Physical Abuse

Azar and her colleagues argue the need for a model which both explains the aetiology of abuse and the developmental disturbances associated with it (Azar 1986, 1989b). She points out that optimal parenting involves more than simply an absence of abuse, and that abuse is only one of a number of forms of rejection and disengagement that can have adverse effects on a child's development. As one mother put it some years ago:

'I don't hit Johnny any more, but I still hate the son-of-a-bitch.' (Kempe and Kempe 1978)

Maltreatment can lead to insecure attachments of a child to his or her primary carer. Insecure attachment, whatever the cause, can produce 'internal working models'—relationships, expectations of others, and self-perceptions—which can be extremely damaging, and which can contribute to intergenerational transmission of abuse, amongst other adverse adult outcomes (see Ainsworth, 1980; Crittenden and Ainsworth 1989; also next section). Ironically, those most vulnerable are probably children whose abuse consists of, or incorporates, psychological maltreatment, as this is less easy to externally attribute to parental aberration, and more likely to be internalised as 'deserved'.

Azar and her colleagues argue that the disadvantage of traditional forms of attachment theory is that, at best, they lack prescriptive value when it comes to intervention. At worst, even reformulated versions imply that the remedy to parenting difficulties that arise from maladaptive forms of attachment may require long-term intervention focused on the parent's relational experiences (see Rogosch *et al.* 1995). For some parents this may be right, and many researchers highlight the need to focus on an abusive parent's own experiences of childhood. However, Azar suggests framing these phenomena in the context of social-cognitive theory, in which *relational schema* — cognitive processes which bias or guide behaviour—replace the less well-defined and less well operationalised *internal working models* proposed by attachment theorists. Both theories are coming from similar directions, with similar assumptions about the relationship between experience and behaviour and to that extent are complementary. However, the processes and mechanisms which feature in the former enjoy more empirical support, and have more direct implications for interventions which have been developed and evaluated, with promising results.

Relational Schema

As human beings we do not simply respond to stimuli, whether external or internal, we interpret them (Bandura 1977). In other words, if a child behaves in a certain way, our reaction will in part depend on how we see it, what we think has precipitated it, what its purpose is, and how appropriate it is. The appropriateness of our response will in part be a function of how accurate our interpretations are. For example, it is possible to completely misread a child's behaviour and respond inappropriately, as when a parent feels their child is 'deliberately trying to provoke' when the explanation may be much less emotionally charged. Further, most parents 'adaptively interpret' much of their children's behaviour—what family therapists might call 'reframing'— so that for example, resistance to a request may be interpreted as a sign of 'an independent spirit'. Most children depend on this 'benefit of the doubt' view of their behaviour, and it is probably an important factor in shaping pro-social behaviour (what cognitive-behavioural workers might refer to as *differential reinforcement*).

Cognitive theorists hypothesise that over time we acquire certain schemas particular to social roles, such as 'parent', 'child', 'self', together with scripts which detail the rules governing how people in such roles should operate and interact (Azar 1997). Schemas denote the particular ways in which people view the world, and themselves. Studies in experimental psychology show that, whilst schema facilitate the processing of information, this functional attribute is accompanied by a bias towards coding and retrieving schema-consistent information, at the expense of counter-schematic information (Robins and Hayes 1993; Goldfried and Robins 1983). Thus, the schemas of depressed people are, in essence, the converse of the 'rose tinted spectacles' of the optimist.

The point about schemas is that they are usually automatic, and rarely conscious. They serve a functional purpose in that they allow us to make 'automatic' and fast judgements, without which it would be very difficult to operate in complex, social situations. Through selective perception, they influence not just how we interpret what we see, but what we see in the first place. Thus, a parent who has developed a negative schema about her son's behaviour ('he is just out to annoy me') will be most likely to notice his 'bad behaviour' and least likely to see his pro-social or 'good' behaviour. Further, when the latter is noticed—or pointed out—it is likely to be interpreted as malevolent i.e. designed to have ulterior motives—'just being like that because he wants something'.

Schemas are themselves shaped by social and cultural norms and personal experience, of which our early relationships with primary care-givers are important, but not to the exclusion of other influences. Those whose child-hoods were abusive and neglectful, and for whom there were no 'protective' or 'remedial' relationships, may develop schemas about themselves (worthless, unlovable, a victim) and the role of parents, which make them vulnerable to treating their own children as they were themselves treated. Azar summarises the impact of schemas as follows:

> 'these schemas . . . shape our processing of the information we encounter in interpersonal situations . . . The sum of such processing colours our perspective on life generally. If our schemas about relationships and the self are positively toned and predictable, the world too is perceived as a safe and positive place where what happens is predictable.' (Azar 1997, p. 85)

As Azar argues, parenting is an active process of socialisation which involves the interpretation of children's behaviour. This interpretation is reflected back to children in ways which shape their behaviour and which makes a significant contribution to the schemas that children themselves develop. In other words, it has a developmental role:

> 'Parents must develop a fine-tuned ability to identify acts in their offspring as meaningful and worthy of response and to provide accurate and predominantly positively-toned information about the self, others, and the world. . . . Positively toned elements in schemas would include a sense of mastery, confidence in one's decisions, and a sense that the world is a relatively predictable (contingent) place. Schemas also need to be flexible, and the very processes involved in revising and reshaping one's views can also be modelled by parents.' (Azar 1997, p. 85–86)

Abusive parents appear to have acquired schemas that are far from positively toned or predictable. This appears to result in, or be accompanied by, a range of cognitive distortions that make it difficult for them accurately to interpret their children's behaviour, and to respond appropriately, in a child-centred way, to the challenges of parenting. Research suggests the following cognitive errors, or assumptions, that distinguish abusive from non-abusive parents:

1. Essentially, they demonstrate an inability to put themselves in their children's shoes (empathy, or 'role reversal').
2. They have unrealistic expectations of their children (Azar and Rohrbeck 1986).
3. They are less likely to track pro-social behaviour (Wahler and Dumas 1989).
4. Abusive parents display a negative attributional bias when interpreting their child's behaviour (Larrance and Twentyman, 1983; Johnston 1996).
5. They hold children more responsible for their behaviour and for bringing about negative outcomes (Larrance and Twentyman, 1983). Bearing in mind that a majority of physically abusive incidents occur within disciplinary contexts, the degree of responsibility attributed to children is important in that it may have a direct bearing on the severity of punishment meted out to them (Dix *et al.*, 1989).

6. They are more likely than others to judge their children's misbehaviour harshly (Chilamkurti and Milner 1993) and to see them as more deviant than other adults perceive them to be (Mash *et al.* 1983).

7. They are less likely to notice or respond to children's cues that they are in need (Crittenden 1981).

8. Abusive parents generally have less well-developed problem-solving skills (Hansen *et al.* 1989), and are generally less able to generate a range of potential solutions.

9. They are less adept at managing stress (Casanova *et al.* 1992) and establishing a support network (Lovell *et al.* 1992), and are more impulsive (Rohrbeck and Twentyman 1986).

According to Azar (1997) it is these cognitive deficits or distortions that increase the potential for anger, aggression, and inept responses in parenting, not least of all because children, especially young children, are frequently likely to infringe parental expectations. Such distortions also detract from the positive aspects of parenting. Abusive parents are less likely to engage in positive interactions with their children, and more likely to use negative, coercive, and rigid methods of control (see Patterson and Reid 1970).

Such parents are unlikely to afford their children the 'scaffolding' required to achieve mastery, and develop a positive sense of self, others and the world (see Meadows 1996). Such parents provide poor role models, are unlikely to adequately stimulate their children's intellectual development, and may increase the risk of children themselves acquiring maladaptive 'scripts' or schema. For Azar, these social-cognitive problems are core aspects of abusive parents, and are at the root of other skill deficits which have also been identified in abusive parents, *viz.*, poor anger control, child management problems, and difficulties in problem-solving.

This social-cognitive model makes sense of the fact that so much physical abuse takes place in the context of disciplinary incidents in which the boundary line between discipline and violence is often confused, both in the abstract and in practice. Reid *et al.* (1981) found that abusive mothers were only half as likely to be able to terminate their children's aversive behaviour immediately compared with other non-distressed mothers who succeeded 85% of the time. An inability successfully to end children's troublesome behaviour with non-physical means makes it more likely that one will resort, via threats, to physical measures which, as the emotional 'temperature' rises, are likely to become more severe and, for young children in particular, more dangerous. Azar's framework for conceptualising abuse explains why some of these incidents arise despite children's behaviour falling well within the realms of the 'normal'. It also suggests a series of cognitively-oriented intervention strategies which may be important not only in effecting change, but in ensuring that changes are maintained, and generalised to other situations in the future, and possibly extended to other children. It also broadens the focus of cognitive-behavioural assessment and intervention with abusive parents towards a more child-centred focus, essentially concerned with optimum child development, which is squarely in keeping with the general trends in research and in the field.

THE PHYSICAL NEGLECT OF CHILDREN

'Typically defined as an act of omission rather than commission, neglect may or may not be intentional. It is sometimes apparent . . . and sometimes nearly invisible until it is too late. Neglect is often fatal, due to inadequate physical protection, nutrition or health care. . . . In some cases, neglect slowly and persistently eats away at children's spirits until they have little will to connect with others or explore the world.' (Erickson and Egeland 1996, p. 4)

Whilst neglect is a frequently defining characteristic of the context in which physical abuse takes place, abuse has attracted most attention from researchers, policy makers and practitioners (Wolock and Horowitz 1984). For a considerable time, even when neglect was a primary focus of concern, this was most often because of physical signs such as accidental injury caused by inadequate care or supervision, or malnourishment. Now, however, in both the U.S.A. and the U.K., cases of child neglect appear to be on the increase. In the U.S.A., the National Incidence Study of Child Abuse and Neglect reported an overall rate of child maltreatment of 1 553 800 cases of demonstrable harm (as opposed to children deemed to be 'at risk'), of which over half—879 000— were cases of neglect (Sedlak and Broadhurst 1996). This same study suggested that the rate of neglect is increasing more quickly than that of physical abuse, with the latter increasing by about 45% between 1986 and 1993, whilst neglect cases increased by almost 100%. Similar patterns are occurring in the U.K. In a study undertaken by Wilding and Thoburn, of 349 child protection cases in one local authority, 64% were purely neglect related. A further 23% of physical abuse cases also included issues of neglect (Wilding and Thoburn 1997). It may be that the seriousness of neglect is once again seeping into professional consciousness, after a lengthy preoccupation with other, more dramatic forms of maltreatment. I say dramatic, but it is also the case that each year children die as a direct result of neglect. A series of public inquiries and Part 8 Case Reviews (see page 228) all testify to the role that neglect has played even in cases where children have died as a result of assault. The investigation into the death of Paul, a fifteen month old boy who was chronically neglected and slowly starved to death by his parents, drives home the potential physical dangerousness of neglect:

'He had lain in urine soaked bedding and clothes for a considerable number of days. Photographs taken after his death show burns over most of his body, derived from urine-stain, plus septicaemia, with septic lesions at the ends of his fingers and toes. In addition, he was suffering from severe pneumonia. It is impossible to imagine the level of suffering that this little boy experienced before his death slowly occurred. (The Bridge Child Development Service: 1995)

More commonly, neglect undermines children's development in ways that are irreversible. It robs them of happiness and security in their childhoods, and may have serious consequences for their adult lives, including their capacity to provide adequate parenting to future generations of children. This is because the threat of significant harm brought about by neglect is as much a function of its psychological impact on children's development, as it is a function of cumulative physical harm. Indeed, there is a growing consensus that the psychological consequences of all types of maltreatment provide a unifying link in their impact on the health and well-being of children and adolescents (Brassard *et al.* 1987; Claussen and Crittenden 1991; Cicchetti and Toth 1995). Evidence is also accruing that *severe and/or persistent* neglect may have a direct impact on children's developmental progress and may well be implicated in developmental delays of various kinds. Neglect is a particularly serious matter in child protection work. Professionals risk becoming immune to signs of inadequate care that is not visibly associated with physical abuse, and taking for granted such serious, long-term and life-chance compromising developmental consequences for children (see for example, The Bridge 1999). It is all too easy to see developmental delay as 'typical' of such disadvantaged families, assuming that problems which may be common amongst the children (or indeed the parents) are therefore 'genetic' rather than indicative of inadequate parenting. In these circumstances, we are unlikely to intervene as we would if similar delays or problems were noticed in our own families, or those of less obviously disadvantaged or 'problem' families. Neglect is probably the category of maltreatment which throws most starkly into relief what is at best a professional blind-spot and at worst a professional 'double-standard'. This desensitisation to the seriousness of neglect has been implicated in child abuse and neglect fatalities (see Bridge Child Care Consulting/Islingon ACPC 1995).

Definitions of Neglect

Attempts to define neglect have, to some extent, created as many problems as they have tried to resolve. Definitions vary according to the different roles and responsibilities of those proposing them, so for example, lawyers are likely to operate more exclusive and precise definitions than welfare workers, or non-neglectful parents (e.g., Polansky *et al.* 1985; Gaudin *et al.* 1996). Key differences arise depending on whether one views neglect from the perspective of the parent and parental behaviour, or from the perspective of the child (see Rose and Meezan 1997).

A Parental Perspective on Neglect

Taking the parent's behaviour as a starting point is likely to expand the scope of any definition of neglect. The assumptions underpinning the view that definitions should focus on parental behaviour are:

(i)   It is possible to identify behaviours which will bring about harm. Some think this is now the case (see Erickson and Egeland 1996) whereas others take a different view (see Besherov 1985 and Giovannoni and Beccera 1979).

(ii) Acts of commission or omission should be labelled 'neglectful' irrespective of whether or not they constitute significant harm or an immediate threat of significant harm. One reason put forward in support of this argument is that only in this way can society take into account the long-term consequences of neglect (see Kadushin 1988).

(iii) Intentionality matters. Parents should not be held accountable for things beyond their control, or which they do not intend. Others argue that intentionality is neither here nor there (see Dubowitz *et al.* 1993). For example, the adverse consequences of maternal depression, or lack of understanding of a child's needs are no less serious for being unintended by the parent.

(iv) Only by focusing on parenting behaviour can one do adequate justice to issues of cultural difference. Cultural factors play an important part in defining neglectful behaviour. For example, Garbarino describes how some Hispanic parents decline to place their infants in car safety seats because they fear they will feel abandoned (Garbarino 1991).

A Child-focused Perspective on Neglect

Taking a child's perspective and defining neglect in terms of its consequences on a child solves a number of problems.

(1) It resolves problems around establishing intentionality.

(2) It acts as a brake on the actions of over-zealous professionals who might otherwise intervene in situations irrespective of any obvious consequences for the child.

(3) Child-focused definitions more easily allow for individual differences in resilience, and other protective factors, but make it more likely that intervention will only occur in those cases in which there is immediate

and clear evidence of physical or emotional harm. This may expose children to longer-term or cumulative adverse consequences which are not identifiable in the short term (Ney *et al.* 1993).

In a review of selected literature on neglect, Rose and Meezan (1997) note that over time, there has been a shift from a focus on parenting behaviours *per se* to an increasing emphasis on the consequences for the child. Thus, there is less concern with home cleanliness and more about the hazards that particular levels of cleanliness might pose to a child's welfare.

Essentially, definitional dilemmas reflect varying perspectives on blame and accountability, and differences of opinion about when, and on what evidence, one should intervene on behalf of a child. Of course, it partly depends on what form of neglect one is talking about, and in the next section we consider various types of neglect, and describe briefly how they are conceptualised. Irrespective of definitions, diminishing child welfare resources mean that families referred for neglect are less and less likely to receive services unless and until the situation is severe. Some writers have pointed out that in America 'once (the) window of opportunity for preventive services has passed, our most widely used intervention is to pull neglecting families into the foster care system' (Duerr-Berrick and Duerr 1997). Once in care, neglected children stay longer than those placed for other reasons (Needell *et al.* 1995), and many others suffer the serious adverse developmental effects of neglect referred to by Erickson and Egeland (Erickson and Egeland, 1996; Wodarski *et al.* 1990). In the U.K., neglect—in the absence of other forms of maltreatment—remains the poor relation of child protection intervention. If the trends of extant research into intergenerational transmission of abuse are correct, this could represent a very short-sighted approach to the deployment of resources, as well as leaving unaddressed the needs of large numbers of children.

Types of Neglect

Neglect can take one or more of the following forms:

- *Physical neglect.* This is most well-known and easily recognised. It can mean lack of appropriate supervision, but most often covers the failure to provide adequate clothing, shelter, or nourishment i.e., a failure to cater for a child's basic physical needs. And of course, in relation to these last issues there is debate about the relative responsibilities of the individual and the society—which tends to lead one back to starting-point discussions about whether the State should intervene in the lives of families where children are being inadequately cared for by parents who find themselves unable to do so due to their socio-economic circumstances.

- *Emotional neglect.* In this volume this is treated as a separate category, partly because this reflects the distinction made in legislation, but also because it is one form of psychological maltreatment which is best dealt with in conjunction with emotional and psychological abuse. It highlights all the definitional problems referred to earlier, and these are discussed in more detail in the following chapter.
- *Medical neglect.* A carer's failure to provide adequate health care or medical treatment for their child(ren). This can include the withholding of medication or the refusal to allow essential surgery. It highlights particular tensions around the clash of religious beliefs with medical opinion, and the dilemmas of parental choice versus children's welfare.
- *Mental health neglect.* As yet, this is essentially an American concern, and refers to those occasions on which children may be deprived of appropriate interventions designed to address behavioural or emotional disorders (see Erickson and Egeland 1996; Hart 1987). In the U.K. this kind of 'neglect' is more likely to be perpetrated by wider social systems (in which help is not forthcoming), and an approach to professional freedom which does not constrain would-be helpers to use evidence-based approaches (see Macdonald 1998).
- *Educational neglect.* Children are deemed subject to educational neglect when they are denied services and provision deemed necessary for their development and well-being.

This volume does not address interventions aimed at redressing educational and medical neglect. It is concerned with problems of physical neglect, including issues of supervision, and research concerning the factors thought to be associated with physical neglect that form the focus of the next section.

Factors Associated with Child Physical Neglect

Problems in defining abuse also hamper research into the causes and consequences of neglect. They both undermine the usefulness of the limited research that has been undertaken to explore factors associated with neglect and attempts to identify optimum strategies for prevention and intervention (Aber and Zigler 1981; Gaudin and Dubowitz, 1997). Further, it is rare to find studies of the correlates of abuse which separate out different facets of maltreatment.

Most studies have explored the determinants of neglect alongside physical abuse, or have examined the antecedents of child maltreatment in general. These studies have sometimes attempted to disinter the particular correlates of different types of abuse, without success. The researchers conducting one of the better studies, the Minnesota Mother-Child Project, concluded:

'Overall, the maltreating parents differed markedly from nonmaltreating parents on many variables, but the differences by specific type of maltreatment were small.' (Erickson and Egeland 1996, p. 14)

In 1989, in recognition of the seriousness of the problem presented by parental neglect, and the paucity of good quality research that focused on this type of maltreatment, the National Center for Child Abuse and Neglect in America funded five studies of family functioning in neglectful families. These studies are quite large, explore neglect in ethnically diverse populations, and have a number of other strengths lacking in previous studies (e.g., comparison groups, multiple measures of key constructs e.g., self-esteem, neglect). However, despite these strengths, the five studies—like their predecessors—are fraught with methodological problems. These may account for some of their discrepant results, which suggest that in general, neglectful families do not clearly differ from non-neglectful or other high risk (e.g., risk for HIV) families. Here is the conclusion of two reviewers of these studies:

'The results . . . suggest that there exists enormous heterogeneity among neglectful families. No clear profile of neglectful family functioning is evident. The unique characteristics of each neglectful family must be recognised, and interventions must be tailored to their individual needs. . . . The results from the in-depth interviews with the neglect families in South Carolina . . . suggest the necessity of understanding the family members' own perspectives on their functioning, their strengths, and areas for improvement. Narrative and solution-focused interventions that emphasize strengths, competencies, and empowerment of families offer promise with neglectful families.' (Gaudin and Dubowitz 1997, p. 55)

Currently, then, research does not allow us to distinguish a particular set of factors which especially highlight families at risk of neglect, rather than, say, physical abuse. So, the many factors identified in Chapter 4 (see Table 4.1) can be implicated in incidents of neglectful parenting, in a number of ways. Given the recognition of the need to look at the interplay of a range of factors at different levels (the ecological framework) and our understanding of cumulative risk (Sroufe and Rutter 1984) this is perhaps not surprising. The search for more specific 'trajectories' may well prove elusive.

That said, amongst the factors listed in Table 4.1 (pages 42–43) poverty, social isolation and stress seem especially salient amongst social factors; of factors designated 'biological', mental illness (particularly maternal depression), substance misuse, and learning disability appear significant, as do the attachment histories of parents, their psychological maturity, their perceptions and attributions regarding children's behaviour and the quality of their relationships with their children (negative affect and empathy). Crittenden (1993, 1999) has suggested a useful way of conceptualising how and why neglectful parenting occurs, which is particularly helpful in terms of assessment and determining how to intervene. It also integrates a number of perspectives on neglectful parenting, including attachment theory, learning theory and cognitive psychology. The next section provides a brief summary of this approach.

Information-processing of Neglectful Parents

The impact of socio-economic factors on abuse and neglect is not to be trivialised, and is discussed in more detail in later chapters. The focus here is on the inter- and intra-personal factors associated with neglect. In the course of their report Pianta and his colleagues described the neglectful mothers in their study as follows:

> '. . . irresponsible or incompetent in managing the day-to-day activities and care of their children. Their responses to interview procedures indicated that they failed to provide for the necessary health care of their children. Observations in the home indicated that they did not provide adequate physical care and did little to protect the children from dangers in the home. For several cases, the children were observed to have extremely poor hygiene and appeared malnourished. Although these mothers might have expressed interest in the well-being of their children, they lacked the skill, knowledge, or understanding to provide consistent, adequate care.' (Pianta *et al.* 1989, p. 227)

Without undermining the importance of other factors, such as poverty and poor housing, Crittenden points out that, at an inter-personal level, there may be a number of reasons why an adult might not respond appropriately to a child. The absence of appropriate parenting skills may be one reason, and this is the rationale behind parent-training approaches. However, there may be other explanations, each of which may pertain to certain patterns of neglect, and which may have different implications for intervention. Let us take these in turn.

1. *A parent may fail accurately to perceive signals that indicate a child's need for attention.* This is particularly likely to occur in parents who are consistently withdrawn, depressed, or psychologically unavailable. It may also contribute to the neglectful behaviour of parents who are learning disabled. As Crittenden points out, diminished affect reduces the flexibility of an individual's response to his or her environment. Child-rearing is an inherently 'affective' experience, particularly when children are young, and a parent's failure to respond to a childs' affective signals (cries, smiles, touch, eye contact etc.) will depress such pro-social ways of behaving, and may eventually result in more aversive patterns of behaviour. This may reinforce the withdrawal of response from a reluctant parent. The end result is the negative cycle of interaction so often

noted by researchers in this field (see Wolock and Horowitz 1979; Crittenden 1988).

For some parents this kind of perceptual exclusion may be the consequence of their own early experiences with attachment figures. If one has not been loved, one may well cope by effectively excluding affective information about relationships from one's 'schemas' and from one's perceptual antennae. Several researchers have highlighted the links between being neglectful parents and having neglectful histories (e.g., Polanski *et al.* 1985) and have suggested that until the needs of neglectful parents are met, it may well be difficult to improve their responsiveness to their own children.

2. *A parent who perceives a signal, may nonetheless misinterpret its significance.* This may arise because the signal loses its value, perhaps through overuse. Crittenden gives the example of attention-seeking children who then have difficulty communicating 'real' need (as opposed to 'background noise'). Intermittent reinforcement (e.g., when a parent occasionally 'gives in') both exacerbates the child's behaviour and reinforces the parent's inclination to 'disattend'. Alternatively a parent may accurately interpret the signal but not see it as their responsibility (e.g., children who are left to 'feed themselves'), perhaps because of age-inappropriate expectations, or because of a belief that to respond would not be appropriate. Finally, parents who have learned to manage their feelings by limiting their expression, are likely to be made uncomfortable by the expression of feelings in others and may leave a child to manage on their own, and to contain them too. This may well form part of an intergenerational repetition of a means of reducing arousal (Eckman 1992).

Crittenden hypothesises three possible childhood routes to faulty attributions in adulthood. First, neglect may leave some children with no exposure to nurturing adults. Having survived its absence they may lack the empathy required to accurately attribute signals and respond to them. Alternatively a child may have had to inhibit their own feelings in order to meet their parents' demands for nurturing. This is one way of securing their parents' attention, but will most likely lead to anger and resentment, sometimes resulting in similar demands placed on their own children to care for them. Finally, some adults may have learned that nothing they do can elicit a predictable and/or loving response, and may continue to be similarly passive with their own children.

3. *A parent may fail to select an appropriate response.* Signals can mean different things, and may require different responses at different stages e.g., a baby's crying could mean hunger, or fatigue, or sickness. An appropriate response to a 10 year old will not necessarily be the same as that to a baby. This may arise through lack of knowledge or skill, and may indicate an inability to seek help, as evidenced by the finding that neglectful parents have very

limited and non-reciprocal social networks (Crittenden 1985; Polanski *et al.* 1985). Alternatively it may well reflect learned helplessness, as parents feel that no response will be effective.

4. *Having chosen a response the parent may fail to implement it.* It is not just a question of having the right response within one's repertoire (e.g., knowing how to play with a child) but also giving it priority over competing needs. Failure here may arise from an inability to prioritise children's needs over their own, or may be attributable to other pressing needs, such as the need to work long hours to make ends meet, or the demands of caring for an ill or disabled family member.

Crittenden's approach offers a useful structure within which to organise assessment and intervention in situations where children are subject to neglect. Her work underlines the importance of attending to the needs of neglectful parents in their own right, as a prerequisite perhaps to effecting changes in the parenting, and highlights the long-standing nature of some of the factors which may precipitate neglect. The idea that these can be remedied in the space of a very time-limited intervention is highly questionable, to say the least, and points to a need to reconsider many current practices in social services. Insofar as neglect is a frequent background factor in physical abuse, and appears to substantially increase the risk of physical abuse (see Ney *et al.* 1993), these factors may be relevant in the majority of child protection cases. Much of Crittenden's work is at a theoretical stage at present, and her ideas (though they stem from earlier research) require testing and developing. However, she points out that to date, our approach to neglect has not yielded much in the way of effective solutions, and these ideas suggest some inherently rational ways forward for some families and some forms of neglect:

> 'our dual perspectives of individual pathology and societal failure have not, in the past 30 years, led to effective solutions to the problem of neglect. A new explanation that can lead to new treatment techniques is needed, and the rudiments of one such approach are offered here. Possibly, these ideas will be sufficiently intriguing to initiate fresh thinking about child neglect. It is the most serious type of maltreatment and the least understood. Careful thought, new policies, and improved interventions can't come too soon.' (Crittenden 1999, p. 67)

PSYCHOLOGICAL MALTREATMENT

Definition of Psychological Maltreatment

This volume uses the generic term 'psychological maltreatment' to encompass emotional abuse and neglect. Some authors have argued the need to distinguish emotional abuse and psychological abuse (see O'Hagan 1995), but in the absence of a secure empirical or theoretical basis on which to do so, such a distinction is difficult to sustain. Attempts to distinguish the two generally rely on broadly similar categories of adult behaviour. Further, whilst at the extremes it is possible to identify patterns of abusive behaviour which adversely effect a child's emotional responsiveness, and those patterns of behaviour which are detrimental to a child's intellectual development, it is generally difficult to separate out these areas of functioning, or to 'ring-fence' certain behaviours as detrimental to one particular aspect of a child's well-being.

Typologies of Psychological Maltreatment

Interest in psychological maltreatment is relatively recent, and therefore is a somewhat under-developed concept (Garrison 1987; Crittendon et al. 1994; Crittendon 1996). As with neglect, a major focus of the literature is around problems of definition and its relationship with other forms of maltreatment, and the failure adequately to resolve these dilemmas partly accounts for the slow progress made in understanding the phenomenon, and in developing effective interventions or decision-making strategies.

Hart et al. (1996) have proposed a six-fold definition of psychological maltreatment (see Table 5.1). It provides an example of an approach which centres on parent behaviours, rather than on demonstrable consequences for children (although it is framed in such a way that it would be applicable to others, e.g., teachers). It also typifies the problems and issues with which researchers and practitioners are grappling, viz.:

(i) perhaps more than other forms of abuse, psychological maltreatment is culturally-bounded. What may be seen as desirable in one culture may be regarded a psychologically abusive in another. Where young babies sleep (alone or in their parents' bed) provides one common example; the role of older children in caring for their younger siblings is another. Further, the consequences of particular actions may vary according to cultural norms. For example, if every girl's movements are restricted, it may not be as psychologically damaging as it might be if one girl's movements were restricted in a cultural setting where this was generally not the case.

(ii) although some have argued for definitions which distinguish psychological from other forms of abuse (e.g., McGee and Wolfe 1991) others argue that this is not easy to do, and that psychological maltreatment often occurs in the context of physical abuse (Egeland et al. 1983; Garbarino and Vondra 1987; Herrenkohl et al. 1983) and neglect. For example, there is frequently a relationship between psychological maltreatment

Table 5.1: Typology of psychological maltreatment

Condition	Examples
Spurning	Belittling, degrading and other non-physical forms of overtly hostile or rejecting treatment. Shaming and/or ridiculing the child for showing normal emotions such as affection, grief, or sorrow. Consistently singling out one child to criticise and punish, to perform most of the household chores, or to receive fewer rewards. Public humiliation.
Terrorising	Placing a child in unpredictable or chaotic circumstances. Placing a child in recognisably dangerous situations. Setting rigid or unrealistic expectations with the threat of loss, harm, or danger if they are not met. Threatening or perpetrating violence against the child. Threatening or perpetrating violence against a child's loved ones or objects.
Isolating	Confining or placing unreasonable limitations on the child's freedom of movement within his or her environment. Placing unreasonable limitations or restrictions on social interactions with peers or adults in the community.
Exploiting Corrupting	Modelling, permitting, or encouraging antisocial behaviour e.g., prostitution, substance misuse. Modelling, permitting, or encouraging developmentally inappropriate behaviour e.g., parentification, infantalisation, living a parent's unfulfilled dreams. Restricting or interfering with cognitive development.
Denying Emotional Responsiveness	Being detached and uninvolved through either incapacity or lack of motivation. Interaction only when absolutely necessary. Failing to express affection, caring, and love for the child.
Mental, Health, Medical and Educational Neglect	Ignoring the need for, failing, or refusing to allow or provide treatment for serious emotional/behavioural problems or needs of the child. Ignoring the need for, failing or refusing to allow or provide treatment for physical health problems or needs of the child. Ignoring the need for, failing or refusing to allow or provide treatment or services for serious education problems or needs of the child.

and physical abuse e.g., 'terrorising' children. Indeed there is a growing consensus that many of the adverse developmental consequences of physical abuse, neglect, and sexual abuse, are psychological in nature (Youngblade and Belsky 1992; Cicchetti and Toth 1997).

(iii) psychological maltreatment is not necessarily intentional. For example, there is potential for 'indirect' forms of psychological maltreatment e.g., when children witness inter-parental violence, or threats against those they love.

(iv) although it is possible for 'one-off' incidents to cause long-term harm to a child's well-being (for example, witnessing a parent being murdered), in general it is the *frequency, persistence* and *duration* of such behaviour that appear instrumental in their adverse consequences, particularly when they occur in the context of hostile, generally unloving relationships. Taking this argument further, some have argued that 'psychological maltreatment' should be seen as the extreme end of a continuum of parenting, marked by 'the most salient, extreme and severe forms of psychologically damaging or limiting care and interactions' (Hart *et al.* 1996). Problems 'beneath' this threshold are best thought of as 'inappropriate, inadequate, or misdirected child-rearing'.

(v) like other forms of abuse, psychological maltreatment is most appropriately viewed within an ecological framework. Amongst the factors which can mediate the occurrence and impact of psychological maltreatment are individual difference, and the quality of relationships. For example:

    (a) children differ in their resilience or vulnerability. Some children are temperamentally 'stimulus hungry' and may see some experiences as challenges and excitements that would terrify another child. Most parents who have a more reticent child would simply tailor their expectations accordingly. Some are unable or apparently unwilling to do this.

    (b) other mediating variables include age, gender, support from others. For example, the same behaviour can have differential impacts on different children, and on children of different ages; the standing of different actions in different societies can also exert an influence.

    (c) some children may be protected against the adverse effects of a psychologically abusive parent, by factors such as high IQ, the presence of another, caring adult, and expressions of positive affect by the abuser (Hart and Brassard 1991; Schaeffer and Lewis 1989). This makes screening or the identification of problems on the basis of parental behaviours particularly difficult and underlines the importance of careful assessment as the basis of sound decision-making.

A U.K. study conducted by Glaser and Prior (1997) identified three tiers of concern which led to children being registered under the category of emotional abuse: (i) harmful parental attributes e.g., mental ill-health, domestic violence, substance misuse. In 69% of cases (59 out of 85 children) these factors were considered to contribute to the risk of significant harm. (ii) forms of ill-treatment such as developmentally inappropriate interaction (42% of children), rejection or degradation (34%), emotional unavailability or neglect (13%), repeated separations or moves (13%), using child for emotional needs of adult(s) (7%) and mis-socialisation and terrorising (2%). (iii) the third tier of concern were indicators of impairment to a child's development, covering: emotional state (e.g., frightened); behaviour (e.g., age-inappropriate responsibility); developmental/educational attainment (e.g., school non-attendance); peer relationships (e.g., withdrawn) and physical state (e.g., poor growth).

Intervening in situations in which abuse is defined purely in terms of categories of parental behaviour is clearly problematic. To do so would require a demonstrable, predictable relationship between such behaviour and identifiable adverse effects on a child's development. Endeavouring to identify psychological maltreatment by focusing on the child's behaviour is, of course, equally problematic, due the range of other factors which may account for such problems. Once again the onus must be on a sound understanding of what is known about the causes and consequences of psychological maltreatment, its relationship to other forms of abuse and neglect, and the relative strengths and weaknesses of given interventions. A functional assessment of each child and family is essential. The longer-term focus of child development fostered by the concept of 'significant harm' encourages a more serious consideration of this form of abuse than might previously have been the case (Lynch and Browne 1997), and places the issue of psychological maltreatment as one worthy of primary prevention, targeted at 'children in need' before it becomes one of child protection (Glaser and Prior 1997).

Factors Associated with Psychological Maltreatment

In general, the research base underpinning our understanding of psychological maltreatment is relatively sparse, compared with that of other forms of maltreatment (Thompson and Kaplan 1993; Hart et al. 1996). The co-terminosity of psychological maltreatment with physical abuse and neglect means that the factors associated with these may also place children at risk of psychological maltreatment. Specifically, there is an emerging consensus that physical abuse, physical neglect and sexual abuse, can themselves be psychologically abusive in their impact on children (see Claussen and Crittenden

1991, Crittenden 1996). Physical neglect, in particular, appears to be highly correlated with psychological maltreatment, specifically cognitive and social/emotional neglect (Claussen and Crittenden 1991).

Much of what was said in relation to physical neglect applies here too. Thus, some forms of psychological maltreatment may arise out of lack of understanding of a child's needs or how best to meet them. Pianta *et al.* described mothers they categorised as psychologically unavailable, 24 months into their study:

> 'These mothers appeared detached and uninvolved with their children, interacting with them only when it appeared necessary. For example, in the problem-solving situation . . . these mothers would ignore their child's cues for help and assistance, offer no encouragement . . . even if the child was failing to perform the task, and would appear comfortable even when the child was highly frustrated. These women took very few steps to protect their children's self-esteem. In general they were withdrawn, displayed flat affect and seemed depressed. There was no indication that (they) derived any pleasure or satisfaction from their relationship with their children. (Pianta *et al.* 1989, p. 227)

It is easy to imagine that this behaviour might be the result of immediate problems in information processing, and that these might have their origin in poor early attachments (see previous chapter). However, it is more difficult to see this as a satisfactory account of the seriously hostile interactions that characterise some parental behaviour. Pianta *et al.* also described this kind of behaviour in mothers during the second year of their study:

> 'Mothers in the hostile/verbally abusive group chronically found fault with their children and criticized them in an extremely harsh fashion. This form of maltreatment involved constant berating and harassment of the child. . . . (During the problem solving task) . . . children . . . would be met with insults when they asked for assistance or would be told "you're so dumb". Other examples include more blatant hostility indicated by a very angry tone of voice or yelling at the child.' (Pianta *et al.* 1989, p. 227)

The close association of verbal and physical abuse may indicate that we need to look at factors associated with physical abuse in order to understand the origins of some psychological abuse of this kind. If so, we have still to ask why some parents 'restrict themselves' to verbal abuse. On the basis of their research, Lesnik-Oberstein *et al.* (1995) suggest that a range of factors at different systemic levels interact to produce psychologically abusive behaviour. They suggest that three major influences shape psychological maltreatment: parental hostility, parental inhibition of overt aggression, and a focusing of parental aggression on children. Each is seen as resulting from an interaction of factors operating at different systemic levels. Thus, parental inhibition of aggression is a function of the interaction of six factors: a poorly developed level of moral reasoning, low cultural inhibition of overt aggression, lack of insight into their own past abuse, substance misuse, the absence of a supportive partner or social network, and a lack of empathy. Whether parents engage solely in verbally abusive behaviour, as opposed to verbally and/or physically abusive behaviour, will depend on the ratio of parental hostility to parental inhibition of aggression. In other words, in a culture which discourages physical aggression, and in the absence of social stressors, a parent who experiences hostile feelings may well restrict their expression to verbal abuse.

NON-ORGANIC FAILURE TO THRIVE

This section ends with a consideration of a condition which has variously been conceptualised as resulting from physical neglect, and from emotional neglect, known as *non-organic failure to thrive*.

Non-organic failure to thrive is the diagnostic classification given to children whose growth falls below a satisfactory weight (usually below the third percentile), height, and general development. These are children whose problems in physical development have no apparent organic cause. As a classification it is rather tautologous, and imprecise, as evidenced by wide ranges in reported incidence (Mayes and Volkmar 1993). Increasingly it is recognised that the divide between those cases with organic explanations for growth failures and those diagnosed as 'non-organic' is considerably less clear-cut, with organic factors being diagnosed in children thought to belong to the latter group (see Mathiesen *et al.* 1989). Early studies appeared to point the finger at inadequate mothering, and this is one area where the introduction of more rigorous research has dramatically shifted our understanding of the aetiology of a problem (see Boddy and Skuse 1994).

At the crux of non-organic failure to thrive are problems in the feeding interaction between parent and child (which is why mothers are so often 'centre-stage'). Psychoanalytic perspectives, together with poor methodology exacerbated this tendency toward 'mother-blaming explanations' (Lachenmeyer and Davidovicz 1987). The origins of the idea that problems associated with mothering might be implicated in non-organic failure to thrive originated in part because of the similarities in this condition with that of infants cared for in institutions (e.g., Bowlby 1951). Mothers of infants who failed to thrive appeared to differ from those of children without problems, in respect of psychopathology, family dysfunction and inadequate nurturing. Although a great deal of research has been conducted into non-organic failure to thrive, much of it is flawed. In many studies it is not possible to be sure that observed differences are not attributable to the consequences of non-organic failure to thrive, rather than contributory factors.

In a review of research, conducted by Boddy and Skuse (1994), the authors concluded that on the basis of the few more methodologically secure studies it is reasonable to conclude that mothers whose children are failing to thrive appear to differ from other mothers in such parenting behaviour as communication and sensitivity i.e., they appear less well-tuned to their children's needs, interact less often and less well. For example, research by Pollitt *et al.* (1975) suggested that mothers whose children were failing-to-thrive engaged in fewer verbal and physical interactions with their infants, were less positively reinforcing and less warm. Drotar *et al.* (1990) showed that in a sample of families referred to hospital, mothers of children who were failing to thrive were less emotionally expressive, less responsible and accepting and less co-operative with their infants. In one of a few studies using a community sample, Heptinstall *et al.* (1987) noted more indifference and anxiety amongst mothers of non-thriving children, compared with controls. These mothers were also more negative in their affect, and were less likely to give instructions, communicate or socialise at mealtimes.

However Boddy and Skuse emphasise that as yet we do not know *why* these differences arise. There appears to be a link between a mother's recall of adverse early experiences and infant failure to thrive, but this is not universal. It may be, as other research suggests, that early adverse experiences make one vulnerable to a range of parenting (see Dowdney *et al.* 1985) or other difficulties (see Andrews *et al.* 1990), of which the problems associated with failure to thrive are only one, but the literature offers no explanation of the mechanism(s) by which this rather than some other difficulty should arise.

Similarly, differences have been noted amongst children who fail to thrive. Difficult temperament (Skuse 1985) and behaviour problems (Pollitt and Eichler 1976, Raynor and Rudolph 1996) have all been associated with non-organic failure to thrive. In a study by Polan *et al.* (1991) children who were failing to thrive tended to express less positive affect than control children. Similar psychosocial stressors would appear to play a role, although once again it is difficult to determine the 'direction' of cause and effect, and we are still left to puzzle over why only some children who are difficult, and/or whose parents are under stress, develop non-organic failure to thrive?

Boddy and Skuse recommend that future research should look more broadly at the range of cases of non-organic failures to thrive, rather than focusing primarily on those who are hospitalised and which might be atypical (only a small percentage of those infants whose growth is less than optimal are referred to a paediatrician). They also recommend exploring some of the developments within mainstream psychology which may help 'unpack' the nature and development of non-organic failure to thrive. This will need to focus on parental behaviour, child behaviour, and broader family and social factors such as couples discord, social isolation and so on. In particular they point to the potential of giving attention to such factors as the role of social cognitive processes in parenting, as these have been shown to guide parental behaviour. For example, Pollitt *et al.* (1978) noted that a mother's ability to perceive and respond appropriately to her infant's signals is an important feature of establishing a routine that is attuned to her child's needs. Similarly mothers who feel strongly about a particular child behaviour are more likely to choose high power strategies for dealing with them (Rubin and Mills 1990). It may be that mothers with very definite views of how babies *should* behave, or be brought up, or what is good for them, are less likely to be able or willing to sacrifice their wishes to those of their infants. Rather in the same way that Crittenden conceptualises neglect generally within an information processing framework (1993), Boddy and Skuse suggest that future research would benefit from a focus on the cognitive and affective processes of parenting: beliefs, emotions, attributions.

'Psychosocial stressors and childhood adversity increase vulnerability to child rearing problems; however, this association is neither inevitable, nor direct. The parent's cognitions about stressful experiences determine *whether* she experiences child rearing problems, and also the *nature* of those problems. . . . a model of parental social cognition has the capacity to explain why stressors such as isolation, or child characteristics such as sleepiness lead to infant malnutrition in some families, while others cope or demonstrate different problems such as abuse or neglect.' (Boddy and Skuse 1994, p. 418)

The nature and quality of parenting, and parent-child interaction appears to be an integral, if little-understood, factor in accounting for non-organic failure to thrive. If untreated, non-organic failure to thrive can be fatal for young infants. It would appear that many children who are not diagnosed as failing to thrive may nonetheless be sustaining an assault on their physical development, and the psychological correlates may have long-lasting consequences for emotional and psychological well-being. This reinforces the general argument made earlier that psychological maltreatment is something which poses a general threat to a child's development. It can do significant harm, but only rarely perhaps is that threat one of immediate harm, in the sense that practitioners are required to consider this term under child protection legislation (see Glaser and Prior 1997). Rather, it highlights the need to anchor preventive efforts in more broad-based work with children in need, as was discussed in more detail in the chapter on primary prevention.

CHILD SEXUAL ABUSE

Definition of Sexual Abuse

There are a number of definitions of sexual abuse, many of which endeavour to capture the nature of the relationship between abuser and victim rather than specify particular behaviour or events. So, for example, we encounter definitions such as that used by Schecter and Roberge (1976), in which sexual abuse is defined as 'The involvement of dependent, developmentally immature children and adolescents in sexually abusive activities they do not fully comprehend, to which they are unable to give informed consent or which violate the social taboos of family roles.' When researchers set out to investigate the incidence and prevalence of abuse, their answers vary depending on how inclusively or exclusively they operationally define sexual abuse e.g. some include any unwanted experience including touching or indecent exposure, whilst others exclude these (see Gorey and Leslie 1997).

The Size of the Problem

As elsewhere, this lack of precision and variability in this area makes it almost impossible to accurately estimate the extent of child sexual abuse (see for example, Holmes and Slap 1998, Fergusson and Mullen 1999). With these cautionary notes in mind, there are some estimates that are both generally acceptable and widely accepted.

Fisher has estimated the incidence (number of new cases) of child sexual abuse within the U.K. as 1 per 1000 children, per annum (Fisher 1998). This figure is based on an analysis of available studies, using different definitions. Prevalence rates (numbers of children who report child sexual abuse at any one time) range from 12–27% for girls and 8–16 % for boys (see for example, Finkelhor et al. 1990). Similarly, in their integrative review, which endeavoured to control for some of the sources of bias referred to above, Gorey and Leslie estimated likely prevalence rates of child sexual abuse to be 22.3% for women and 8.5 % for men (Gorey and Leslie 1997; see also Volgetanz et al. 1999).

In their review of the epidemiological literature on the prevalence of child sexual abuse, Fergusson and Mullen conclude that the experience of unwanted sexual attention is commonplace, and that between 5% and 10% of children are exposed to serious sexually abusive acts, defined as actual or attempted penetration (Fergusson and Mullen 1999). Estimates from other Canadian researchers place the likelihood of childhood sexual abuse at one in ten (MacMillan et al. 1997). Similar estimates have been made in relation to the U.K. (Fisher 1994). Whilst numerically many more girls are sexually abused than boys, the latter comprise a substantial number (Fergusson and Mullen 1999). Holmes and Slap go further in their review, claiming that the 'sexual abuse of boys is common, under-reported, under-recognized, and under-treated' (Holmes and Slap 1998).

Even allowing for the problems in accurate accounts of prevalence and incidence, child sexual abuse appears to be a sizeable social problem with serious consequences for those children who fall victim to this form of abuse (see Chapter 6). In the U.K., Marshall has estimated that as of 1993 approximately 260 000 men over the age of 20 had been convicted of a sexual offence against a child, and sexual abuse of children comprised the majority of all serious sexual offences committed by men under the age of 40 (Marshall 1997).

Recently we have begun to take on board the fact that child sexual abuse is not confined to adult men, but that women, children and young people also commit sexual abuse (see Morrison *et al.* 1994; Erooga and Masson 1998). Studies such as those conducted by Abel *et al.* (1987), Abel and Rouleau (1990), Hindman (1988) and Thomas (1981) reveal that many adult males convicted of sex offences against children, began their offending in their teenage years. These data, obtained retrospectively from clinical samples, must be treated cautiously. But other sources confirm the seriousness of the problem of child and adolescent perpetrators. For example, official statistics in the U.K. show that in 1994 almost one fifth (1500) of all those found guilty of, or cautioned for, sexual offences (7400) were aged between 10 and 17. Marshall estimated that one third of convicted sex offenders had committed their first offence before the age of 19 (Marshall 1997). Puri and his colleagues found that sexual offences accounted for 26% of those index offences for which adolescent offenders were institutionalised in England (Puri *et al.* 1996). As yet, we do not know whether the factors which predispose young people to commit sexual offences against children are the same as those which shape the longer-term, adult perpetrator (see Vizard *et al.* 1995). Research suggests that a majority of children and young people who commit sexual offences do not go on to become adult offenders (ATSA 1997).

Factors Associated with the Sexual Abuse of Children

Problems of definition are exacerbated by the well-rehearsed difficulties in relying on official statistics, which at best give a serious underestimate of offences, and do not include abuse which is either not detected or not reported (see Russell 1984). This means that only a minority of offenders come to the attention of the criminal justice system and/or the helping professions, a minority of these are convicted, and those convicted may have admitted to a lesser charge, masking not only the extent of offending but also its seriousness (Fisher 1994). Similarly only a small percentage of those who have been subjected to sexual abuse are known to the helping professions. Therefore, research which relies on these two groups for unravelling this particular problem may well be working with very unrepresentative samples. As we have seen in relation to other forms of maltreatment, this is always a reason for caution. There have been some attempts to overcome these problems by taking an epidemiological approach. Here, researchers survey larger groups of the wider population and use statistical techniques to try to identify those factors that distinguish offenders from non-offenders, victims from non-victims, and to explore the relationship between particular kinds of experiences (at particular times and in particular circumstances) and their short- and long-term sequelae.

But even here, all is not straightforward. As in other areas, different studies frequently produce contrary findings, and one is well advised to consider the research trends insofar as these are carefully put together and analysed. This presents additional problems because, as well as the technical and ethical challenges inherent in such research, researchers often fail either to specify their particular approach, or to develop a common approach, or to establish mechanisms for verifying reports of abuse. This makes it difficult to review the literature and draw meaningful conclusions. Here are the observations of Holmes and Slap (1998) when they reviewed the literature on the sexual abuse of boys:

> 'The literature was small and methodologically limited. Methods of eliciting abuse histories frequently were poorly described or done subjectively, defini-tions of abuse varied widely, sampling techniques were generally poor . . . Con-sequently, prevalence estimates were discrepant, associations confounded and causal inferences not feasible.' (Holmes and Slap 1998, pp. 1859–1860)

Although this was written specifically about the state of play in relation to our understanding of the sexual abuse of boys (a rather under-researched area) the conclusions apply to most areas in this field.

Research into the factors which differentiate those who sexually abuse children from sex offenders in general and from non-offenders, has tended to run in parallel with developments in model-building (how these factors inter-relate) and the development and evaluation of interventions. Whilst not unusual, this does mean that these three activities—all of which are important in the development of evidence-based practice—are somewhat out-of-step with one another. At present we know something (with varying degrees of uncertainty) about what characterises those who sexually abuse children and what differentiates them from other groups. We possibly know a little more about what factors appear to be associated with 'offending' (used here to describe the act of abuse, rather than as a legal category for those successfully prosecuted) and we have some indications of the correlates of effective programmes. This section concentrates on what we do and don't know about those who sexually abuse children, and about whether or not it is possible to identify whether particular groups of children are more vulnerable than others to becoming the victims of sexual abuse.

As indicated earlier, it can be highly misleading to draw conclusions from individual studies and it is important to endeavour to identify research trends and to develop an approach to research synthesis which enables us to make sense of apparently disparate results across studies and to answer such questions as: Why do some people who have been abused as children go on to abuse when the majority do not? Is it the case that some circumstances offset the worst consequences of sexual abuse whereas others exacerbate them? And so on. In the absence of available systematic reviews, what follows is a summary of what appears to be the received wisdom at present. This is an area where little integrative work has been undertaken, where such work may not always be possible, and where the picture as we currently see it may well change as it comes into clearer focus. One particular area which remains relatively un-researched, is that of women who sexually abuse, and indeed the problem of women sexual perpetrators has only very recently begun to receive appropriate attention. In a summary of studies published between 1990 and 1996, Ferguson and Mullen point out that whilst almost all female victims have been sexually abused by male perpetrators (between 92–99%), this estimate drops (to between 65–86%) for male victims (Fergusson and Mullen 1999). Whilst still very much a minority, Ferguson and Mullen also point out there is evidence of under-reporting of sexual abuse by women, largely as a result of a lack of recognition (see Peluso and Putnam 1996). Unless explicitly stated otherwise, the following summary addresses what is known about male sexual abusers. Most of the points are based on work with adult male offenders, and where they relate to child and adolescent sexual offenders this is indicated. We know relatively little, as yet, about the continuities and discontinuities between adolescent and adult patterns of sex offending.

Sex Offenders

Personality Factors

There appears to be no one set of personality factors which consistently differentiate between those who commit sexual offences against children and those who do not, nor any clear correlation between particular forms of psychopathology and offending (see Murphy and Smith 1996). That is to say, there appears to be no 'typical' child sex offender. Some studies have suggested that recidivists (those who go on to re-offend) are more likely to have anti-social lifestyles and psychopathic personalities (Hanson and Harris 1998; Rice *et al.* 1991; Maletsky 1993; Marques *et al.* 1994), but others indicate that up to 25% of incest offenders show no abnormality of personality (Scott and Stone 1986; Langevin *et al.* 1985). Studies looking for patterns of personality types sometimes make the mistake of grouping data and identifying more homogeneity than in fact pertains; they often use non-standardised measures, and rarely use control groups (Murphy and Smith 1996). To date, the evidence is that sex offenders who abuse children present with a range of personality profiles and a wide range of psychopathology. Personality and psychopathology may be important considerations in designing interventions, because they may impact upon the responsiveness of offenders (see Hughes, Hogue and Hollin 1999), but they do not necessarily help us in predicting or describing those at risk of offending (Murphy and Smith 1996).

Socio-demographic Characteristics

Those who commit sexual offences against children are comparable to the populations from which they are drawn in relation to factors such as intelligence, age, ethnicity, psychiatric status and educational achievement (see Wolf 1985). However, there are signs within the growing literature on juvenile sexual offenders that larger numbers than might be expected have learning problems or learning disabilities (see Lane and Lobanov-Rostovsky 1997; Manocha and Mezey 1998; Allam *et al.* 1997). Thompson and Brown caution that this might be an artefact of the relative lack of privacy of the learning disabled, their greater tendency towards impulsive offending, often in public places, and perhaps a naivety when challenged, compared with non-disabled offenders (Thompson and Brown 1997, see also Thompson 1997 and O'Callaghan 1998).

Victim–Perpetrator Relationships

Studies published between 1990 and 1995 indicate that the majority of sexual offences against children are committed against children outside the family of the perpetrator. Up to half of offences are, however, committed against children *known* to the perpetrator. Child sexual abuse perpetrated by natural parents appears relatively rare, with estimates ranging from between 1.5–16% (Ferguson and Mullen 1999). Whilst the proportion of sexual offences committed by step-fathers is comparable to that of natural parents, the fact that step-fathers are a much smaller group means that they are more likely to commit child sexual abuse.

Victim Preferences

It is probably misleading to assume that offenders can be categorised according to their victim preferences (e.g., boy or girl, intra-familial or extra-familial). Whilst this may be the case for a large number of offenders, Abel *et al.* (1987) showed that 23% of offenders committed offences against both family and non-family members, and a similar percentage offended against both boys and girls (see also Fisher and Maier 1998). These findings may be attributable to the highly deviant nature of the participants in some studies, as others have reported much lower rates of 'crossover' (e.g., Beech *et al.* 1998), but this is an area awaiting further data.

The Enmeshment Myth

Although a dominant clinical perception, there is no strong empirical evidence that those who commit sexual offences against children belong to families where there is enmeshment among family members, or role confusion (e.g., where the daughter assumes the maternal role) or lack of clear sexual boundaries (see Conte 1985). Such hypotheses assume a distinction between intra-familial and extra-familial abuse which empirical data do not support (Abel *et al.* 1988). Forty-nine per cent of incestuous fathers and stepfathers referred for outpatient treatment in Abel's study also admitted to sexually abusing children outside the family. Indeed, a substantial minority were also raping adult women whilst sexually abusing their children (Abel *et al.* 1988). Nonetheless, there is likely to be a need for family-focused interventions, aimed at addressing problems within the family (co-existing with abuse) or in helping families manage the fact of abuse, and in protecting children from further offences (see Bentovim 1991). Again, the kind of family to which an offender belongs, may have implications for the kind of approach required (Murphy and Smith 1996) and decisions about safety (Epps 1999).

Dysfunctional Families

Data from descriptive studies suggest that adolescent sex offenders often grow up in dysfunctional families, marked by inadequate and inconsistent care, with high rates of parental separation and divorce, having been exposed to violence between adult partners (Manocha and Mezey 1998; Richardson *et al.* 1995). Such studies also point to associations with known parental criminality, illicit substance misuse and mental illness, a history of abuse and neglect—although support for these vary between studies and their methodological limitations make it difficult to draw firm conclusions. If these associations exist, it is unclear how they operate.

Maker *et al.* analysed data from a questionnaire-based survey of 130 college women, looking at the predictive value of such variables (Maker *et al.* 1999). They collected information on: parental violence, overall family functioning, parental sociopathy (criminal behaviour, lying, stealing, arrests, incidents of violence), parental drug use, parental alcoholism and childhood sexual abuse. Their analysis of the data indicated that, at least for this sample, parental sociopathy was a stronger predictor of childhood sexual abuse than either parental substance use or family dysfunction, and when co-morbid risk factors are assessed simultaneously (i.e., together, rather than one by one) sociopathy was the only predictor of childhood sexual abuse. These researchers conclude that parental sociopathy is a critical antecedent of sexual abuse, although they stress (i) that their research was methodologically limited as it relied on retrospective accounts of one group of women; (ii) that even though it was a strong predictor, sociopathy only accounted for a modest amount of the variance between those women who reported childhood sexual abuse and those who did not. Therefore, other risk factors were operating that were not examined in this study. The authors hypothesise that other family factors that appear to be associated with increased risk of abuse are typically those which are linked to sociopathy, *viz.* substance misuse, criminality, anti-social behaviour (Maker 1999). They also hypothesise that sociopathy, rather than drug or alcohol misuse, may account for the 'disinhibition' attributed to the latter, as sociopathy is marked by an absence of such affects as guilt, shame or anxiety. Similarly, whereas some researchers have suggested that a dysfunctional family environment, characterised by stress, poor communication, conflict and issues of control and power set the scene for enhanced risk of childhood sexual abuse (see Finkelhor 1980), Maker *et al.* offer an alternative account of this association. They observe that maternal sociopathy may sometimes lead directly to sexual abuse, but might more generally reduce a mother's capacity 'to provide adequate nurturance, limits, boundaries and rules to protect her children from sexual exploitation' (Maker *et al.* 1999). Similarly, the absence of a safe and nurturing social environment may increase the risk of extra-familial sexual abuse as parents with anti-social behaviour problems are more likely to mix with other sociopathic adults, increasing risk of exposure to potential sexual abusers. The fact that most children are sexually abused by those outside the family but known to the family supports this formulation of the data, according to Maker *et al.*

Biological Factors

To date, there are no clear biological factors implicated in sex offences against children, or other adults, although relevant research is sparse, and at a very rudimentary level.

Childhood Victimisation

Although a popular idea amongst practitioners, there is little evidence to support the notion that offenders were themselves child victims of sexual offences. Extant studies estimate that approximately 10–15% of male adults were abused as children (e.g., Finkelhor 1990), and some 30% of child sex offenders (e.g., Freund *et al.* 1990) with the inescapable conclusion that the majority of sex offenders were not themselves victims. However, it may be that those who have been sexually abused as children are at increased risk of becoming a perpetrator. This is not necessarily because of the abuse itself but because of factors associated with it, such as increased sexual deviance or chaotic family circumstances (Hanson 1990). Several studies point tentatively towards the possibility that living with intrafamilial violence (whether as a victim or as a witness) and experiencing discontinuity of care (e.g., losing a parent figure, or family breakdown) may be important factors in predisposing sexually abused boys to abuse others (see Skuse *et al.* 1998; Ryan *et al.* 1996).

Deviant Sexual Arousal

Data from studies which have examined the arousal patterns of sex offenders are generally inconclusive. For example, some studies provide evidence of deviant arousal in incest offenders (Murphy *et al.* 1986) whilst others report no such differences (Marshall *et al.* 1986). On balance, the research evidence suggests that in terms of sexual arousal to presented images (measured by circumferential or volumetric penile erection) incest offenders respond more as non-offenders than non-incestuous offenders. However, such measures are not wholly reliable, and the data are difficult to interpret. They may be useful in monitoring progress in intervention, but are not reliable indicators regarding whether or not particular individuals meet certain profiles (Murphy and Peters 1992).

Social Skills

The evidence about the relationship between social skills and sexual abuse is unclear (Beckett 1994; Towl and Crighton 1996). In a review of the social competence of sexual offenders, Stermac *et al.* (1990) concluded that on self-report measures, those who committed offences against children were less assertive than other sex offenders, e.g., rapists, and other non-sex offenders. However, on other ratings (by peers and external observers) these differences were not sustained. There is some evidence that those who commit offences against children lack significant social and interpersonal skills, such as initiating and sustaining conversations with adults, and generally feel more at ease with children than with adults (e.g., Araji and Finkelhor 1986; Williams and Finkelhor 1990). The contribution of such skill deficits is poorly understood, but there is evidence that for some offenders, the lack of key social skills is a contributory factor in their offending. At present, there are elements of social skills training in most intervention programmes, not least of all because these tend to be 'pre-packaged' or 'formulaic' programmes delivered on a group basis (see Chapter 11), but what is needed is a more detailed and specific approach to researching those aspects of social skills where deficits appear to be implicated in particular kinds of offending. Similarly, in work with offenders, a more individualised approach to addressing skills deficits—where they are a contributory factor in offending—is required. Insofar as such skills are an important pre-requisite of developing and maintaining appropriate inter-personal and sexual relationships with adults, they are likely to justify their place in most treatment programmes.

Ability to Problem-solve

Also in the study by Stermac *et al.*, those who committed sexual offences against children could generate solutions to a problem but were less likely to select adequate solutions, suggesting a need to focus on the offender's perceptions, as well as (or rather than) their social competence, which is a typical focus of intervention (see below). An inability to problem-solve is one of a number of cognitive factors associated with sexual offending, others being cognitive distortions and a lack of victim empathy (Stermac *et al.* 1990).

Empathy

Lack of empathy has been postulated as a contributory factor to child sexual abuse, in that it acts as a disinhibitor. In general, the function of empathy as an *inhibitor* of behaviour is well established (see Bandura 1973; Feshbach and Feschbach 1982), and the development of empathy for the victims of child sexual abuse is a well-established feature of therapeutic programmes (see Beckett *et al.* 1998, Knopp *et al.* 1992). Hildebran and Pithers have summarised the situation as follows:

> 'Victim empathy gives [the sex offender] the pivotal reason for not reoffending, for, with empathy, he can no longer not perceive his victim's pain.' (Hildebran and Pithers 1989, p. 238)

Cognitive Distortions

A pattern of cognitive distortions typically characterises sex offenders in general. These are ways of thinking that encourage, or which do not inhibit, exploitative relationships, including sexual offending. Attitudes and ways of thinking are acquired as a result of learning, either from our parents, or significant others and from peers. Typically, these are reinforced or cued from the social and cultural climate, for example by the exploitation of children in pornography (see Chapter 5 for an exposition related to physical abuse). The sorts of cognitive distortions that differentiate sexual offenders are those which either deny an event, or its significance (harm, or intent to harm) and/or which locate the responsibility elsewhere, often with the victim. Here is one typology of the explanatory statements provided by child sexual offenders: (i) a denial that anything happened; (ii) a denial of responsibility (something happened but it wasn't my idea); (iii) denial of sexual intent ('something happened, it was my idea, but it wasn't sexual'); (iv) denial of wrongfulness ('something happened, it was my idea, it was sexual, but it wasn't wrong'), and (v) denial of self-determination (something happened, it was my idea, it was sexual and it was wrong, but there were extenuating circumstances) (Pollack and Hashmall 1990, Blumenthal *et al.* 1999). It is thought that offenders typically rely on such cognitions to trivialise their actions, and minimise the impact on their victims (see Ward *et al.* 1997), although Ward *et al.* point out that there are problems in assessing both their existence and their influence. This is because most research explores cognitions *after* the offence has been committed, therefore these post-offence cognitions may not be representative of pre-offence or offence-contemporaneous cognitions. Further, there is a strong social desirability bias in questionnaire data provided by sexual offenders, which may undermine their validity (see Haywood *et al.* 1994; Langevin 1991). Finally insofar as patterns of cognition reflect underlying 'schema' (see Chapter 5) they may not be accessible to offenders to report.

Nonetheless, attention to cognitive distortions is a mainstay of treatment programmes (see Chapter 11). Effective challenges to these beliefs requires not only that their content is challenged, but that sex offenders are enabled to feel something of the pain and terror that their actions inflict on their victims, i.e. empathy (Prentky 1996). Research undertaken by Blumenthal *et al.* (1999) suggests that child sexual offenders are more likely than adult sex offenders to defend their offending by more entrenched cognitive distortions. They also caution that research in this area is in its early stages, and that even within categories ('child sex offenders' or 'adult sexual offenders) there is considerable heterogeneity, and that there may be considerable scope for refinement in our understanding of the role of cognitive distortions in those who sexually abuse children, and their relationship to other factors.

Social Anxiety

One of the factors thought to be implicated in sexual offences against children is a high level of social anxiety, in particular a fear of being criticised and rejected by others. There is some empirical support for this (e.g., Groth 1982; Overholser and Beck 1986). In a study comparing the cognitions of incestuous offenders, extra-familial sexual offenders, rapists, non-sexual offenders and lay persons, Hayashino *et al.* found that fear of negative evaluations was significantly higher in both incestuous and extra-familial child molesters (Hayashino *et al.* 1995). This was the only area of cognition in which such a distinction was found in both groups. In this study, only extra-familial offenders evidenced other kinds of cognitive distortions or level of empathy.

As with most research in this area, this was a small study, and the attempt to analyse factors according to category of child sex offender (i.e., incestuous versus extra-familial) may not be wholly sensible given the available evidence that offenders do not fall neatly into such categories. However, the comparisons with other kinds of offender (i.e., rapists and non-sexual offenders) and lay persons revealed some interesting data. In particular, the results indicated that 25% of lay persons endorsed several cognitive distortions e.g., that a child who does not resist an adult's sexual advances really wants to have sex with the adult. Almost 20% reported the likelihood of engaging in sexual activity with a child if assured they would not be punished. The authors are aware that their attempt to screen out child molesters from this group may have been inadequate, but suggest that equally as probable is the possibility that such views amongst 'non-offending' lay persons reflect wider societal views regarding the acceptability of involving children in sexual activity (Hayashino et al. 1995).

Anger and Aggression

Anger and associated aggression is evident in many forms of sex offending, but its role in child sexual abuse is not well understood. It may be particularly relevant where childhood victimisation has resulted in schema which predispose to anger, and which may be triggered by real or imagined provocation.

Impulsivity and Sexual Arousal

It is not at all certain that the impulses or desires that contribute to sexual offending are restricted to offenders (see Briere and Runtz 1989). In view of the contributory factors of social norms, and stereotypes, this may not be surprising. What may distinguish offenders from those who do not offend is the absence of inhibitory mechanisms, both internal (poor impulse control) and external (under-socialisation—or the consequence of external disinhibitors such as alcohol).

Recidivism

As far as we can ascertain at present, more people commit sexual offences, including sexual offences against children, than go on to commit repeated offences. It is important to know what factors differentiate those who are likely to commit further offences from those who are not, in order to accurately assess risk, and to target treatment strategies efficiently. The different approach taken by individual researchers (i.e., different data sources, time scales etc.) make it difficult to accurately estimate rates of recidivism, and to link these with particular characteristics or circumstances associated with particular groups of offenders. Perkins *et al.* (1998) have suggested that predictor variables can be classified as:

- static—historical and unchangeable, such as previous offence history;
- dynamic (stable)—potentially changeable but relatively stable, such as personality characteristics;
- dynamic (acute)—features which can change rapidly such as mood or intoxication.

Different researchers have looked at different kinds and combinations of factors. As Perkins *et al.* point out, if static factors are either not specified or not controlled for, it becomes particularly difficult to assess the effectiveness of treatment.

Perkins *et al.* summarise the evidence from a number of studies which have examined the actuarial associations between sexual recidivism and characteristics of offenders and their offending histories as shown in Table 5.2.

Table 5.2

Study: authors and focus	Location	Factors identified
Fisher and Thornton 1993, *Convicted sex offenders*	UK	Any previous sexual convictions. Four or more previous convictions of any kind. Any conviction for non-sexual violence. Sexual convictions involving three or more victims. High Score on the Psychopathy Checklist-Revised (PLC-R) (Hare 1991).
Hare 1980; 1991 *PCL-R*	Canada	Interpersonal and affective traits (Factor 1). Socially deviant lifestyle (Factor 2).
Abel *et al.* 1988 *Child molesters*	USA	Assaulting boys and girls. Committing both contact and non-contact abuse. Assaulting both family and non-family members. Failure to accept increased communication with adults as a goal. Being divorced.
Rice *et al.* 1991 *Extrafamilial child molesters*	Canada	Offender never having been married. Previous prison admissions. Previous property convictions. Diagnosis of personality disorder. Deviant sexual preference for children (assessed using PPG).

The variety of factors identified in Table 5.2 highlights the problems for those seeking to assess risk. However, there are some common threads, and some studies such as those of Fisher and Thornton (1993) and Hare (1991) have resulted in the development of some useful tools in risk assessment. Hanson and Bussiere's meta-analysis of 98 reports providing data on 28 805 sex offenders and 165 potential predictor variables, suggests that the best predictors of sexual recidivism are:

- static variables relating to the pattern and type of previous offending (e.g., extra-familial abuse, abuse of boys), followed by:
- dynamic predictors relating to deviant sexual preferences and failure to complete treatment.

Children who are Sexually Abused

Mullen and Fergusson have surveyed those studies which have attempted to explore whether or not there are particular characteristics or situational factors which place children at increased risk of child sexual abuse (Fergusson and Mullen 1999). They identify the following trends:

(1) In contrast to other forms of abuse and neglect, there are no clear associations between social class and child sexual abuse (Fergusson *et al.* 1996; Fleming *et al.* 1997).
(2) There are associations between child sexual abuse and measures of family dysfunction, including:
     - marital discord, parental divorce and separation, marital conflict;
     - patterns of family change, especially the presence of step-parents in the family;
     - parental adjustment, particularly alcoholism and criminality;
     - measures of parental attachment.

The ways in which these factors may increase the vulnerability of children within them have been discussed above.

Despite these associations, there is no evidence to suggest that such factors could be used to identify children at risk. A prospective study by Fergusson and his colleagues highlighted the folly of trying to do so. They collected measures of family and social circumstances which allowed them to identify a number of individual and family predictors of child sexual abuse, including gender, marital conflict, parental attachment and bonding, and parental problems (Fergusson *et al.* 1996). Although it was possible to identify groups who were high risk (children with up to a 25.8% risk of child sexual abuse) and low risk (children with a risk of only 1.8%), even amongst the high risk group, the majority of children were not, in fact, sexually abused. In other words, the 'false positive' rates from such attempts are unacceptable for such endeavours to be of any use.

Models of Child Sexual Abuse

There are a number of models which attempt to explain the ways in which these, and other, less well-evidenced, factors conspire to precipitate sexual abuse against children. This chapter reviews two which enjoy some support and appear to do justice to a range of factors, including social and cultural features or pressures, and which have some connection with current programmes of intervention. They are the well-known model by Finkelhor (1984), and that of Prentky and his colleagues (Prenty 1996; Prentky *et al.* 1989).

Finkelhor has proposed a model which both purports to explain how it is that some adults become sexually interested in children and to describe the process whereby such offences are committed. Three factors are thought to contribute to our understanding of why some people commit sexual abuse, and comprise the first of four preconditions of child sexual abuse. They are:

(a) *emotional congruence.* This theory posits that sex offenders find their non-sexual and emotional needs are best met by sexual activity with children. Children therefore have a special meaning. A number of explanations have been put forward to explain this. One suggestion is that such men (the theory really only addresses males offending) find children less threatening than other adults. A study by Howells provides some support for this (Howells 1979). Other theories are more psychoanalytic in orientation and focus on such problems as: impaired emotional and psychosexual development with a resultant need to control; a narcissistic tendency which results in perpetrators identifying with the self as a young child, and a need to re-enact early experiences of sexual abuse in an attempt to come to terms with it. Few of these suggestions enjoy strong empirical support but are attempts to make sense of a common finding that relationships with children provide many child sexual abusers with particular emotional gratification.

(b) *sexual arousal.* A sexual attraction to children. At present the reasons why some men are sexually aroused by children are poorly understood. A majority of those who sexually abuse children are also aroused by stimuli concerning adults (Barbaree and Marshall 1989); previous childhood sexual abuse holds only for a minority of sexual abusers, and attempts to identify biological variables is at best inconclusive (see Flor-Henry *et al.* 1991, Hucker *et al.* 1986). However, sexual arousal to children—whatever its origins—is an important factor in the perpetration of child sexual abuse, and an important focus of intervention.

(c) *blockage.* Factors which interfere with the development of appropriate adult–adult relationships. Empirically this is perhaps the weakest part of Finkelhor's conceptualisation. It is probably the case that many child sexual abusers have poor relationships with adults, but this is not true of all, and the reasons why this should be are not certain e.g., evidence about the role of social skills deficits is mixed. However, it may be that whatever explains the particular emotional significance held by children for perpetrators may also point to qualitative problems in the ability to form and maintain satisfying adult relationships which sometimes manifests itself as lack of skills etc. but which sometimes might be less visible.

These three factors comprise the first of Finkelhor's preconditions for the occurrence of child sexual abuse, and effectively address motivational issues. The remaining pre-conditions are:

(a) *overcoming internal inhibitions.* In order to engage in sexual activity with children, an individual must overcome any internal, socially conditioned inhibitions against this. Cognitive distortions which allow the perpetrator to justify his/her activities play a major role in sexual offending against children, and are seen as Finkelhor as the first of three barriers to be overcome.

(b) *overcoming external inhibitors.* In order to realise a desire to sexually assault, an offender must devise a set of circumstances in which the opportunity for such activity arises. Although some offending clearly happens opportunistically, particularly in the case of young sexual offenders, the majority of offences perpetrated by adults appears to be planned for. This can be a long-term endeavour, and is referred to by Wolf as 'planning and grooming' (see Wolf 1985 for an alternative model). Implications for intervention lie in helping an offender to recognise this aspect of his offending pattern, to identify risk situations and to develop strategies for either avoiding them or leaving them.

(c) *overcoming the resistance of the child.* Finally, offenders need to persuade children to allow them to offend. This too can be a long-term and planned endeavour, in which the abuser cultivates the relationship with the child and uses persuasion, bribes and threats to achieve his/her aims.

In this model then, offenders are conceptualised as adults who find relationships with children less threatening than those with adults (see Howells 1979), and who enjoy children's dependent and relatively weak status. They are, for reasons not well understood, sexually attracted to children, and have difficulties in establishing and sustaining relationships with other adults. In order for these predisposing factors to lead to abuse, the taboos against sexual activity with children must be weakened or over-ruled by overcoming internal and external inhibitions. Cognitive distortions of the kind described above, in which children are seen as inviting abuse, or benefiting from it (or at least not being harmed), may contribute to the breakdown of internal inhibitions, as may alcohol or substance misuse. External inhibitions may be overcome by cultivating relationships with children, and securing a situation in which abuse can take place. Threatening or bribing a child to stay quiet constitute the 'final' piece of this particular explanatory jig-saw, or 'offending map'. The strength of Finkelhor's model is its accessibility to practitioners and researchers, and the scaffolding it provides upon which to hang research questions, and tackle treatment issues. However, as yet it lacks the empirical support that would be ideal, and in and of itself does not prescribe the detail of optimum programmes of intervention.

Prentky and his colleagues are developing a more complex model which takes into account a range of variables such as (i) degree of fixation (pre-occupation with particular categories of victim); (ii) social competence; (iii) amount of contact with the child; (iv) meaning of the contact (sexual only, or social and sexual); (v) degree of physical injury, and (vi) degree of sadism. The model is constructed around two axes, the first of which involves a dichotomous rating on the first two dimensions (degree of fixation and social competence) yielding four subgroups. The second axis comprises those variables relevant to the degree and nature of contact with children. The validity and generalisation of this model is currently being tested, but promises to shed some light on differences in the developmental histories of particular forms of abuse (Knight and Prentky 1990) and may be helpful in directing future research and practice.

6

CONSEQUENCES OF MALTREATMENT

An increasingly detailed picture is beginning to emerge of the short- and long-term consequences of physical abuse and neglect, psychological maltreatment and sexual abuse. A growing number of prospective studies avoid many of the confounding problems associated with retrospective studies, for example, problems of recall, failure to disclose, biased samples and the difficulties of separating out the effects of abuse from other factors such as family discord, or parental illness. This increases the confidence we can have in what these studies suggest are the sequelae of abuse.

The consequences of abuse appear to be a function of a number of factors, including: type(s) of abuse, severity and frequency of abuse, age of child, gender and availability of protective factors which function to increase a child's resilience (e.g., Fonagy *et al*. 1994). The absence of adverse consequences in the *immediate* aftermath of maltreatment may be indicative that no consequences have occurred, perhaps due to a child's resilience or to other protective factors in his or her environment. Alternatively it may belie an increased risk for the development of psychosocial problems in later years. These may be triggered when an individual has to negotiate key developmental tasks, e.g., forming intimate relationships, managing inter-personal conflict, becoming a parent, and so on.

There are a number of detailed reviews on the developmental sequelae of child abuse and neglect (see for example Trickett and McBride-Chany 1995). A number of studies focus upon particular relationships, e.g., between physical abuse and the development of aggressive behaviour and attempt to explore the mechanisms whereby adverse consequences are mediated and, again, what factors protect children (see Weiss *et al*. 1992; Romans *et al*. 1995). However, it is generally recognised that children can undergo very similar experiences and yet be differently affected (a phenomenon captured in the concept of 'multifinality') and others can have vastly different experiences and yet end up with common developmental outcomes (referred to as the 'equifinality'). It is unlikely, therefore, that we shall ever be able accurately to predict the particular outcomes of specific experiences, and there is some evidence that attempts by researchers to do so have been misplaced (see Rind *et al.* 1998 for a review).

It is also important to bear in mind that few children experience only one form of abuse, and that accompanying psychological maltreatment, or psychological and emotional stress, may account for some of the adverse consequences of other forms of abuse and neglect (see Claussen and Crittenden 1991). Indeed, there is a growing body of research which suggests that at least one of the possible mechanisms whereby abuse and neglect have a deleterious effect on child development may be via their effects on the development of the brain and the nervous system. Reviewing the available evidence from neurobiological studies, Glaser concludes that there is considerable evidence for changes in brain function as a result of maltreatment (Glaser 2000), many of which are associated with, or attributable to, a range of stress responses which maltreatment triggers in children. Some of the neurological changes which these stressors can bring about may go some way to explaining some of the emotional and behavioural difficulties which such children manifest, including hyperarousal, aggression, dissociative reactions, educational under-achievement and so on. Previous research concentrated primarily on how deficits in a child's environment (e.g., lack of stimulation or nurture, appropriate learning opportunities) might affect development. Such environmental deficits are thought to be particularly crucial at a particular time, that is to say, that to some extent a child's optimal development depends on opportunities being available during particular development 'windows', which—if missed—are difficult, if not impossible to redress (Glaser 2000). It is not appropriate to go into the detail of these studies here, not least of all because there is not an emergent trend (apart from the possibility that a stress reaction functions as a common denominator which itself might be mediated by compensatory factors in a child's life). Suffice it to say that some studies suggest that the protective factors associated with differential outcomes in children may themselves be associated with the effects of buffers on brain functioning e.g., some researchers have suggested that secure attachment may serve to protect the developing brain from exposure to raised levels of certain hormones which can otherwise cause damage to the brain during its greatest period of developmental vulnerability.

Rather than conclude that because we are talking about neurobiological processes, we are in a determinist setting which renders the idea of preventive or remediative intervention somewhat dubious, it is worth considering an alternative view, put by Glaser as follows:

'Since brain development is integrally related to environmental factors, active early intervention (e.g., Zeahnah and Larrieu 1998) offers the greatest hope for children's future. The evidence for the protective effects of secure attachment in the face of stress clearly indicates a target for concern and treatment.' (Glaser 2000, p. 111)

Against this background, this brief overview considers the kinds of adverse outcomes that have been associated with particular types of maltreatment. Bearing in mind the caveats, particularly those around equifinality and multifinality, this chapter is organised around the putative consequences of each form of maltreatment with regard to: physical and mental health; cognitive and emotional development and behavioural consequences. It considers both the initial (or short-term) impact that maltreatment can effect, as well as the longer-term (or distal) consequences that may occur, some-times in the absence of apparent adverse consequences around the time of the abuse or neglect.

THE PHYSICAL ABUSE OF CHILDREN

In addition to the injuries that children can and do sustain as a result of physical abuse, there is evidence that children's health and development suffer as a result of physical punishment and abuse (see Augoustinos, 1987), and neurological impairments have also been observed (see Lewis *et al.* 1989). Kolko hypothesises that the effects of child physical abuse may impact upon a child's health in much the same way as spouse abuse has been shown to be correlated with poor health (Kolko 1986; Gelles and Straus 1990).

Cognitive and Academic Development

In addition to its potential to cause neurological damage, physical abuse appears to have the potential to seriously compromise children's intellectual and academic development. Studies of physically abused and 'mixed' groups of infants and young children have shown cognitive developmental delays and poor academic progress in early life (Aber and Allen 1987; Trickett 1993; Vondra *et al.* 1990). These school problems continue into middle childhood and adolescence (Trickett 1997).

Social and Emotional Development

Child physical abuse is associated with the development of negative affect in abused children and adolescents (e.g., Schneider-Rosen and Cicchetti 1984).

It is reckoned that such environments condition maltreated children to become sensitised to negative affective cues that acquire particular salience, living as they do in contexts of stress and threat. In a study of children's emotional reactions to, and processing of, negatively or positively valenced stimuli (e.g., a happy or an angry face) Pollak *et al.* identified electrophysiological differences between physically abused and non-abused children which suggested that abused children were more attuned to respond efficiently to negative cues (Pollak *et al.* 1997). They observe that this may well be an adaptive reaction in stressful environments, but such a bias toward negative affect, and diminished responsiveness to positive affect (also shown) are not necessarily adaptive in the long-term (see Rogosh *et al.* 1995):

> 'Such processes may allow children to tailor adaptive behavioural responses to meet the challenges presented by their environments, yet provide costly and ultimately maladaptive solutions that contribute to maltreated children's social-cognitive difficulties and increased risk of psychopathology.' (Pollak *et al.* 1997, p. 784)

And indeed, such problems have been noted in the research literature (e.g., Gaensbauer and Hiatt 1984; Sroufe 1979).

Abused and neglected children are also more likely to see themselves in a neutral or negative light. If not remedied, this may be an early precursor to the development of low self-esteem (Schneider-Rosen and Cicchetti 1991). Abused and neglected children use fewer emotion-specific language words, make fewer verbal references to physiological states and negative affect (Beeghly and Cicchetti 1994). As they grow and develop, these difficulties generalise to their relationships with peers, with whom they demonstrate difficulties in picking up distress signals and to whom they more often respond with hostility (see Main and George 1985). In general, they are less likely to develop pro-social behaviour, which also impacts adversely on their peer relationships. Young abused children appear to engage in more solitary, repetitive play than their peers, and are less likely to initiate positive interaction with them (see Allessandri 1991 and Haskett and Kistner 1991). Problems in social competence mark older children (Trickett 1997).

Physically abused children are more likely to develop aggressive (see Ammerman 1989; Kolko 1992), and other externalising behaviour problems such as rule violations and oppositional behaviour, both of which put them at risk of delinquency (Widom 1990). However, the methodological problems associated with the bulk of this literature mean it is not easy to be certain that it is the abuse that is responsible for these adverse outcomes, rather than other, contemporaneous problems such as witnessing parental violence (see Edleson 1999).

Long-term Physical and Mental Health

Within the context of a longitudinal study conducted in America, Silverman and her colleagues examined the correlates and long-term sequelae of child physical and sexual abuse (Silverman *et al.* 1996). They report 'alarming rates of psychopathology and co-occurring disorders' amongst both groups, who reported significantly more incidents of major depression, post-traumatic stress disorder, and anti-social behaviour. Those who were physically abused were more likely to have developed drug abuse dependence, compared to non-abused peers. Four-fifths ($n = 8$) of physically abused young men, and nearly three-fifths ($n = 7$) met criteria for one or more *DSM-111^R* (1987 Diagnostic and Statistical Manual of Mental Disorders III: Revised Edition, Washington, DC: American Psychiatric Association) disorders, with increasing risk for those who had suffered more than one form of abuse. As the authors are at pains to note, 'both forms of abuse were strongly associated with poor mental health'. The study was not designed as a child abuse study, and suffers some methodological problems, not least of all its small sample size. It does not claim to demonstrate a causal connection between these abuse and adverse outcomes, but the correlational evidence is strong, and supported by a number of other studies which suggest that adults who were physically abused as children are at increased risk for externalising and internalising problems, such as anti-social and aggressive behaviour (men and women) and depression and anxiety (especially women) (Trickett 1997). Not surprisingly, some studies indicate that those children exposed to sustained abuse over a long period are particularly vulnerable to the development of a range of psychiatric problems (see Green 1981; 1983).

THE PHYSICAL NEGLECT OF CHILDREN

Despite the limited amount of research conducted on the consequences of maltreatment, what there is suggests that neglected children probably fare worse than children suffering other forms of maltreatment in terms of adverse consequences (English 1995, Eckenrode *et al.* 1993, Erickson *et al.* 1989). This is probably because neglected children are those for whom a range of basic developmental needs remain unmet. Infants and young children are particularly dependent on their parents and may have fewer sources of compensatory relationships compared with older children. Poor quality parental care and/or the emotional unavailability of parents at these crucial early stages can impact upon children's views of themselves, others and relationships, as well as upon their own behaviour and emotional development, in ways which stack the odds against them in future years.

Cognitive and Academic Development

Compared with matched comparison peers, neglected children have been observed to perform less well on measures on language ability and intelligence (see Crouch and Milner 1993 for a more detailed review of these, and other findings). In a comparison of abused, neglected, abused *and* neglected, and non-abused preschool children, only neglect emerged as a significant predictor for measures of auditory comprehension and verbal ability, suggesting it may play a crucial role in the relationship between maltreatment in general, and language delays (Allen and Oliver 1982). A study by Fox *et al.* (1988) suggests that severity of neglect may be an important factor in determining its impact. Gowan followed a group of pre-school children for two years (Gowan 1993) and concluded that the quality of psychological care predicted IQ and language abilities, particularly receptive language, of children at age 2 and 3 years. Children in lower income groups showed a deterioration in IQ scores over time, whether in the maltreated group or the non-maltreated groups, but children who had been physically neglected had significantly lower scores, and at 3 years, those who had been inadequately cared for, either physically, psychologically or both, showed less ability to engage in age-appropriate play (Gowan 1993).

In a study of school-age maltreated children (Howing *et al.* 1993), neglected children showed even more extreme academic delays than those who had been physically abused, although they had no apparent socio-emotional difficulties. The results are somewhat insecure in their interpretation because the researchers failed to match the comparison groups on a number of key variables that one might assume would be influential, such as ethnicity and family size.

It is likely that neglect affects children's intellectual and linguistic abilities primarily via the lack of stimulation which occurs in neglectful parenting (Allen and Oliver 1982). However, once again the current body of research evidence makes it difficult to attribute these consequences unequivocally to neglect, rather than other co-terminus problems, or to account for their effect if they have a causal role.

Social and Emotional Development

Neglected children, together with all maltreated children, are at risk of developing insecure attachments with those who might be expected to look after them, and in particular are frequently classified as having avoidant or resistant attachments (e.g., Crittenden 1992; Egeland and Sroufe 1981; Lamb *et al.* 1985). Observational studies suggest that neglected children are more passive and withdrawn, remaining isolated during play time (Crittenden

1992). Like physically abused children, neglected pre-school children tend to exhibit less pro-social behaviour than non-abused peers, and appear generally more apathetic and withdrawn, and passive recipients of social interaction (Egeland *et al.* 1983).

However, over time, neglected children are also at risk of developing behavioural problems, which may account for the disparate results of some other studies which focus on older children. Crittenden has suggested that neglected children may seek compensatory stimulation resulting in active exploratory behaviour (Crittenden 1988a). More recently, in an analysis of different forms of neglect, she has hypothesised that children whose neglect takes the form of disorganisation rather than emotional unavailability, and who live in families where affect is dominant, may learn that 'what pays off' is behaviour of a similarly high emotional valence, resulting in patterns of behaviour that are both self-centred and coercive (Crittenden 1999, see also Patterson 1982).

Reviewing the available literature, Crouch and Milner conclude that the relationship between neglect and behavioural difficulties and aggression in preschool and school-age children is equivocal, and they note that few studies have taken seriously the potential influence of gender (Crouch and Milner 1993).

Similar ambiguity exists for the impact of neglect on the development of delinquent behaviour in older children and young adults. Analysis of prospective data by Widom and her colleagues suggest that boys who are abused or neglected in childhood are at increased risk of delinquency, adult criminality and violent criminal behaviour (Widom 1991; Rivera and Widom 1990), although they also point out that the majority of neglected and abused children do not go on to engage in delinquent behaviour.

A study of adult symptamatology associated with types of abuse suggests that this 'pattern' continues to adulthood, with low self-esteem being associated with women who were neglected in childhood (Briere and Runtz 1990). This otherwise interesting study is limited by its retrospective nature and its focus on women only.

In a longitudinal study of families at risk for maltreatment, Egeland and Sroufe (1991) concluded that children who experienced neglect were more likely to display more negative and less positive affect from as early as two years of age. Further, those who suffered neglect, but no abuse, displayed more frustration, and were more likely directly to express anger towards their parents. At 42 months, these children were less able to problem-solve, and were reported to display less effective coping behaviour. The authors describe these children as having 'the least positive and most negative affect' of all types of maltreated children included in their study.

Long-term Physical and Mental Health

Little is known about the long-term health-related consequences of child physical neglect. Clearly, neglect in childhood can result in malnourishment and illness due to lack of adequate housing and clothing, and so on. Malnourishment (rather than the neglect which caused it) is itself implicated in a range of health problems. Few studies which have examined the long-term consequences of abuse and neglect, even in retrospective studies, have included neglect as a separate category (although some have included psychological maltreatment). The extent to which the findings of these more general studies, which do not differentiate neglect, apply to those who experience this form of maltreatment alone is not therefore clear. However, it is not unreasonable to suppose that the psychological neglect that so often, though not invariably, accompanies physical neglect, may have adverse consequences for adult mental health.

THE PSYCHOLOGICAL MALTREATMENT OF CHILDREN

As indicated in numerous places throughout this volume, the psychological correlates of physical abuse, sexual abuse and physical neglect, are increasingly thought to be mediated in large part by their psychological and/or emotional impact on children. As Glaser's review suggests, it may well be the stress that maltreatment elicits, and the absence or availability of environmental or personal 'buffers' that determine how deleterious the effects of any form of maltreatment will be. In other words, psychological correlates of maltreatment may well account for a range of sequelae following all forms of abuse, depending on a child's processing of what is happening to him or her, and the alternative forms of support and nurturance available.

Cognitive and Academic Development

Psychological maltreatment was associated with a decline in cognitive ability and problem-solving capacity in infants and pre-school children in the study conducted by Egeland and his associates (Egeland and Erickson 1987; Erickson and Egeland 1987; Erickson et al. 1989). Even when socioeconomic indicators of disadvantage are controlled for, psychologically maltreated children do notably less well than their non-abused peers with regard to educational achievement (Hart and Brassard 1991; Erickson and Egeland 1987).

Social and Emotional Development

In a study of physically abusive and neglectful families, together with two control groups (one comprising children in mental health treatments, the other drawn from the community), Claussen and Crittenden examined the contribution of psychological maltreatment to a range of child outcomes (Claussen and Crittenden 1991). They reported that (i) psychological maltreatment was present in almost all cases of physical abuse, and (ii) the degree of psychological maltreatment, rather than the degree of physical injury, predicted psychosocial and behavioural problems in children. This also applied to those children in the comparison groups who had not (all) been physically abused.

In a longitudinal study (Erickson et al. 1989), children whose mothers were deemed 'psychologically unavailable' exhibited a number of behavioural problems, including self-abusive behaviour, anxiety, and other indicators of developing psychopathology.

Long-term Physical and Mental Health

Only one study to date, that of Moeller et al. (1993), has explored the differential effects of physical, sexual and emotional abuse, and their cumulative impacts where they are conjoint—as they so often are. Moeller and her colleagues ascertained that in their sample of 668 women attending a gynaecological practice in the U.S.A., half reported childhood abuse. Over one third (250 respondents) reported severe emotional distress in childhood, including: an extreme level of tension in the household more than 25% of the time (79%); frequent, violent fighting between parents (45%); repeated rejection of self (28%); exposure to repeated, life-endangering threats (17%); and 21% recalled types of emotional abuse such as parental suicide attempts, alcoholic parents beating and killing other people, threatened abandonment (e.g., being sent to a *new foster home [sic]*), and mentally ill parents raging in public (Moeller et al. 1993).

This clinical study provides suggestive evidence that both physical and sexual abuse have serious adverse consequences for the physical and mental well-being of women. Multiple forms of abuse increased risk, but those who had experienced psychological maltreatment were more likely to have sought help from therapists, or personal confidants. The most helpful group to whom these women turned were reportedly therapists (43%), followed by friends (36%)—possibly reflecting a distinct North American bias in terms of service provision and service use. A most worrying finding of this study was that only 4% of all the women who reported a history of childhood abuse had received intervention *as a child*. Those who had received help, had obtained it as the result of seeking it in adulthood. This is clearly an area which merits serious consideration given the nature of the sequelae reported in this study.

CHILD SEXUAL ABUSE

The impact of childhood sexual abuse is thought to be mediated by a range of external factors, including the nature of the abuse, its severity, frequency and duration, the relationship of the victim to the perpetrator, the numbers of perpetrators, whether or not coercion or physical force were used, and the degree of support, particularly maternal support, subsequently available to the child (Green 1993; Kendall-Tackett *et al.* 1993; Romans *et al.* 1995). Other studies testify to the importance of more subjective factors, such as the extent to which victims of childhood sexual abuse hold themselves responsible for the abuse (see Weaver and Clum 1995) and other factors which augment the resilience of victims to adverse events. Included in the latter are a sense of control over one's life ('internal locus of control') and an optimistic outlook (see Spacarrelli 1994, Himelein and McElrath 1996). The emotional climate of the family in which the victim lives may also play a role in exacerbating or minimising the impact of abuse, as well as being associated with its prevalence (Faust *et al.* 1995; Nash *et al.* 1993a). Few studies to date have examined the impact of such a range of factors using non-clinical samples i.e., samples of people who have been sexually abused in childhood but have not presented to health or psychological services with symptoms. In one such study undertaken by Lange *et al.* (1999) the researchers found, in a sample of over 400 women recruited via an advertisement for women who had had unwanted sexual experiences in childhood, that severity of abuse (number of different types of abusive acts) was the most important objective factor (that is to say, descriptor of the abuse) associated with the development of adult psychopathology. The authors also established the significance of the victim's subjective characteristics and the atmosphere in the family of origin as strong predictors of psychopathology. Lange *et al.*, found an association between feelings of guilt and psychopathology, even when victims attributed responsibility for their abuse to the perpetrator. This is in contrast to other studies which have suggested that the attribution of responsibility is a key factor (see Morrow and Sorell 1989, and Mennen and Meadow 1994). This underlines the need for those working with victims of abuse to focus not only on external attributions but on feelings of worth and self-blame.

Fewer studies have been conducted on the immediate impact of childhood sexual abuse on children and on their subsequent development, although the number is growing (see Kendall-Tackett *et al.* 1993). One of the findings to emerge from reviews of these studies is the diversity of symptoms which have been identified in separate studies, the absence of any one symptom which characterises a majority of sexually abused children, and the large proportion of children (around one third) who show no obvious effects. It is currently not possible to say whether or not these last children are truly asymptomatic (one possibility is that studies may not always include measures of all relevant symptoms), whether these might be children who are particularly resilient and/or who have more in the way of psychological, emotional and social support, or whether adverse consequences of their abuse are likely to manifest themselves at subsequent stages of development, when their experiences are likely to carry more meaning e.g., developing close relationships in adolescence.

Bearing the complexities of this area of research in mind, this brief over-view draws especially on reviews by Trickett (1997), Green (1993) and Kendall-Tackett *et al.* (1993) and endeavours to remind readers of the problems associated with the majority of these studies.

Cognitive and Academic Development

In her review of the literature, Trickett concluded that there is little secure evidence regarding the cognitive and academic consequences of childhood sexual abuse on very young children (Trickett 1997). She identified only one study reporting developmental delays in girls, but not boys, and the sample size was very small (White *et al.* 1988). In middle childhood and adolescence the evidence is more mixed, with some studies reporting problems at school (e.g., Tong *et al.* 1987; Trickett *et al.* 1994) whilst others not (Eckenrode *et al.* 1993). Trickett's conclusion is that these differences appear to be a function of the measures used in studies, with teacher and parent ratings generally producing evidence of problems, and academic grades failing to do so. Most studies which have examined IQ have ascertained deficits in sexually abused and physically abused children (e.g., Trickett 1993). Many studies show a high level of attention deficit hyperactivity disorders among sexually abused, physically abused and 'mixed' groups of children (see Famularo *et al.* 1992; Kolko *et al.* 1990).

Social and Emotional Development

The consequences of sexual abuse on social and emotional well-being and development is better documented. Young children and children in middle years evidence a range of internalising problems, and inappropriate sexual behaviour (Freidrich *et al.* 1987; White *et al.* 1988). Sexually abused children are most likely to have problems of social withdrawal and isolation. These problems have implications for peer relations, which are identified as a problem throughout childhood. Children who have been sexually abused also exhibit high levels of dissociation (a psychophysiological process that produces a disturbance in the normally integrative functions of memory and identity) (Hill *et al.* 1989). Adolescents are at increased risk for suicidal or self-injurious behaviour (Kendall-Tackett *et al.* 1993) and are likely to engage in sexual activity at an early age (Kendall-Tackett *et al.* 1993), as are some younger children (see Deblinger *et al.* 1989). Trickett summarises the results as follows:

> 'One consistent finding, with important ramifications for interpersonal competence is that sexually abused children from early ages exhibit unusual and inappropriate sexual behaviour. Sexual activity seems to start at an early age and may include promiscuity. . . . there is more and more evidence of a link between sexual abuse in childhood and pregnancy during adolescence. This is one of the few instances in which, for the present at least, an outcome (sexual maladaptation) is associated unequivocally with only one type of maltreatment (sexual abuse).' (Trickett 1997, p. 409)

Children whose response to the trauma of sexual abuse includes behavioural problems can find themselves at increased risk of delinquency if these are not dealt with, and the underlying problems resolved.

Long-term Physical and Mental Health

For reasons discussed earlier, the evidence of long-term effects, particularly on mental health, is difficult to assess at present. Clinical studies suggest that women sexually abused as children have a higher incidence of somatic complaints, including headaches, stomach-aches, and abdominal pain (Greenwald *et al.* 1990). Childhood sexual abuse has also been implicated in increased risk of drug or alcohol misuse (Cole *et al.* 1992). Others indicate that adults who were sexually abused as children are at increased risk of a range of externalising and internalising problems, including aggressive and anti-social behaviour, anxiety and depression and low self-esteem (see Black *et al.* 1994, Jehu 1988, Jumper 1995, Beitchman *et al.*, 1992, Mullen *et al.* 1993). However, reviews by Rind and Tromovitch (1997), Finkelhor *et al.* (1990) and Higgins and McCabe (1994) augur caution. Roosa and his colleagues point out that differences between these and other studies/reviews may be attributable to a range of factors including: differences in definition, whether or not researchers attended to whether or not sexual experiences were wanted or unwanted (rather than merely defining abuse in terms of age), whether or not studies controlled for other co-existing problems which might themselves be associated with adult mental health independently of abuse (e.g., family factors such as partner conflict, family break-up) or to differences in samples (Roosa *et al.* 1999). Roosa *et al.* also point out that few studies to date have explored the potential mediating impact of ethnicity in determining the effects of childhood sexual abuse. In a study using a reliable and valid measure of sexual abuse which focused exclusively on unwanted sexual events and which assessed the severity of the abuse, Roosa and his colleagues explored the relationship between child sexual abuse and depression in young women from four ethnic groups in America. The study also controlled for factors often shown to be related to adult depression. The results suggested that 33% of women from each group (non-Hispanic white, African American, Mexican American and Native American) had experienced similar patterns of childhood sexual abuse, with about 20% of each group reporting rape. Their results are discussed in detail but their major conclusions were that severity of abuse was significantly related to depressive symptoms only for non-Hispanic whites and Mexican Americans. The data are difficult to interpret but they hypothesise that perhaps the high levels of stress and poverty amongst the other two groups may minimise the likelihood of any one factor making a measurable impact on adjustment. They highlight the complexities involved and stress the urgency of research which takes ethnicity into account as an important variable in understanding the impact of childhood sexual abuse, how it might be reacted to, and how one might therefore appropriately respond. Interestingly, child physical abuse was the strongest predictor of adult depression and the only significant predictor for each group. They note its association with a wide range of adult adjustment problems and suggest this may be because it is more likely to be a chronic problem. Again, they stress the need for future research into the consequences of child sexual abuse to control for the effects of child physical abuse.

In relation to the impact of sexual abuse on intimate relationships and sexual adjustment the jury is 'still out' in terms of evidence. The study by Briere and Runtz—referred to earlier—concluded that sexual abuse was specifically related to later sexual behaviour problems (e.g., getting into trouble because of sexual behaviour, using sex to obtain one's own way), unlike physical abuse or psychological maltreatment. The limits of this study were discussed earlier. Other studies are similarly limited, but evidence from clinical samples suggest that sexual abuse can result in sexual problems (Jehu *et al.* 1984), interpersonal problems (Briere and Zaidi 1989), anxiety (Fergusson *et al.* 1996), depression (Bifulco *et al.* 1991; Briere and Runtz 1987), substance misuse disorders (Bushnell *et al.* 1992; Fergusson *et al.* 1996; Mullen *et al.* 1993) and attempted suicide or self-harm (Fergusson *et al.* 1996; Mullen *et al.* 1993; Peters and Range 1995). As with other forms of abuse, severity, age of onset and duration of abuse, force, nature and quality of the relationship with the abuser, and level of maternal support are correlated with severity of outcome (see above, and see Nash *et al.* 1993a; Kendall-Tackett *et al.* 1993; Lynskey and Fergusson 1997; Ketring and Feinauer 1999).

There is evidence from one study that women who were sexually abused are likely to regard themselves more negatively as parents, and to use more physical punishment strategies (Banyard 1997).

Trickett's review is located within the framework of examining the effects of physical and sexual abuse on the development of social competence in children. As she says, this forces one to consider the 'whole developing child' rather than focusing on clusters of 'symptoms' (Trickett 1997). A corollary of this approach is the need to move from interventions which focus on individual victims, to those which attend to interpersonal and cognitive competencies. It also points to the role that agencies other than social work agencies might have in addressing these concerns. We discuss some of these in Part C. A number of authors have proposed that the impact of childhood sexual abuse is best understood within a post-traumatic stress (PTSD) framework (see Wolfe *et al.* 1989) and this has informed the development of some promising interventions (see Chapter 10).

Holmes and Slap reviewed the particular consequences of sexual abuse of boys. They suggest, on the basis of those large-sample studies available, that sequelae fall into three categories: psychological distress, substance abuse and sexually related problems e.g., hypersexuality, sexually aggressive behaviour, confused sexual identity (Holmes and Slap 1998).

RESILIENCE

The relatively uncertain picture concerning the links between particular forms of abuse and neglect is exacerbated by our limited understanding of the factors which make some children more resilient than others. Across categories of maltreatment it is the case that not all those who experience childhood victimisation go on to develop problems, either in the short or longer term. Understanding what factors influence or shape resilience is important in developing strategies for intervention and preventive endeavours (Spaccarelli and Kim 1995). Identifying those factors is, however, not straightforward and the research which has been done to date is not without its problems. As well as the, by now well rehearsed, problem of differing definitions of resilience (not to mention risk, or maltreatment), there are other methodological challenges and shortcomings. These include:

- *sample selection.* For example, children are often identified via biased sources such as social services child protection agencies, and are therefore amongst the more 'extreme' cases.
- *confounding factors.* Factors which may be associated with differences in the way children respond, for example, age or developmental stage at the time of abuse.

- *defining competence*. Competence in particular areas is typically used as a measure of resilience, but one which may vary across studies. Some studies use single measures e.g., lack of depression, or academic achievement, others use multiple measures which they combine to produce an overall competence rating.
- *source and type of data*. Evidence suggests that the source of information about resilience (or competence) will vary according to the respondent. So, for example, a child may be seen as competent by a parent or teacher, but not by other significant adults. As Scott Heller *et al.* (1999) point out, researchers have found that children rate themselves higher on measures of social competence than others rate them (Kaufman *et al.* 1994; Vondra *et al.* 1989). Similarly the type of data is important, with a need to gather data on external functioning (e.g., academic achievement, social competence) and internal functioning (e.g., anxiety, depression). *When* data are collected they may also be important, as memory and current difficulties can adversely influence the accuracy of retrospectively recalled experiences. This highlights the importance of the next methodological issue, *viz.*, research design.
- *longitudinal versus cross-sectional research*. Resilience may well be a 'fluid' rather than a 'fixed' capacity in children (see Herrenkohl *et al.* 1994). That is to say, children may be resilient in some circumstances when faced with some adversities, but not in others (see Cicchetti and Toth 1995). Therefore it is important to identify children who have been maltreated at the time of maltreatment, or shortly thereafter, and follow them over time, if one is to obtain as accurate a picture as is possible about the range of factors that appear to be correlated with resilience and how they interact.
- *protective factors and processes*. Finally, some studies examine single factors and processes, where others study a range. These are usually conceptualised according to a tripartite framework developed by Werner (1989) and Luthar and Zigler (1991), covering: (i) dispositional/temperamental attributes of the child (for example, responsiveness, intellectual ability), (ii) a warm and secure family relationship, and (iii) the availability of extra-familial support.

In a useful review article, Heller and her colleagues discuss these methodological issues in some detail, and proceed to summarise the results of existing research, commenting on the methodological shortcomings of each (Heller *et al.* 1999). This is a good source article. On the basis of the available studies they conclude that the profile of the individual who is resilient in the face of maltreatment is someone who probably has a high level of cognitive ability, a developed sense of self-esteem and self-worth, and a high level of ego-resilience and ego-control. By the last they mean individuals who are 'reflective, persistent, attentive, dependable, planful and relaxed' (Cicchetti *et al.* 1993, Heller *et al.* 1999). Girls who show resilience in the face of sexual abuse are likely to show an internal locus of control for good events (atypical for girls more generally, compared with boys—see Beal 1994) and to make external attributions of blame for what happened. For children in early childhood, those who demonstrate resilience to the consequences of maltreatment are likely to be those who enjoy a source of sensitive care-giving, whether through foster care, adaptive family status change (e.g., departure of abuser) or a significant adult within or outside the family. Other factors which may feature in the lives of resilient individuals are: a structured school environment, involvement in a religious community, or extracurricular activities. However, this admittedly tentative list comes with a number of health warnings. First, the authors point out that it is unclear which factors or processes (or combination thereof) is necessary to effect or enhance resilience in maltreated children. Nor do we know much about the impact of individual differences such as race, class or gender, and research has yet to adequately take these into account.

Heller *et al.* conclude that it is currently 'difficult, if not impossible' to ascertain which protective factors are causally related to which risk factors (Zimmerman and Arunkumar 1994). They go further, and endorse Rutter's view that what is now needed is research that attends to the developmental processes that promote adaptive functioning (Rutter 1990). They point out that negative outcomes are rarely associated with one specific risk factor, and that the number of factors present is probably more significant i.e., the more risk factors the more significant their impact. They argue that a better bet would be to explore and identify the underlying developmental processes which these less specific factors impact upon. So, whilst we now have the basis for further research, we are less secure in what we can confidently do to minimise the adverse consequences of abuse and neglect. One thing that seems fairly secure is the desirability of helping children to recover (or maintain) their sense of worth, presuming, that these children have lived in relationships where this has been established i.e., have enjoyed secure attachments. They point out that a host of factors happen to help or hinder this process. Some factors (like temperament) are biologically determined, whilst others are environmentally determined, like a caring adult. Ensuring that children have as much stability as possible, at home and in school (including those children in care), that they have access to supportive and caring adults, have help and encouragement to develop to the maximum of their academic and social abilities, are amongst the things that the professional may have *some* leverage on. Certainly, the consequences of abuse and neglect, particularly when severe and/or persistent, are such that these are the least that children should be able to expect of those who are there to help. Particular therapeutic endeavours which may contribute towards their recovery and which may bolster their resilience, are discussed in Chapter 10.

PART C
Evidence-based Approaches

7

PRIMARY PREVENTION

With the exception of programmes aimed at preventing the sexual abuse of children and young people, few primary interventions target one particular form of maltreatment. In part this reflects the difficulties raised in Chapter 2, such as problems of definition, but it also signifies that programmes aimed at reducing the likelihood of abuse and neglect generally do so in the context of aiming to bring about overall improvements in developmental outcomes for children. This also applies, to some extent, to interventions aimed at secondary prevention.

It is also indicative of the sheer paucity of research in this important area. For example, despite the frequency with which governments launch expensive social interventions aimed at improving children's welfare, few are introduced within a rigorous evaluation framework. One hopes that the evaluation of the Comprehensive Child Development Programmes in the U.S.A. and of Sure Start in the U.K., will prove exceptions to this.

This Chapter considers what evidence there is for the effectiveness of interventions broadly designed to improve child welfare and thereby to reduce the risk of, or impact of, abuse and neglect. It then goes on to consider programmes designed to promote children's safety in relation to the risk of abduction and/or sexual abuse. Because such programmes generally focus only on the potential victims of sexual abuse they only feature in this Chapter on primary prevention.

Why Primary Prevention?

The evidence for the effectiveness of interventions which follow the occurrence or identification of abuse and neglect is extremely limited, as will become clear from Chapter 9. Our apparently limited inability to prevent further abuse once it has occurred, or successfully to address its adverse consequences (often because of resource shortfalls) are some of the reasons to consider the possibility that prevention might be a better bet, could we but manage the switch in resources that such a move would necessitate. However, there are other reasons too:

(i)   Abusive and neglectful acts are only some of the many events which threaten healthy development and optimum outcomes for children. They are closely related to other factors, such as economic and social stress, inadequate support, or ill-health. Primary prevention strategies typically focus on children's well-being in general and the correlates of good parenting, provided in the context of supportive communities and enabling social and economic policies. Almost by definition they are designed to address the problems that can occur at the macro and meso-levels of social organisation, and at the interface between formal and informal networks, families and individuals.

(ii) Primary prevention programmes highlight the important role of agencies other than social welfare agencies in preventing child abuse and neglect. The limited resources of social services in general and child protection agencies in particular, mean that staff are often constrained to work at the level of tertiary prevention, with (for some) an all-too-remote possibility of working with some families at high risk. Even if they were not, were we to be able to 'rewind' the life-histories of those families whose children are at risk or who have been maltreated, we would find that in most cases early indicators of these 'child abuse trajectories' were evident in other social systems e.g., play-groups, schools, primary health care. Even if these settings require assistance from those with qualifications in youth work, social work or clinical or educational psychology, it would probably make more sense if this help was available *within* those systems, rather than separately. Often, changes in the operation of these systems could ease the pressure on families, or contribute to the resolution of problems in ways that would be more readily acceptable to families. Problems identified at earlier stages are generally more amenable to successful intervention. Closer involvement of social systems with parents and families could also go some way to offsetting some of the adverse consequences of such factors as poverty, poor housing, stress and ill health (see following Chapter).

(iii) Because of their broader and generally more positive focus, primary preventive programmes more easily avoid the stigmatising features of interventions that are designed to address extant problems with individuals already labelled as abusive or neglectful.

However, a major factor militating against many interventions in this area is their cost. Because many potential forms of primary prevention are designed to be offered to whole communities or populations (e.g., all new parents) their adoption could incur a level of expenditure that would be difficult to demonstrate as cost-effective if reduction of abuse and neglect is the sole outcome measure (Holtermann 1997). Currently, these problems of cost are exacerbated because we know relatively little about the effectiveness of many primary preventive strategies (Daro 1996). Most broad-based social interventions are therefore targeted at impoverished communities, or communities which are in some other ways deemed to be 'at risk'. Insofar as some of these programmes represent a rather 'grey' area between primary or secondary prevention (that is to say, they might be grouped under either heading) they could have been dealt with in either this Chapter or the following one.

PHYSICAL ABUSE AND NEGLECT

The Scope for Primary Prevention

'Do we want to prevent child abuse? Do we want to prevent sexism? Racism? Ageism? Or other forms of victimization? If we do, we must redistribute social and economic power. It is as simple, and as difficult, as that.' (G. W. Albee, 1980, p. 117)

Child physical abuse is only one form of family violence, and one of many forms of oppression that are underpinned by inequality. In 1985 Gelles and Cornell identified a number of areas of activity as particularly appropriate for primary prevention of physical abuse. The following formulation of their list is somewhat modified to account for more recent research and theoretical developments, and to extend their analysis to take into account some aspects of physical neglect:

- the reduction of socially determined, violence-provoking stress, such as poverty and inequality;
- the promotion of social organisation and adequate networks of family support;
- educational programs that reduce the likelihood of abuse and neglect, including those which aim to:
  - eliminate norms that legitimate and glorify violence in society and the family;
  - promote anti-sexist norms, values and expectations;
  - break the cycle of violence in the family by teaching alternatives to violence as a way of controlling children, and managing conflict;
  - increase understanding of children's needs and how to meet these.

Tackling the effects of poverty, or enabling parents to cope with them, are key components of many primary prevention interventions. More parents in poverty care adequately for their children than do not and it is therefore important never to make unconsidered and uncritical assumptions about the relationship between poverty and neglect in particular. On the other hand, poverty can exacerbate a range of other stressors, and it can indicate increased risk for other kinds of vulnerability such as those discussed later in this chapter. A majority of primary prevention strategies describe themselves as targeting physical abuse *and* neglect. This is largely because the understanding of how socio-economic factors contribute towards neglect is generally limited, and restricted to a view of neglect that characterises it as a consequence of parents who would care adequately for their children if they had the necessary skills, support and resources. As we saw in Chapter 5 this is only part of the picture when it comes to making sense of neglectful parenting, but it is nonetheless one part. The majority of the programmes discussed in the first half of this Chapter are therefore very broad-based in their aims and approaches, partly reflecting their more general 'welfare' orientation. Some specifically target child abuse and neglect, others do so more indirectly. All enjoy a coherent rationale for the approaches taken, though few have been evaluated at the level of rigour that would be 'first choice'. Some are in the process of being evaluated.

Reducing Socially Determined Violence-provoking Stress

Poverty is undoubtedly associated with child maltreatment, although its influence is by no means a straightforward or inevitable one. The absurdity of making simple causal assumptions is evident when one considers the scandalously large numbers of children brought up in poverty who are nonetheless, loved and cared for, and well-socialised within their families of origin. However, poverty undoubtedly impacts on the lives of individuals both at a community-level and often, indirectly, via the social and economic decline of neighbourhoods (Drake and Pandey 1996). We are unsure of *how* poverty interacts with other variables to dramatically increase the risk of abuse in a particular family. At the community level, it appears that poverty is associated with reduced levels of social cohesion and social organisation, leaving families devoid of informal, and even formal, networks of support. Inadequate income influences the material quality of life parents can provide for their children (home, diet, clothing) and the social and educational environments in which children grow up. The cumulatively stressful effects of economic and social hardship can precipitate or exacerbate personal or interpersonal difficulties, thereby impacting on the quality of parent-child, and other family relations. Some parents *may* be in poverty as a result of their limited educational achievement, which in turn *may* be indicative of a limited ability to deal with day to day problems. In other words, poverty can act as a 'marker' or 'magnifier' of other problems which more directly result in mal-treatment.

It is worth repeating that poverty does not cause neglect or abuse. Many poor families do their utmost to provide their children with the kind of environment in which to realise their potential. Further the imbalance in child protection figures of families in poverty may be the result of the ability of more wealthy families to stay out of the system, or to buy their way out of trouble e.g., via child minders, nannies, boarding schools etc. But, irrespective of this, and despite the fact that it is only a relatively small percentage of poor parents who abuse or neglect their children, the resource implications are sizeable, and a much larger number of children are bearing the developmental costs of policies which leave large numbers of families in poverty, and which have resulted in increased gaps between the poorest and those well-off.

Therefore, despite differing views about the magnitude of the impact of poverty and inequality on children's health and development, and the mechanisms whereby poverty has its effect, there is little disagreement that it is a key factor in bringing about poor outcomes in the health and development of children (see Davey-Smith and Egger, 1986; Roberts 1997; Gelles 1992). It is not surprising therefore, that a serious contender for primary prevention is a series of changes aimed at redressing inequality, or—minimally—improving the socio-economic contexts in which our poorer children are raised.

The relevance of economic and social reform for the prevention of physical neglect is highlighted by the following conclusion reached by authors who have undertaken a review of recent research in this field:

'Prevention of child neglect requires the implementation of public social policies and programs that target the root causes of poverty: poor education, teen parenthood, unwanted pregnancies, unemployment, and substance abuse. Low-income single mothers also need adequate financial assistance or job training services to be able to provide adequate nurturance and care for their children. Welfare reform is essential to provide incentives and remove barriers to family stability.' (Gaudin and Dubowitz 1997, p. 56)

The failure to intervene in these important areas has been summed up by one American writer as amounting to 'collective neglect' (Hamburg, 1992).

Increasing Family Support

In the absence of nationally co-ordinated fiscal policies aimed at promoting the welfare of children generally, many social interventions aim to help families increase their incomes, or limit the effects of poverty, in the course of providing other forms of family support.

Child protection referrals are rarely randomly distributed across towns or cities, or rural communities. Rather they tend to cluster in particular communities (Garbarino and Kostelny 1992; Garbarino and Sherman 1980). There may be many reasons for this, but one hypothesis regarding the influence of poverty on child abuse is that its negative consequences are mediated by means of its impact on social organisation at the level of neighbourhood and community (Garbarino and Sherman 1980; Coulton *et al.* 1995). It is this, some argue, rather than poverty *per se*, which distinguishes those neighbourhoods which are 'high risk' in terms of child abuse (Garbarino and Kostelny, 1992; 1993). Similarly, it is argued, this might explain why another factor appears to be highly correlated with abuse and neglect, *viz.* social isolation (Thompson 1994). In terms of primary prevention, both analyses invite community-based interventions, albeit of somewhat different emphases.

Communities with high levels of social organisation are marked by a range of locally-based formal and informal networks, institutions, and organisations which help support families in the tasks of socialising children and young people. The availability and 'mix' of these networks vary in both rich and poor communities. However, in relatively wealthy communities, any decline in informal networks, which might arise from increased mobility for example (people following jobs and moving away from friends and family), may to some extent be compensated for by the availability of formal provision and the ability to purchase, for example, child care, leisure and so on. This is less likely to be so in more impoverished areas. In these communities, there is some evidence that as the geographical boundaries of impoverished communities grow, the availability and quality of formal provision effectively (or in fact) shrinks (Bursik and Grasmick 1993). Those agencies that do exist often fail to work collaboratively, to link with community groups, and to work strategically to provide comprehensive services (Pugh and McQuail 1995). These failings are often exacerbated by shrinking resources. In the U.S.A. and the U.K., some initiatives have therefore been specifically targeted at increasing the co-ordination and collaboration of formal support services across health, education and welfare.

Augmenting Formal Support Networks

In America, the reduction of child abuse and neglect is an integral part of a large and growing number of community-based initiatives aimed at improving the lives of children and families in poverty by improving the range and co-ordination of health and welfare services. These demonstration projects are specifically designed 'to address the pervasive needs of low-income children and families and to combat the fragmentation of existing programs that serve them' (Smith and Lopez 1994). In part they endeavour to improve children's welfare by maximising the opportunities for parents to improve their educational qualifications and secure employment that will enable them to be economically self-sufficient. They aim to promote such educational achievement and economic and social self-sufficiency through the provision of 'intensive, comprehensive, and continuous support to both children and families from a child's birth until entry into school' (Smith and Lopez 1994). All programmes are subject to a series of evaluations, which are not yet complete.

By law, these programmes (known as Comprehensive Child Development Programmes) provide, either directly or by contract, a number of core services for families:

1. early childhood education and development services for all pre-school age children;
2. early intervention for children with, or at risk for, developmental delays or disabilities;
3. nutritional services for children and families;
4. child care that meets state licensing standards;
5. child health services (medical and dental);
6. prenatal care for pregnant women;
7. mental health services for children and adults;
8. substance abuse education and treatment;
9. parental education in child development, health, nutrition, and parenting;
10. vocational training and other education related to obtaining employment or employment that pays more, has a benefit package, or both.

(Smith and Lopez, cited in Striefal *et al.* 1998)

Beyond this, projects develop in accordance with the needs of the local context, and the wishes of participating families and community groups.

Clearly, improving inter-agency working is particularly important in a policy context where a mixed economy of welfare has been the norm, where state aid is by no means adequate and where the numbers of agencies operating within health, education and welfare are generally more numerous and more independent than is the case in the U.K. However, these projects are about more than *just* effective inter-agency working. Their primary prevention focus means that a range of agencies are needed to plan and deliver a co-ordinated approach to the range of problems that can jeopardise children's optimum development. Although the above list reads like a description of welfare provision to which U.K. families are entitled, it is worth noting the paucity of UK provision in some areas (e.g., substance abuse education and treatment), and the high threshold criteria which operate in others (e.g., mental health services). The U.K. government's Sure Start initiative has very similar aims, and—like the Comprehensive Child Development Programmes—the projects it is supporting will be subject to evaluation over a reasonable period of time. How rigorous that evaluation will be remains to be seen.

Augmenting Informal Support Networks

Social isolation appears to be characteristic of many abusive families (Seagull 1987). Again, some researchers see this as, in part, one of the consequences of a lack of community organisation or coherence. Others have pointed out that for a number of reasons some parents do not establish links with support systems that are available, whether these be with local groups or more informal networks (Coohey 1996). Wahler has provided evidence to suggest that mothers who are socially isolated are more likely to use physical punishment. A series of studies suggested that the use of physical punishment increases on days when there is little contact with others, or when contact with others involves conflict (Wahler and Afton 1980; Wahler 1980). Commenting on the societal values and influences which contribute to social isolation, in particular the value placed on 'individualism' and 'achievement' in the West, Garbarino observes:

> 'Altogether, our excessive and unrealistic valuing of independence sets us up for unhappiness, and our children for impaired development. For example, depression often comes from social dislocation and produces neglectful child-care (Weissman and Paykel 1974). This depression results in part from the macrosystem.' (Garbarino 1992, p. 57)

The socially isolated parent or family is deprived of naturally occurring opportunities to learn from others, to give and receive support, recognition and feedback on how they are doing. The socially isolated family has no social 'mirror' in which to see their progress reflected, valued and enjoyed. Although in child protection this impact is largely discussed in terms of the impact on parents' ability adequately to parent their children, such separation and alienation can also take its toll on broader aspects of a child's development as families remain poorly linked and integrated with key services and institutions e.g., education, health (Garbarino and Long 1992), and problems or deficiencies in extra-familial systems impact upon relationships and experiences within the family (Whittaker 1983). Clearly, then, there is ample rationale for endeavouring to develop and maintain support networks for families who live in communities where these are limited, and to facilitate the integration of families who are socially isolated. Agencies providing formal support services often have a key role in facilitating and nurturing such developments in informal networks, not least of all because these are best placed to provide naturally occurring, acceptable, esteem-boosting and long-term sources of support. Garbarino and Long put it thus:

'To support and protect families and professionals, we must lose ourselves in the social landscape, blend in with the human terrain, and become part of the natural social systems of families and communities. At present, far too much of what we call the human-service system sticks out above the natural social horizon or is out of harmony with the social scene it seeks to aid.' (Garbarino and Long 1992, p. 260)

They suggest that there are four key steps in achieving this goal: first, recognising the limits of professionalism. Secondly, offering consultation to families and communities, rather than 'expert' help. This is something that community workers have always recognised and is increasingly being emphasised in more recent concepts such as 'empowerment' and 'working in partnership'. Thirdly, they argue that advocacy is a key strategy in ensuring not only that appropriate services are provided and maintained at the community level, but also that those services function in a family-centred and/or child centred way. Finally, they urge providers to ensure that intervention programs target the strengths of families and communities, and build on this. In building on this, they argue for effective, inexpensive, locally relevant, simple and sustainable projects which are compatible with—if moving away from—existing values (Garbarino and Long 1992). Within the U.K. this approach is more typically adopted by the voluntary sector, and such a blueprint is certainly detectable in projects such as those undertaken by Barnardo's, a national children' charity. More limited attempts to improve informal support networks is a feature of many child abuse programmes, at all levels of prevention.

Some primary prevention strategies endeavour to combine interventions relevant to the stresses of poverty and social isolation with those which attempt to empower families to overcome some aspects of adversity. Broadly speaking, they aim to:

(i)   alleviate social and economic pressure where possible;
(ii)   enhance informal *and* formal networks, thus reducing social isolation;
(iii) offer help/opportunities for parents to improve particular skills such as parenting; child-management; social skills (so enhancing economic opportunities); literacy, and so on.

Such projects typically target both formal and informal support networks. Because of their rootedness in local neighbourhoods, many projects have strong community-development aspects. These approaches have received renewed attention in recent years (see Cannan and Warren 1997) and emphasise the importance of community work and community development skills in primary prevention. Related to this general philosophical approach, projects typically have a strong, positive emphasis on promoting child and family well-being, and on working collaboratively, which perhaps accounts for their popularity among users who see them as sources of support and empowerment. In the U.K., voluntary organisations make a particular contribution to this area of work, with local authorities more usually focusing on those families for whom abuse is an identified problem.

The problem is that, as Garbarino and Long observed in 1992, few if any of these programmes are ever evaluated, and none rigorously. A recent evaluation of a multi-disciplinary, community-based, collaborative child abuse prevention programme in Canada, which aimed to provide family support via formal services and informal contacts, describes itself as 'formative' and 'primarily qualitative' (Onyskiw and Harrison 1999). Given the costs of services, it is indeed a pity that such services do not combine innovative development with 'good-enough' evaluation. To the extent that some of the projects within Sure Start also aim to combine these strategies, this should provide a source of future evidence about the success of such endeavours. Such evaluations are certainly much needed.

One area with a combined focus on improving formal service provision, and using the latter to enhance informal support and to achieve the broader aims listed earlier, has been home visiting programmes. In this volume, these are discussed in the next Chapter, as the majority describe themselves as targeting high risk groups, such as poor, teenage, single parents. However, Guterman has argued, that in as much as some of these studies do not screen individuals (for example, using checklists to ascertain the presence or absence of individual-level risk markers), and often make their interventions available to all members of a demographically based group or population, that these studies could be described as 'universal provision', which is in essence, primary prevention interventions (Guterman 1999). The reason that the issue is an important one is not just cost or cost-effectiveness, but that programmes provided to particular groups are more vulnerable than mainstream provision in times of financial retrenchment. In a review published at the end of 1999 Guterman identified 19 controlled trials whose aims included prevention of child maltreatment and which used outcome measures relating to physical abuse and/or neglect e.g., child protective services reports or close proxy measures of parenting. Using meta-analytic techniques Guterman concluded that all studies demonstrated clinically significant measures of effectiveness in reducing child maltreatment, using the measures deployed. Further, the 11 studies that used 'population-based' enrolment strategies (what we could consider primary prevention studies) generally did better than those which screened their sample using an individualised approach to risk assessment. Guterman's view is that our poor track record in being able accurately to target high risk *individuals* (see Lyons *et al.* 1996), together with the additional costs this imposes and the stigmatisation which often goes hand-in-hand with such programmes, makes these less than cost-effective, and generally less desirable than population-based programmes. Clearly, this is not to say that these cannot be targeted at high risk *communities* or ·

groups as some of the most successful programmes have done (see following Chapter), and within this more universal approach we should perhaps seek to increase the range and intensity of services for those families within these groups who appear most needy. Such programmes also have to focus on ways of engaging those most in need of support, and factors associated with success in this, and other related areas, are discussed in the next Chapter. The kind of studies that Guterman reviews, and the review itself, epitomise the kind of evaluative approaches that are needed to determine the effectiveness of primary prevention strategies and to inform decision-making in this area. The last word on the topic of family support is left with him:

> 'Among the most consistently identified etiological influences in child mal-treatment across studies are community-based, meso and macro-level factors such as economic impoverishment, social network deficits, and neighbourhood exigencies (e.g., . . . Guterman 1997; . . . Thompson 1995; Thyen, *et al.* 1997; Zuravin 1989). Perhaps for these reasons the U.S. Advisory Board on Child Abuse and Neglect highlighted a community-based over an individual approach to the problem, noting that we must:
>
>> . . . strive diligently to overcome the isolation created by the demands of modern life and exacerbated by the ravages of poverty. We must tear down the wall that divide us by race, class, and age, and we must create caring communities that support the families and shelter the children within them. (U.S. Advisory Board on Child Abuse and Neglect, 1993, pp. 81–82)' (Guterman 1999, pp. 879–880)

Day Care and Early Education

There has been a long-standing interest in the capacity of educational inter-ventions to redress inequality or to offset the developmental consequences of social disadvantage. There is now sufficient evidence of the effectiveness of good quality day care and pre-school education, in promoting a range of good outcomes for children, for it to be considered in terms of a major social intervention in the U.K. (see Zoritch *et al.* 1997; Sylva 1994). Although the 'return' for the investment needs to be measured across generations, there is now promising signs from a series of well-evaluated American programmes, such as the Perry Pre-School Project (one of the Head Start programmes), that such an investment would prove socially and economically cost-effective (Holtermann, 1992; Duncan *et al.* 1995; Campbell and Taylor, 1995).

Data from a number of cohort studies testify to a range of protective factors for children from poor socio-economic circumstances, of which a positive experience of education is one. The National Survey of Health and Development for example, suggests that one of the most important of these is *parental interest in, and enthusiasm for, their education.* It may well be that this will emerge as a crucial factor in some of the home visiting programmes discussed in the following Chapter, as researchers undertake longer-term follow-up studies of these interventions. For parents who may themselves have had dispiriting educational experiences, to be able to enter their child's school without feeling intimidated, to value their child's attainments, and to be in a position to give their child a hand with school work, is likely to have a beneficial effect on children's well-being and have positive long term outcomes. For example:

- children fortunate enough to have this help tend strongly to do better in cognitive tests, and in educational attainment (Douglas 1986);
- in due course, such children, as adults, were more likely than were others to be enthusiastic about their own children's education (Wadsworth, 1986; 1991);
- parental enthusiasm also helps to fend off the risk to educational attainment presented by parental divorce and separation (Wadsworth and Maclean, 1986);
- the importance of educational attainment is seen in all aspects of adult life. Those with 'A' levels (or training equivalent) qualifications or above had much better chances in health (Braddon, et al., 1988; Kuh and Wadsworth, 1993; Kuh and Cooper, 1992; Mann et al., 1992) as well as in occupation and income (Kuh and Wadsworth 1991; Wadsworth 1991).

Further evidence comes from a series of experimental evaluations of the impact of pre-school educational programmes on a range of outcomes for disadvantaged children in America. No such evaluations have occurred within the U.K., but there seems no reason to think that the benefits that have accrued to American children would not be replicated, given a faithful replication of the intervention—something which does not appear to be an integral feature of moves to promote education for all children aged 3 and over within the U.K.

The evidence also suggests that it is not the case that 'any educational experience' will produce these results for disadvantaged children. Current plans to expand educational provision to all children when they reach their third birthday is unlikely to mark a major provision in an area of unmet need, unless attention is paid to the *content* and *process* of educational provision, as well as to numbers of children provided for. It is the *active-learning component* of particular pre-school programmes (e.g., play/do/review) that appears to account for their effectiveness in providing children with long-lasting academic, cognitive and social gains. These programmes (staffed by skilled workers) stretch children 'towards the outer bounds of their own competence', and shape their motivation and sense of self-efficacy. Here is Sylva's succinct description of the curriculum:

'In the High/Scope curriculum children learn to be self-critical, without shame, to set high goals while seeking objective feedback. There is a deliberate encouragement to reflect on efforts and agency, encouragement to develop persistence in the face of failure and calm acceptance of errors.' (Sylva 1994, p. 142)

The essential features of this programme are:

- an effective curriculum for participating children *and their families*;
- daily two and a half hour sessions for children Monday to Friday;
- weekly one and a half hour home visits to parents and/or parent group meetings, in which staff acknowledge and support parents as actual partners in the education of their children and model active learning principles for them;
- a high staff–child ratio: 1 adult trained in early childhood education to 10 (or preferably 8) children;
- an active-learning approach, drawing on the child development ideas of Jean Piaget, emphasises that children are active learners who learn best from activities that they themselves plan, carry out, and then review. The role of adults is to observe, support, and extend children' activities in the following ways:
    - by arranging and equipping interest areas in the learning environment
    - maintaining a daily routine which permits children to plan, carry out and review their own activities
    - by joining in their plans, asking appropriate questions that extend their plans and help them to think about their activities.
- Using as a framework a set of active learning *key experiences* derived from child development theory, adults encourage children to engage in play activities that involve making choices and solving problems, and that otherwise contribute to their intellectual, social and physical development. These key experiences are not culture-specific, and do not entail the use or reliance on resource books or the use of standardised tests and workbooks that dominate traditional approaches. There are 10 categories:
    - creative representation
    - language and literacy
    - social relations and personal initiative
    - movement
    - music
    - classification (recognising similarities and differences)
    - seriation (creating series and patterns)
    - number
    - space
    - time.

Each category includes several key experiences, for example, *social relations and personal initiative* includes:

- making and expressing choices, plans, and decisions
- solving problems encountered in play
- taking care of one's own needs
- expressing feelings in words
- participating in group routines
- being sensitive to the feelings, interests and needs of others.
- building relationships with adults and children
- creating and experiencing collaborative play
- dealing with social conflict.

Other characteristics of the intervention are:

- parent involvement
- pre-service staff training
- adequate staff salaries and benefits
- on-going training and adequate supervision from supervisors or consultants who know the curriculum
- appropriate space and materials
- health and nutrition services.

(Schweinhart *et al.*1993, p. 7)

The positive experience of school which these programmes seem to engender, appears to reduce the likelihood of early school failure and placement in special education—key turning points in the lives of many children. The generally positive attitude to school developed by these programmes has also been shown to be protective against later risk of maladjustment and delinquency. In summary then:

'Early childhood education may be viewed as an innovative mental health strategy that affects many risk and protective factors (Weissberg, Caplan and Harwood 1991).' (Sylva 1994, p. 143)

The apparent significance of the *content* and *process* of the curricula in delivering such positive outcomes (in contrast to other programmes) raises the question of whether educational initiatives that primarily endeavour to extend the availability of pre-school education to larger numbers of children in fact run the risk of exposing ever increasing numbers of children to experiences of early failure and disenfranchisement.

Besides offering children important social and developmental opportunities (not to mention fun), access to high quality day care affords parents a much needed opportunity for respite from an arduous task, and for pursuing others of importance. It offers a chance for improving employment opportunities, or obtaining work, with the possibility of relieving economic stress.

Evidence for the effectiveness of these programmes and their potential impact on abuse and neglect is summarised in the following assessment from two reviewers of early childhood programmes:

> 'Parents made positive changes in their own educational and employment levels and showed reductions in child abuse and neglect. Early childhood programs clearly do help overcome the barriers imposed by impoverishment.' (Campbell and Taylor 1996, p. 78)

Parental involvement is not just an incidental ingredient that produces welcome side-effects. It appears to be an essential mediator of good outcomes for children from disadvantaged backgrounds, perhaps reflecting the kind of parental involvement that socially advantaged children take for granted. It emphasises the importance of locating early education interventions in a broader framework of investment in family support.

Educational Approaches

In principle, educational approaches could be used as part of a range of interventions aimed at primary prevention. Possible targets include:

- teaching parenting skills;
- preventing teenage pregnancy;
- teaching conflict negotiation skills to young people;
- promoting values which eschew violence, sexism and racism.

They can range from the provision of information that features in many parent-education classes, to more intentional strategies of social influence such as those which feature in anti-sexism or anti-violence programmes, and which emphasise the importance of skill acquisition. Many primary prevention interventions in the fields of health and social welfare are predicated on the assumption that knowledge and information can be sufficient to bring about behavioural change. There is, in fact, a great deal of evidence to cast doubt on this assumption, but nonetheless when lack of information or knowledge *is* a factor, it clearly makes sense to address it. For example, many societies are now structured in ways which do not ensure that young people acquire certain key skills in the course of growing up. Family demography now frequently means that young people have no experience of child care, and few opportunities to acquire parenting skills by modelling on others. Looked-after children (and others) often know little about how to cope with the demands of daily living (e.g., budgeting, planning, maintaining employment). Similarly, peer and other pressures on young people, lack of social skills such as assertion or skills such as asking for and using contraception, can combine to result in unwanted pregnancy. Particularly for such problem areas, there is good reason to consider the mainstream or broad-based provision of programmes which might address some of these gaps. Such an approach might go some way towards 'normalising' expectations that, for example, parenting skills are not genetically endowed, but need to be acquired, or that parents need and should expect support. To transmit these messages, and to provide core information at times when people are not up-against it, when they have not been identified as 'a failure' or 'difficult' and whilst they are in environments which do not stigmatise, may offer an opportunity to prevent the development of problems. More likely, it may make subsequent intervention more acceptable.

Even in these circumstances, it is probably sensible to combine information with opportunities to acquire, practice and consolidate the skills necessary to make use of that information. Often it is in these areas, rather than lack of knowledge, that people have deficits. Interventions need not be 'all or nothing' however, and it may be that seeding improvements in knowledge and understanding can provide a basis on which to build. For that reason it may well be sensible to address important areas which we have reason to believe are weak points in our socialisation of young people and in preparing them for adult roles.

A majority of these programmes would be more suited to development by agencies other than social work or social care agencies. For example, if we are successfully to promote attitudes that challenge violence and sexism, and programmes which develop pro-social interpersonal skills, then this will probably require more than one or two short interventions in the course of a young person's education. Indeed it should probably be a pervasive part of children's socialisation, and suggests that schools should play a key role in taking forward the types of intervention that are currently confined to high risk groups. Resources are clearly restrained in all areas, but it might be possible to change the content or emphasis within extant personal development curricula which already have a place within the mainstream of education. This would then also have the added benefit of 'normalising' them. Such topics are often already covered in areas such as personal education, but for the reasons outlined earlier, a reliance on information and discussion is probably insufficient. It is important to remember that we currently know very little about 'what works' in this regard, and should take seriously the messages from areas such as health promotion regarding the challenging gap between giving people information and expecting to see that acted upon. This important datum appears to be under-appreciated in the design of programmes and in their evaluation i.e., choice of outcome measures.

In fact, there are few evaluations of educational programmes related to physical abuse and neglect which have a primary prevention focus. The majority are evaluations of programmes directed at parents, or professionals or communities, which endeavour to raise *awareness* of child abuse, and the problems associated with it (for example parenting problems). The overall aim of programmes is to enable adults to identify abusive or potentially abusive situations at an early stage in their development and to respond appropriately and more effectively. The majority of these studies are American. Few evaluations deploy appropriate and specific outcome measures, or are sufficiently well-designed and executed to allow any firm conclusion about their effectiveness (see Gough 1993 for a more extended discussion).

Parenting Programmes

There has been a steady recognition of the need to assist a number of parents in acquiring the skills of 'good-enough' parenting, and interventions which aim to achieve this are often a feature of the composite approaches discussed earlier e.g., part of formal support and informal support. As this focus of parent training runs across categories of prevention, discussion of this particular intervention is deferred to the next Chapter.

PSYCHOLOGICAL MALTREATMENT

As far as it has been possible to ascertain, no interventions have been evaluated which are targeted at the primary prevention of psychological abuse. Possible reasons for this were discussed earlier in this chapter. However, it may be that other kinds of interventions focused on children may act in ways that offset the adverse psychological consequences of abuse, and other factors which damage children's healthy development. It provides another 'take' on the potential role of schools.

Hart *et al.* (1996) have pointed out that school personnel 'are the most reliable source of compensatory relationships and role models for children who otherwise do not have good relationships or positive role models in their lives'. Further, schools are 'therapeutic environments in that they promote achievement and attainment of pro-social development in children, even when mental health problems, illness, and family pathology are present'. It may well be that programmes which aim to promote social cohesion and educational achievement in schools, will incidentally (and perhaps by design) offer children at risk of abuse and neglect a set of experiences that will protect them against the adverse effects of abuse and neglect. This is especially important when one remembers that psychological maltreatment is thought to be a major mechanism through which all forms of abuse and neglect harm children's development. Such programmes have been developed as part of initiatives to promote social cohesion within communities in the U.S.A. (Connell *et al.* 1996), and the Joseph Rowntree Foundation is currently sponsoring a U.K. replication (*Communities that Care UK*).

SEXUAL ABUSE

The task of identifying effective interventions aimed at the primary prevention of child sexual abuse is made easier by the existence of a number of carefully considered reviews (Carroll *et al.* 1992; Finkelhor and Strapko 1992; MacMillan *et al.* 1994b) and a recent meta-analysis (Rispens *et al.* 1997). The following summary draws particularly on the reviews by MacMillan *et al.* (1994) and Rispens *et al.* (1997), beginning with an account of the MacMillan *et al.* review.

MacMillan and her colleagues identified 19 controlled trials relevant to primary prevention of child sexual abuse, published in English language journals between January 1979 and May 1993 inclusive (MacMillan *et al.* 1994b). All programmes were educational, with most targeting the prevention of sexual victimisation in general. Two studies focused on the prevention of abduction and sexual abuse by strangers (Fryer *et al.* 1987a,b; Poche *et al.* 1988). Three were aimed at the prevention of both physical and sexual abuse (Nibert *et al.* 1989; Peraino 1990; Wolfe *et al.* 1986). Eighteen of the 19 studies evaluated interventions directed at children. Three studies compared interventions directed at children alone, with child-directed interventions *plus* an intervention directed at teachers (Hazzard *et al.* 1991; Kolko *et al.* 1987; Kolko *et al.* 1989). One study evaluated a programme directed solely at teachers (Kleemeier *et al.* 1988) and another examined the use of a training programme aimed at parents (Kolko *et al.* 1987). The interventions included:

- verbal instruction
- verbal instruction plus behavioural training
- verbal instruction plus film or video
- verbal instruction plus film or video plus behavioural training
- verbal instruction plus simulation
- a play.

Several studies compared the relative effectiveness of these alternatives and combinations of approaches (with or without parents or teachers) which is why the number of interventions totals more than the number of studies. Outcome measures deployed in these studies tended to cluster around knowledge (usually measured by the use of questionnaires) or skills thought to relate to prevention, typically assessed by verbal response to vignettes or, in a couple of studies, to simulated conditions e.g., stranger approach. Only two studies included data on child disclosure of sexual abuse (Hazzard *et al.* 1991; Kolko *et al.* 1987; 1989).

MacMillan and her colleagues conclude that there is evidence that educational programmes targeted at children can effect improvements in their knowledge. On the basis of evidence from children's responses to post-intervention vignettes, or their behaviour in post-intervention simulations, these interventions also appear to enhance prevention. However, their effectiveness in preventing abuse *per se* is unknown. Further, even when these data are collected, researchers do not say (or know) whether reports of abuse or inappropriate touching took place before, during or after the programme. This, coupled with an absence of data regarding children in the control groups, and the lack of randomisation in some studies, means it is simply not possible to draw any conclusions in this regard. It is not surprising that the reviewers conclude that, whilst there is evidence that improvements can occur in both these spheres (knowledge and skills), it remains to be ascertained whether or not these lead to prevention in real-life situations. We simply do not know whether (i) improved knowledge or conceptual understanding, (ii) a child's ability to say what one *could* or *should* do when faced with a hypothetical situation, or (iii) what a child does in response to a simulated incident, in fact mean that they *will* act accordingly in a situation of real threat.

In order to undertake a meta-analysis of outcome studies it is necessary to have data on the degree of change from pre-intervention to post-intervention, referred to as measures of effect. Rispens *et al.* (1997) conducted a meta-analysis of randomised controlled trials which concentrated on two effect measures: knowledge of sexual abuse concepts and acquisition of self-protection skills, and looked at changes at post-intervention (ranging from immediately after intervention to 2 months later) and at follow-up (measured from 1–6 months after the post-test). As a result of these particular inclusion/exclusion criteria (i.e., the outcome measures), four studies that were included by MacMillan and her colleagues were excluded because they did not provide information on these measures of programme effects. This eliminated the study directed at teachers only in MacMillan *et al.*'s review (Kleemeier *et al.* 1988) and reduced the number of studies focused on children (Fryer *et al.* 1987a,b; Poche *et al.* 1988; Nibert *et al.* 1989). Rispens *et al.* identified 6 further studies, only one of which met the inclusion criteria, *viz.* an intervention and control group, sufficient data to calculate an effect size, outcome measures covering knowledge of child abuse concepts and acquisition of self-protection skills (Oldfield *et al.* 1996).

The total number of children in the experimental and control groups for whom post-test data were available was 2436 and 1544 respectively. At follow-up these numbers were 1180 and 520 children respectively. Their conclusions were as follows:

- All studies yielded positive results at the end of the programme (post-test). Children of all ages benefit from these programmes in relation to improved knowledge and self-protection skills.
- At follow-up these improvements are not maintained at their original, post-intervention level, but still represent significant changes. In other words, there is a evidence of a 'wash-out' effect.
- Programmes that include specific behavioural training in self-protection skills are more effective.
- Longer/more intensive programmes achieve better results.

> 'Programs that focus on skills training, allowing sufficient time for children to integrate these self-protection skills into their cognitive repertoire, are to be preferred. Since the decrease of follow-up effect size indicates that program effects may fade, it may be wise to repeat the program at regular intervals.' (Rispens *et al.* 1997, p. 983)

- Younger children generally demonstrate greater gains immediately following a programme, but these 'fade' at follow-up, adding weight to the argument that there should be more opportunity for repeated learning.
- Those studies which provided data on socio-economic status (50%) suggest that children from lower socio-economic groups benefit most from preventive programmes (see also Finkelhor and Dziuba-Leatherman 1995). However there is also evidence of a 'fading' of effects over time, with between-class differences at follow-up being much smaller. This suggests that, like age, low socio-economic status may be associated with poor retention of knowledge and skills.
- There is no evidence on the transferability of knowledge and 'proxy' skills to real life situations in which children are at risk of sexual abuse.

There are increasing numbers of evaluative studies which are concerned with examining particular aspects of programmes, such as the specifics of content and format. Wurtele *et al.* (1989) compared the relative effectiveness of a 'feelings-based' intervention (in which children were encouraged to use their feelings to distinguish good and bad touches) with that of a behavioural skills training programme (in which children were taught about the appropriateness of other people's behaviour). Both programmes were effective in promoting personal safety skills compared with a control (receiving instruction if other areas of safety e.g., road and fire safety) but the behavioural skills training group was deemed to be less confusing for pre-school children. More attention needs to be paid to developing programmes which are tailored to the developmental age of children, particularly their cognitive ability.

Primary prevention programmes of the sort described above have reasonably been criticised for placing the responsibility of prevention on the shoulders of potential victims (see Melton 1992; Cohn 1986). There is some merit in these arguments, and certainly we should invest in ensuring reduction of threats to children's welfare wherever possible. That said, there is also merit in equipping children in general self-protection skills that can stand them in good, long-term stead in a social context which *de facto* contains threats of violence and intimidation (Asdigan and Finkelhor 1995). What we need to establish is what strategies can reliably achieve this 'in real life'.

IMPLICATIONS FOR POLICY AND PRACTICE

1. Whilst many primary prevention strategies have yet to demonstrate their effectiveness or cost-effectiveness, there are some clearly emerging trends that merit consideration.
2. Providing informal and formal support networks to families in need (in communities in need) may well contribute to a net reduction in risk of maltreatment to children. It will almost certainly enhance the quality of their childhood experiences, within the family, school and community. Although we know that social isolation is associated with maltreatment, we do not have a clear picture as yet about how it impacts on parenting or why it is that some parents are more isolated than others, irrespective of the communities in which they reside. That said, it is generally accepted that all parents need support in bringing up children and providing adequate care, and this may be rationale enough for service provision in this area. However, in terms of whether such provision makes a difference to rates of maltreatment, the jury is—at best—out.
3. Pre-school day care and education of the kind which characterises High Scope may well have a range of benefits to children's development and well-being. The evidence suggests that children who are afforded this opportunity to succeed have a better chance of moving out of poverty, of avoiding delinquency and of becoming adequate (and non-maltreating) parents. This highlights the necessity of a multi-professional and multi-departmental approach to primary prevention of child abuse and neglect. One of the major challenges facing those who seek to refocus services away from a preoccupation with 'hard-end' child protection work (tertiary prevention) towards helping those whose problems may only just have begun, but where the odds are perhaps stacked against them, is the fact that in order to do this, agencies other than child protection services need to take the reins. Education's investment at time one will result in social services savings at time two. Leaving aside the human cost (which should take precedence) the reality is that there are currently limited financial or political incentives to adopt such a broad based approach.

4. Insofar as parenting is not genetically endowed, but encompasses (in part) a range of knowledge and skills, it is theoretically sound to make parent-training available to new parents, or to parents who may be encountering difficulties with a particular child or set of circumstances. However, as yet we know almost nothing of the effectiveness or cost-effectiveness of such programmes—when targeted at communities rather than high risk groups.

5. In relation to child maltreatment, most community-based educational programmes have focused their attention on raising awareness of child abuse and neglect, and persuading communities to intervene early. There is little evidence of their effectiveness.

6. Educational programmes aimed at enhancing children's self-protection skills in respect of sexual abuse provide evidence of the general effectiveness of such programmes at increasing knowledge over the course of the intervention. Cognitive-behavioural programmes, with their emphasis on skill acquisition and rehearsal, do particularly well. Overall, however, such gains in knowledge and analogue skills (changes in skills measured in artificial simulations or role plays) do not appear to persist over time, with the implication that such programmes may need to be repeated at regular intervals to sustain changes. Most significantly there is, as yet, no evidence that such programmes in fact help children to protect themselves in situations of real threat.

8

SECONDARY PREVENTION

The categories of primary and secondary prevention have been interpreted quite strictly, so that this Chapter considers evidence of *What works* in relation to work with parents who are thought to be at high risk of abuse or neglect, but where this has not yet occurred. It is important to bear in mind that some authors, including some of those whose work is discussed in this Chapter, categorise some such interventions as *primary prevention* (e.g., Stevenson *et al.* 1988; MacMillan *et al.* 1994a,b; Clémant and Tourginy, 1997) so the conclusions drawn in this review may appear to differ from those of other writers i.e., studies supporting conclusions about effective secondary prevention may elsewhere be used in support of primary prevention.

Secondary prevention programmes which show up well in the evaluation literature are characterised by a clear rationale, based on what we currently understand about both the causes and triggers of child physical abuse. The components of these successful interventions are usually multi-faceted, and aimed at addressing a range of factors associated with enhanced risk. In this respect they, too, draw heavily upon social and ecological models of child maltreatment, seeing child maltreatment as stemming from a matrix of factors such as poverty, from social disadvantage, from diminished social resources to manage those stresses, from personal difficulties in dealing with key aspects of parenting (see Barth 1989 for an example) and from the failure of social systems to interact in ways that support and assist families, or to recognise when things are well. Programmes often comprise elements of education or parent-training, social and emotional support, and assistance to cope with the stress. There are some promising trends in this area of prevention. However:

- only a few interventions have been rigorously evaluated,
- because they are directed at factors associated with child abuse, they rarely collect data on abusive behaviour *per se*. This means that little is known about the effectiveness of these programmes at reducing the occurrence of physical abuse and neglect.

Why Secondary Prevention?

Whilst it is particularly difficult to demonstrate the cost-effectiveness of primary preventive strategies, this problem eases as we target interventions at those most at risk of developing particular problems. Essentially this is the rationale for screening groups at high risk within health services. Of course, the benefit of this approach depends on our ability to accurately identify those at risk, and to be able to provide effective preventive services. Our improved, as yet imperfect knowledge, of some of the factors which interact to increase the risk of child abuse and neglect, affords an opportunity to design interventions which, at least conceptually, have a chance of effecting change in areas over which we have sóme influence. This is one reason for placing an emphasis on secondary prevention. Others include:

(i)   our limited success with post-maltreatment interventions (*tertiary prevention*) means it remains preferable to endeavour to pre-empt the development of problems. This also maximises the chances of good developmental outcomes for children;

(ii) in some circumstances this can be done without reference to child protection services, thereby maintaining the positive emphasis on child and family well-being that makes primary prevention such an attractive option (see page 118);

(iii) we now have some promising indicators that some interventions can effect the changes we are seeking, and reduce the incidence of child maltreatment.

Not surprisingly, we again encounter some problems in this literature. Whilst we may be better able to identify some individuals and groups as being at risk of maltreatment, it seems that as we move into the areas of secondary and tertiary prevention problems arise in relation to the families recruited to the studies. Distinctions between those 'at risk' and those who are deemed to have in fact physically or psychologically mistreated their children can become rather blurred, particularly as one moves away from physical injury *per se*. Many studies feature 'mixed' samples rather than samples which fall wholly into an 'at risk' or 'abusive' category, not least because many studies rely on referrals to and from child protection agencies where the categorisation of families is often a difficult professional judgement. The technical challenges of conducting research in this field may make these problems difficult to avoid, but again it means that one has to be cautious in interpreting the results.

For example, such problems may result in a negative bias. If, as we shall see, there is a dearth of evidence of effective interventions with parents who have an established history or record of abuse, it may well be that the apparent 'strength' of secondary interventions is masked by their inclusion in evaluation studies. Such parents may need *different* interventions, or interventions that are more intense and longer-term. These problems are exacerbated in studies that have not used experimental methods (and which therefore have no control over such sources of bias), have not used appropriate selection criteria, have not taken care to describe their samples, or—where applicable— have failed to match groups carefully. Finally, as in the previous chapter, many interventions aimed at prevention with high risk groups, do not distinguish between preventing physical abuse, physical neglect, or emotional and psychological maltreatment.

Such factors make the task of grouping studies a difficult one, and other reviewers may make different judgements to those exercised here. Generally, this Chapter considers only those studies which purport to focus wholly or predominantly on high risk groups, and which appear on the whole to have achieved this in their sampling procedures.

PHYSICAL ABUSE AND NEGLECT OF CHILDREN

The Scope for Secondary Prevention

Effective secondary prevention hinges on our ability to reliably identify factors which place individuals or groups at increased risk of abuse. In some areas, such as prenatal screening, there is evidence that this can be done to a fair degree of accuracy and there is mounting evidence that we can subsequently intervene effectively. In other areas the evidence about recognising high risk individuals is more mixed and frequently lacks the clarification that prospective, experimental studies can provide. In these studies, whereby we identify those we think are at risk, and allocate them to two groups (preferably randomly) only one of which receives the intervention under scrutiny, it is possible to see—with the passage of time—whether we were right in our screening procedures, and whether our interventions make the desired difference.

In principle, the range of problems that might be targeted within the concept of secondary prevention is considerable, given the range of factors associated with increased risk. For example, we know that the children of teenage mothers are at greater risk of inadequate child care and child maltreatment, so targeting those with unwanted or unplanned pregnancies would fall within this remit. So too, do interventions aimed at breaking the apparent cycle of inter-generational abuse and neglect, by endeavouring to equip vulnerable (high risk) young people with the skills and attitudes necessary to develop non-violent means of negotiating conflict and managing the inevitable stresses of later adult life in general, and intimate relationships in particular.

There is also considerable overlap between the sorts of problems that primary and secondary prevention aim to tackle, for example poverty, social isolation, parenting difficulties etc. Interventions deployed in both have been more extensively and rigorously researched in the context of secondary prevention, and this Chapter emphasises those interventions which the evidence suggests 'work'.

HOME VISITING

One of the most developed areas of secondary prevention has been that of identifying women thought to be at risk of problems with parenting, including abuse and neglect, and providing a variety of forms of assistance during and/or after pregnancy, and for varying lengths of time thereafter. The majority of these programmes comprise home visiting by a trained nurse, paraprofessional or lay person and focus on helping (i) to shape parenting skills, (ii) to enhance the parent–child relationship, and (iii) to improve relationships with informal and formal networks (for example, via social skills training). In general terms, the programmes focus on interpersonal relationships within and outside the family, and endeavour to pre-empt or help remedy problems as they arise. Not all studies have a well-developed theoretical and/or empirical rationale. We discuss one that does later in this section, which also enjoys the best evidence of effectiveness.

A number of authors have reviewed reports of the effectiveness of these interventions. These reviews have been of varying degrees of rigour. Each uses different inclusion criteria, and—although they generally conclude that there is evidence to support the effectiveness of home visiting—they differ in the strength of the conclusions they draw (Olds and Kitzman 1993; MacMillan 1994a; Clémant and Tourginy 1997). Despite being a little out-of-date in terms of available studies, the methodologically most secure review to date remains that conducted by MacMillan and her colleagues. Some of the researchers included in her review have since published further reports, covering the extension and replication of the programme to different populations (see Olds 1997). Their results confirm, rather than challenge, the conclusions drawn by Macmillan and her colleagues.

Using a clearly specified search strategy MacMillan et al. identified 11 prospective experimental and quasi-experimental trials published in English language journals between January 1979 and May 1993. Within the studies, the following interventions were assessed, either in comparison with another, or with no intervention other than the usual services available (Table 8.1).

Although they represent the most rigorous studies in this field, and encompass interventions usually evaluated using less stringent designs, the authors identify a number of serious problems. First, few studies were

Table 8.1

Intervention(s) studied	Number of studies	Relevant studies
Home visits—trained nurses.	2	Olds *et al.* 1986; Gray *et al.* 1979a,b
Home visits—paraprofessionals.	3	Siegal *et al.* 1980; Barth 1991; Wolfe *et al.*, 1988
Home visits—community mothers.	1	Hardy and Streett 1989
Home visits *plus* intensive paediatric contact.	1	Gray *et al.* 1979a,b;
Home visits *plus* enhanced mother–child contact during postpartum period.	1	Siegal *et al.* 1980
Enhanced mother–child contact during postpartum period.	1	O'Connor *et al.* 1980
Social work following discharge to women regarded at risk for child abuse.	1	Lealman *et al.* 1983;
Early intervention behavioural parent-training for mother-child pairs.	1	Barth 1991
Comparison of two programmes, one described as a 'life-skills, esteem-building program', the other as a life-skills programme combined with parent-training.	1	Resnick 1985
Free transportation to appointments for regular prenatal and well-child care.	1	Olds *et al.* 1986

devoid of methodological problems, with only one or two reaching the level of methodological quality one would wish to see.* The work by Olds *et al.*, and Hardy and Streett provide exceptions, and Olds' work is considered later. Secondly, not all studies provided adequate descriptions of the *content* of the intervention e.g., what the home visitors *did*. Thirdly, although most studies used outcome measures considered relevant to child maltreatment, few used more direct measures e.g., reports of abuse. Fourthly, as can be seen above, the range of interventions, coupled with variations in duration and frequency of contact, meant it was not possible to pool these studies statistically. Only two studies which included outcome measures of direct relevance to child maltreatment demonstrated positive effects (Olds *et al.* 1986 and Hardy and Streett 1989). One of these was what we are categorising as secondary prevention (Olds *et al.* 1986), the other was primary prevention

---

* Each study was rated for methodological quality in such a way that the maximum score was '25'. Only one study obtained '23' (Olds *et al.* 1986) and a further two reached '19' (Barth 1991; Hardy and Streett, 1989). Whilst some factors undermine the confidence we can place in studies more than others, this gives some indication of the problems inherent in assuming that published material (i.e., research) is 'sound'.

(Hardy and Streett 1989). Fortunately these are the strongest studies, which have since been replicated in other populations (see Olds 1997) and for which a longer-term follow-up is now available (see Olds *et al.* 1994).

Of all the interventions under scrutiny, only one secondary prevention programme—a fairly long-term programme of visiting by trained nurses, begun during pregnancy—seemed effective in preventing abuse and neglect. Other interventions appeared to make, at best, no difference. Here is the conclusion reached by MacMillan *et al.*:

> 'among the prenatal and early childhood intervention programs, according to the outcomes assessed in this overview, long-term visitation has been shown effective in the prevention of child physical abuse and neglect among families with one or more of single parenthood, poverty, and teenage parent status (Hardy and Streett, 1989; Olds *et al.*, 1986). The evidence regarding the effectiveness of interventions of short-term home visitation, early and extended postpartum contact, intensive paediatric contact, use of a drop-in-centre, classroom education and parent training remains inconclusive.' (MacMillan *et al.* 1994a, p. 852)

These appropriately restrained conclusions mirror those of other reviewers who found little encouragement in the results of earlier, often less rigorous, studies (Combs-Orme *et al.* 1985; Olds and Kitzman, 1990, 1993), but with a touch more optimism. Given that only one particular form of home visiting appears to be particularly effective, it is worth examining in some detail.

Correlates of Effective Home Visiting

Olds and his colleagues have conducted a series of studies into the effectiveness of their home visiting programme. This has developed over the course of the last 20 years, which itself poses interesting problems about disinterring 'what' exactly 'works'. However, unlike many social interventions they provide a very well-articulated rationale for the programme's ingredients, and a detailed description of what precisely their home visitors do. It is difficult to summarise, but the following list of features provides a flavour:

(i)   it was specifically designed to improve the following aspects of maternal and child functioning:
   - outcomes of pregnancy
   - qualities of care-giving (including associated child health and developmental problems)
   - maternal life-course development (helping mothers return to education, or work, and to plan any future pregnancies);
(ii) preventing child maltreatment was an explicit aim of the programme;

(iii)   the programme was grounded in an ecological framework, which con-
        ceptualised the adequacy of care provided by parents as a function of
        other relationships, and the wider social context. Home visitors therefore
        focused attention on the social and material environment of families, and
        aimed to promote informal networks of friends and family members
        who could provide reliable sources of material and emotional support;
(iv)   home visitors also linked mothers with formal provision if informal
        sources of help were unavailable, and helped them develop the skills
        necessary for using these effectively;
(v)   mothers were seen as developing persons, and the primary focus of the
        intervention. In other words, the primary route to improving the life
        chances of both parent and child lay in working with the mother to
        foster a sense of optimism about herself, her capacity to develop as a
        person as well as a parent, and the possibilities of change;
(vi)   in the course of its development, the programme has gradually paid
        more attention to theories of human attachment, and to the perceived
        importance of self-efficacy theory i.e., that human behaviour is partly a
        function of how effective people perceive themselves to be. The latter
        has brought about an emphasis on behaviour rehearsal and reinforce-
        ment, rather than a reliance on information and discussion, and
        problem-solving. The former has had particular relevance to the
        process of helping, stressing the importance of:
        • establishing an empathic relationship between mother and home
          visitor
        • reviewing with caregivers' their own child-rearing histories
        • the development of an explicit focus on promoting a sensitive,
          responsive, and engaged caregiving in the early years of a child's
          life;
(vii)   mothers received an average of nine visits during their pregnancy and
        23 visits (SD = 15) from birth through the second year of the child's life.

This truncated account illustrates the care taken to ensure a 'logical fit' (see
Macdonald and Sheldon 1992) between what the home visitors were doing,
and a range of factors implicated in child maltreatment, that fell within their
potential sphere of influence.

The original study, begun in 1977 in New York, randomly allocated 400
women to either a home visiting condition or to a control group that received
free transportation to ante-natal care, and screening alone. Of the women,
85% either had low incomes, were unmarried, or were teenage. None had
had a previous live birth, and the sample was predominantly composed of
white clients (however, the programme has since been run with ethnically
diverse populations, with similar results—see below). Because of its broad
focus on child and maternal health, the researchers have a wealth of outcome

data, from smoking reduction through to abuse reports. A recent publication reports the following findings for white mothers, in relation to child maltreatment, injuries, and qualities of parenting:

- 19% of the poor, unmarried teenagers in the control group abused or neglected their children, as compared with 4% of poor, unmarried teenagers who were home visited;
- independent observations of mother–child interaction, home conditions, and medical records corroborate these data;
- the impact of the programme on child maltreatment appears to have been further moderated by women's sense of control over their life circumstances when they enrolled in the programme. Rates of child maltreatment were substantially higher for mothers in the comparison group who were assessed as having a poor sense of control. The programme appears to have reduced risk for such mothers in the group that received the home visiting service;
- between their 24th and 48th month of life, children of home-visited women were 40% less likely to visit a physician for an injury or ingestion (poisoning) than those in the comparison group;
- during the two years following the programme there were no differences noted in referrals for child maltreatment. However, during this period parents who were visited at home paid 87% fewer visits to a physician for injury or ingestion than those in the comparison group; lived in homes with fewer safety hazards, and in homes which were deemed to be more conducive to their intellectual and emotional development as measured through home-based assessments (Olds *et al.* 1995). The authors also point out that child maltreatment in the comparison group is likely to be under-detected, and over-detected in the experimental group due to the increased surveillance of child abuse and neglect which the project effected.

The authors speculate that perhaps even longer periods of visits are required in order to make a long-term impact on child abuse and neglect. Given (i) the changing demands that are placed on parents as their children develop, and the ongoing need to acquire new, age-appropriate knowledge and parenting skills, and (ii) the long-standing nature of many of the problems faced by vulnerable families, it may well be that—as in many other areas of child protection work (see next Chapter)—longer-term interventions merit serious consideration.

Are these results sustained with ethnically diverse populations? As indicated earlier, this programme has been replicated in a predominantly low-income, predominantly black (African American) population in an urban area (Memphis, Tennessee), and was similarly assessed. The results, now published, show a similar pattern of results. Improvements in maternal life-course were noted, as measured by subsequent pregnancies and births, although there were no differences in educational achievement or length of employment. As Olds and his colleagues point out, the Memphis sample was a considerably more 'at risk' one, with 98% unmarried and all from poor families. The home-visited families in Memphis had fewer health care visits for injuries and ingestions, especially amongst those families deemed to be most at risk. This study also replicated improvements in child care and mother–child interaction, and Olds and his colleagues report that while these findings were 'strong enough to emerge as program "main effects" (they) were concentrated among women with lower levels of psychological resources at the time of registration'. They go on:

'The effects were also seen in children's behavior toward their mothers; children of nurse-visited mothers with few psychological resources were observed to be more responsive and communicative toward their mothers than were their control counterparts in the comparison group.' (Olds *et al.* 1999, pp. 59–60)

The Child Development Programme

Walter Barker has developed and evaluated a number of home visiting programmes across the U.K. The *Child Development Programme* appears more limited than that of Olds and his colleagues (known as the *Prenatal and Early Infancy Project*), comprising essentially a source of social support for first-time mothers to help and encourage them in the tasks of parenting. This support was provided originally by specially trained health visitors, known as 'first parent visitors'. It has subsequently been provided by experienced volunteers ('community mothers') who receive support, some training, and small financial recompense. The core elements of the programme are:

- An emphasis on enabling or empowering parents, to give them a sense of control over their lives and over their children's upbringing.
- 'First parent visitors' are encouraged to develop a sense of 'total equality' in their relationships with the parents (Barker 1994) e.g., to work collaboratively with parents, and to their concerns rather than any they, as workers, might have.
- The programme focuses on all areas of a child's development, health and nutrition.
- They use semi-structured methods, a visiting form, and illustrated materials including informative cartoons suggesting strategies for tackling many of the scores of child care and child-rearing issues which typically arise. Parents are encouraged to set themselves developmental, dietary, health or other tasks to carry out with their children in the coming month.

- Emphasis is also placed on the health and well-being of the mother, in her role as a woman with her own interests and future and not merely as the mother of her children.
- Enhancing the role of the father/partner is also a focus of this programme.
- Some of the work may be done in groups, in order to promote social support and possibly to encourage community involvement.

Effectiveness

Two randomised controlled trials have been conducted on the effectiveness of this programme. The first focused on trained health visitors (Barker 1988), the other, more recent example, examined the effectiveness of the programme using specially trained volunteer mothers from the community (Johnson et al. 1993). Other evidence comes from the analyses of longitudinal data gathered on the very large numbers of families served by the programme each year (Barker estimates that some 20000 new families are brought into this programme each year, most of them living in social stress areas, Barker 1994).

Results of the studies indicate an improvement on a variety of home environmental factors, such as language and cognitive improvements, the nutrition of children who have, by proxy, received this help, as well as reductions in substantive child abuse and neglect. For example, Johnson et al. (1993) randomised controlled trial of the effectiveness of community mothers showed that programme children were more likely to have received all of their primary immunisations during their first year of life, less likely to begin cow's milk before 26 weeks, and kept longer on formula feeds than control children. They were also more likely to be read to daily. At the end of the study, programme mothers were less likely to be tired or to feel miserable. These results are in keeping with the findings of the main study programme (see Barker 1988 and 1994). Barker attributes the success of the project to the involvement of lay people, 'community mothers', whom he believes are more acceptable to new parents, and are more likely to be able to understand and assist them in relevant ways. This raises an important issue, which is considered next.

Professionals or Lay Helpers?

A question that frequently rises in the prevention literature, is whether or not the involvement of lay people is more effective than professional help? The discussion has a wider relevance than home visiting, but we discuss it here because these studies raise the issue rather starkly, and because Olds and his colleagues have manipulated this particular factor in subsequent trials, with mothers from a variety of ethnic backgrounds, and preliminary results are now being discussed in general terms, though not yet available in detailed form (Olds 1997).

The case for the deployment of paraprofessionals—lay helpers—to work in areas which do not require the technical skills of trained professionals, share some of the components of the advantages of groupwork. Paraprofessionals, because of their shared experiences, are thought better placed to provide more empathetic, genuine and street-credible help than that offered by professional trained staff; they can offer suggestions which are better-rooted in the experience of users, and are less likely to appear judgemental. They also provide a source of believable modelling—in other words, they convey the possibility that things can change and improve. Discussing this issue, Daro observes that the final review of the 'Fair Start' programme in the U.S.A. (the High Scope programme) noted that clients 'were more open, relaxed and responsible with the lay workers than they would have been with professionals' (Larner 1990), but that they sometimes had difficulty providing the range of help that was required in the areas of health care, child care, and mental health services, partly due to the high demand for mental health services (Daro 1996).

Olds and Henderson (1990) reported that some parents were reluctant to confide in helpers from their community, for fear of loss of privacy and a view that professionals were more effective at helping users communicate with other services. In frankness, the answer to 'what works best?' in terms of professional or lay help is that we don't know. In their 1993 review of research on home visiting, Olds and Kitzman summarise the experimental evidence as follows:

> 'It is our clinical experience that mothers are particularly concerned about their physical health during pregnancy and the physical health of their newborns. Consequently, they especially value nurses as home visitors because of nurses' abilities to address their concerns about health.
> The challenge in these programs is for the visitors to build upon parents' pressing and immediate concerns and to forge a long-range commitment to their own growth and development and of the improved care of their child. Future research should explore these topics as factors predicting the success of home visiting programs for low-income, at risk families.'
>
> (Olds and Kitzman 1993, p. 87)

Olds and Kitzman also point out that it is the hardest to reach who require the most sensitive and persistent efforts to establish a relationship. Ironically, as is so often the case, they point out that most home visiting programmes have established policies which require the termination of efforts for those who are persistently 'not at home'. In all probability this is a question that ought not to be framed in terms of either/or, but that service providers should think carefully about what they are trying to do, and who would (therefore) be most appropriate in terms of skill and efficiency (cost).

Longer-term Effectiveness?

In the United States, the Department of Justice has espoused a development policy aimed at reducing violent crime, gang, and drug activity in targeted high-crime neighbourhoods, and promoting social and economic revival. Olds and his colleagues were asked to disseminate their programme as part of this strategy, because of its 'potential for reducing the rates of delinquency, crime, and violence among children as they mature' (Olds *et al.* 1997). These are high hopes. Of particular significance is the attention that Olds and his colleagues are going to give to the process of dissemination. All too frequently the impressive results of one-off, or 'demonstration' projects atrophy when adopted as routine practice. One of the challenges of 'what works' is to take well-evaluated interventions and apply them in such a way that their effectiveness is retained. This latest series of evaluations should therefore shed important light on an area about which little is known.

PARENTING PROGRAMMES

The Rationale and Evidence-base

The rationale for parenting programmes is three-fold.

(i) Parenting skills are learned. Most of us acquire these skills on the basis of our own experience as children and from observing others. Many of us modify the parenting styles to which we have been exposed in the light of changing social views, information (e.g., about the nutritional needs of children), or as a reaction to things we perceive as 'unfair' or 'inappropriate'. But for many adults, their own experience of parenting does not provide an adequate starting point for satisfactory parenting, and this is often compounded by the relatively few opportunities available for compensatory learning.

(ii) Children are born 'different' in ways that can cause their parents difficulties, particularly if parenting styles are 'fixed' or inflexible (Thomas *et al.* 1968; Chess and Thomas 1990; Prior 1992). Some children are temperamentally more challenging than others and are generally more difficult to manage. When there is a clash between parenting style and a child's temperamental 'bent' then the parent–child relationship can be particularly fraught.

(iii) Some children develop patterns of behaviour that can prove extraordinarily challenging to manage. This may have its origins in a difficult temperament which is not successfully negotiated, or may be more generally shaped by environmental factors such as lax discipline, poor socialisation, coercive patterns of family interaction (Patterson 1982). Comparisons between families who are not experiencing child management problems and those who have been referred to agencies for help with a range of difficulties (including child abuse) have identified the following differences in the behavioural profiles of parents and children:

Parents:

- give more commands than their non-referred counterparts, and do so in a threatening, angry or nagging way;
- engage in more criticism of their children's behaviour;
- respond to their children with more negative behaviours in general (e.g., shouting) and more often supply negative consequences to their children's behaviour, whether deviant or not.

Children labelled 'aggressive' (or 'disruptive', 'antisocial' or 'conduct disordered'):

- generally display higher rates of 'coercive behaviours' such as hitting, issuing commands, yelling, humiliating and teasing;
- for children beyond infancy a clustering of problems is the rule rather than the exception, comprising a combination of the aforementioned behaviours with destructiveness, temper tantrums, and non-compliance;
- such children exhibit a corresponding lack of desirable behaviours such as laughing and talking, independent activity and 'positive attention' e.g., listening interestedly, admiring;
- there is some evidence that children from a range of 'distressed' family types (including the children of divorcing parents) are more difficult than their counterparts from undistressed families, and pose especial challenges to the task of parenting.

The picture is aptly summed up by Patterson (1976) as one in which the families of 'problem' children are characterised by a high rate of coercive interaction.

(iv) High levels of negative emotion can distort parents' judgements about their children's behaviour, increase their negative expectations, disrupt their ability to monitor and attend to their children's behaviour, and disrupt their ability to problem-solve and think clearly about child-rearing conflicts (Patterson 1982; Dix 1991). Most parents take steps to regulate both their emotional arousal and its expression, for example parents typically make decisions about whether or not (or to what extent) to express their anger to children, and limit their feelings by appraising the motivation, age and circumstances under which an anger-eliciting action took place. Some parents who abuse their children do not do this adequately, or alternatively, have not developed the strategies necessary to control these feelings.

Aims and Objectives of Parenting Programmes

Broadly speaking, parent training programmes endeavour to address these problem areas. Fundamentally, they aim to enhance parents abilities to manage their children's behaviour, to reduce conflict and confrontation whilst increasing compliance, co-operation and pleasant interaction, and generally to alter the balance of reward and punishment in favour of the former. This may entail any combination of the following:

- providing information about child development, health, hygiene, safety etc;
- helping parents reconsider and reframe 'age-inappropriate' expectations and misattributions ('he's doing it to wind me up');
- enhancing the quality of child–parent relationships by, for example, teaching play skills, structuring the day so that they set aside some time for themselves and their child(ren);
- developing parents' ability to monitor and track their children's behaviour and respond appropriately, including the management of challenging behaviour;
- increasing support networks.

However, there is great variation in the 'recipes' to be found in the literature (Polster et al. 1987; Smith 1996) and it is important when endeavouring to reproduce effective programmes reported in research, to identify exactly what was done in the name of 'parent training', as well as whether or not it has been soundly evaluated. In fact, few programmes of any formula have been subjected to rigorous scrutiny (see Barlow 1997). Of these, only a handful involve work with parents deemed to be at 'high risk'.

Parent-training for Child Management Problems

We begin by reviewing what we know about those programmes which have as their aim the amelioration of child behaviour problems. We start here for three reasons: (i) child management is a frequent factor in child physical abuse, which is often triggered by disciplinary situations that get out of hand, (ii) knowing 'what works' in terms of child management is therefore directly relevant, even if only one aspect of a more complex situation; and (iii) knowing the difficulties that workers have encountered in less challenging situations should help in the development of more acceptable and accessible programmes. In primary prevention parenting programmes often centre on child management strategies. We take Barlow's recent review as a starting point.

Barlow systematically reviewed the effectiveness of parent-training programmes in improving behaviour problems in children aged 3–10 years. Her inclusion criteria were as follows:

- studies should be randomised controlled trials, in which participants were randomised to an experimental and control group (either wait-list; no-treatment, or placebo control). Studies comparing two different therapeutic regimes but with no control group were excluded;
- studies should focus on children aged 3–10, where the primary problem was one of 'conduct disorders' and where at least one of the problems was 'externalising' in nature e.g., temper tantrums, aggression, non-compliance;
- studies should include at least one 'group-based' parent training programme;
- studies should include at least one standardised child behaviour outcome measure.

(Barlow 1997, p. 7)

The review covered the years 1970 to 1997. Programmes were grouped into three broad categories (although these had marked 'within-type' variations): skills training (behavioural and social learning-based), educational (Parent Effectiveness Programmes [PET]), and relationship (Adlerian). The results were as follows:

- group-based programmes generally produced superior results to individual programmes;
- behavioural programmes produced superior results to either Adlerian or PET programmes;
- one study showed that a behavioural programme produced significant changes in child behaviour irrespective of the method of administration i.e., group or individual: telephone or home visits). Barlow writes:

'While the number of parents participating in the treatment groups in this trial were small, this result may testify to the robustness of the behavioural method in producing positive changes.' (Barlow 1997, p. 36)

In conclusion:

'Overall, while all group-based parent-training programmes produced changes in children's behaviour using both parent-report outcome measures and independent observations of children's behaviour, the behavioural programmes produced effect sizes of a much greater magnitude than the remaining programmes. This finding was consistent with the earlier results of [other] overviews (Cedar and Levant 1990; Todres and Bunston 1993; Serketich and Dumas 1996).' (Barlow 1997, p. 37)

These generally positive conclusions need to be tempered by an appreciation of the methodological problems that beset even these relatively robust studies. However, in terms of the available evidence, cognitive-behavioural methods are the intervention of choice for parents whose difficulties include child behaviour problems, or who use inappropriate means of punishment, both in terms of their rationale, and their efficacy. We therefore turn to the particular focus and content of these programmes next.

Cognitive-behavioural Parent-training

Cognitive-behavioural approaches to parent-training for parents with young children (say, under 10 years old) have at their core the following strategies:

- emphasising the importance of establishing the ground rules and boundaries of acceptable family behaviour, so that children have a growing appreciation of a *plan* against which to assess their own behaviour;
- helping parents to acquire an understanding of what they can reasonably expect from their children; expecting too much or too little of children of a given age being a common underlying problem;
- teaching parents to give clear, unambiguous instructions—'James, I want you to . . .';
- training in contingency management skills—to recognise and reinforce desired behaviour and to 'punish' unwanted behaviour by responding appropriately e.g., ignoring, using non-physical means of punishment such as time-out (a more organised and manageable form of 'Go to your bedroom'). Consistency is a key factor.

The theoretical base of these strategies lies in the learning theories, including social learning theory. Generally, they emphasise the fact that the acquisition of skills requires more than just insight or discussion—although these may be important—and that one of the most effective means of acquiring skills is through modelling: watching someone else perform a skill and using it successfully, replicating it ('in one's own words' so to speak), practising it, and modifying one's performance in the light of feedback (either verbal feedback from others, or through 'environmental' feedback i.e., when it does not produce quite the effect we had intended or hoped). In recent years these approaches have broadened to include a focus on parent–child and adult relationships, and on the emotional and cognitive factors that underlie family problems. We return to these later.

We do not spend much time in this volume reviewing the obstacles to evidence-based practice. These are, by now, well-rehearsed (see Macdonald 1998). However, one problem worth registering here is the antipathy towards cognitive-behavioural approaches that has, historically, permeated social work, and indeed other helping professions. Practitioners often prefer less allegedly mechanical alternatives, (although there are few evidence-based alternatives) and interventions which pose fewer allegedly ethical dilemmas. An appreciation of the complexity of cognitive-behavioural assessment and case planning would soon dispel any notion of their being 'mechanistic'. Consideration of their efficacy should raise the question of the ethics of not using them as the 'approach of choice' with a wide range of parenting difficulties and child behaviour problems.

Parent-training with 'At Risk' Families

Despite the success of parent-training in helping families whose children have behaviour problems, a number of studies have recorded quite high drop-out rates (Griest *et al*. 1980) and a failure of successful results to last for any appreciable length of time beyond the end of intervention or to generalise to new problems (Griest and Forehand 1982). Exploration of the reasons for this have identified a number of factors which appear to be responsible, and which suggest that these are generally attributable to researchers and/or workers adopting too narrow an approach to complex problems. The kinds of families for whom parent-training is unlikely to be a *sufficient* response to parent–child problems are those where one or more of the following pertain:

- poor parental adjustment, particularly maternal depression (Rickard *et al*. 1980; McMahon *et al*. 1981; McMahon 1982)
- maternal stress and low socio-economic status (Dumas and Wahler 1983; Kazdin 1990)
- social isolation of mother (Dumas and Wahler 1983; Wahler 1980)
- relationship problems (O'Leary and Emery 1983)
- extrafamilial conflict (Wahler 1980)
- the problems are severe and/or long-standing (McAuley and McAuley 1980)
- parental misperception of the deviance of their children's behaviour (Lobitz and Johnson 1975; Griest *et al*. 1980; Larrance and Twentyman 1982; Reid *et al*. 1987).

It is clear that these factors are more often present than not in the families with whom social work agencies are likely to be involved. Three things follow:

(i) the complexity and entrenchment of many of these difficulties indicate the importance of a move away from time-limited approaches with multi-problem families. The development of longer-term work has shown dividends in work with families of pre-adolescent anti-social children in contrast with time-limited programmes (Patterson *et al*. 1982). Once more, this is in keeping with the professional wisdom of social workers, but is at odds with the popularity of 'task-centred' approaches, and may need to be fought for in terms of its cost-effectiveness.

(ii) the complexity of family problems, and the adverse circumstances with which parents so frequently have to contend, mean that we need broad-based approaches to assessment and intervention, which address a range of difficulties. The evidence regarding how best to respond still favours cognitive-behavioural approaches, but applied to this wider range of problems. There is some support too for family therapy approaches. The other components of what is essentially a behavioural family therapy approach (Griest and Wells 1983; Thyer 1989) are discussed in the following Chapter.

(iii) given the dependence of these programmes on the active participation of at least one parent, this intervention is inapplicable when offered on a voluntary basis and where parents are unwilling to participate. It *has* been shown to be effective with court-ordered parents in the U.S.A. however, and it is important to remember that motivation is, we would argue, in large part the responsibility of the workers 'selling' the approach. We consider this issue in more detail, next.

The PARTNERS Project

The absence of research with 'real' families, facing 'real' problems (Weisz 1997) and the high drop-out rates reported in most studies have led some to conclude that such parenting programmes are least effective with those who are thought to need them most. Webster-Stratton has a refreshing alternative perspective:

> 'Such families have been described . . . in short, (as) unreachable. However, these families might well describe traditional clinic-based programs as "unreachable". Clinical programs may be too far away from home, too expensive, insensitive, distant, inflexible in terms of scheduling and content, foreign in terms of language (literally or figuratively), blaming or critical of their lifestyle. A cost-benefit analysis would in all likelihood, reveal that the costs to these clients of receiving treatment far outweigh the potential benefits—even though they do genuinely want to do what is best for their children. Perhaps this population has been "unreachable" not because of their own characteristics, but because of the characteristics they have been offered. (Webster-Stratton 1998, p. 184)

It is generally accepted that successful outcomes in work with families in difficulty are significantly influenced by therapist variables (Alexander *et al.* 1976; Patterson *et al.* 1982). Relationships skills and an ability to structure interviews and the work undertaken have been found to account for differential outcomes (Alexander *et al.* 1976). Webster-Stratton and Herbert (1993;

1994) suggest that when trainers present themselves as 'experts' this may create or reinforce feelings of failure or guilt in parents. Further, if therapists work too directively or prescriptively, they may foster dependency and inhibit that sense of self-efficacy which seems to be so important to success, and to the generalisation and maintenance of change (Bandura 1977). Therefore, they advocate a model of parent-training that is social learning in its theoretical and technical framework, but which pays close attention to the processes that will facilitate the engagement of families and maximise their chances of positive outcomes of meaning to them.

One such a programme was offered to 210 families enrolled in Head Start, a federally funded pre-school programme available to children whose parents are receiving welfare, and which has been described as 'an ideal natural national laboratory for conducting child abuse and neglect treatment and prevention research' (National Research Council, 1993, and Fantuzzo *et al.* 1997). Research conducted by Webster-Stratton has demonstrated the high incidence of harsh, critical discipline amongst Head Start parents, and the high risk of conduct disorders (Webster-Stratton 1998). Eight Head Start centres were randomly assigned to the parent-training programme (PARTNERS) *plus* Head Start, or to Head Start only. This cognitive-behavioural programme (designed in conjunction with teachers and parents) comprised eight sessions covering: (1) How to Play with Your Child, (2) How to Help Your Child Learn, (3) Effective Praise and Encouragement, (4) How to Motivate Your Child, (5) Effective Limit Setting, (6) How to Follow Through with Limits and Rules, (7) Handling Common Misbehaviours, and (8) Problem-Solving.

A range of outcome indicators were used, including independent observation of parent–child interaction and of child behaviour in the classroom, as well as teacher and parent reports of child behaviour, plus interviews. Results were as follows:

- PARTNERS mothers:
  - made significantly fewer critical remarks, used less physically negative discipline, and were more positive, appropriate and consistent in their disciplinary style when compared with control mothers;
  - perceived their family service workers as more supportive than did control mothers;
  - were reported (by teachers) as more involved in their children's education than controls;
- PARTNERS children were observed at home:
  - to exhibit fewer negative behaviours than control children;
  - to be less non-compliant than control children;
  - to demonstrate a more positive affect and more pro-social behaviour than control children.

In addition, there was markedly less 'drop-out' amongst PARTNERS mothers (88% of whom attended more than two-thirds of the session, and only 12% of whom attended fewer than 12%), and a very high level of consumer satisfaction. Given the fact that the programme content was not markedly different from that of others, Webster-Stratton examines a range of other 'non-specific' factors. Possible contenders are:

- involving parents and 'significant others' (Head Start staff) in planning from the outset;
- using and training trainers who had credibility with parents (i.e., who were culturally and linguistically representative of the parents; already associated with Head Start);
- actively encouraging the participation of all parents within the Head Start programme;
- making sure the programme was accessible and feasible (via convenient physical location, quality child care arrangements);
- providing incentives for participating in the study. Cash payments helped offset the added demands of evaluation (which often reduce participation, see Spoth and Redmond, 1995) and may have helped maintain high levels of attendance. However, end of programme evaluations from parents indicated that 96% of them would have participated even if they had not been given the financial incentive;
- providing dinner (to parents and children) enabled parents to collect children at 5.00 p.m. from day care and still turn up to a 6.00 p.m. meeting, often with their partner;
- the collaborative nature of the programme. In the non-hierarchical, non-blaming relationship between trainer and parents, the latter 'function as experts concerning their child, their particular family, and their community, and the trainer functions as expert concerning child development, family dynamics in general, behaviour management principles, and so on.' (Webster-Stratton 1998). This modus operandi is extended to the running of the group, making it a safe place for parents to share their problems, their ideas, and to take risks;
- trainers demonstrated high empathy, warmth and genuineness e.g., more 'interested friend' than 'aloof expert';
- the group setting which offered an antidote to social isolation and boosted the confidence of participants, some of whom went on to consider participating in other kinds of groups, such as Parent Teacher Association boards. The group setting also promoted collaborative problem-solving, a key factor in the generalisation of change;
- a focus on building support networks outside and within the home— being a person as well as a parent;
- the use of video modelling, designed to be used to facilitate group

discussion and problem-solving. Videos show parents of different ages, cultures, sexes, temperaments, and socio-economic groups, interacting with their children in a range of natural situations. The 130 vignettes illustrate parents 'getting it right' as well as 'getting it wrong';

- the low-stress use of role-play;
- home assignments (helping to translate the 'theory' into 'practice'), and self-management;
- use of readings and tapes (for non-readers) covering the programme;
- judicious use of humour which helped to defuse anxiety and build rapport;
- reframing difficult behaviour in positive terms (e.g., as the result of a psychological or emotional drive);
- positive expectations of parents, and positive reinforcement;
- core principles of good group work (see Rose 1986).

There are two possible ways to respond to this long list. First, we can take the position that as we don't know *which* of these factors, if any, were jointly or severally responsible for an impressive set of findings, we should 'wait and see' before adjusting our practice. However, it is worth remembering that research in other areas has underlined the importance of most of these. More important, however, we can reflect that there is little here that we would not expect for ourselves, were we in the position of requiring assistance and that it is the least we can attend to in the development and delivery of services to others—generally less demanding and in greater need.

ANGER MANAGEMENT

Families in which child abuse occurs are often characterised by low levels of pleasant exchanges and high rates of aggressive behaviour on the part of parents and child(ren). This can result in the all too common 'spiralling' in which, in response to a child's misdemeanour: the parent shouts; the child continues; a parent threatens; the child goes on in either the same way or (typically) his/her behaviour gets worse; parent smacks, child retaliates with verbal and/or physical abuse; parent 'lets fly'.

Parent-training generally aims to break this cycle early on by equipping parents with more effective management strategies. However, sometimes, the problem lies less with skill deficits of this kind, than in a parent's self-control being insufficient for the challenge. In most cases, what distinguishes child abusing families from non-abusing families is not angry feelings or impulses, but that most of the time the majority of parents can contain these. Some parents can't, or fail to. One of the aims of anger-management strategies is to equip the parent with impulse or anger control—usually in combination with child-management skills. Of the parents who attended Webster-Stratton's PARTNERS programme, 45% said they would welcome training in anger management.

Anger control training offers a promising avenue for continued research (Barth *et al.* 1983). Training typically involves the following steps:

1. Teaching parents to identify cues that presage an angry response. These may be physiological: tension, shaking, 'going hot'; or situational: provocative situations such as the supermarket, where the parent feels particularly vulnerable to embarrassment. Some cues overlap both such as tiredness, pre-menstrual tension, financial worry.
2. Teaching parents how to relax when these cues are identified and to use various coping strategies. These might include: deep breathing; engaging in an alternative activity; trying to divert the child; changing the way he or she thinks about the situation e.g., providing them with information about age-appropriate expectations of children.

Choosing alternative courses of action presupposes the ability to think constructively about a situation, to decide what courses of action could be taken and to choose which would be best. Often, abusing parents are unable to generate alternative (non-aggressive) responses to situations in which their children provoke their anger. The resulting stress and frustration contribute to their aggressive outbursts. Like child-management strategies, problem-solving can be *taught,* and this has been one component that several self-control training programmes have used.

Unfortunately, because programmes with abusing parents so often include a number of intervention strategies (reflecting an appreciation of the urgency and multifaceted nature of the problem) it is often difficult to say which procedures are in fact (the most) effective or responsible for the successful outcomes reported. Whiteman *et al.* (1987) compared the effectiveness of four interventions conducted by social workers:

(i)   cognitive restructuring (aimed at rectifying misattributions of children's behaviour such as 'he's doing that to annoy me');
(ii) problem-solving skills (learning to think of alternative ways of resolving conflicts or dilemmas);
(iii) relaxation (staying calm so the parent will be less likely to hit out);
(iv) a combination of relaxation, cognitive restructuring *and* problem-solving skills.

Fifty-five families in which child abuse had been committed, or the parents were at risk of such behaviour, were randomly assigned to the above four groups and a control group which received agency services but no experimental interventions. The results showed a reduction in anger measures for those in the experimental groups, with the composite group doing best.

Whilst this study relied rather heavily on self-report and role-play measures, rather than observed real-life situations, their findings are in keeping with a number of other good quality studies conducted by psychologists.

There is evidence that groups may enhance the effectiveness or appeal of these approaches (Nomellini and Katz, 1983; Barth *et al.*, 1983). Groups may be a valuable source of social contact for clients, and indeed reducing social isolation was one of the aims of a study by Wahler (1980). This ascertained that parents' use of physical punishment was significantly correlated with the number of contacts they enjoyed with friends on any one day i.e., the more such contacts the fewer the incidents of physical punishment. The group setting also gives an opportunity to provide parents with a variety of coping models, feedback and support for change endeavours.

Finally a cautionary note. One of the dangers of résumés of effective strategies is that they tempt practitioners to adopt a 'tool-box' approach to intervention. If there is one thing that the better studies teach us is that careful assessment is (almost) all. Because the aim of anger-management strategies is to help individuals identify the build-up of aggression from its earliest signs—when they are most likely to be able to intervene success-fully—this approach is, by definition, contraindicated for those whose temper, coupled with physical violence, is 'instantaneous', and—except insofar as it is a pattern of behaviour known to exist—unpredictable.

BREAKING THE CYCLE OF VIOLENCE

Four factors seem to be implicated in the intergenerational cycle of violence:

(i) Children who witness persistent parental violence or whose parents resort to violence as a disciplinary tool or as strategy for conflict resolution, are at risk of repeating such behaviour as adults (Peled and Edleson 1995).

(ii) Children who have been victimised can develop 'hostile beliefs and power assertive behaviour with regard to male–female relationships' (Wolfe and McGee, 1994), which are reinforced by societal pressures towards highly gendered and sexist patterns of human interaction.

(iii) Earlier patterns of learned behaviour may be more entrenched so that when we encounter certain problem situations (such as relationship con-flict) we are likely to fall back on the strategies we first learned, including those internalised from our experiences as children (Wolfe *et al.* 1997).

(iv) Wider social factors, such as a general exposure to violence (see Emery 1989; Jaffe *et al.* 1990) and power relations (see Dobash and Dobash 1992), particularly the active devaluation of women (Sudermann *et al.* 1995).

These factors have informed the development of programmes designed to break this pattern of violence, by addressing these factors in a systematic way, focusing on the relational contexts in which violence occurs (see Jaffe *et al.* 1992). Their starting point is that one's ability to successfully develop and sustain nurturing relationships, and to negotiate the stresses and strains of intimate relationships, will be inversely correlated with the likelihood of violence. In this regard, they highlight the importance of attachment theory in the development of supportive and violence-free relationships, and point to adolescence as a time when young people are seeking and developing new attachment relationships (Wolfe *et al.* 1997; Feiring, 1995). Mid-adolescence is, therefore, an optimum time in which to try to intervene in patterns of relationships conflict (Wolfe *et al.* 1997).

> 'Adolescence represents a crucial link in the prevention of violence in relationships because it is both an important time for relationship formation and a period in which the scars of childhood can impair normal adjustment.' (Wolfe *et al.* 1997, p. 113)

This hypothesis is enhanced by evidence that abuse among 'teen dating partners is as common as, and resembles, that of adult relationships (Gelles 1997; Girshick 1993; Walker 1989)

The Youth Relationships Project (YRP)

The *YRP* aims to prevent violence in close relationships (peer, and dating) and to promote positive, egalitarian relationships (Pittman *et al.* 1998). It is run by two co-facilitators, one male one female, who model appropriate sharing of power. The original project was targeted at young people in mid-adolescence (14–16) who were deemed to be at risk for violence by means of a history of child maltreatment, including: (a) witnessing domestic violence; (b) physical abuse; (c) sexual abuse, (d) emotional abuse, (e) physical or emotional neglect, and who were thereby known to child protective services. However, the authors point out the desirability of recruiting young people in a way that does not label them as in need of 'treatment', but which enables them to present the programme as one of health promotion. They are therefore exploring (i) more general recruitment and (ii) involving schools, both of which will take them more into the area of primary prevention. The results summarised below, pertain to the original study.

The 18 weekly session course has four aims:

(i)   to increase participants' understanding of power, and its role in relationship violence;
(ii) to develop the skills needed to build healthy relationships and to recognise and respond to abuse in their own relationship;
(iii) to understand the societal influences and pressures that can lead to violence and to develop skills to respond to those influences;

(iv) to consolidating learning of new attitudes and skills and increasing competency through community involvement and social action.

The principles of developing group cohesion and collaboration underpin the process of the project. Each two hour session incorporates five stages: teach, show, practice, reinforce, and apply (McWhirter *et al.* 1993). Skills are taught via a mix of role-play, demonstrations, panel discussions provided by community advocates (for example, those previously engaged in violence), videos, small group discussions and exercises. There is an emphasis on positive, pro-social alternatives to violence, and the programme allows for a major input from adolescents themselves. This emphasis on attitudes *and behaviour* is what makes this project singular.

Effectiveness?

At present only process data are available for this project. These are positive, and attest to the 'rightness of fit' between the programme model and the experience of the young people involved. Evaluation of this and other projects are in progress, and will include data on the quality of extant relationships, and analogue data (video-taped simulations) on the competence of participants to negotiate conflicts, compared with controls. At present, therefore, one has to categorise this as a *promising approach*, with a strong evidence-based rationale, appropriately broad-based, and incorporating a range of strategies most likely to maximise the chances of change, and their maintenance and generalisation (rarely do health promotion interventions address these last two issues). There appears to be no U.K. equivalent.

PSYCHOLOGICAL MALTREATMENT

Perhaps because it is easier to identify parents at risk of maltreatment, than to say what form of abuse will ensue, secondary prevention strategies rarely target psychological abuse *per se*. The majority of studies aimed at physical abuse and neglect will have some relevance to many areas of psychological maltreatment. So, for example, enhancing a parent's understanding of child development may effect a shift in parental thinking and expectations which impact on the way a parent perceives his or her child, and how they feel toward him or her. Anger-management techniques can be used to divert verbal hostility as well as physical aggression. However, there are some interventions that specifically address factors which are correlated with the development of problems associated with psychological maltreatment, and we discuss these briefly here.

Early problems with bonding may be a factor in a range of emotionally abusive parent–child relationships. Difficulties in bonding may be apparent in early feeding problems between mothers and their new-borns, lack of enjoyment and even aversion to physically intimate contact such as cuddling, nursing, bathing and changing. Interventions which help mothers to feel more positively towards their infants, and to develop more intimate and positive relationships are likely to reduce the risk of future maltreatment. Such programmes have been evaluated in the treatment of mothers whose infants are failing to thrive (see Chapter 5), but could perhaps usefully be adapted to the wider population of mothers who experience such difficulties.

Programmes typically comprise teaching mothers how to hold their babies in ways that make them feel secure; maintaining eye contact with them during feeding, and smiling at the baby. Mothers may not feel like doing this, and need to be reassured that, in some circumstances, changes of feeling follow changes in behaviour. Babies whose mothers handle them in these ways are more likely to be responsive, and rewarding. For unresponsive babies, Nugent advises that mothers should withold feed until the baby makes eye-contact, and then reward him or her by giving them the bottle (or breast) immediately (Nugent 1996). Fahlberg provides similar advice about promoting attachment using touch, play and voice tone etc. (Fahlberg 1991).

Having said this, it may well be that mothers who are at high risk of psychologically maltreating their children are themselves emotionally needy. In the absence of better evidence to support the implementation of such programmes the best advice is to make a careful assessment of the origins of these problems. If unresolved issues of personal need transpire, it may well be more appropriate to focus primarily on the needs of the mother, in order to best secure the needs of the child. This is eminently reasonable, and an approach we would advocate on those grounds as long as the child's well-being remains the primary concern. The evidential base, as we defined it at the outset, is relatively thin however, even in terms of non-experimental studies or case studies (single case designs), and this work requires careful monitoring and evaluation.

IMPLICATIONS FOR POLICY AND PRACTICE

1. Effective secondary prevention measures depend on our ability to accurately identify factors that place people at increased risk for maltreatment, either as children or as parents.
2. Home visiting programmes have a particularly good track record in enhancing a range of developmental outcomes for mothers and children. The approach that has been evaluated by Olds and his colleagues suggest that the risk of accidental injury and of child abuse and neglect can also be reduced. His programme, which has been evaluated over a twenty year period and in a range of communities, is distinguished by being grounded

in an ecological framework, by focusing on mothers as developing persons as well as their children, by endeavouring to promote a sensitive, responsive and engaged parenting in the early years, and emphasising the importance of skill development, rather than information giving and discussion. It is constructed around the theories of attachment, social learning and self-efficacy.

3. Parenting programmes have been successful in reducing the risk of maltreatment in high risk families. Parenting programmes are most effective when they are group-based rather than individual, they are cognitive-behavioural in design rather than primarily based on relationship work, and when they recognise the importance of process variables in successful outcomes. The PARTNERS programme provides a particularly good example of the integration of cognitive-behavioural interventions, group work and the importance of attending to the expectations that inform and shape patterns of parenting, both good parenting and inadequate or damaging parenting.

4. Parenting programmes are rarely sufficient when there are a number of problems in the family, and especially when these are long-standing. In these circumstances, more broad-based and multi-faceted programmes will be required and interventions may need to be of a longer-term nature. Cognitive-behavioural approaches enjoy a good track record in relation to a range of other problems which may be relevant in working with maltreating families e.g., substance and alcohol misuse, relationship difficulties, depression.

5. Anger control training for some parents offers a promising approach. However, there is no evidence that it will be appropriate as a single or major intervention where violence is severe and long-standing, or where there is little opportunity to intervene in the process between arousal and overt aggression. In families where domestic violence is an issue or where children are directly on the receiving end of intentional physical violence (as opposed, say, to the result of disciplinary incidents 'gone wrong') such an approach should only be used when indicated by a careful assessment. Even then it should be used with great caution and careful monitoring, and with due regard to the safety of children.

9

TERTIARY PREVENTION

PHYSICAL ABUSE AND NEGLECT

'On the one hand, certain intervention efforts aimed at identified maltreating parents and children are useful and relatively successful if implemented properly. On the other hand, the utility of such intervention must be weighed against the very high costs (in human suffering as well as financial) of efforts that focus on reversing longstanding problems *that have worsened to the point of abuse or neglect.*' (Wolfe and Wekerle 1993, p. 497)

'Although there is no shortage of papers on child abuse in all its forms, it appears that we still do not know a lot about how to treat parents who physically abuse their children, if judged by the number of papers on this subject, and their results.' (Oates and Bross 1995, p. 470)

The first quote represents the conclusion of an overview of studies that evaluated interventions aimed at parents and/or children, and which met the following criteria:

- used a control group or a controlled design;
- provided an adequate report of details of intervention to permit evaluation;
- had no major methodological or analytical flaws;
- presented findings pertinent to a specified set of criteria for intervention concerned with the perceived needs of maltreated children, and the problems that contribute to maltreatment.

These were fairly modest criteria, and although the authors do not state the criteria they used to assess the methodological quality of studies, they identified only five studies of child-focused interventions that met these criteria. A further eleven studies met the criteria for parent-focused interventions. They do not specify the period covered by their review.

The second quote is the conclusion of another review which covered studies published between 1983 and 1992. Oates and Bross identified only 25 papers in 10 years which met the following criteria:

- more than five subjects in the sample;
- one of three methods of comparison (randomisation, matched control group or the use of a pre- and post-measure of effectiveness);
- at least 15% of the subjects in the sample known to have been physically abused (as opposed to neglected).

Of these studies, 13 covered interventions aimed at helping abused children, the remaining 12 evaluated interventions aimed at helping parents. None of these were concerned with routine service provision. Excluding primary prevention studies Gough's overview of the literature covering a similar period (between 1980–1992) identified around 20 intervention studies featuring control or comparison groups. Few of these were focused on tertiary intervention, and none were concerned with routine service provision (Gough 1993). In such an important area of policy and practice, the routine call for more research of adequate quality to guide practice, appears to have been largely unheeded.

Given the paucity of studies, and the methodological problems that accompany many of them (*e.g.*, small sample sizes, high drop-out rates, inadequate outcome indicators, no follow-up), it is difficult to conclude anything other than that the available evidence-base underpinning what I shall term therapeutic (as opposed to administrative or legal) interventions in child protection, is wafer-thin. It is all the more serious then, that the evidence that *is* available is so rarely advocated, so rarely acted upon, and the requisite practice skills so rarely taught on professional courses.

One of the points of consensus in all the reviews to date, is that behavioural and cognitive-behavioural approaches have much to offer to the problems which need to be addressed if abuse and neglect are to be prevented from recurring in a range of circumstances. Here are extracts from the reviews:

'The evidence favouring successful interventions to meet the needs of caregivers is abundant for the cognitive-behavioural approaches. With the exception of issues related to lifestyle, of which there is little mention, such studies report consistent success in helping maltreating parents improve several of the conditions that predispose them to abusive and neglectful treatment.' (Wolfe and Wekerle 1993, pp. 489–490)

'The results of the behavioural studies are impressive. Many of the experimentally controlled studies experienced methodological problems such as subject attrition, but the studies are still more rigorous than many other studies considered in this review. The results also run counter to the trend reported in several other chapters that the more rigorous the evaluation the less positive the findings reported.' (Gough 1993, p. 127)

Remember this earlier example of one of the challenges to promoting evidence-based practice in this field:

> 'Suppose, for example, we adopt a very strict criterion and consider only those methods which have been tested using the protocols of experimental research. We will quickly discover that they are very few in number and restricted almost entirely to behavioural techniques which train parents to use less abusive forms of discipline (or, more generally, make available a wider range of parenting skills).' (Paley 1990, M-3-1)

In other words, to set quality standards for evidence may take us in directions we would prefer not to go. This is an important consideration, particularly for social work educators, research funders, and those responsible for organisational policy.

USING COGNITIVE-BEHAVIOURAL INTERVENTIONS TO PREVENT THE RECURRENCE OF ABUSE AND NEGLECT

In general then, the cognitive-behavioural approaches discussed in the previous chapter comprise a good starting point for developing interventions designed to prevent the recurrence of a variety of forms of abuse and neglect. Programmes typically combine parent training with self-management techniques (such as anger-control) and problem-solving, and increasingly these are delivered in contexts which also attend to the broader social context in which children and families live. Rather than rehearse the detail of these techniques (covered in the previous chapter), this section provides some examples of their application to situations in which parents have already abused and/or neglected their children.

Working in Difficult Circumstances

As long ago as 1981 Wolfe and his colleagues reported the successful use of cognitive-behavioural assessment and intervention to reduce the risk of further abuse by parents who had been ordered to comply with 'treatment' following substantiated complaints of child abuse, or circumstantial evidence of high risk. Parents had either been court-ordered, or had been obliged to attend in order to avoid court action by the child protection agency involved. Their intervention comprised:

A.   A group-based element. Parents met one evening per week for 2 hours, over eight weeks. It had three main components:

A.1. *Developing an understanding of child development and child management.* Parents met in a group to develop their knowledge of child development and child management. A manual *Parents are Teachers* (Becker 1971) was provided to participants, and this was used as the basis for training and evaluation. One of the authors has experience as a social worker of using this manual with child-abusing parents (Macdonald) with positive results. Video-tapes were used to explore issues, and parents were provided with behavioural principles as applied to parenting e.g. positive reinforcement, time out, shaping, appropriate punishment.

A.2. *Problem-solving and modelling of appropriate child management.* Using video-taped examples of typical child management problems, parents learned to problem-solve and to develop appropriate management techniques, drawing on behavioural principles.

A.3. *Self-control training.* Parents were taught deep muscle relaxation and learned anger-management techniques, using the strategies described in the last chapter.

B. *Individualised home-based training procedures.* Essentially, weekly home visits by the project co-ordinator (a clinical psychology graduate student) facilitated the generalisation and maintenance of skills and knowledge acquired in the group. This was done by asking parents (i) to identify one child-related problem and to record it during the following week, (ii) to select a target situation and decide on a positive approach to its resolution, (iii) to rehearse it with the co-ordinator and the child (if appropriate). This was done in an incremental fashion, beginning with less challenging problems. The authors report that 'the majority of the families attained skill proficiency after eight home sessions (an average of 8.9 professional hours in the home per family)'.

The effects of this intervention were compared with those of standard services provided to a wait-list control. These comprised regular biweekly monitoring of the child's safety in the home, and/or the provision of community resources (e.g., welfare support, homemaker services) during the same period. Small sample size is a problem in this study, with only 8 families in each group. However, it is unusual in combining an experimental design with a wide range of relevant outcome measures, including observational measures of child management skills (using the Parent–Child Interaction Form), parental report (using the Eyeberg Child Behaviour Inventory), the views of referral agencies and reported incidents of child abuse.

Effectiveness

The results show that those families who participated in the programme made significant improvements in their child management skills, reported fewer child-behavior problems and were seen by caseworkers as having noticeably fewer problems. One year on, none of the eight families who had been involved in the programme had been reported or suspected of child abuse or maltreatment, and all cases had been closed in the year following the programme, on the basis that the families were viewed as functioning effectively. This was also the case for the six control cases who subsequently entered the programme. Of the two that did not, one had a further reported incident of abuse, and the other remained under the supervision of the child protection agency and the court.

Other sources of evidence of the effectiveness of such approaches can be found in Crimmins *et al.* 1984; Egan 1983; Wolfe and Sandler 1981; Wolfe *et al.* 1981, 1982. Some of these are case studies in which the evaluation and work are organised experimentally and controlled using single-case designs. However, whilst there are more outcome studies of cognitive-behavioural approaches in tertiary prevention than there are studies of other approaches, controlled *group* studies are still relatively few in number.

UK Examples

The bulk of work in this area has been conducted in the United States, and the implications of this is a frequently occurring theme in discussions about evidence-based practice. In an earlier chapter a case was made for paying attention to American studies (see Chapter 2). What follows is a discussion of two U.K. examples of the application of behavioural techniques, neither of which produced conclusive, positive results, but both of which illustrate a number of important issues.

One of the first U.K. attempts to rigorously evaluate the use of behavioural approaches in the tertiary prevention of abuse was that of Smith and Rachman in 1984. They examined the 'value-added' of a behavioural approach to routine child protection services (i.e., monitoring, practical help and counselling). During a 16 month period, all cases of child physical abuse were referred to the project, providing the families and social workers concerned were agreeable. The specific behavioural interventions varied according to the needs of the family, but included a variety of child management skills (such as the use of differential reinforcement, time out, and token systems etc.), relaxation training, assertion training, anger control, behavioural treatment of depression, structured approaches to problems involving social skills (e.g., job hunting, visiting dentists or family planning clinics). However, the study suffered high attrition, which precluded a conclusive outcome. The most valuable aspect of the authors' report is the detailed account of some of the work undertaken, the problems they encountered, and their discussion of the implications of these results. These issues are discussed again later on.

A second study of interest is that of Nicol *et al.* (1988) who undertook a randomised controlled trial examining the relative effectiveness of an intervention they termed 'brief focused casework' and play therapy.

Criteria for Participation. Participation was confined to families where:

(i) actual physical abuse had been inflicted on the child;
(ii) family life was marked by significant conflict. An inability to successfully end children's troublesome behaviour with non-physical means makes it more likely that there will be a resort, via threats, to physical measures; as the emotional 'temperature' rises, these are likely to become more severe and, for young children in particular, more dangerous. The researchers were keen to evaluate the use of behavioural methods in cases where this appeared to be a major feature.
(iii) families were typical of those worked with by child protection social workers. The study was a co-operative endeavour between a child psychiatry service and an N.S.P.C.C. special unit and the authors say it represented a move away from the 'long-term intensive support' traditionally provided by the latter agency.

The Intervention. 'Brief focused casework' was essentially the use of behavioural methods of proven efficacy in this area (see Wolfe *et al.* 1981) within a casework (advice, support, practical help) approach. Intervention occurred up to three times per week over 6–8 weeks.

The sample. Thirty-eight families were randomly allocated to the two interventions. Fourteen were single parents and 11 were divorced, and in all but 5 families the main wage-earner was unemployed.

Assessment and Outcome Measures. Included in the assessment was direct and systematic observation of each families interaction style, in the home. Seven observation sessions were conducted per family, each of which included at least two blocks of observation per family member (five minutes each). The use of direct observation adds particular strength to judgements about actual, as opposed to reported, change.

Attrition. Attrition was high, 45% of families dropped out between assessment and the follow-up assessment, equally divided between the two groups. Reasons ranged from family break-up to those who 'changed their minds'. No information is given about the distribution of reasons between the two groups, making this differential drop-out even more problematic.

Results. The results were as follows:

- Taking fathers, mothers and children together, no significant changes occurred before and after intervention in the rates of positive behaviours for either group.
- Family members in the brief focused casework group showed a lessening of coercive behaviours.
- Examined separately, only one difference emerged, namely that after play therapy fathers evidenced *less* positive interaction with their children (perhaps they irritated them more by wanting to play . . .).
- When the results are analysed in terms of improvement (pre-post changes) brief focused casework appeared to have reduced coercive behaviours and improved rates of positive behaviour when family members are combined, but not when analysed separately.
- In terms of outcomes (a measure of the final state of the problem), there were no significant differences.

Discussion. As with the Smith and Rachman's study, our ability to draw firm conclusions is limited by the small sample size, the high rate of attrition, and the apparent absence of blind-ratings by observers, about whom we are given no information. In contrast with the Smith and Rachman study there was no follow-up period, and no attempt made to evaluate outcomes in terms of future abusive incidents. The original rationale for the intervention, *viz.* its reputable track record in reducing coercive interaction and its beneficial effect on abusive incidents, is ignored beyond the introduction.

Implications for UK Context

Should we conclude that such approaches are either not appropriate to the U.K. context, or not appropriate in tertiary prevention? With the caveat that the evidence-base is generally too thin to make strong statements, the following points are presented for consideration.

(i)   The inconclusiveness of both of these studies is, in part, attributable to the technical challenges of conducting experimental evaluations in this field. Studies both here and in the United States bear testimony to these. As Smith and Rachman observe:

> 'The results . . . indicate that it is feasible to carry out a full, complete evaluation, given considerable resources and even more considerable endurance and patience.' (Smith and Rachman 1984, p. 349)

are, of course, commenting on the challenges of recruiting and taining families to therapeutic programmes, something that is dised further below. As a matter of urgency we need more, larger, better designed and executed trials than we currently have available, with 'clinical' samples and with relevant outcome indicators.

(ii) The results of the Smith and Rachman study were promising, though by no means conclusive. It is not unusual for these methods, and most others, to be conceptualised as short-term, focused interventions, as it was in the Nicol *et al.* study. What was striking about the Smith and Rachman study was that not only was the intervention provided on an intensive basis, but it was provided over many months. Many researchers (e.g., Wolfe and Wekerle 1993; McAuley and McAuley 1977) suggest that long-standing, complex problems may generally yield less optimum outcomes, and may well require long-term, as well as intensive patterns of intervention. This is in contrast to the general trend in psychotherapeutic literature which suggests that if change is to occur it usually does so within the first twelve weeks of an intervention, and that thereafter the gains are marginal (see Rachman and Wilson 1980; Macdonald and Sheldon 1992). The dominance of task-centred approaches, whilst appropriate for many situations, may need to give way to longer-term programmes of support, punctuated periodically by more intensive periods of more focused activity.

(iii) Not only are long-standing problems more intractable and less amenable to change, but the characteristics and situations of abusing and neglectful families are such that unexpected problems and crises and changes of circumstance are probably the norm, rather than the exception—what previous generations of social workers might have labelled 'multi-problem' or 'chaotic' families. In these circumstances, the use of cognitive-behavioural approaches is best integrated within a broad-based approach in which the worker can adjust and manage the 'therapeutic intervention' in ways that accommodate other concerns. This may be a broad-based casework approach or a community-oriented approach which addresses problems such as social isolation, socio-economic problems and so forth.

(iv) Further, it may be that in child protection, cognitive-behavioural approaches might prove more effective in the hands of appropriately trained social workers who, unlike most other professionals, are used to community-based and home-based settings and to working with seriously up-against-it families whose circumstances are constantly changing, often in critical and unpredictable ways. It is easier to integrate this training within the broad-based training social workers currently receive, than to bolt the latter on to more exclusively 'clinical' courses.

(v) One of the things commented on by Smith and Rachman and Nicol *et al.* was the time it took to establish trusting and working relationships between the behavioural worker and the families concerned. Workers in the former study appear to have been more successful in achieving this, perhaps because of their longer-term involvement.

It is difficult to separate secondary and tertiary studies, because of a pervasive tendency to 'mix' populations of carers who are thought definitely to have abused their children with those thought at 'high risk' of such abuse. Taken together the evidence supports the further consideration, development, and evaluation of cognitive-behavioural approaches within this field. In tertiary prevention there are particular gaps in our knowledge, and particular challenges—both to service provision and evaluation. Attrition (and lack of co-operation) is a major problem for both. This section concludes with a brief consideration of some promising approaches to involving and retaining families in therapeutic work.

Issues in Working with Abusive Parents

Working behaviourally with parents who have been deemed to have abused their children can present difficulties insofar as the emphasis on a detailed assessment and monitoring of progress may make parents feel that they are potentially providing evidence which may be 'used in evidence against them' at a future state. Further, many parents are constrained to accept advice or help for behaviours they may not themselves perceive as problematic. Whilst few families are formally obliged to attend programmes in the U.K., many comply somewhat reluctantly with would-be helpers. Work by Reid and his colleagues provide some useful suggestions for working with families in difficult circumstances (Reid *et al.* 1981). They suggest:

(i)   whilst it is important to acknowledge the seriousness of the abusive incidents it is advisable to focus assessment and intervention on the problems the parents face daily in managing their children. As well as being less off-putting to parents, this is therapeutically more useful as it is these daily hassles which set the scene for the more serious, but generally rarer, abusive incidents;

(ii) rather than entering irresolvable debates with families about *whether* abuse occurred, focus on those areas of parenting which place them under most stress;

(iii) rather than enter into conflict over the legitimacy of statutory intervention, endeavour to empathise with the pain and stigma that go with child protection investigations, and about the frustrations that parents feel when they feel forced to resort to physical punishment as a means of controlling their children;

(iv) share with parents what advantages might accrue from participation and collaboration, making clear to parents the reasons behind each phase of assessment and intervention, thereby offering some reassurance about the purpose behind information gathering. It may be a truism to say

that if a question or request is not pertinent it is impertinent, but this is a maxim that could usefully be born in mind by those using assessment schedules;
(v) begin with assessment of problems that are of concern to parents and which they can see the potential benefit of tackling.

Learning-disabled Parents: a Particular Opportunity

One area where there is promising evidence on the effectiveness of cognitive-behavioural approaches to parent-training is in relation to parents with learning disabilities. Learning-disabled parents face especial problems in parenting which are thought to contribute to problems of neglect, developmental delay and behaviour problems in their children (Tymchuk and Feldman 1991; Feldman and Walton-Allen, 1997). Learning-disabled parents are more likely to have their children removed from their care than other parents. This reflects prejudice, but also indicates the parenting difficulties that learning disabled people encounter in the absence of appropriate support from informal and formal networks (Feldman 1998). Some studies have indicated that learning disabled parents experience high levels of stress and depression, which may contribute to their parenting difficulties (Feldman *et al.* 1997), and these may arise, in part, from the adverse social circumstances in which they often live. Children of learning disabled parents are themselves at risk of developmental delay (Reed and Reed 1965; Scally 1957; Feldman and Walter-Allen 1997) and may need compensatory social and educational experiences, in addition to interventions aimed at improving their general level of care and stimulation.

Feldman describes a home-based parent-training intervention designed to help learning disabled parents improve their parenting skills, and reduce the risk of child neglect, developmental delays, and behaviour problems. Trained parent education therapists visited participants homes twice weekly (more often if necessary, and for new-borns). Therapists had degrees in psychology or early childhood studies, and knowledge of behavioural skill training and parent-training methods. Referrals came from child welfare agencies, doctors, families, and parents themselves. Often referrals were court-related. Most of those referred were mothers, of whom 50% lived alone.

In addition to parenting skills training, the staff provided ongoing counselling, stress management, community living and social skills training. The programme was sensitively and carefully structured, and made use of direct observation, modelling, instruction, and reinforcement. Training was pitched at the skills required for caring for a child at the age relevant to the family. Trainers in Feldman's programme worked closely with other agencies and saw their work as an essential component of a multi-agency approach.

A number of evaluations are available, from single-case evaluations to randomised controlled trials (Feldman *et al.*, 1992a,b; 1993; 1989a,b). The latter were possible because the rate of referrals outstripped the team's capacity to provide training. One study focused on the training of basic child-care skills for infants and toddlers (1–23 months); the other evaluated the effects of teaching parents to be more responsive and reinforcing to their children (Feldman *et al.* 1993). This resulted in a range of improvements, and increased family preservation. The control groups were of the 'wait-list' variety, so these parents received help later. In the second study, parents were helped to increase specific interaction skills known to be associated with optimum child language development e.g., praising, imitating, expanding a child's vocalisations, talking and looking at the child when interacting, and providing physical affection (Feldman 1998). Before training, both groups of parents performed significantly less well than a comparison group of mothers without learning disabilities. Before training, children of learning disabled mothers were vocalising significantly less than a comparison group of age-matched children whose mothers did not have learning disabilities, and significantly fewer were talking. It took a mean of 45 weeks (range: 17–89) to teach the requisite skills to the level performed by mothers without learning disabilities. After training:

(i)   only control group parents remained significantly below the performance of comparison mothers with regard to total parent interactions;

(ii) during the parent-training, child vocalisations and verbalisations in the intervention group improved above any anticipated levels of maturation (these were controlled for by the control group), placing them on a par with children whose mothers had no intellectual disabilities;

(iii) compared with control children, intervention children scored significantly higher on post-test language and social items of the Bayley Scales of Infant Development, and began talking sooner;

(iv) similar changes occurred in the control groups children once their parents were offered training;

(v)   informal observations and analyses of audio-tapes suggest that interactional training resulted in qualitative improvements in mother–child interaction.

Although these data need to be interpreted cautiously, it would appear that child removal also dropped considerably in this study from 78–20%, up to 3 years after participating in the programme.

Feldman and his colleagues do not regard parent training as a panacea, and are aware that other interventions, such as specialised pre-school programmes, may have more to offer some children whose parents are learning disabled. However, they rightly highlight the need for specialised and carefully tailored interventions to help with problems faced by those without learning disabilities. They are developing a range of programmes aimed at particular developmental and parenting challenges, and evaluating strategies to ensure maintenance and generalisation. A problem with parent-training as a 'one-off' is that the skills necessary to care for a one-year old baby will not suffice to meet the needs of a toddler, or eight year old. Parents with learning disabilities may need long-term help and support that is shaped by the developmental needs of the child.

BEHAVIOURAL FAMILY THERAPY

It will be clear from the preceding sections that few applications of cognitive-behavioural approaches are restricted to child management skills. Families in trouble are likely to need help with relationship problems, problems of depression and/or low self-esteem, substance misuse, as well as the socio-economic troubles which are of such importance. An appreciation of the role played by these other factors in the aetiology and maintenance of family problems, including abuse, has influenced the development of two rather broader-based approaches to cognitive-behavioural assessment and inter-vention. The first is known as behavioural family therapy (see Griest and Wells 1983; Thyer 1989). The second is styled ecobehavioural.

Behavioural family therapy differs from conventional family therapy methods in a number of respects:

(i)   it has a strong evaluative basis and a history of empirical evaluation;
(ii) its aim is to help families, but does not necessitate the involvement of all members in intervention, since it is hypothesised—in line with systems theory—that if an individual's problems can arise via complex family dynamics, the latter can be influenced via planned change endeavours with individuals alone. This is not to suggest, for example, that efforts should not be made to engage fathers in work whenever possible, but it does emphasis that even if they are not present that their influence is important—providing an antidote to 'mother-blaming', and that even when key actors are unwilling or unable to participate, that not all is lost (compare Thomas and Santa 1982);
(iii) it does not reify the abstract notion of a 'family':

> 'It must be recognised that there is no such thing as a family entity. There-fore, a family cannot cause anything to happen. Individuals influence one another and their environment. This occurs among those who live together as a group—as a family—and it occurs among individuals who reside among different groups.' (Hudson and Harrison 1986, p. 85)

Such an approach, which emphasises an interactional assessment, is necessarily informed by a concern for the *meanings* which family relationships carry for particular groups;

(iv) the approach is based on the principles of social learning theory (Bandura 1977);

(v) the central aspects of the model are the use of structured, behavioural exchange programmes to increase positive behaviours and communication; problem-solving and the use of contingency contracting (Wodarski and Thyer 1989).

Behavioural family therapy is an approach based on the premise that many factors conspire to produce abuse and neglect, that a number of these factors are located within the family (or can be intervened with at the level of the family), and that cognitive-behavioural approaches are effective ways of intervening in these difficulties.

The evaluation base of this approach then, more often lies in reports of work directed at specific, relevant aspects of family functioning, from inter-parental conflict, to alcohol misuse or depression, rather than in studies which describe the work as 'behavioural family therapy'. Indeed one author has observed that whilst the term eco-behavioural (which subsumes behavioural family therapy) is helpful in emphasising the importance of attending to the multiplicity of factors associated with abuse and neglect, it is misleading in suggesting that a behavioural approach *per se* does not require, or adopt such a broad focus (Gambrill 1989). The evidence-base of such an approach is very broad indeed, although we still lack sufficient studies which clearly explore the use of these techniques (and any other approach) with families where abuse and/or neglect has occurred. Family-based behavioural approaches have also been evaluated in the context of these broader, eco-behavioural approaches, and these are discussed next.

ECO-BEHAVIOURAL APPROACHES

Project 12-Ways

The name is derived from the 12 core services which were described in the original programme proposal: parent–child training, stress reduction for parents, basic skill training for the children, money management training, social support, home safety training, multiple-setting behaviour manage-ment '*in situ*', health and nutrition, problem-solving, couples counselling, alcohol abuse referral, and single mother services. Considerable importance was placed on '*in situ*' assessment and delivery of services, in order to maximise the generalisation and maintenance of newly learned skills across

behaviours, settings and time, and to make it easier for families to participate. The following table gives a flavour of the profile of services offered to
families during the first two years of the programme.

Table 9.1: Services offered in Project 12-Ways

Service	% of families	
	1980	1981
Parent–child training	42	66
Stress reduction and assertiveness training	17	16
Self-control training	10	21
Basic skills training for children (e.g., with developmental delays)	21	27
Leisure time counselling (enhancing family life and relationships)	5	21
Couples counselling	—	7
Alcoholism treatment or referral	3	3
Social support groups	5	17
Job-finding training	7	13
Money management	6	18
Health maintenance and nutrition training	—	14
Home safety training	—	14
Multiple setting behavioural management training	11	32
Prevention services (single mothers)	16	30

The project has utilised case studies ('clinical data'), single case experimental designs and matched-group comparisons in the documentation of its
effects (see Wesch and Lutzker 1991). Single-case evaluations have provided
evidence of the project's effectiveness in tackling a range of problems assessed
as contributing to child abuse and neglect, and these are summarised in
Table 9.2.

Table 9.2: Single case evaluations relevant to interventions used in Project 12-Ways

parent-training	Dachman *et al.* 1984
stress reduction	Campbell *et al.* 1983
couples counselling	Campbell *et al.* 1983
home safety assessment and hazard reduction	Tertinger *et al.* 1984; Barone *et al.* 1986
infant stimulation and health care skills	Lutzker *et al.* 1988
affect training	Lutzker *et al.* 1985
home cleanliness and nutrition	Sarber *et al.* 1983

Programme Effectiveness

Approximately 50–100 families *per annum* were served by the project
between 1979 and 1985. Once each year since 1980, Project 12-Ways has submitted the names of their selected group of project families and those of

matched comparison families to the body responsible for collating records on reports of abuse and neglect. A five-year follow up of more than 700 families, 352 of which had received services from Project 12-Ways show that Project 12-Ways families had consistently lower rates of abuse across all years, except one (1981, when the rate was similar to that of the control group, Lutzker and Rice 1987). In another report, Lutzker makes the case that those families who receive services from Project 12-Ways are significantly less likely to be reported again for child abuse and neglect up to 4 years after services (Lutzker and Rice 1984), even when—as in some of the evaluations—it was ascertained that project families had more severe problems than their control counterparts. However, the authors note that over time, the incidence of reported abuse increases for both groups, and the gap between them, whilst still statistically significant, looks clinically less impressive (an overall recidivism rate of 21.3% for Project 12-Ways families, compared with 28.5% for those in the comparison group). In other words, there seems to be what they call a 'wash-out' effect over time. They note that this may reflect the fact that some families either dropped out of the project, or had not been successfully helped to resolve identified problems. Alternatively, they suggest it points to the need for 'booster services' or additional support to these families, in order to maintain the early differences between the group. Both hypotheses are plausible and both merit further exploration. Certainly, the latter is in keeping with a general trend within the literature suggesting the need for longer-term interventions in tertiary, and possibly secondary prevention. A detailed account of an eco-behavioural programme, including strategies for training staff, developing assessment schedules that allow careful tailoring of programmes and monitoring of progress, and trouble-shooting a range of problems that can occur, can be found in a paper by Donohue and Van Hasselt (1999).

Project Ecosystems

Eco-behaviourally-based services have also been made available to parents who have children with learning disabilities (Lutzker and Campbell 1994). This project, located in California, provides services for families with a child with developmental disabilities. It also works with children or adults in residential care whose behaviour is such that they are at risk of a more restrictive setting. It is not a service aimed at abusive parents, and strictly speaking it does not belong in this Chapter. However, a large number of the families served by Project 12-Ways (which was targeted at abusive and neglectful parents) did have children with developmental disabilities, or had parents who were themselves learning disabled. The particular challenges this presented was one factor which led to the development of a programme specially designed to serve the needs of families with developmentally disabled children:

Project Ecosystems. The project is described here because of its implications for work with abusive and neglectful families where the stresses and strains of caring for a learning disabled child or children, contribute to poor parenting and abuse. The core services in *Project Ecosystems* are:

• *Planned activities training.* This provides an alternative to formal contingency management—in which the parent is taught to reinforce desirable behaviour and punish/reduce unwanted behaviour. Planned activities training focuses on affect (tone, command style, talking to children at eye-to-eye level, active and passive touch, and subtle aspects of contingency management), structured activities, and 'incidental teaching'. In other words, rather than having a structured parent-training component, workers organise a series of activities which provide pegs on which to hang the teaching of these skills, but whose primary focus is on the parent–child relationship. This approach appears to be preferred by parents (a view based on practice experience) and there is some evidence that it is equally as effective (Harrold *et al.* 1992; Lutzker and Campbell 1994).

• *Basic skills training.* Some basic skills are taught directly to children, and some are taught to parents for them to teach to their children. Behaviour therapists have a well-established track record of successfully teaching even complex skills to learning disabled children (and teaching parents to teach) as well as such skills as feeding, using the toilet, communication, hygiene, safety and self-help skills. Campbell and Lutzker report a case study with a child whose very serious challenging behaviours (severe temper tantrums and property destruction) were eliminated by providing the parent and child with functional communication skills.

• *Behavioural paediatrics.* Working with parents to enable them to comply with the medical regimens of their children e.g., using asthma medication, managing worries and fears about visiting hospitals and associated behavioural problems, managing hyperventilation by relaxation.

• *Stress reduction.* Stress and depression are frequent problems associated with parenting children with developmental disabilities (Dyson 1991). Sometimes these are a result of management problems, sometimes they are triggered by the prospect of other interventions such as counselling or the use of behaviour management procedures. Lutzker and his colleagues have developed two approaches to stress management which are suitable to adults and children. One of these, behaviour relaxation therapy, does not depend on the use of imagery (see Poppen 1988).

• *Problem solving and counselling.* These are core aspects of working with stressed families.

This particular project is not being evaluated using a comparison group, so conclusions must be tentative. However, Lutzker and Campbell report that during the first six years of its operation, Project Ecosystems saw over 300 families. Of these, less than 1% of children were placed into more restrictive settings. Service users rate it highly, as do other professionals, and the average cost of the programme is $1500 per family (somewhat cheaper than other services) and compares very favourably to the cost of residential care. The evidence of the single-case experimental evaluations is persuasive.

FAMILY THERAPY

Judging by the popularity of training courses, and the general literature, family therapy is a much-used intervention in secondary and tertiary prevention. Family therapy approaches are many and varied. Here is a summary of the principles underpinning family therapy approaches:

> 'The family is viewed not simply as a collection of individuals but as a rule-governed system and an organised group that transcends the sum of its separate elements.' (Hazelrigg *et al.* 1987, p. 428)

In viewing families as systems, in which member's behaviour is influenced by that of others, family therapists conceptualise the problems experienced by individual family members as symptomatic of system 'malfunctioning'. Systems theory recognises that a family has to evolve and adapt to the developmental changes of its members (for example adolescence), changes within the family (children leaving home, death and so on), and changes outside of it (unemployment, changes in social networks). Family systems are continuously endeavouring to both maintain the status quo and accommodate change (for example, failing to change family rules in recognition of growing children can result in disputes). If they do not manage to strike the balance between the two, problems can occur. Similarly, if a sub-system within the family (for example the parental-subsystem) fails to operate as it should then this will result in one or more family members behaving in ways that—in the short-term—are likely to keep the system functioning, albeit not in a healthy way. For example, a child's behaviour problems may serve to distract parents from their marital problems, or even keep together a family threatened with break-up. From a systems perspective, offering such parents child management training is unlikely to be helpful, unless their relationship problems are also addressed. This is because it is argued that the child's behaviour is the symptom rather than the cause.

Key therapeutic strategies in family therapy include: *joining*—establishing a bond between therapist and family members, either singly or as a whole; *reframing*—a process whereby a new meaning is assigned to a piece of behaviour, a relationship or series of interactions—for example, helping someone view positively something they hitherto viewed negatively; and *prescribing tasks or rituals*. The latter recognises that much of family life rests on ritualistic patterns of behaviour and ways of interaction. Asking people to do things differently—sometimes as a one-off, and sometimes as a new ritual—can serve a number of functions, summarised by Sutcliffe *et al.* (1985) as follows: to support competence, to increase skills, to differentiate roles, challenge stereotypes, introduce rewards, and promote proximity or challenge enmeshment (inappropriate closeness or lack of appropriate boundaries between members of different subsystems e.g., parent and child). Clearly this list is by no means exhaustive and different schools emphasise different techniques.

Whilst a number of evaluations of family therapy have appeared in the literature during the past twenty years, statements about its effectiveness as a social intervention in child protection work are hampered for the following reasons:

- Whilst a number of meta-analyses of the effectiveness of family therapy have been conducted, these are problematic insofar as they cover a range of problems (from childhood neurosis to alcoholism for example). Adding apples and oranges in this way probably limits the usefulness of the results of meta-analysis, whatever they are.
- This problem is exacerbated by the tendency to lump together different family therapy approaches. In a meta-analysis conducted by Hazelrigg *et al.* (1987) only one approach featured in more than one study. This raises the question as to whether different family therapy approaches amount to different interventions *per se*.
- A further problem concerns the way that studies are categorised within meta-analyses. For example Markus *et al.* (1990) describes 18 of the 19 studies included in their meta-analysis as 'behavioural'—labels which would be disputed by many of the authors of the studies analysed.
- There is within family therapy, as elsewhere, a view that it is misguided to think that these approaches can, or should be subjected to scientific scrutiny of the kind advocated in this book. This problem is illustrated in a recent review of the effects of Milan Family Therapy in which Carr (1991) reviews ten studies of the use of this approach. The Milan approach is a school of therapy developed in Italy. It has contributed a particular set of techniques to family therapy such as circular interviewing, triadic questioning, and the practice of developing hypotheses about family dysfunction prior to the first interview, which are then tested. Carr is criticised by a leading exponent of the approach who believes the

endeavour to assess effectiveness is important but technically impossible due to the constantly evolving nature of the approach.

'In fact it is precisely the constant, rapid evolution in our way of working and doing therapy that is one of the main reasons which has discouraged us from carrying on at least one of the many quantitative follow-up projects we planned, and sometimes even started, in these last years: our problematic pathology consists in a persistent and repetitive feeling that what we were doing a couple of years earlier was junk!' (Selvini 1991, p. 265)

• Taking mainstream family therapy approaches, we have as yet only slender evidence of the effectiveness of this. This was the conclusion of Hazelrigg and her colleagues:

'there are too few studies in the literature to reach any definitive conclusions distinguishing between the types of alternative treatments. Before concluding that family therapies are better treatments than other forms of therapy, more and better research must be conducted comparing family therapies with both attention/placebo treatments and viable treatment alternatives.' (Hazelrigg et al. 1987, p. 439)

• Finally, evaluations of family therapy's effectiveness with problems of child abuse and neglect are hard to find.

There are, however, some evaluations, although there is only one study of acceptable methodological quality which is of potential relevance to working with maltreating families (Brunk et al. 1987). The authors do not, however, include subsequent incidents of child abuse amongst their outcome indicators, and have no follow-up. This seriously limits the security of the findings.

In 1987 Brunk and her colleagues compared the effectiveness of parent-training and multisystemic therapy—systemic family therapy which encompassed attention to the role of cognitive and extrafamilial variables in maintaining problem behaviours, in this case child abuse and neglect. Eighteen abusive and 15 neglectful families were randomly allocated to either parent-training (run in groups) or multisystemic family therapy (conducted in the home). Each programme operated for 1.5 hours per week over 8 weeks. The authors used both self-report and observational measures (videotapes of parent–child interaction), and data were collected by research staff who were 'blind' to the hypotheses being tested and to the interventions provided to families—a rare occurrence which enhances the attributive confidence of the study. With this in mind, the impact of intervention was assessed at three levels: individual functioning, family relations, and stress/social support. In fact the authors are admirably cautious about the attributive confidence of this study in general, pointing out that the design did not permit a comparison with 'no-treatment', and did not control for expectancy effects or the demand characteristics of the therapeutic context (people often report and behave differently simply because of the context in which they find themselves).

In brief, both interventions appeared to bring about statistically significant improvements in the following areas: parental psychiatric symptomotology, overall stress, and the severity of identified problems. Pre-post-test comparisons suggested that parent-training was most effective in reducing identified social problems (perhaps because of the group format) and multisystemic family therapy had the edge on restructuring parent–child relationships, and facilitated positive change in those behaviour problems that differentiate maltreating families from non-problem families (Crittenden, 1981).

The study highlights another problem in outcome research, namely, the points of comparison researchers seek to test. Even in 1987, it is surprising that Brunk and her colleagues should have selected 'parent-training'—a relatively simple and pre-programmed package, of proven effectiveness, for child-management *simpliciter*—to compare with multisystemic family therapy (which included instruction in child management) which conceptually addressed the multi-faceted nature of child abuse and neglect. A more reasonable comparison might have been with a similarly broad-based intervention—behavioural family therapy or (because of its recognition that child abuse is located within a number of social systems) an *ecobehavioural* approach. Whilst these approaches currently enjoy limited support as effective strategies within tertiary prevention, this is more than that available for systemic family therapy. Both merit further investigation and evaluation, but the eco-behavioural approaches generally have a stronger empirical rationale, and use interventions of demonstrated effectiveness in a planned way across a wider range of problems. They also enjoy more support in evaluations of their application in secondary prevention, and in dealing with problems related to abuse such as child behaviour problems. They are also less mystical than the majority of family approaches.

Before leaving this approach, two things are worth noting, based on U.K. research. First, traditional family therapy approaches do not come cheap given (i) the number of people involved (often up to four per session) and their seniority (though whether this is necessary is a moot point); and (ii) given the high number of 'no-shows' and drop-outs from therapy (see Howe 1989). Any evaluation of this approach should include an assessment of its cost-effectiveness *vis-a-vis* other approaches. Second, as attrition rates suggest, it is not always a popular approach, particularly (as Howe's study suggests) amongst families at the sharper end. This finding introduces a note of tension between the views of users—with whom we are supposed to work in partnership—and the preferences of professional staff. It may pose a challenge to our working practices in terms of *what* we do, or merely point to a need to attend more closely to *how* we present what we do to clients.

SOCIAL NETWORK INTERVENTIONS

This section concludes with a consideration of another approach whose popularity is disproportionate to the available evidence, but which is worth considering given its rationale, and the evidence that is available. Social network interventions are those which explicitly aim to address the problems of abuse and neglect by increasing the amount and quality of social support available to needy and socially isolated parents. Only one controlled study has been conducted to date, but it is methodologically quite secure, and is one of the few studies primarily to target the needs of neglectful parents.

Gaudin *et al.* (1990) randomly assigned 88 families for whom neglect was a verified problem, to one of two groups. All families were selected from the caseloads of social workers working for the Department of Family and Children's Services in Georgia. Those that were allocated to the control condition continued to receive the services of their caseworker. The remainder were allocated to one of the project social workers who had total case management and intervention responsibility (i.e. 'holistic' care management) for the families on their caseloads. These workers:

(i) Undertook an assessment, which included:
   (a) *network assessment*: assessment of existing community formal and informal support available to parents in general; and an individual assessment of a family's informal support network, covering size, composition, and supportiveness;
   (b) *psychosocial assessment*: comprising interviews with parents and children to identify the range of problems facing a family, across a range of settings (school, home, housing, substance misuse, debt, unemployment etc.).
(ii) Identified significant material and psycho-social barriers to the development of supportive networks e.g., lack of telephone, poor verbal and social skills, poor self-esteem, unresolved conflicts with family members of neighbours.
(iii) Agreed goals for intervention with the family. These ranged from immediate physical goals such as obtaining adequate housing, food or clothing, to improving relationships. Network goals included: enhancing parents' verbal and social skills, increasing the size of the support network, and reducing conflict.
(iv) Intervened using five discrete social network interventions along with professional casework/case management activities that included

extensive advocacy and brokering of formal services. Social network interventions included:

(a) personal networking. Direct interventions to promote family members' existing or potential relationships with family member, friends, neighbours or work associate;

(b) establishing mutual aid groups which focused on teaching parenting and more broadly based social skills, to develop mutual problem-sharing, problem-solving and to enhance self-esteem;

(c) volunteer linking. Recruiting and training volunteers to do tasks akin to 'family aides' in the U.K.;

(d) recruiting neighbours as informal helpers. These people were paid a small sum, and received support and weekly guidance of the social workers;

(e) social skills training.

A number of overviews of tertiary prevention interventions have identified extreme difficulties in preventing the recurrence of maltreatment, particularly in neglectful families (Daro 1988). The results of this study then, are particularly encouraging.

Results

At six months:

- families in the experimental group were significantly improved in respect of three measures used in the study, all of which have established reliability and validity: the Child Neglect Severity Scale (Edgington *et al.* 1980); the Indicators of the Caretaking Environment for Children Scale (Halper and Jones 1981) and the Childhood Level of Living Scale (Polansky *et al.* 1981). No changes were noted for those in the control group.
- parents in the experimental group had significantly more appropriate expectations of their children and were less reliant on corporal punishment than control parents.
- experimental families reported significantly larger, and more supportive networks than at baseline. No such changes were reported for control families.

At 12 months:

- Highly significant changes were reported for experimental families on measures of parenting adequacy. No significant changes reported for control families.
- Families who received the social network interventions moved out of the neglectful category into marginally adequate parenting. Control families remained neglectful in their parenting practices.

- Experimental parents evidence significant improvements in their age-appropriate expectations of children, their empathetic understanding of them, and their use of corporal punishment. No such changes occurred for control families. Nonetheless the improvements in the experimental group still left these families below the average for non-neglectful adults.
- Experimental families experienced significant increases in the size of their support networks, while the networks of the control families remained essentially unchanged.
- Both groups reported a statistically significant increase in the perceived supportiveness of social networks, but these increases were greater and more significant for experimental families.

The results of this study are encouraging and point to the potential of a focus on enhancing social networks in work with poor neglectful families, in both multi-racial urban and rural settings. As the authors sum up, 80% of those who received nine months of intervention or more, improved their parenting from neglectful or severely neglectful on the standardized parenting measures to marginally adequate parenting, and almost 60% of cases were closed because of improved parenting. In terms of outcome studies, these results are at the 'top' end of positive results. However, they point to a number of problems, partly with the study, and partly in terms of implications for mainstream or routine practice. Firstly, in terms of the study, all the participants were voluntary, so it is doubtful whether these results would generalise to reluctant or resistant parents. Secondly, there was a high drop-out rate due to the extreme mobility of the families involved. This is a characteristic of many neglectful families, but presents a particular challenge to this way of working. In terms of the implications for mainstream practice, these are the messages from the study.

Implications for Practice

(i) Social networking is a promising approach in tertiary prevention, as in primary prevention (see Chapter 7).

(ii) In the context of tertiary prevention, it appears important to combine it with intensive casework, advocacy and case management, all of which were deemed essential in this study, particularly in the early stages of relationship-building with families.

> 'Social network members, volunteer parent aides, and natural helpers are effective supplements, but not substitutes for professional helping with the socially, emotionally and materially impoverished neglectful family.'
> (Gaudin et al. 1990, p. 120)

(iii) To intervene effectively by strengthening support networks requires frequent, consistent professional consultation for problem solving and support.
(iv) Successful implementation depends on:
   • manageable caseloads of 20 or less;
   • well-trained social workers with a combination of knowledge and skills that include (in one role):
      (a) case management,
      (b) individual casework/counselling,
      (c) group leadership,
      (d) advocacy, mediation,
      (e) supervision and consultation with volunteers, and
      (f) community relations skills.
(v) In tertiary prevention, longer-term, intensive programmes, which are multi-faceted (in keeping with the range of problems that families both present, and encounter), and which include a focus on skill development, as well as the concrete problems of daily living, are needed to effect change.

This is not the first time that the training needs of professionals or the need for longer-term intervention in the lives of abusive or neglectful families, appear in the child protection literature. One of the challenges to effective tertiary prevention—already sufficiently challenging—is to train social work staff in skills which have a sound evidence-base and which they can deploy in appropriate circumstances, over an appropriate length of time, and in appropriate concentration. This is increasingly difficult in a climate of resource shortage. However, in terms of both effectiveness and cost-effectiveness, those who advocate such approaches are probably more 'realistic' than those who say it is unrealistic in such a climate to even think in these terms.

It is quite unrealistic to expect families with long-term histories of cumulative problems and disadvantage, to overcome these in the course of a few weeks, however skilled the would-be helper. Whether a child can safely be left in a family for the length of time it might take to effect change and secure his or her safety or well-being is a decision that needs to be made in each case, and the answer will depend on a range of factors including his or her age, and the assessed risk of significant harm. Knowing that effective intervention may take one year or more in seriously damaged families who are not functioning at a level to secure their child's well-being may be an important datum in these decisions.

PSYCHOLOGICAL MALTREATMENT

Only one study has been identified which explicitly addresses tertiary pre-vention of psychological maltreatment (Iwaniec 1997). Iwaniec compared the effectiveness of individual parent training, with individual parent training *plus* group parent training, with 20 emotionally abusive and neglectful families in Belfast. Families were referred by the Paediatric Assessment Centre, outpatient clinics, and local authority senior social workers. The first ten families were assigned to the 'individual parent training' condition, the second ten to the 'individual *plus* group training condition'. Both groups appear comparable, and included single, step-parent and intact families, and families from working class and middle class backgrounds. Of the five families described as 'black' (no further information) three were in the individual parent training group.

Parents in the individual parent training group met with workers weekly, usually in the family home. The content of sessions and 'between session assignments' was agreed weekly between parents and workers. The training covered:

1. Developmental counselling (aimed at developing age-appropriate expectations). Training materials were developed by Iwaniec and Herbert at the Child Treatment Research Unit at the University of Leicester, and are available from Iwaniec at Queen's University, Belfast.
2. Improving parent–child interaction and relationships. Parents were encouraged to explore their attitudes and feelings about their child and to put them in interactional contexts, with an emphasis on understanding the antecedents of problem behaviour. Appropriate play and interactional skills were modelled and rehearsed using video feedback and planned activities. Training materials were based on McAuley and McAuley (1977) and Webster-Stratton (1991).
3. Managing children's and parent's problematic behaviour using behavioural approaches.

In this study individual parent training focused mainly on children's needs. Iwaniec was interested to see if the addition of a group component would augment the effectiveness of training by addressing the personal needs of emotionally abusive parents, who often suffer from low self-esteem and high anxiety or stress levels, have poor anger-control and problem solving skills, and are socially isolated (Iwaniec 1997). A feature of this study is the lengths to which workers went to secure parental attendance at the group (e.g., pre-group discussions with each member, transport, single-session evaluations). It was successful in preventing any drop-outs (although not all participants attended every session), and in involving fathers (this was also the case with the individual parent training). The group met once a week for 10 sessions, each session lasting 2 hours. After each session there was social space (coffee and cake) and a play group was run by two social work students to free parents during the group. In addition to providing a forum for 'mutual support, encouragement and exchange of ideas' this structured group aimed to develop:

- stress management
- self-control
- problem solving

Results

More parents *in the individual plus group training* component made a satis-factory level of improvement (compared with a moderate improvement in the *individual training* condition) in targeted areas, *viz.* social isolation, self-control, relaxation and problem solving. Parents in this group (individual *plus* group training component) also scored slightly lower on anxiety and depression scales, suggesting that the social contact facilitated by the group had a beneficial effect. Both groups demonstrated: (i) improvement on measures of anxiety and depression, (ii) improvements in levels of stress, (iii) reductions in emotionally abusive behaviours (88–12%, and 99–1% respectively). Both groups of parents gave positive evaluations of the content and process of the interventions. The study had a two year follow up period. Fathers were most active and constructive when work was done within the family (both groups) but were less enamoured of group work, with the exception of problem solving and stress management exercises. Other foci they saw as 'women's stuff'.

So, both individual parent-training and individual parent–training *plus* group work, were successful in bringing about improvements in parent–child relationships. Nonetheless, in keeping with other areas of child protection, Iwaniec observes that parents whose wider needs were addressed in the groups, did better in the long term than those who only had individual training. Whilst parents in both groups were clear that the parent-training had helped them, parents who had also been involved in group work, attributed their improvement as much to their hard work, greater optimism, and increased self-efficacy (Iwaniec 1997). This is in keeping with the recommendations of other researchers. So, a promising study. Unfortunately the account of the study is very poor, and there are a number of methodological (or reporting) weaknesses that mean we should treat the results with some caution. The report tells us little about the nature of the problems which led to referral. The rationale for the measures used is not clear, and there are some questions about the appropriateness of some areas of the data analysis, and therefore of the conclusions drawn. For example, Iwaniec collapses some categories of response which may inflate the positive results.

In cases of serious maltreatment, it might be worth considering an approach which combines family work of the type described by Iwaniec with therapeutic services for children who have suffered abuse or neglect (e.g., Garbarino *et al.* 1996; Crittenden 1999; Glaser 1993). The next Chapter considers the evidence for interventions directed at the effects of abuse and neglect. Parallel interventions may be particularly important when children are sustaining serious psychological maltreatment, and would benefit from compensatory nurturing, in an environment which affirms their worth and helps to promote positive images of themselves as young people who can cope with adversity.

IMPLICATIONS FOR POLICY AND PRACTICE

1. Cognitive-behavioural approaches are an important source of help for preventing the recurrence of abuse and neglect. Cognitive-behavioural studies demonstrate that long-standing, complex problems may require longer-term programmes of support as well as intensive periods of task-centred activity. They are most effective when integrated within a broad based and flexible approach.
2. Cognitive-behavioural parent training appears to be effective for parents with learning disabilities.
3. Families in trouble are likely to need help with a number of problems in addition to child management skills. Behavioural family therapy and eco-behavioural therapy are two broad based approaches which enjoy some empirical support.
4. The effectiveness of other forms of family therapy, such as systemic family therapy, is not yet clear but merits further investigation.
5. In cases of serious maltreatment, programmes which combine family work and day care services show some promise.

10

HELPING CHILDREN WHO HAVE BEEN ABUSED OR NEGLECTED

There is no shortage of descriptive accounts of work with children who have been physically or sexually abused, or who have been physically, emotionally or psychologically neglected. There is, however, a near-scandalous dearth of rigorous studies of the effects of these particular interventions in the lives of these most vulnerable of children. One hears many accounts of successful outcomes of play therapy, group work, counselling, adventure holidays. The issue, however, is that we should know better by now than to assume that all is therefore well when we use these approaches with children in general, or that even when we bear witness to positive outcomes, that these are the result of our interventions. The history of the helping professions shows that we are invariably over-optimistic about our influence; hopelessly unrealistic about our potential for harm, and that in general, the more rigorous the evaluation the less impressive are our apparent achievements (Oakley 2000).

This Chapter is more soberly based on a search for studies which used controlled groups or, at least, comparison groups. The search was a particularly dispiriting one and the absence of good quality evaluation should, in all honesty, be a source of serious professional disquiet. Damaged children deserve something rather better than what Barbara Wootton described as professionals (in her example, social workers) 'dabbling their fingers self-approvingly in the stuff of other people's souls' (Wootton 1959 p. 279, quoting Virginia Woolf). Included in this chapter are one or two examples of non-experimental research studies. These are included *only* because they were carefully described, enjoyed a good theoretical and/or empirical rationale, and seemed—within the restraints of their design—to provide evidence of potential efficacy. Nonetheless, they should be regarded cautiously, and as much as springboards for more rigorous research, than as a sound basis for practice. Any practice initiatives derived from research should, in any case, be subject to careful monitoring and review (for example, one can never be sure that the gap between the circumstances of an original study and the real-world settings into which interventions are exported, will be an easy one to bridge). When such initiatives concern vulnerable children, great care must be taken to ensure that our help, however, well-intentioned, however skilled the workers, however needy the child, does not in fact make matters worse. Before describing what interventions there are which enjoy some persuasive evidential base, let us review the extent of the difficulties we face in this area, drawing on earlier work by Fantuzzo.

In 1990 Fantuzzo reported an extensive literature search for studies of the effectiveness of interventions intended to ameliorate the adverse effects of child abuse and neglect, and to prevent a range of longer-term adverse consequences for children's development. A search of over 1500 articles from relevant computer data bases yielded only two studies that met what he described as 'minimal standards of experimental design' (i.e., random assignment) and included dependent variables derived from the child-maltreatment research literature. One was a study he had conducted with colleagues, and which is described below. The other was a study we have already discussed in Chapter 9, by Nicol (Nicol *et al.* 1988) which compared the effects of brief focused casework with play therapy. As Fantuzzo goes on to say, this last study does not really 'count' as in this study, play therapy was 'not taken seriously and served more as a placebo control condition than a serious treatment alternative' (Fantuzzo 1990). The author's conclusion is:

> 'This is clearly a case of *child neglect*. To date, behavioral and social scientists have neglected to provide child victims with empirically tested treatment strategies based on scientific assessment of their unique needs.' (Fantuzzo 1990, p. 317)

Ten years on, the situation has not greatly improved. A shortage of resources means that children rarely receive tailored help to meet their needs, except perhaps that which is expected to happen routinely in the course of out-of-home placements. The exception to this is possibly in cases of sexual abuse, but even here the absence of research, as in other areas of maltreatment, is striking.

CHILD PHYSICAL ABUSE

Most outcome studies in this field examine services provided to maltreated children in day centres, which combine a range of group activities with individual therapy, and these have been described in detail in Chapter 1 (Culp *et al.* 1987a,b; 1991). In these studies, and most other day treatment studies (see also Ayoub 1991; Bradley *et al.* 1986; Gabel *et al.* 1988, 1990; Sack *et al.* 1987) programmes have been offered to both physically abused and neglected children, and several studies included children 'at risk' of maltreatment as well as those who had been maltreated. All these factors make the interpretation of these studies somewhat difficult, but in general it appears that these composite interventions, which provide a safe, structured, nurturing environment, and which are intentionally geared towards addressing the specific sequelae of abuse, are most successful.

In a non-experimental study of a therapeutic pre-school for physically abused and sexually abused children, 24 children described as having sufficiently serious development delays and problematic behaviour to be judged unsuitable to enter mainstream schooling were enrolled in Project KEEPSAFE (Kempe Early Education Project Serving Abused Families) (Oates *et al.* 1995). This project aimed to provide a physically and psychologically safe environment, and to provide each child with the knowledge and pre-academic skills required for entry into mainstream school. The rationale for this is that success at school is a major protective factor to offset childhood disadvantage (see Macdonald and Roberts 1996). In addition to a carefully structured routine and a curriculum designed to meet these aims, the project included a case-management system whereby one teacher was responsible for each child's case, including the provision of home visits. These were designed to provide support to caregivers (six children were in foster care at the point of enrolment), and to improve the quality of interaction between the child and the caregiver.

Of the 22 children old enough for school at the end of twelve months, 79% were enrolled in mainstream schools (33% in regular classrooms and 46% into special education). Only 12% required residential placements. Results from a range of standardised developmental tests showed that the majority of the children made developmental gains at a faster rate than would be expected. In the absence of a control or comparison groups, these results should be treated cautiously, but they mirror the trends of group comparison studies such as those by Culp and his colleagues. What is different about this programme is the addition of home visiting in an attempt to influence and integrate factors in both the major contexts of children's lives. This approach certainly merits more careful, controlled research.

CHILD PHYSICAL NEGLECT

Apathy, passivity, and social withdrawal are amongst the documented effects of child physical neglect, along with behaviour problems and academic delay (Crittenden 1981; Egeland *et al.* 1983; Wodarski *et al.* 1990). Some of the projects discussed earlier in this Chapter have included interventions aimed at helping neglected children (see Project 12-Ways above). The majority of therapeutic day-care programmes discussed in the previous section included neglected children in their samples, and should be considered too, although in the absence of separate analysis this should be done cautiously. A few studies have focused specifically on the needs of neglected children, or identified neglected children as a sub-sample of those for whom services were provided (see Fantuzzo 1990; Fantuzzo *et al.* 1987, 1988).

These studies provide a good example of an incremental approach to service development and evaluation, beginning with single-case designs (Fantuzzo *et al.* 1987), and moving in a step-wise fashion to randomised controlled trials (Fantuzzo *et al.* 1988, Davis and Fantuzzo 1989). They are concerned with the development of social interaction skills in withdrawn, maltreated children. The interventions were provided in a day centre and comprised attempts to initiate social interaction with neglected children, first using specially trained 'peers', then comparing this intervention to interaction initiated by adults, and finally comparing the relative effects of adult- and peer-social initiation with (i) withdrawn neglected children, (ii) aggressive physically abused children, and (iii) withdrawn non-maltreated children. All the children were pre-school children.

The results showed that children respond more positively to peer-initiated interactions, which resulted in significant increases in positive social behaviour across a range of settings. In contrast, children who received adult-initiated interactions displayed a significant decrease in social behaviour after treatment. Puzzlingly perhaps, a moderate increase in the negative behaviour of withdrawn children occurred alongside increases in positive interactions. Physically aggressive/abused children, showed a preference for the adults, and initiated play with them more frequently. A salutary lesson perhaps.

In a more recent study, Fantuzzo and colleagues randomly allocated 46 socially withdrawn Head Start children, of whom 22 had been physically abused or neglected, to two groups. In the experimental group, children were paired with 'resilient' peers who, under the supervision of the class-room teacher, initiated play. Results show that these children demonstrated significant increases in positive interaction peer play, and a decrease in solitary play for all withdrawn children, both those who had been mal-treated, and those who had not. These improvements were maintained at two months follow-up (Fantuzzo *et al.* 1996).

Conclusions

There are clear trends in the tertiary prevention literature favouring cognitive-behavioural approaches to a range of problems associated with child physical abuse and neglect. At their most successful, interventions are multi-faceted, and pay careful attention to process factors, such as the careful engagement of families, particularly parents, who either may not share the same view of what is happening as professionals, or who may feel victimised by the protection process. Work with abused children is most successful when the sequelae of abuse are specifically targeted.

PSYCHOLOGICAL MALTREATMENT

In their 1995 overview, Becker *et al.* began their section on the treatment of psychologically maltreated children with the sentence:

> 'There are currently no empirical studies on the treatment of psychologically maltreated children.' (Becker *et al.* 1995, p. 29)

Given that psychological maltreatment is increasingly recognised as the mechanism whereby other forms of abuse bring about adverse developmental outcomes, it is perhaps surprising that this is the case. In practice, most children who receive help for psychological abuse are likely to be in substitute care, rather than with their families of origin. Again, sexually abused children may be the exception to this. Certainly it is possible to identify aspects of day treatment programmes which address the psychological and emotional impact of maltreatment. However, given the immense damage caused by psychological maltreatment, typically inflicted over a long period of time, the absence of outcome studies of interventions designed to address the needs of this vulnerable group is professionally unacceptable. Insofar as seriously maltreated young people may be removed from the care of their parents, then the success of substitute care arrangements in remedying the effects of this kind of abuse and neglect should be *specifically* addressed in outcome *research.*

SEXUAL ABUSE

The sheer numbers of children who are sexually abused make it all the more worrying that only a handful of evaluation studies can be found, few of which are of sufficient quality to provide practitioners with a firm evidence base upon which they can depend in the development of services. This is in sharp contrast to the hundreds of accounts of interventions and therapeutic programmes that are to be found in the literature (see for example Kolko 1987; Friedrich 1991). As earlier reviewers of the literature wryly observed, this is particularly regrettable given that sexual abuse was arguably one of the first clinical problems confronting the emerging discipline of psycho-therapy (O'Donohue and Elliott 1992).

Child-focused tertiary interventions are typically concerned to minimise the adverse short- and long-term consequences of sexual abuse. Insofar as childhood sexual abuse can increase the risk of revictimisation (Fromuth and Burkhart 1987)—and in a minority of cases the risk of future perpetration of abuse—they *may* also serve a secondary prevention function. The format and content of programmes vary enormously. The most common formats are individual and group therapies, but family-based approaches are also reported. The content of programmes ranges from play therapy, through psychotherapy, to cognitive-behavioural therapies and family therapy. It is not possible to make any authoritative statement about *what works* in this important area, because of the near-absence of sound research. However, some approaches are more conceptually and empirically coherent than others, and enjoy suggestive support from quasi-experimental studies, pre-post test evaluations, and single case designs. We discuss these later. First we take a brief look at some of the specific problems with outcome research in this field.

Obstacles to Evidence-based Practice in Helping Sexually Abused Children

As Finkelhor and Berliner (1995) have observed, sexual abuse is an event, rather than a disorder. The possible consequences of sexual abuse are many and varied, and not easily predictable. Therefore, the fact that someone has been sexually abused is minimally helpful as an indicator of someone need-ing a particular form of help, and this presents major challenges to those endeavouring to develop and evaluate treatment programmes. Once again, this highlights the importance of a careful assessment of the impact of the abuse on the child and family. In order to maximise the likelihood of an appropriate response, Swenson and Hanson recommend that this should be:

- comprehensive;
- multifaceted (i.e., including multiple methods of data collection across different settings, and using multiple respondents);
- cover not just the abusive incident(s) but a complete social history, including a child's history of trauma and of mental health and behaviour problems;
- draw on a range of standardised instruments, including those specifically designed to identify the sequelae of sexual abuse.

This is partly because it is difficult to disinter problems that have arisen as a direct result of abuse from those which either pre-dated it, or are the consequence of related problems, such as family dysfunction. Whilst some problems may respond to certain interventions whatever their origins, others may require carefully tailored interventions, as when behaviour problems are the result of abuse, and may reflect a child's lack of trust or sense of betrayal by a non-offending parent.

Such issues are too rarely attended to in outcome research, making the results of studies difficult to interpret. Other problems are:

1. Some children are referred because they have been abused, not because they have identifiable problems. Should these children be included in evaluations (their presence may 'depress' the apparent effectiveness of programmes)? Finkelhor and Berliner (1995) suggest their exclusion is probably desirable for short-term outcome studies, but that they should not be excluded from outcome research in general, because of their risk of deterioration.

2. A related concern is that some of the problems associated with sexual abuse do not manifest themselves immediately. The debate hinges on whether early intervention can prevent the development of these problems, or whether they are the result of particular developmental challenges (e.g., establishing intimate relationships) that may not be amenable to early intervention. This problem (and also the evidence that some children 'deteriorate' before they improve) points to the need for long follow-up periods in outcome research and multiple assessments—very unfashionable amongst most research funding bodies at the moment.

3. A range of factors such as parental support (Everson *et al.* 1989), maternal upset (Newberger *et al.* 1993) and family functioning (Conte and Schuerman 1987) are good predictors of the extent to which sexual abuse results in adverse consequences, and the speed with which children and family members recover. In addition to underlining the need for experimental studies that can control for these important background variables, this also raises the question of where intervention is best targeted. A view that programmes which focus on the child and the parent(s) are best placed to secure good outcomes, have led to a number of promising trends in the literature (see below).

4. In general, evaluations need to examine (and programme developers consider):

   • the relative contribution of the length and duration of treatment;
   • the content (the 'logical fit' between the way the problem is conceptualised and the proposed response—see Macdonald and Sheldon 1992), and how they are expected to result in the desired outcomes;
   • the outcome measures used (which should be relevant to the abuse-specific effects of sexual abuse, see above);

- the relative impact of interventions on sub-groups of children within programmes, rather than rely solely on group means and significance tests.

5. There are a number of practical challenges in gathering appropriate data in this area, such as the concern that talking to children might constrain them to relive experiences and concerns which they have begun to come to terms with. This may be particularly the case if 'third party' researchers are gathering the data; but delegating the task to therapists or others familiar to the child may lessen the response rate (Monck 1998) and pose other problems of bias.

Evidence About What Works

These problems are explored in a review of interventions in this field conducted by Finkelhor and Berliner in 1995. It is a narrative review, so lacks the sophistication of that conducted by MacMillan *et al.* (1994b) or Rispens (1997). However it is an appropriately cautious review, and we take this as our starting point. It is broadly in line with earlier reviews by Beutler *et al.* (1994) and O'Donohue and Elliott (1992).

Finkelhor and Berliner identified only three randomised controlled trials, five 'other-treatment' controlled trials and five quasi-experimental outcome studies concerning the effectiveness of child-focused interventions addressing the therapeutic needs of sexually abused children (Finkelhor and Berliner 1995). They also identified seventeen pre-post test design studies. Their inclusion criteria were absolutely minimal. Studies needed to include:

- some quantitative measure(s), used at two points in time subsequent to the disclosure of the abuse;
- at least five or more evaluated children having received treatment during that interval.

This led to the exclusion of single case experimental designs, and—unfortunately—to the inclusion of a number of follow-up studies of abused children in studies that were not intended to evaluate interventions *per se*, for example studies that looked at the effect of court testimony. Studies included in the review covered a range of interventions, including sex education, music therapy, family therapy, group therapy and cognitive behavioural interventions.

Finkelhor and Berliner note that all-but-one of the pre-test post-test evaluations tended to demonstrate improvements in sexually abused children, but that within such designs, these cannot be confidently attributed to the intervention rather than the passage of time. The contribution of these studies to evidence-based practice lies primarily in their negative results.

They suggest that certain problems, such as 'externalising' problem behaviours (aggression, acting out etc.), and sexual symptamatology (e.g., sexualised behaviour) are less amenable to change within general therapeutic approaches (see Lanktree and Briere 1995, and Nelki and Waters 1988).

Of the more rigorous studies, three of the five quasi-experimental studies showed no advantages for those receiving help compared with a control group. The no-treatment randomised controlled trials however, showed significant improvements for children, although the authors caution that they are all small-scale, two are unpublished (Burke 1988; Perez 1988) and the third used an 'unconventional approach' (group therapy plus sex education) which they say—although they do not say why—undermines its scientific weight (Verleur *et al.* 1986). The five 'other-treatment' controls showed no clear advantages for one approach over another, with the exception of a study by Cohen and Mannarino who compared the effects of group supportive therapy with group-based 'abuse-specific' therapy for pre-school children (Cohen and Mannarino 1996). Results favoured the latter.

Their review does not systematically address the relative impacts of these different approaches, partly because so little information is given in individual studies, and partly because the evidence-base is so small. Their general conclusion is that there is no overall support for either individual or group formats, but that the study by Cohen and Mannarino lends support to a growing consensus that an important element of effective interventions is that they are, at least in part, 'abuse-specific' (Finkelhor and Berliner 1995). This was also the hallmark of a later study, published after the review, this time with children aged 7–13 years (Deblinger *et al.* 1996). It is to the merits of 'abuse-specific therapy' that we now turn.

Abuse-specific Therapy

Although all treatment programmes are concerned to prevent the adverse consequences of abuse, not all interventions are organised around the abuse experience. *Abuse-specific* or *trauma-specific* interventions are those which are specifically designed to promote the emotional and cognitive processing of the abusive events, to reduce the acute abuse-related consequences, to restore or maintain normal development, and to reduce the risk of future abuse-related problems in adjustment (see Berliner 1991 and 1997; Berliner and Wheeler 1987).

The rationale for at least including an abuse-specific component in the treatment of sexually abused children is that although children react differently, sexual abuse *per se* often causes emotional and behavioural problems. Some problems, such as sexualised behaviour, differentiate sexually abused children from other clinical and non-clinical samples (Friedrich 1993). Others, such as post-traumatic stress disorder, are more prevalent amongst sexually abused children (McCleer *et al.* 1992; Wolfe *et al.* 1989). Further, it is likely that the longer-term consequences of sexual abuse are mediated by the ways in which children cope psychologically and emotionally. They may cope by avoidance behaviour, which may leave them vulnerable to later problems, or by developing negative attributions about themselves and others:

> 'Janoff-Bulmann (1989) advances a trauma theory positing that significant, disturbing events that threaten bodily integrity have the potential to alter basic assumptions about self, others, and the world. Psychological adaptation to negative cognitive schemata for safety, trust, power, esteem, and intimacy, that are acquired as a result of traumatic experiences can lead to psychiatric disorders and interfere with normal functioning (McCann, Sakheim, and Abrahamson, 1988).' (Berliner 1997, p. 158)

Negative and abuse-related attributions by sexually abused children appear to be correlated with the level of a child's self-reported psychological problems such as anxiety, depression, and self-esteem (Mannarino and Cohen 1996). Such self-reports occur in the absence of parental reports of sexual or behavioural problems (Spacarelli 1995). This may support the provision of some time-focused intervention even when children appear to have no problems following abuse, although this is a complex issue. Broadly speaking the components of abuse-specific therapy are:

- educational: providing information about the nature of sexual abuse and the range of likely consequences;
- the facilitation of the expression of a range of abuse-related feelings;
- identifying and correcting distorted or maladaptive cognitions;
- teaching anxiety-management skills;
- equipping children with self-protection skills;
- interventions directed at managing problematic behaviours associated with the abuse.

Such an approach may be targeted at children, or at their parents. The rationale for including parents hinges on the importance of family support to coping, recovery, and protecting against long-term adverse consequences. Sexual abuse can be a serious stressor to non-offending parents and siblings. Enabling them better to understand abuse, and manage the immediate consequences is crucial in establishing a maximally supportive environment (Masten *et al.* 1991; Berliner 1997). There is some evidence that programmes which offer help to parents and to children simultaneously are more beneficial than those with a focus on either parents or children.

The broader literature is replete with examples of techniques that can be incorporated within such a therapeutic framework, and as yet there is no clear evidence from studies with this population that one is superior to another. Many of the programmes incorporate cognitive-behavioural methods because they enjoy broad-based support from evaluations of their application to similar problems e.g., fears, anxiety, aggression, depression and low self-esteem (see Stauffer and Deblinger 1996). These approaches feature in the two studies by Cohen and Mannarino (1996) and Deblinger *et al.* (1996) and we provide a brief summary of these studies next.

Two Studies

Deblinger et al. 1996

The conceptual approach used in this study was based on that of post-traumatic stress disorder (see Wilson and Keane 1997). This is on the basis that many children referred for mental health services following sexual abuse are diagnosed as suffering from post-traumatic stress, and many others exhibit partial symptoms. The researchers compared the effects of a cognitive-behavioural approach designed to target these symptoms (*viz.* intrusive thoughts, constricted affect, avoidance, and sleep disturbance) to the standard therapeutic care available within the community. One hundred children were randomly assigned to one of four conditions:

(i) *community control condition.* Parents in this group received information about their children's symptom patterns and were strongly encouraged to seek therapy; and child protection workers, or the victim witness co-ordinator (cf., victim support worker) were asked to assist families with referrals.

(ii) *Experimental condition 1: Child-only intervention.* In this group, children were seen in twelve 45 minute individual sessions. The intervention included the following cognitive-behavioural methods: gradual exposure, modelling, education, coping, and body safety skills training. Gradual exposure (described as the 'cornerstone' of the intervention) aimed to help children break the associations frequently made between highly negative emotions and abuse-related thoughts, discussion and other reminders. One of the reasons why anxieties and phobias are often resistant to change, is that one way of coping with them is avoidance. In the attempt to protect children who have been sexually abused, parents often shield them from abuse-related stimuli or discussion, thus preventing children from experiencing situations which enable them to process their abusive experiences. Parents received occasional updates on their child's progress and the workers answered any questions or concerns they had. However, structured parent-training was not provided to these parents.

(iii) *Experimental condition 2: Non-offending parent intervention.* Twelve weekly group sessions of 45 minutes long, in which parents were taught the therapeutic skills deployed by the therapists in the child-only group. Mothers learned to reduce their children's fears and avoidance behaviours through the use of modelling, gradual exposure, and cognitive processing exercises. They also learned to analyse their interactions with their children behaviourally, identifying situations in which they might inadvertently have shaped or maintained problems associated with the abuse. Child management skills were then taught to help parents change these unhelpful patterns of interaction.

(iv) *Experimental condition 3: Combined parent and child intervention.* In this condition sessions lasted 80–90 minutes, weekly over 12 weeks. Parents and children were seen separately for the first 40–45 minutes, and then jointly for 30 minutes.

Results

- Mothers assigned to treatment (parent-only and parent–child conditions) described significantly greater decreases in their children's externalising behaviours (e.g., aggression, acting out), reported greater use of effective own parenting skills than those assigned to the community or child-only conditions.
- Similarly children whose mothers were assigned to treatment (parent-only and parent–child conditions) reported significantly less depression than those children assigned to the community or child-only conditions.
- Children assigned to treatment (child-only and parent and child) exhibited significantly fewer PTSD symptoms than children not so assigned (i.e., parent-only and community).
- A statistical analysis of outcomes for those children in the community group who did receive treatment ($n = 12$) with those who did not ($n = 10$) showed that those receiving treatment did no better than those without. This confirms other studies suggesting that general treatment strategies which are not 'abuse-focused' are not effective for this group (Goodman *et al.* 1992; Oates *et al.* 1994).
- Follow-up data are not yet available.

Implications

(i) Non-offending mothers should be engaged in the treatment of their sexually abused children whenever possible, particularly when children are exhibiting externalising behavioural difficulties or depressive symptomatology. It appears that enhanced parenting skills may result in decreased behavioural difficulties. This is in line with general trends in cognitive-behavioural research (Kazdin 1987; McMahon and Wells 1989).

(ii) Mothers' involvement may be an important factor in helping children adjust following sexual abuse. Their involvement may be tangible evidence to children that they have their mothers' support, and this may be the mechanism whereby their depression is lessened. The coping strategies that are taught as part and parcel of cognitive behavioural interventions may increase parental self-efficacy, which may encourage their children to develop similarly functional patterns of coping.

(iii) Gradual exposure appears to be influential in bringing about a reduction in PTSD symptomatology. It appears that there is some merit in involving professional staff in this process, rather than delegating this to mothers who are themselves emotionally involved.

(iv) The content of treatment is important. Abuse-specific therapy should be considered as an important component of strategies designed to help children who have been sexually abused.

Cohen and Mannarino (1996)

In this study, 67 sexually abused pre-school children and their parents were randomly assigned to one of the following:

(1) *Cognitive behavioural intervention.* Children and parents in this group received 12 individual sessions targeted at common problems/symptoms associated with sexual abuse and a number of themes and issues that have been shown to be prevalent and predictive of problems in older sexually abused children. Work with parents addressed:

- ambivalence in belief about the child's abuse
- ambivalent feelings towards the perpetrator
- attributions regarding the abuse
- feeling that the child is 'damaged'
- providing appropriate emotional support to the child
- management of inappropriate child behaviours (including regressive and sexual behaviours)
- management of fear and anxiety
- parental issues related to their own history of abuse (if applicable) and
- legal issues.

Work with children addressed:

- identification of appropriate versus inappropriate touching
- attributions regarding the abuse
- ambivalent feelings toward the perpetrator
- regressive and inappropriate behaviours
- fear and anxiety

- safety education and
- assertiveness training.

(2) *Non-directive supportive therapy.* This was designed to control for the non-specific aspects of therapy, such as the amount of contact with a therapist, support from an understanding professional and the passage of time. It is also designed to reduce loneliness, isolation, hopelessness and anxiety by providing support to mother and child. The therapist:

- established and maintained three basic components of the therapeutic bond: the working alliance, empathic resonance and mutual affiliation
- used reflective listening
- provided appropriate empathy
- provided supportive statements, clarification and encouragement
- could help the client to examine alternatives through non-directive interventions (e.g., 'Is there no other way you could think about that?').

Results

(1) The cognitive-behavioural intervention (CBI) was more effective than non-directive supportive therapy (NSI) in reducing problems associated with sexual abuse, including sexualised behaviour problems.

(2) Considering only those children whose problems were in the clinical range at pre-intervention, the results showed that after intervention, 56% of children who had received CBI had improved to an extent that these behaviours were within the normal range, compared with only 22% of those who received NSI. These changes were more dramatic on specific scales such as those measuring externalising (65–12%) and internalising (60% compared with 11%) behaviour.

(3) Six children were removed from the NSI group because of the persistence of serious, sexually inappropriate behaviours. Had they remained in the group, the relative changes for this problem area would have been more extreme:

> 'We believe it is clinically significant that although many of the children in the (CBI) group had these sexually inappropriate behaviors as well, the (CBI) intervention was apparently effective in eliminating them within two treatment sessions, thus preventing the need to remove any (participants) from CBI.' (Cohen and Mannarino 1996, p. 48)

(4) Both groups experienced modest improvement in social competence.

(5) There were no significant differences between the groups in terms of parental satisfaction.

Conclusions

Whilst outcome studies in general suggest that sexually abused children benefit from a range of interventions, few studies have been conducted which allow us to control for the passage of time, or for the relative merits of particular aspects of composite programmes. Those that exist suggest that interventions which focus specifically on the trauma of the sexual abuse itself, and directly target the sequelae of abuse, are more likely to be effective than those that do not. Of the interventions for which there are rigorous outcome studies, cognitive-behavioural approaches appear to have much to offer, and in terms of dealing with sexualised and externalising behaviours, should be considered as an important component of any programme.

Finally, one issue that has not received much attention, but which deserves consideration, is the help that might be offered to parents (non-offending parents) whose children are thought to have been sexually abused, at the time this comes to light. Parental support is thought to be correlated with a positive outcome for children coping with the experience of sexual abuse (see Conte and Schuerman 1987; Everson *et al.* 1989), but it is also the case that many parents have difficulties coming to terms with what has happened to their child. They may not know what to expect of an investigation. If sexual abuse has occurred, they may not understand what effects the abuse might have for their child. They may find their child's response difficult to manage, not knowing what to say or do, and of course, they may themselves have difficulty coping with the reality and the aftermath of the disclosure. Few studies have sought to find out what would best facilitate a supportive response from a parent, both for the parent's own benefit, but also because of the importance to the child's outcomes. One exploratory study of parents referred to a treatment study, revealed that parents experienced serious levels of distress which had a negative impact on their relationship with their child, and that the treatment agency did not cater for the needs of the parent (Davies 1995). Jinich and Litrownik (1999) randomly assigned 87 mothers of children between 4–12 years of age, who had been referred for assessment for sexual abuse at a Child Protection Centre in San Diego. Whilst the children were being interviewed, mothers who agreed to participate in the study were assigned to one of two groups. Those in the experimental group were shown a 22 minute tape in which a local TV News Anchorwoman presented:

'specific information about the short- and long-term psychological and behavioural effects commonly seen in sexually abused children, common reactions of parents were identified, and the importance of how parents responded was emphasized. . . . Following this introductory section that let mothers know it was natural for them to be experiencing a variety of feelings (i.e., distress, anger, guilt), that they may not know what to do, and recognizing that they wanted to help their child, a number of specific supportive responses was presented.' (Jinich and Litrownik 1999, p. 180)

The responses suggested to parents were presented using the acronym 'BRAVE', representing five supportive behavioural approaches:

1. Believe your child;
2. Reach out and comfort your child;
3. Assure your child that they are not to blame;
4. Validate your child's feelings;
5. Encourage your child to talk about what happened.

These were demonstrated using five different actors in a variety of contexts (mother–child, father–child, mealtimes, bedtime etc.). Parents assigned to the control condition watched a 22 minute videotape that provided general information about services at the Centre for Child Protection, Children's Hospital and so on. Parents were observed relating to their children when they were reunited after an initial interview with a social worker, and again following the child's interview. In addition, mothers were interviewed one week later, during which they were asked about the helpfulness of the interview, and a number of measures were administered designed to determine parental knowledge, attitudes and skills, as well as child functioning. The structured observation periods were used to assess levels of supportive verbal behaviours (statements of reassurance, and statements of encouragement to the child to talk about his or her feelings or the interview) and supportive non-verbal behaviours (hugging, kissing, holding hands etc.). Children were also interviewed using a structured interview designed to explore their perceptions about parental support (*Children's Impact of Traumatic Events Scale-Revised*, CITES-R, Wolfe and Gentile 1992).

Results for this brief, early intervention for non-offending parents of children thought to have been sexually abused are very promising, though not conclusive. Following the video, mothers in the experimental group showed more knowledge about how to respond to their child in a supportive way and were more likely to engage in supportive responses when their child joined them after their interview (raters who evaluated tapes of mother–child interactions did not know which video had been seen by which mothers). At one-week follow-up there was some evidence that the intervention, although aimed at mothers, may have made a difference to the children too, insofar as children whose mothers had watched the intervention video reported having more positive feelings about their parents non-supportive responses than those in the control group. However, at follow-up, many of the post-interview differences were either not statistically significant or had disappeared. The authors reflect that there may be a number of reasons for this, including the relatively small sample size and the possible insensitivity of some of the measures used, given that in this study the majority of mothers believed their children. Their follow-up period of one week may also have been inadequate to detect changes over time (although it seems appropriate if one is seeking to ascertain differences in knowledge and attitude during a critical period). Lastly, there was some evidence that for all mothers (experiential and control) those who were more distressed by what had happened, and who appeared to hold their child responsible engaged in more non-supportive behaviours towards their children, and vice versa. This is clearly an area where there is scope for development, and may provide a window of opportunity for very cost-effective interventions which might help minimise the adverse consequences of the potential trauma of child sexual abuse.

11

WORK WITH SEX OFFENDERS

There is no dearth of literature on the factors considered to be associated with sexual abuse, on patterns of sexual offending, or on the treatment of sex offenders. However, when one sorts this literature against criteria such as methodological rigour and validity, one is left with only a handful of studies which are not easy to distil. This is, in part, because of a variety of differences between them, such as varying definitions of abuse. But more fundamentally, there are some other, difficult-to-avoid problems, such as the fact that the easiest group of child abusers to access for research purposes are those who have been convicted of offences, and yet there is very good reason to think that convicted sex offenders are, in fact, a very small proportion of the wider group of people who sexually abuse children. This being so, we do not know how representative are sex offenders of sexual abusers in general. Also, too often the nature of sexual offending receives scant attention, and an assumption is made that all sexual offending has similar roots, similar maintaining factors, and is amenable (or not) to the same therapeutic interventions. Such a 'blunt' approach to the area minimises opportunities to develop a more secure knowledge base upon which to develop and evaluate interventions.

This chapter considers the evidence for the effectiveness of those interventions currently in use with sex offenders. It draws particularly on two reviews, one a systematic review which concentrated solely on evidence from randomised controlled trials (White *et al.* 1998), the other a more inclusive overview of studies which extended its inclusion criteria beyond randomised controlled trials and critically appraised the findings of earlier reviews (Perkins *et al.* 1998). Before considering this evidence, it is worth reviewing the rationale for the core psychosocial components typically found within programmes designed to prevent sexual offenders from committing further offences. This summary review builds on the material presented in Chapter 5. There are alternative interventions, such as drug treatments designed to lower testosterone levels, and surgical castration, and these are discussed below. Programmes designed for sex offenders are invariably referred to as 'treatment' programmes.

Evaluations can be divided into two broad categories, only one of which really addresses recidivism as an outcome. Most studies seek to evaluate the impact of intervention on those factors which are thought to influence offending, such as cognitive distortions, levels of empathy, social anxiety etc. We cannot conclude from these studies whether or not the intervention has made a difference to the likelihood of re-offending, unless of course, the authors follow the progress of these participants. When studies follow participants over time, ideally long periods of time, to ascertain whether or not there are any detectable differences in post-intervention levels of offending, then these become 'outcome studies' proper. It is high quality examples of the latter that are few and far between.

Generally speaking, most programmes which evidence positive effects, whether in terms of outcomes or impact on factors thought to be associated with sexual offending, are cognitive-behavioural (see Kelly 1982; Marshall et al. 1991; Perkins et al. 1998), and the majority of current programmes which incorporate psychosocial elements are built on theories of learning. These include behavioural treatments aimed at teaching offenders to control or modify aspects of their behaviour, such as sexual arousal, and cognitive therapies aimed at tackling distorted thinking. Here is a summary of the components of cognitive-behavioural programmes, the problems they seek to address, and their underpinning rationale.

1. *Addressing denial and minimisation.* This is often the starting point for programmes. Unless offenders recognise the unacceptability of their offending, and its seriousness, they will be unlikely to engage fully in a programme aimed to change their behaviour, and will not be able to develop the kind of understanding of their behaviour that forms the basis of behaviour change (Salter 1988). Techniques used to tackle denial and minimisation include placing offenders in a group context with other offenders who have (i) already begun to acknowledge the extent and seriousness of their offending, and (ii) are well-placed to challenge the denials of others, as they are intimately familiar with the strategies used to maintain a veneer of innocence or having inflicted minimum harm.

2. *Enhancing victim empathy.* As indicated in Chapter 5, sex offenders often demonstrate little empathy for their victims, and often attribute to them the responsibility for the offending. It is thought that enhancing empathy with victims will help offenders to realise the magnitude of their offences, and will provide an inhibitory 'brake' on the likelihood of future offending. Techniques used include: role reversal; education (watching videos or reading scripts written by victims); work in pairs and groups, using tasks

which require participants to 'put themselves in the shoes' of others, and accurately feeding back their views, experiences; writing 'victim apology' letters; and so on.

3. *Tackling distorted thinking.* Because distorted thinking is thought to play a major part in the self-justification of their behaviour, and in the subsequent minimisation of guilt and responsibility, this is a major target of intervention. Essentially, offenders are helped to identify maladaptive patterns of thinking, and then helped to develop more appropriate patterns of thinking. Offenders are helped to recognise distorted thinking in a number of ways. One means is via the kinds of exercises referred to above, in which reflecting on the experiences of victims might highlight these. Another strategy is requiring offenders to provide a blow-by-blow account of their offence cycle, taking individual offences, and saying what the circumstances were before, during and after the offence. In this context 'circumstances' include what the offender was thinking and feeling. Using material from a diary can provide an alternative source of thoughts and feelings, perhaps more reliable as long as accurately reported, because not suffering from retrospective bias. Once an offender's particular pattern of distorted thinking has been identified, this is challenged by staff and, if treatment is group-based (as the majority is) by other group members. This teaches offenders (via a process of modelling) the skills involved in tracking and challenging their own distorted cognitions.

4. *Addressing anger and aggression.* In dealing with rapists, problems of anger and aggression are more commonplace and form a mainstream feature of treatment. It is less clear what role anger plays in child molestation, but some child molesters intentionally inflict injury on their victims, and some researchers have hypothesised that this may be attributable to feelings of generalised anger towards children in general, perhaps as a result of experiences of childhood victimisation (i.e., of witnessing or experiencing domestic violence and/or physical abuse). In these circumstances cognitive behavioural strategies aimed at helping offenders to manage and contain anger (see Chapter 8) and relapse prevention skills (see below) are the key strategies used. Also, where childhood victimisation is thought to be a factor, some programmes include group or individual elements aimed at helping the offender come to terms with these traumatic events, by understanding them, making more accurate attributions of blame and responsibility, and so on.

5. *Changing deviant sexual fantasies.* Deviant sexual fantasies (e.g., sexual fantasies involving children, fantasies involving inflicting physical pain) are thought to provide a major antecedent condition in the offence cycle of sexual abuse. (see Quinsey and Earls 1990). They are therefore a core target of programmes aimed at preventing recidivism. Typically, such fantasies have been developed in conjunction with, and reinforced by, mastur-

bation. Such fantasies are highly arousing, and are thought to provide a major motivational trigger for sexual offending. There are two kinds of techniques used. The first are geared towards minimising deviant sexual arousal. The others are designed to increase appropriate arousal. Most are based on classical conditional. Techniques most commonly used to minimise deviant sexual arousal include:

- *covert sensitisation*—the offender is asked to imagine himself in the context of his deviant fantasy, and whilst engaged in this fantasy, he is presented with a psychologically aversive image such as being apprehended, being in court with his mother in the public gallery, or with a physically aversive experience such as being sick. Over time, this 'pairing' of the fantasy with an aversive correlate, is aimed at response inhibition. Its efficacy is uncertain.
- *aversion therapy*—this is the most commonly used strategy. Whilst engaging in his fantasy, the offender is presented with an aversive experience such as a noxious odour, or a previously agreed level of electric shock (the level being determined by the offender, the timing being determined by the therapist).

Techniques used to develop and/or increase more appropriate forms of sexual arousal include:

- *systematic desensitisation*—essentially, introducing more appropriate images (e.g., of adults) to offenders whilst in a state of arousal. The aim is for the offender to maintain arousal. Over time, it is hypothesised that this 'pairing' of arousal with non-deviant images or fantasies will help shape non-deviant patterns of sexual arousal and behaviour.
- *orgasmic reconditioning*—timing the presentation (or bringing to mind) of an appropriate fantasy to coincide with the reinforcement of orgasm.

6. *Addressing social skills deficits*. Insofar as men who sexually abuse children have social skills deficits which prevent them establishing appropriate intimate relationships with other adults, it is clearly sensible to include interventions aimed at addressing these deficits, which include under-assertiveness, problems in initiating and sustaining conversations, shyness, and anxiety (Fisher and Beech 1998). Most programmes include a focus on these potential skills deficits, and the major techniques are those of social skills training, i.e., modelling, behavioural rehearsal and feedback. Relaxation training, systematic desensitisation and sex education may also play a part.

7. *Relapse prevention*. This is increasingly recognised as a key part of effective strategies. Repeat offences can and do occur some considerable time after an offender has completed a programme (see Hanson *et al.* 1993). Therefore, it is important to help offenders to recognise the development of

antecedent conditions which may place them at risk of re-offending. This might include helping them to identify high risk situations (such as being alone with children) and helping them to develop strategies for resisting or avoiding such opportunities; to identify times and circumstances of increased vulnerability e.g., social isolation, low mood; or to avoid those particular triggers associated with their own offending histories e.g., alcohol or drug misuse, exposure to paedophile friends, pornographic literature and so on.

Most programmes contain some or all of these 'ingredients'. Whilst generally these cognitive-behavioural packages are promising, as will be seen from the evidence below, much less is known about what particular elements are particularly salient in reducing re-offending. More importantly, these interventions are most frequently delivered as part of a group-work programme. This makes a great deal of intuitive and practical sense. Joining a sex offenders group involves some recognition of their offending by participants and provides a milieu in which 'normal' social interactions can be reinforced and deviant behaviour and cognitions most effectively challenged. However, the formulaic approach which group-based treatment demands, means that these are rarely tailored to the particular profiles associated with individual offenders (see Beckett *et al.* 1994). Further, some interventions such as fantasy modification are not amenable to group-based provision—beyond the provision of information to offenders about the role of fantasy in sexual offending—and often remain unaddressed unless offenders also have access to individual therapy. In all, it may well be that important features of participants' offending are not adequately addressed in these programmes. Minimally, this underscores the importance of careful and detailed assessments, monitoring and evaluation of the progress of individuals who participate in group-based programmes, and sufficient flexibility within treatment settings to address any needs which are not catered for within the main programme.

The following section considers the available evidence from randomised controlled trials.

EVIDENCE FROM SYSTEMATIC REVIEWS

White *et al.* published a systematic review of studies concerned with the effectiveness of sex offender programmes. They restricted their international review, published in the Cochrane Library (White *et al.* 1998), to randomised controlled trials which evaluated the treatment of adults who have been convicted for sexual offences and/or disorders of sexual preference. The latter included:

- bestiality (involving animals);
- child sexual abuse and incest (intrafamilial child sexual abuse);
- exhibitionism or indecent exposure;
- fetishism (using non-living objects);
- frottage or frotteurism (touching or rubbing a non-consenting person);
- sado-masochism and bondage and discipline (being humiliated, beaten, bound or otherwise made to suffer or causing psychological or physical suffering to another which is sexually exciting to the perpetrator);
- transvestism and crossdressing (wearing clothing belonging to the opposite sex);
- voyeurism (observing an unsuspecting person, usually a stranger in an intimate circumstance, for example undressing or engaged in sexual intercourse); and
- rape.

The authors acknowledge that rape is often seen as a crime of violence rather than a sexual offence, but included it in this review. Their list highlights some of the decision-points that researchers and/or authors need to make when dealing with the subject of sexual offending, and one does not need to labour the point that different decisions make it very difficult to 'synthesise' work across the field. White *et al.* considered both antilibidinal drugs (a common form of treatment) and psychological interventions aimed at reducing the target sexual acts, urges or thoughts of offenders or patients (people presenting with problems they wish to change). Drug treatments included:

- testosterone lowering drugs: (i) stilboestrol (an oral synthetic non-steroidal aestrogen), (ii) oestrogen pellets (planted subcutaneously), (iii) medroxyprogesterone acetate (an oral or intramuscular injection synthetic progesterone that lowers testosterone levels) and (iv) cyproterone acetate (an oral antiandrogen that blocks the production of, and opposes the action of testerone);
- antipsychotics: any drug usually given for the purposes of management of pyschotic illnesses such as schizophrenia;
- bromides;
- surgical castration.

Psychological interventions included:

- behaviour therapy of any type;
- relapse prevention. The authors describe this as involving a 'comprehensive multimodal group of interventions aimed at preventing relapse by developing skills to avoid reoffence in the future. These include identifying high risk situations and include cognitive behavioural training, decision matrices, relaxation training and stress and anger management,

attendance at therapeutic community meetings and leisure/recreational activity. Individuals also receive treatment for drug or alcohol problems, and behaviour therapy for sexual deviation.' The latter includes aversion therapy, masturbatory satiation or orgasmic reconditioning (see Beech *et al.* 1998).

The authors sought to compare the effects of any of these treatments against a 'placebo' where possible (e.g., drug treatments) or to 'standard care'. They were primarily interested in whether or not any of these interventions impacted on recidivism (whether in terms of behaviour, thought or urges to act) and whether or not people stayed with the treatment. They also looked at other outcomes such as death, other forms of criminal offence, mental state (using standardised measures), patient satisfaction, side effects and cost effectiveness. An exhaustive search of the international literature identified 70 studies of which 58 were excluded (56 because they turned out not to be randomised controlled trials, 2 more because they did not meet other review criteria). At the time of publication nine studies were awaiting assessment by the reviewers, who had approached the authors for data needed for inclusion in the review (or in some cases decisions about eligibility for inclusion). The three remaining studies were included in the review. These three studies covered: antilibidinal management (a comparison of medroxyprogesterone plus imaginal desensitisation with imaginal desensitisation alone); relapse prevention (of the kind described above and compared with no-treatment), and group therapy (a ten year follow up of intensive probation plus group therapy versus intensive probation alone). In brief, the results provide little for our comfort. The authors conclude that there is no data to support the use of antilibidinal drugs and that nondescript group therapy adds nothing to probation, which itself is ineffective (White *et al.* 1998):

> 'At this stage there is no trial-based evidence to strongly support the use of any treatment of sex offenders or those with disorders of sexual preference. . . . Trials should be simple and long, stretching over years if not decades.' (White *et al.* 1998, p. 19)

The most promising approach was that of relapse prevention, but in the relevant study the only clear result was in relation to the prevention of further non-sexual violence rather than sexual offending. Other problems with the RCTs reviewed by White *et al.* include: (i) an absence of a sufficiently long post-intervention follow-up (Marques *et al.* 1994); (ii) the absence of a close 'logical fit' between the interventions under scrutiny and what we know of the likely need for a broad based approach targeted at the criminogenic needs of perpetrators (McConaghy *et al.* 1988); and (iii) the lack of 'logical fit' in relation to matching the nature of interventions to the specific needs of study participants (Macdonald and Sheldon 1992).

Prior to this review, Hall had undertaken a meta-analyses of randomised controlled trials relevant to the management of sex offenders, and found a 'small but robust effect size for treatment versus comparison conditions' (Hall 1995). However, although a meta-analysis, Hall's review included a number of studies which White *et al.* excluded from their review because they had insufficient methodological rigour i.e., were thought prone to bias, and used statistical analysis which are also thought more prone to bias than their own (White *et al.* 1995). In their non-systematic review of the literature, Perkins *et al.* observe that whilst Hall's review concluded that there were medium sized effects on sexual recidivism of cognitive-behavioural approaches and of hormonal treatments, the magnitude of the effect was lowest for those studies using randomisation or matched control groups (Perkins *et al.* 1998). With this salutory reminder of the impact of study design on evidence of effectiveness, the next section considers evidence from less systematic reviews, and non-experimental studies.

EVIDENCE FROM LESS SYSTEMATIC REVIEWS

Gloomy news on the whole. However, some have argued that the treatment of sex offenders is an area where randomised controlled trials (RCTs) are quite difficult to conduct, not least of all because of the relatively small samples available to the researcher, and the heterogeneous nature of sex offenders may well mask effects if some interventions are more likely to be effective (theoretically at least) with certain kinds of offender. Further, treatment strategies are often a matter of national or service policy i.e., all offenders receive a particular intervention 'package' as a matter of course, limiting the scope for experimental methodology. On this basis, when Perkins and his colleagues conducted a review of sex offender treatment programmes they extended their inclusion criteria and considered other, non-RCT studies, at the same time highlighting the limitations of those studies they examined.

They begin their review of treatment evaluations by considering impact studies, i.e., studies which have focused on the effectiveness of particular interventions designed to bring about changes in factors thought to be associated with offending e.g., cognitive distortions, victim empathy, low self-esteem (see Chapter 5). These are important insofar as they highlight (i) whether a particular intervention achieves what it is designed to achieve, (ii) whether these changes last over time, and across settings (e.g., from prison to community) and (iii) whether success is associated with reduced rates of recidivism. They draw on two studies focusing on U.K. sex offender treatment programmes, one community based (Beckett *et al.* 1998) and the other prison based (Beech *et al.* 1998).

FINDINGS FROM IMPACT STUDIES

The study by Beckett *et al.* (1994) examined the progress of 59 men participating in six community-based sex offender programmes, run by probation departments, and one residential programme. Programmes were of the cognitive-behavioural kind described above. With regard to probation-based programmes, data were collected before the participants joined and again after they had had 54 hours of treatment (to allow comparisons between programmes which were otherwise of varying lengths, 54 hours being the shortest). Men participating in the residential programme were interviewed before they entered the programme and again at the end, on average after 462 hours of therapy. Before treatment the authors report that the child abusers in their study differed significantly from a comparison group of non-offenders:

'They were typically emotionally isolated individuals, lacking in self confidence, underassertive, poor at appreciating the perspective of others, and ill-equipped to deal with emotional distress. They characteristically denied or minimised the full extent of their sexual offending and problems. A significant proportion were found to have: little empathy for their victims; strong emotional attachments to children and a range of distorted attitudes and beliefs, where they portrayed children as able to consent to, and not be harmed by, sexual contact with adults . . .

The men with the most problems in these areas tended to be the most serious offenders. They were more likely to have: abused against a number of victims; committed a previous sexual offence; committed extrafamilial, or both intra- and extrafamilial offences; committed offences against both boys and girls; and report having been abused as children.' Beckett *et al.* 1994, p. 5)

Pre-post the evidence suggests the programmes had a varied impact on offenders, depending on length of treatment, seriousness of offences, levels of sexual deviancy and skills of therapist. In particular:

- 54% of the sample of men studied (across seven programmes) showed a treatment effect, however these men tended to be amongst the least serious offenders, and had profiles indistinguishable from the non-offending sample on most measures used.
- Some men got worse. In particular, 23% became more blaming of their victims. The authors hypothesise that this may be because they were pushed too soon to undertake work on enhancing empathy. The authors suggest that if undertaken too soon it may be counter-therapeutic, as offenders who have not accepted the consequences of their behaviour may well try to cope by becoming defensive and resorting to victim blaming.
- Short-term treatment significantly enhanced the willingness of less deviant offenders to admit to their offences and to sexual problems. It reduced the

extent to which they sought to justify their offending and reduced their distorted thinking about children and sexuality. It made no impact on highly deviant men.

- Long-term treatment made an impact on highly deviant men, leading to desirable changes in admission of offences, offender justifications, distorted thinking, and improvements in self-esteem, assertiveness and intimacy skills. 65% of men in the long-term residential programme showed a treatment effect.
- Short-term programmes had a good overall success rate (59%) but the majority of participants on these programmes were originally classed as 'low deviancy' (60%).
- Groups with 'rolling programmes' (with group members joining and leaving) and the group which had a co-working programme (intensive groups being led by staff from the sex offending team and staff from the probation teams) had the lowest overall success rate (33%). The researchers suggest this might be because the participants from this group had not completed some of the work that formed part of their programme.

The authors conclude that work with serious offenders must be intensive and long-term, and this is echoed elsewhere. They noted that not all programmes adequately assessed their clients, with the danger that they were discharged without showing signs of improvement in key areas. They comment on the need to develop programmes designed specially for child molesters (rather than grouping these offenders with others, e.g., adult rapists) and note with concern the absence of detailed fantasy modification work. In addition to the undesirability of attempting this work in a group context, they point to inadequately trained staff, and generally observe the need for highly trained and supported staff , with adequate resources. On the evidence of the differential outcomes for highly deviant men and treatment length, the authors recommend the setting up of a small number of specialised residential programmes for such offenders (Beckett et al. 1998).

A similar programme, aimed at increasing offenders' motivation to avoid further offences, and to provide them with the self-management skills necessary to achieve this, has also been evaluated in this way. As with the community-based programmes, these are largely cognitive-behavioural in philosophy and content, and are provided in groups. The programmes are therefore 'core' programmes, rather than individually tailored to the needs or circumstances of individual offenders (beyond what is possible within a group-based programme). At the time the research was conducted, there was a move away from relatively short programmes (80 hours) to programmes comprising 160 hours of treatment. This enabled the research team to compare the relative impact of increased exposure to treatment. One hundred men were enrolled in the study, from six prisons, and the impact of attention to victim empathy (not a feature of the original programme) and improved relapse prevention. Eighty-two of these men were child abusers, and the study provides pre-post data on 77. A nine-month follow up, in which 56 men from the original sample agreed to participate, also allowed the team to examine offenders post-release circumstances and levels of support, and their perceptions of the programme.

Baseline data were available on offence history, risk assessment, personality, use of alcohol, level of intellectual functioning and personal history, plus pre-treatment assessment of factors thought to be associated with offending e.g., cognitive distortions, self-esteem. On the basis of available data the researchers grouped the men into four categories: high deviancy / high denial; high deviancy / low denial; low deviancy / high denial and low deviancy / low denial (see Beech *et al.* 1998). Drawing on recent statistical work in this area (Hanson and Lambert 1996), the team devised a means of assigning an overall treatment score, as well as changes in relation to core areas. This attempts to measure not only changes in pro-offending attitudes (the primary targets of the programme) but the extent to which there is improvement in social competence/acceptance of accountability. These were examined as a function of offenders' pre-treatment status in terms of deviance and denial, and with regard to length of treatment .

This impact evaluation showed significant changes in measures of pro-offending attitudes e.g., levels of admitted sexual offending increased, levels of offence-related cognitive distortions reduced, and relapse prevention knowledge increased (Beech *et al.* 1998). Again, the least deviant offenders—measured in terms of levels of pre-disposing personality factors and offence-related cognitive distortions—showed most improvement on related measures. However, although both low deviancy groups showed reductions in pro-offending attitudes, only 20% of those who showed high denial at the outset of treatment showed an *overall treatment effect*. Only nine of those judged to be high deviance/high denial responded to treatment, most of these in the shorter programmes. Put another way, of the 24 men who did not respond to treatment, as measured in this study, 21 of them were classified as 'high deviancy' prior to treatment. Treatment duration appeared not to make much difference for low deviancy/low denial men, 59% of whom showed improvement in terms of overall treatment effect. However, longer exposure to treatment made little difference for low deviancy/high denial men and high deviancy men, with few men in either group providing evidence of an overall treatment effect (17% and 14% respectively). The researchers speculate that the probable discrepancy between the more significant changes in pro-offending attitudes and 'overall treatment effect' is related to the fact that the core of the programme is designed to focus on these factors, rather than address social competence. More recent developments may address this gap. They also observe that whilst positive changes were maintained at nine months follow up for those in prison, this was not the case for those participating in community-based programmes unless participants had received the 160 hour as opposed to the 80 hour treatment programme (Beech *et al.* 1998). Of course, these studies do not directly address the 'bottom-line' issue of the impact of these programmes on recidivism.

EVIDENCE FROM SINGLE OUTCOME STUDIES

When considering outcome studies Perkins *et al.* point out that in general terms, interventions targeted at offending behaviours of all kinds have shown moderate and reliable results where criminogenic needs are addressed i.e., offender characteristics empirically related to offending. Studies which do not, show little or no evidence of effect (see Gendreau 1996). Based on work by Marshall (1994, 1996), Thornton *et al.* (1996) and Ward and Hudson (1998), Perkins *et al.* provide a summary list of the likely criminogenic needs of sex offenders.

As might be anticipated from earlier discussions, in the area of sexual offending, these include:

- deviant sexual arousal/sexual preoccupation
- weak commitment to avoid future offending
- cognitive distortions which justify or support offending
- dysfunctional schemas, possibly linked to early attachment experiences
- limited or inappropriate understanding of and reactions to victim distress
- difficulty recognising personal risk factors
- difficulty generating coping strategies to manage risk factors, and difficulty in implementing them
- deficits in problem-solving skills relevant to risk factors
- poor emotional control
- emotional loneliness/lack of social support
- limited or inappropriate intimacy skills
- impulsive, antisocial lifestyle
- history of drug or alcohol misuse.

Earlier reviews of interventions with sex offenders have had mixed results. A narrative review by Furby *et al.* (1989) found little evidence to support the effectiveness of such work; but a review by McGrath suggested that intervention has a chance of succeeding where offenders acknowledge their offending and accept responsibility for it, see their offending as a problem which they wish to stop and are willing participants in treatment (McGrath 1991). A more rigorous review, using meta-analytic techniques (the statistical synthesis of study results) by Hall concluded that there was some evidence that cognitive-behavioural and hormonal treatments could achieve moderate success in preventing sexual recidivism (Hall 1995). However, as Perkins *et al.* point out, as in other areas, the measured effects were least where studies used either randomised controlled trial designs, or matched group comparisons. Similarly, in reviewing the literature pertaining to work with adolescent sex offenders, Camp and Thyer could only identify eleven studies which met their minimal requirement of having reported specific outcomes measures to determine programme effectiveness, together with details about their validity and reliability (Camp and Thyer 1993). There were few controlled studies, and the evidence that few offenders who complete programmes go on to commit further sexual offences is difficult to interpret because of the background empirical data suggesting that recidivism of adolescent sex offenders is relatively rare (see Davis and Leitenberg 1987).

CONCLUSIONS

At the time of writing, it would be difficult to make strong claims for the effectiveness of any kind of therapeutic intervention with sex offenders, as assessed by rate of re-offending, even when measured solely in terms of recorded offences. However, the evidence gives some justification for what Perkins *et al.* refer to as 'cautious optimism' in relation to the kinds of cognitive-behavioural programmes described earlier. A number of studies indicate a brake on re-offending (see Marques 1998; Marshall *et al.* 1991), and a tendency for 'graduates' of such programmes who do offend to commit less serious offences. That said, evaluations to date also suggest that the most serious offenders are the most difficult to help, and that longer programmes are most effective in developing the relapse prevention skills necessary to reduce relapse rates. Evidence from both impact studies and outcome studies suggest that some things could be done to optimise the likely effectiveness of cognitive-behavioural programmes with sex offenders. The work by Beech *et al.* (1998) suggests that even low deviance offenders with high levels of denial require more intense help than is currently on offer in prison based programmes within the U.K. They suggest that assessments should be developed to identify this category of men; and that a special treatment module should be developed to tackle their denial before progress to the main programme. This is one example of a more general need to develop programmes which, whilst cost-effective, and drawing on the undoubted benefits of group-based approaches, more carefully target the particular needs of individual offenders, where these are not already catered for within the group programme. Programmes also need to attend to gaps, such as the under-emphasis within U.K. programmes on certain criminogenic factors associated with social competence (e.g., low self-esteem, emotional identifi- cation with children). For offenders for whom these areas are significant in the offending patterns, additional provision may be required e.g., fantasy modification. Beech *et al.* also recommend that programmes should incorporate systematic testing of the progress of individual offenders, in order to identify those who do not show the reductions in pro-offending attitudes that are expected, and that these men should be asked to repeat the programme. This is an important point, as completion of a therapeutic programme is not synonymous with change. Finally, although the greatest risk for recidivism appears to be within the first five to ten years, there is evidence that recidivism can occur some ten to thirty one years after release (see Hanson *et al.* 1993). Therefore, it may well be important to consider the provision of 'maintenance' programmes, alongside continued monitoring and supervision.

PART D
Assessment and Evidence-based Practice

12

CHALLENGES TO EVIDENCE-BASED ASSESSMENT

'At no point between 1980 and 1993 did the department learn any more about the family's history, despite these early significant leads.' (The Evening Standard)

'Indeed throughout all our dealings with the family one can find nothing that could be recognized as a full or systematic assessment.' (The Bridge Report)

In the absence of a sound assessment, it is impossible to develop an evidence-based approach to child care and child protection. This crucial activity—too often noticeable by its absence—is the subject of this final section of the book. Knowing 'what works' or what interventions enjoy most empirical support, is not enough to ensure good outcomes. Minimally, workers need to be able to identify when a particular intervention is appropriate for a particular family or individual, and how it should be implemented. And of course, the design and implementation of a programme of work within this field is likely to be a skilled activity. Getting it right depends on an ability to undertake good quality assessments, based on what is known about child maltreatment as well as what is known about effective practice. Therefore, this section covers a range of issues relevant to assessment, from the seemingly rather obvious (that assessments should be undertaken as the basis of child protection work) to more clearly complex issues about assessing risk or dangerousness. Child protection is a complex area of activity. Some of the issues discussed here, particularly in the last Chapter, are quite challenging, and may make for a 'slower read' than earlier Chapters. I hope readers will bear with me in this, as they are all of fundamental relevance to this area of work, and to the development of an evidence-based approach to child protection.

ASSESSMENT

Assessment should be an organised, purposeful activity which comprises a discrete phase of work, as near to the point of referral as possible, and revised as and when appropriate. One of the disturbing facts to emerge from a series of child abuse inquiries is the apparent absence of any attempt by those responsible to undertake a full assessment of a particular case *at any point*. By not doing so, the workers robbed themselves of the opportunity to map out the family's history and build up an accurate (or at least more complete) picture of what was going on in the family, its significance and implications for decision making. They thereby failed to identify or to appreciate the risks inherent within the case, and failed to see or understand important information which would have acted as warning signs, and which would assuredly (in some cases) have prompted a change of direction. Similar conclusions have been reached by Sanders *et al.* in their content-analysis of 21 Part 8 Case Reviews*:

> 'A considerable number of Reviews referred to the lack of assessment as a basis for planning. Assessments were either simply not undertaken, or where undertaken were insufficiently structured to be useful.' (Sanders *et al.* 1999, pp. 263)

As they go on to point out, this is not a new concern, and as far back as 1986, the Social Services Inspectorate was highlighting the need for a more structured and systematic approach to assessment in child protection cases (Social Services Inspectorate 1986), a call to be repeated in 1991 by Noyes, who observed that assessment 'is consistently missing from the practice of the cases described in the inquiries' (Department of Health 1991). That same study highlighted a number of other errors that are commonly found when investigations are conducted into child abuse fatalities. Some of these are organisational and are concerned with the communication between professionals (or its absence) and with multidisciplinary decision-making; others concern the appropriateness of training for particular professionals; inadequate supervision, and so on. Yet others are of more psychological, cognitive and perceptual nature. Psychologists have known for some time of a range of systematic and random errors and sources of bias which can undermine the quality of assessment and decision-making. Since Sheldon's contribution to a collection of papers considering issues arising out of the death of Jasmine Beckford (Sheldon 1987) a recognition of these has gradually seeped into the social work and child protection literatures (see for

---

* Part 8 Case Reviews are those reports of investigations into the untoward death of children at the hands of their carers. Part 8 refers to Part 8 of *Working Together* (Home Office, Department of Health, Department of Education and Science and Welsh Office, 1989) which lays on Area Child Protection Committees the responsibilities of holding an independent investigation in cases of child death, or where there is an issue of public concern.

example Munro 1998 and 1999). This and the following Chapter draw attention to examples of those fundamental errors and biases which can lead to flawed or inadequate assessments, and which can lead professional staff to draw erroneous conclusions, sometimes with fatal consequences. These challenges are present irrespective of what assessment framework one adopts, although some approaches may well be more prone to problems than others. This chapter is concerned with a more fundamental issue which, at first sight, might appear to be a truism. It is the need for a separate assessment stage in the process of helping or protecting children in need, and for a view of assessment as a skilled activity, rather than one which merely involves the collecting of information from a range of sources, and in relation to a range of issues. In both this and the following Chapter, the major focus is on social work, although the points raised apply to professional staff from all disciplinary backgrounds. The focus on social work arises from their pivotal position in decision-making and service provision in general, and to the fact that in some countries (such as the U.K.) they have a lead role in the statutory apparatus of child protection.

Taking a Structured Approach to Assessment

The absence of assessment is not a phenomenon peculiar to cases in which there have been unintended and tragic outcomes. We know very little about the extent to which the errors which appear to be implicated in fatal failures in child protection are, in fact, common-place (see Macdonald 1990). However, there is some indication that the failure to undertake an adequate assessment is a too-common occurrence in routine work. In two research projects which involved the scrutiny of large numbers of case files, the existence of an assessment—either recognisable as an assessment (with regard to is structure, coverage and content) or labelled as such (irrespective of the quality) was the exception rather than the rule*. When recognisable assessments existed, they were typically the product of a specially commissioned piece of work, yet still not necessarily of a high quality. Findings of one of these studies which included an analysis of *Comprehensive Assessments*[†] are presented below. Further, in the course of providing post-qualification training to social workers (in areas ranging from evidence-based child protection to cognitive-behavioural methods), it is not unusual to find oneself being asked to engage in what can only be described as 'remedial' work in this area. It seems that, in the U.K. at least, many social workers are ill-prepared by their qualifying courses for this important area of work.

* These were projects undertaken by the present author, one in 1995 in the South-East of England, the other in 1999 in the South West.
[†] Assessments undertaken in accordance with U.K. Government Guidance.

One of the possible explanations for the apparent absence of assessment as a beginning stage of the professional response to referrals is the pervasive notion that assessment is an *ongoing process*. This is one of a number of areas where the recognition of one factor obscures the importance of others. It is certainly the case as new information comes to light, or circumstances change, that an assessment undertaken at a particular point in time will need to be revised. This is *not*, however, a reason for not seeing assessment as an important *first* phase, in which one seeks to make sense of the set of circumstances which have brought a particular child and his or her family into contact with social services. Further, it is *not* a reason to abandon the idea that assessment (subject to other pressures which will be discussed below) is something which should be undertaken and completed *before* decisions are made about the best way forward. Minimally, a detailed assessment is the only sure-footed way of ensuring that we pay adequate attention to the uniqueness of individual cases, that we maximise our chances of coming to a good understanding of what is going on and what it might therefore be logical or rational to do by way of response. Often, and especially in the majority of child protection cases which do not go anywhere near a court room (in which case assessments are often produced by a number of sources), it is only the social worker who is in a position to undertake, or co-ordinate, an assessment, or offer any service. Therefore, this is a priority area for professional and organisational development.

A Framework Approach

Steps taken to improve this situation have not necessarily had the effects intended. A commonly-deployed strategy is to promote a framework within which it is recommended that assessments be undertaken. Insofar as these act as elbow checklists which nudge and ensure that key areas of information are covered, they are a useful tool. However, as a strategy for producing detailed assessments of a high standard they suffer from a number of problems. These are considered in this section.

In 1988 the U.K. Department of Health produced guidance on undertaking a comprehensive assessment. This became known colloquially as the 'Orange Book' because of the colour of its cover (DoH 1988). It aimed to encourage recognition of the need for good quality assessments in child protection, assessments which paid particular attention to children's development and parents' capacity to respond to children's needs. As such, it was organised in a series of sections, attending to particular areas of potential relevance e.g., emotional development of child, the couple relationship and family interactions, physical conditions. In the hands of skilled practitioners it undoubtedly made a contribution to enhancing the quality of assessments undertaken, but it also appears to have had some unintended consequences. Experience of the use of the 'Orange Book' led to the following conclusions being drawn by the Department of Health:

'. . . over the years concerns have arisen about the use made of *Protecting Children*. Inspections and research have shown that sometimes the guide was followed mechanistically and used as a check list, without any differentiation according to the child's or family's circumstances. Assessment was regarded as an event rather than as a process and services were withheld awaiting the completion of an assessment. In some authorities an all or nothing approach was found: either very detailed comprehensive assessments were carried out or there was no record of any analysis of the child and the family's situation.' (DoH 2000)

In 2000 the 'Orange Book' was replaced by a new framework for assessment (which will probably be known as the 'Purple Book' . . .). The new guidance reflects a re-conceptualisation of child protection within the U.K. from one in which children at risk of abuse or neglect (or 'significant harm' as the U.K. legislation frames it) were dealt with as a distinct group, toward one in which they are seen as one particular subset of a larger group of children 'in need'. Thus the guidance is entitled *Framework for the Assessment of Children in Need and their Families* (DoH 2000). Appropriately it emphasises that assessment is an important plank in work with *all* children in need, and an important step in promoting their well-being. It also stresses the importance of working in partnership with children and families, and working collaboratively on an inter-disciplinary basis. However, insofar as this ideological shift towards a view of children at risk as primarily 'children in need' encourages workers to take their eye 'off the protection ball' (see later sections on bias and error) it may carry with it some risks for children whose most pressing needs are for protection. This remains to be seen. What is of primary interest here is how the new guidance attempts to establish good practice in assessment by providing a detailed framework, including a time-frame, for use by practitioners.

The guidance describes the legislation, responsibilities and principles underlying the work of social services departments in promoting and safe-guarding children's welfare and assessing children's needs (DoH 2000) and introduces the framework and assessment process being developed. For the first time, time-scales are set out for the completion of initial assessments (described as a 'brief assessment' of each child referred to social services) and a 'core assessment', described as:

'. . . an in-depth assessment which addresses the central or most important aspects of the needs of a child and the capacity of his or her parents or care-givers to respond appropriately to these needs within the wider family and community context.' (DoH 2000)

This definition illustrates the orientation of the guidance towards an eco-logical approach, emphasising child development, parenting capacity and family and environmental factors. Further detailed guidance on assessment will take the form of proforma documents which will help social workers gather appropriate age-related information, and for the first time the poten-tial value of standardised measures is acknowledged. This change of approach and emphasis is not solely due to a wish to adopt a more integrated approach to children in need. It is intended that this new guidance will ensure that assessment is something done for *all* children referred to social services. Combined with regular inspection and audit one can be optimistic that in the U.K., assessment will assume a more focal point in children and families social work than it enjoyed towards the end of the twentieth century. The central question is, however, whether or not this will guarantee good quality assessments or useful assessments.

Certainly the guidance, in conjunction with other developments, will pro-vide a useful framework covering key areas. It also nods in the direction of evidence-based knowledge. However, one of the problems with the earlier guidance was less the adequacy of the framework itself, but rather that it gave the impression that assessment was purely a matter of the collection of information. Indeed, the fact that assessments undertaken within this guidance were referred to as 'comprehensive' assessments rather accurately sums up the dangers. The limits of such an approach are discussed next.

The Limits of a Framework Approach

As part of a larger project, a detailed analysis was undertaken of eighteen comprehensive assessments, randomly selected from four family centres in one local authority. These were specially commissioned assessments under-taken at the request of child protection case conferences. They were, therefore, explicitly oriented towards child protection assessment; were undertaken by staff who specialised in this work (alongside other areas of work with children and families) and who had time to give this area of work the attention it deserved. They all worked to the 'Orange Book'—although they used it in a myriad of ways—and the majority of assessments were under-taken over a period of weeks. These assessments were read independently by two people, one the present author, the other a senior member of staff employed by the local authority with a responsibility for quality assurance. The assessments were scrutinised using a content-analysis schedule of questions, such as: 'Is the purpose of the assessment stated clearly?'. The judgements of both assessors were compared and any differences resolved by discussion (there were, in fact, few disagreements). The following impor-tant features emerged:

- *Purpose of the assessment.* Rarely was there a clearly stated rationale or purpose for an assessment. Some had been commissioned following a case conference as part of a Protection Plan (though how it was to contribute to this was not clear). Only one half of the assessments were linked explicitly to some statement of concern, for example one assessment stated:

    'The causes for concern are: (i) continuing parental conflict; (ii) the risk of physical aggression between the parents; (iii) the misuse of alcohol; and (iv) the children's involvement in the latter.'

    This however, was rare. The lack of specific direction to these assessments (a theme to be returned to) appeared to have an adverse effect on their planning, execution and subsequent content. Rarely did they specifically address the circumstances which led professionals to be concerned about the welfare of the children. Without a clear understanding of the basic purpose of an assessment, and its place in relation to a particular family, it is easy to understand why a majority of these reports comprised a collection of information organised under a variety of headings, with little in the way of 'joined-up' interpretation.
- *Reasons for referral.* Only seven reports covered the events which led to the children coming to the attention of the local authority, and usually this information appeared *en passant* and had to be disinterred from the text. Its significance is that it is hard to imagine that parents have a firm sense of *why* assessment is being undertaken if it rarely, if ever, addressed the reasons for their embroilment in the State mechanisms of child protection. In eight records there was no mention of the reasons the children were known to social services (let alone why their names might be on the Child Protection Register) and in the remaining three there were elements of such an account only, but these were not addressed specifically.
- *Family composition.* Summary information about family composition makes easier the process of digesting more complex information about families and should be a standard feature of any assessment. Only 11 of the 18 reports provided such a résumé. When they did, they were generally well done, often using a genogram which was also used as a tool in the assessment process i.e., could be used as a basis for seeing, exploring and understanding relationships and patterns of behaviour within a family (see DoH 2000).
- *Social history.* In most cases readers could only identify *elements* of a social history ($n = 8$) and only material that could be so described in 2 cases. There was no sense of how a particular child had come to be where he or she was, what had happened to him or her and to their family, who and what was significant in their lives, and so on. No assessment included a chronology of what had happened to the family. The significance of this is

dealt with in the following Chapter on risk assessment, but readers can deduce from that discussion the value of pulling together as complete a picture as is available of a family when issues of concern are raised. What is clear from analyses of Part 8 Case reviews is that rarely did decision makers base their decision on a complete picture of the facts as they were (potentially) known. It makes no sense to wait for an untoward incident to make use of such an important, and relatively easy, assessment tool. The majority of these assessments related to families where there were such concerns, and yet this important overview was absent in all.

- *Development of problems.* Only two assessments provided an *aetiological* account of how problems had developed over time, with two others providing a partial account. The remaining cases demonstrated no such bringing together of social, psychological and practical concerns, no identification of patterns in the development of problems, and factors in the current circumstances of clients which maintain them (see below). Understanding the way problems develop, what strategies people have tried to resolve them, and with what effect, provide important levers on deciding what it might be sensible to do to tackle them in the future. It is helpful in enabling clients make sense of how they come to be in the difficult situations in which they now find themselves, and how much responsibility they may need to shoulder—or not. It also clarifies the level of cumulative risk that children have been exposed to, and this is essential in making judgements about current or future levels of risk.

- *Current difficulties.* Only eight assessments contained anything resembling an account of current difficulties, and many of these provided this only in an indirect way, i.e., not as a separate section or particular focus. Five others gave some partial account, very much embedded in the text, and five records appeared not to address this at all. The failure of most assessments to address these issues was exacerbated by their failure to consider what factors in the 'here and now' work to compound problems and prevent their resolution. At best one found statements to the effect that clients need to 'work to resolve issues' without saying anything very much about what those issues were, or what their resolution might look like (see below), or what would need to change in order to facilitate this. In only four cases were these important issues explicitly addressed, and in three it was not addressed at all.

- *Nature and causes of maltreatment.* Few assessments explored a range of explanations for causes of concern, or gave due consideration to whether or not the incidents which had brought the family to the attention of social services were indeed indicative of abuse or neglect (all these assessments resulted from child protection investigations). In seven cases the nature of the problems were such that an exploration of alternative explanations was not deemed necessary by those analysing the assessments, but in seven others such explanations were not considered when they might have been justified. In other words, in some assessments social workers pursue one line of explanation where others merit consideration. Another way of putting it might be to say that the explanations explored by assessments appeared to be theory-driven. Assessments were shaped by workers' favoured hypotheses rather than by the circumstances of the case, or what is known about certain kinds of social problem. This might not be so problematic were it not for the fact that these influences were implicit rather than explicit. In only one case was any reference made to theoretical/empirical data to support an interpretation, and this was drawn from systems theory. This assessment was alone in making transparent the links between the theoretical framework being used and the conclusions being drawn from the available information. There was little evidence that workers sought to challenge their interpretation of material e.g., someone with a systems-orientation did not consider alternative accounts, or what might comprise a refutation of her hypothesis.

- *Multi-disciplinary assessments.* These problems were exacerbated by the fact that these assessments rarely integrated information from other professionals involved in the case. One of the most consistent findings of child abuse inquiries and, in the U.K., Part 8 Case Reviews, is that across agency files there is typically a wealth of pertinent and indeed, vital, information that is never brought together in one place. Even in case conferences, each participant is inclined to talk from a basis of his or her opinions, or perceived knowledge, of the child and family, without sharing the information on which that might be based (see Meehl 1995). More serious, perhaps, many practitioners do not take the time to familiarise themselves with the detailed history of a case, and so may be forming judgements not only in the absence of information from other professional sources, but also in the absence of information available in their own records.
- *Source of assessment.* Rarely was it possible to identify who had contributed to the assessment (i.e., how many people were involved), what the sources of evidence were (e.g., interview, direct observation,) or where information had been gathered. This meant that the reader was unable to determine the likely validity and/or reliability of the assessment. In other words, it is less transparent than it should be, less open to challenge or verification.
- *Assessing children.* Rarely was information provided on *how* children were assessed, with only two cases providing clear information about interview techniques (these had been undertaken by drama therapists). In 13 cases it was unclear how children had been worked with, if at all, and only in a few could one safely assume that the standard question and answer interview—when used—was appropriate. In the remaining cases, information was 'buried in the text' in one, and not applicable in two.

- *Children's views.* Nowhere was there any first hand record of the views of the children. They did not seek to include the child's view, even where this might have been possible: this, despite the legal requirement to 'ascertain the wishes and feelings' of children. In other words, the assessment process at best represented the interests of the child as perceived by adults, and usually professionals.
- *Attitudes of family members towards assessment.* Given that the quality of information and its interpretation are influenced by the attitudes of those who are the subjects of such endeavours, it is important to record the views of family members on the process of assessment and on the conclusions drawn by those conducting it. However, this was a rarity in the assessment documents we examined, with only two recording the views of the family regarding the assessment *per se.* Not surprisingly perhaps, these concerned the views of families who were not enthused by the process. Sometimes attached reports contained references to varying degrees of commitment or work on the part of parents, but did not provide any information as to how they *perceived* the assessment, its purpose or implications for their welfare or that of their children, or to what extent they saw it as something with which they would be advised to comply but of no direct benefit to them. The new DoH guidance provides suggestions as to what parents should be told, which should go some way to addressing this particular issue. It also stresses the importance of ascertaining the meaning of events, including assessment, for each person involved in the assessment.
- *Prescriptive value.* The value of assessment lies in its ability to direct future action—soundly. In only two of the 18 assessments reviewed was there thought to be anything approaching a clear plan. One of those concluded:

> "(i) We would recommend that care proceedings be instigated by the local authority as a matter of urgency and that the possibility of an EPO (Emergency Protection Order) be taken if the children's whereabouts can be established. That consideration be given to a residential assessment to include T and the children. That K be invited to be a part of this assessment.
> (ii) That the residential assessment consider the viability of the children remaining with their parents in the future based upon T and K's ability to realise their parental responsibilities and to be able to recognise that the children's welfare is paramount."

It has to be said that this only meets a minimum requirement in terms of specificity of recommendations. Neither recommendation says how these proposals—for yet more assessment (at the end of a 15 page assessment which has taken eight months to complete, and is amongst the best)—will address the concerns set out at the outset. The other assessment with an explicit plan of action contained the following four recommendations:

"(i) It has been noted that the psychiatric assessment has not begun. Depending on the outcome of this assessment it might be appropriate for D to have the opportunity of addressing her past experiences and making sense of them. This would free D to focus more clearly on the areas of her parenting that she wishes to change.

(ii) In terms of family interactions, F and D (*parents*) need to understand themselves what it is they want to be different and how will they know when this has been achieved.

(iii) Whilst commending D and F for wanting to do this on their own, it is our view that they have made good use of feedback during this assessment. We feel therefore they would benefit from working alongside a professional who would draw on their strengths, provide feedback and enable them to set manageable goals.

(iv) P would benefit from continuing individual work with a social worker to support her during the period D and F are focusing on their own relationship. Emphasis placed on helping P (*child*) adopt a more age appropriate role and helping her express herself without recourse to physical outburst."

Clearly, this is not ideal (what exactly constitutes 'addressing past experiences and making sense of them'?, what is the nature of the 'support' to be?) but it does contain some recommendations which pertain to problems identified in the assessment, and does include *some* sense of how it would address them. The majority of others were even less specific:

"(a) The parents need to work together as a parenting couple
(b) D's negative role in the family needs to be addressed
(c) D's carers need to focus on her needs and work towards meeting these consistently"

The difficulty in the above recommendations of one comprehensive assessment is, apart from their almost Rorschachian vagueness, the fact that one of D's carers is acknowledged to be most unlikely to co-operate with social services at all. Imagine a medical assessment on a serious drug abuser concluding that Mr. S needs to address his health problems.

- *Justifying recommendations.* Only five assessments provided any rationale for the recommendations made. In some assessments, the recommendations were 'multi-purpose', 'fit-any-family' recommendations which seemed just to appear at the end of the document. These typically concerned family members needing to 'work through' unresolved difficulties before they could address extant concerns, or come to terms with less-than-specific problems. Taken in conjunction with some of the review case conferences that were analysed in the same research project there was also a considerable sense of decisional-drift in these cases, despite the structure imposed on them by case-conference proformas.

- *Format and content.* The format and content of assessments appeared to be determined (i) in part by the DoH guidelines, often cited at the outset of the assessment record; and (ii) the style of the worker(s) responsible. The former appeared to account for an emphasis on individual profiles rather than a pulling-together of how problems evolved and what maintains them, and contributes to the tendency to follow a 'set formula'. In their extreme, some assessments actually recorded questions taken from the 'Orange Book' and the answer given by parents in response to these questions when put to them. The assessments made extremely difficult reading and offered little in the way of understanding of what has been going on. Many were very short. One can only hope they did not appear as bizarre to those on the receiving end of the assessment process as they did to those endeavouring to make sense of the outcome.

- *Formulaic assessments.* The occurrence of 'set formula' assessments was, in fact, striking. The result appeared to be an approach to assessment which, in fishing terms, had more in common with trawling than with angling. It is as if assessors believed that if certain areas are explored then something will emerge from the data collected that will be of relevance to understanding the family, its problems, the risk posed to children, and the likely courses of remedial action open to them (or not)—the problem of inductionism (see Hempel 1966). The DoH guidelines which underpinned these assessments endeavoured to provide a template of good practice, showing the areas of family functioning which might need to be explored in order to arrive at a comprehensive picture of what, if anything, is going wrong and which can be used to inform decision-making and the planning of intervention. But in order to make good use of this guidance, workers need to understand the significance of certain information, know when to pursue certain avenues of investigation and not others (when a question is not pertinent it is likely to be impertinent e.g., it is not always pertinent to ask couples about their sex lives), know what sense to make of information they obtain, and so on. Without this, all that is likely to happen is that more and more information is obtained but no more light is shed. These assessments are lengthy, costly, and sometimes only result in recommendations for further assessment. Good quality and comprehensive are not interchangeable terms.

In other words, providing staff with frameworks for assessment may be a necessary step towards improving assessments for some, but is unlikely to be sufficient, even when these lead inextricably towards an ecological framework of the kind that is so clearly essential. This is because frameworks are really only *aide-memoirs*, or organising principles, and tools are only useful when used knowledgeably and purposefully. Neither can ensure that questions will be asked because the practitioner knows why they are important (or not asked because they are irrelevant) nor that he or she will know how to interpret the information collected. One of the striking things about the assessments discussed above was that frequently there was a lot of information gathered that was either irrelevant or—more worryingly—was relevant but not recognised as such because it had been elicited *only* because it was covered in 'the Orange Book assessment'. Thus, it is highly unlikely that the new guidance will, in and of itself, deliver the improvements for children's welfare and safety that it seeks.

Conclusions

Assessment is a skilled activity which requires a sound knowledge base of the factors associated with child maltreatment (or any other reason for referral). This knowledge should direct assessment so that relevant information is collected, from appropriate sources, in appropriate ways, is accurately interpreted and appropriate judgements made. Assessment frameworks may ensure that workers address the range of potential factors relevant to developing a good understanding of what is happening within a family, and/or how this is affecting a particular child, but these are unlikely to be sufficient to guarantee an evidence-based approach to assessment.

Insofar as even the best assessments are only 'guesses' about what is happening in a family, we can rarely guarantee that they will be accurate. Good assessments, therefore, are formulated in such a way as to be readily open to revision in the light of new information, and without a loss of face. This is not, however, just another way of saying that assessment is an 'ongoing' process. One of the striking features of many child abuse inquiries is the unwillingness or inability of professional staff to change their minds about a family, *despite* quite dramatic changes of circumstances or considerable amounts of new information which should have alerted them that their view of a particular family or situation was misguided. Invariably this was not because the workers were deliberately ignoring such changes, nor was it because they were unconcerned about the quality of their work. Rather, they were vulnerable, as we all are, to a range of factors than can result in error and misjudgement. Examples of common errors are explored next, together with a discussion of what steps one might take to guard against them or minimise their impact.

BIAS AND ERROR

Human beings seek meaning in almost any set of circumstances, or faced with any event. It is not only a perfectly normal human tendency but one which is very difficult to reign in. For example, it is impossible, when in a meeting from which someone leaves unexpectedly, *not* to find oneself running through a series of possible explanations. It is impossible not to try to work out why a friend walked past one in the street without acknowledging you ('she didn't see me', 'I've upset her' 'she's in a hurry'). Simply to observe and note the phenomena and *not* try to understand them, *not* to explain them, is nigh impossible. In other words, we cannot just 'observe' the world and see events neutrally or objectively; not even photographers can pull it off. To think that we can is, itself, a fundamental error.

Insofar as assessment is an attempt to make sense of what is going on, to understand why and how things have come about and what their implications are, it is quintessentially a search for meaning. What can go wrong? At the risk of engendering a sense of learned helplessness, the answer to this question is 'quite a lot'. Assessments can be biased in a number of ways: (i) we can attend to the wrong data and ignore other important data, (ii) we can underestimate the significance of particular pieces of information and overestimate that of others, (iii) we can make a number of errors in interpreting information and drawing conclusions from it. This Section reviews some commonly occurring sources of such bias and error, and considers steps that we might take to minimise their influence. It begins by considering what can go wrong before we reach the stage of evaluating or assessing the information we collect.

Perceptual Errors

Our brains intervene in what might otherwise seem a relatively simply process, that of perception and information gathering. In other words, we do not merely see with our eyes, or hear with our ears, but we process such stimuli in ways which is active, and which often reflects previous experience. Consider Figure 12.1:

It is very difficult to constrain oneself to see the lines as equivalent in length, although they most certainly are. The source of the illusion lies in the brain. Whilst the illusion does not depend on eye movement (scanning) experiments have shown that people tend to overestimate the extent of eye movement necessary to scan the line with the fins pointing outwards, resulting in the conclusion that it must be longer. The source of this error appears to lie with previous experience of judging sizes and distances in a cultural context that is highly angular (Gregory 1966, Petersik 1982). The Nekker Cube provides another example in Figure 12.2.

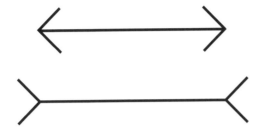

Figure 12.1 The Müller–Lyer illusion

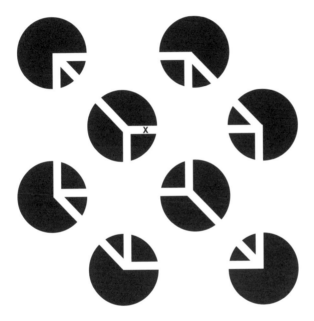

Figure 12.2 Necker cube

Here one can see a cube, which can be viewed two different ways, depending on whether you see the 'x' on the top front edge of the cube or on its rear face. Sometimes the cube appears superimposed on the circles; at other times it seems the circles are holes and the cube floats behind the page. Indeed, the cube looks noticeably whiter than the paper behind it. The problem, of course, is that this cube has no physical existence beyond its representation in our brains (Gregory 1970). The brain makes sense of the data before us in an instant and automatically—and in this case erroneously. The speed and automaticity of response is such that unless we have good cause (e.g., we are presented with an illusion which we 'know' cannot exist) we do not question what we think we 'see' or 'hear'. Thus, when we read a situation wrongly, we are not particularly programmed to question what we see, our brains are wired for survival, and detailed weighing of evidence is—in evolutionary terms—a recently acquired software update. Thus, when a social worker interviewed the family of Kimberley Carlisle, he was reassured that all was well. This was his description of their departure from the department, which he observed:

> 'I walked with the family to the door of the building, and watched as they walked across the road to where their old car was parked. I still have a clear mental picture of the way in which they all walked across the road and got into the car, parents holding children by the hand, children leaping around in the car as they got in, laughing, shouting and playing happily with each other. It was almost an archetype for a happy family scene.' (A Child in Mind 1987, pp. 108–110)

Kimberley was later killed by her step-father. With the benefit of hindsight the subsequent inquiry saw the social worker as having been 'deceived' in this incident, though perhaps the error lay in assuming that abusing families have no happy moments. The misjudgement was exacerbated by an organisational failure to ensure that perceptions of the family were challenged by other information. Other errors are particularly relevant to the assessment of risk and these are discussed in a later section.

Perceptual Bias

Perceptual bias or, in relation to human interaction, 'observation bias', denotes a tendency to see things and people in a particular way, based either on what we are told about them beforehand or on the basis of certain features. For example, in a study conducted in the 1980s it was shown that if interviewers are told that their interviewee was 'extroverted' their questioning was of a kind that elicited confirmatory evidence. The same was true when the interviewers were told their interviewee was 'introverted' (Snyder and White 1981). Other studies have demonstrated that the following features and mannerisms, amongst others, can elicit observation bias from social workers and other helping professionals: status as a young white woman (Kurtz et al. 1989), class (Franklin 1986), race (Cousins et al. 1986) and personal attractiveness (Johnson et al. 1986). It is not difficult to understand how such biases can distort and do distort all aspects of social services delivery, including assessment. This has been well-documented (see for example Bhat et al. 1988). In its crudest form it is the observational pull of stereotypes. This tendency to group things or people on the basis of superficial similarity is also referred to as the 'representative heuristic' (see below). In Jasmine Beckford's case the social workers did not question the fact that they had not seen her for some months, and took the explanation ('she's with her grandmother') to be a positive indicator of the extended care one would expect to find from an African Caribbean grandmother, rather than as a warning sign that all might not be well. What they did not do was visit the grandmother and check the validity of their conclusions. In more subtle forms it may well reflect our own learning histories, preferences and dislikes. The removal into care of large numbers of children by social workers who unquestioningly accepted the claim of two paediatricians that they could accurately diagnose child sexual abuse, and their subsequent interpretation of attempts to invalidate these diagnoses as effectively evidence in its favour, is another, more extreme example (HMSO 1992). Of course it also highlights the influence that the source of information can have on its perceived validity (high status doctors, low status social worker).

Knowing about such factors is therefore helpful, but the point about observational bias is that we do not always know when it is happening. Our feelings or convictions are frequently so strong that we are unlikely to think 'Ah this must be an example of observational bias . . .'. Therefore, because these tendencies are at least semi-reflexive, we need to take extraordinary observational, cognitive, and behavioural and institutional precautions against them. Again, a structured approach to assessment and recording, which seeks evidence both for and against a particular impression or judgement is essential, and a supervisory pattern which seeks to challenge our views is also important (see below). Observational bias is particularly dangerous because of the dominance of first impressions.

The Dominance of 'First Impressions'

One well-known problem in assessments of all kinds is our tendency to form early judgements which dominate subsequent work. The reasons for this are those discussed earlier. Thus, when assessing the eligibility of prospective foster parents, for example, it is difficult not to come to a view within the first few minutes of a first interview. That is fine, as long as (a) one has strategies in place to ensure that that view (whether positive or negative) is open to challenge in the light of new information, (b) information is sought which could challenge an established view, and (c) that information is correctly checked and evaluated. It is here that the problems begin. First, our initial judgements are often highly resilient to change. Once formulated, they tend to mould subsequent information-gathering in a confirmatory, rather than disconfirmatory way. In other words, having decided in the first five minutes that 'this couple' would make good foster parents, it takes considerable skill and discipline to go about an assessment in such a way that it does not merely comprise a supporting framework for such an early judgement. In foster parent assessments, the combination of a framework approach together with scrutiny by independent panels can go some way towards ensuring this. It is less easy when practitioners are more 'free range' and involved in assessments whose purpose is less precise and where the criteria are less well prescribed. Thus, the social worker for Neil Howlett decided at the first interview that he was not at risk from his mother, but that his brother—who was seen as the family scapegoat—was. This rather speedily formed judgement, based on an initial assessment, effectively pre-empted a full decision and formed the basis of a course of action which was to see Neil dead at the hands of his mother some four months later. His brother had been taken into care. The inquiry report comments that the conclusion 'jumped to' by the social worker had been accepted uncritically by other staff, despite the fact that in the history of contact with the family, professional concern had always focused on Neil (Birmingham City Council 1976).

Schemas and Memory

We know from the work of cognitive psychologists that the tendency of the brain to 'organise' material and to make sense of it, also intrudes onto other areas relevant to assessment, namely, memory. Try the following thought experiment. You attend the GP's surgery for a five minute consultation. You speak for about 90 seconds (a 'good innings' for a patient) and he or she talks to you about your complaint, makes some suggestions, and perhaps prescribes some drugs which s/he tells you about and how to use. You leave the surgery. Ten minutes later a friend asks you what the GP said. How much detail do you recall? The answer will, of course, vary a little depending on your powers of retention, on what has happened in the interim (more information about something else, crowding out the other) and how complicated or detailed the consultation was. Typically, however, we only remember key elements, and not always all of these. This is in stark contrast to the amount of information we often expect clients to take on board in a session which might last upwards of an hour, but that's another story. The Inuit folktale reproduced below is part of a long series of experiments conducted by Bartlett on memory. If you want a powerful example of how our brains take a very active role in organising information then read the following extract aloud to one or two colleagues (no notes) and ask them at a later point to reproduce as much of it as they can. Otherwise, read it to yourself, go and do something else for twenty minutes, and then try it yourself.

Bartlett's War of the Ghosts Story

War of the Ghosts

One night two young men from Egulac went down to the river to hunt seals, and while they were there it became foggy and calm. Then they heard war-cries and they thought: 'Maybe this is a war-party'. They escaped to the shore and hid behind a log. Now canoes came up, and they heard the noise of paddles, and saw one canoe coming up to them. There were five men in the canoe, and they said:

'What do you think? We wish to take you along. We are going up the river to make war on the people.'

One of the young men said: 'I have no arrows'.

'Arrows are in the canoe', they said.

'I will not go along, I might be killed. My relatives do not know where I have gone. But you' he said, turning to the other, 'may go with them.'

So one of the young men went, but the other returned home.

And the warriors went on up the river to a town on the other side of Kalama. The people came down to the water, and they began to fight, and many were killed. But presently the young man heard one of the warriors say: 'Quick let us go home: that Indian has been hit,' Now he thought: 'Oh, they are ghosts.' He did not feel sick, but they said he had been shot.

So the canoes went back to Egulac, and the young man went ashore to his house, and made a fire. And he told everybody and said: 'Behold I accompanied the ghosts, and we went to fight. Many of our fellows were killed, and many of those who attacked us were killed. They said I was hit, and I did not feel sick.'

He told it all, and then he became quiet. When the sun rose he fell down. Something black came out his mouth. His face became contorted. The people jumped up and cried.

He was dead.   (From Bartlett 1932)

In Barlett's series of experiments the following pattern emerged:

- the story is immediately foreshortened by omissions;
- the phraseology is altered to fit the listener's own ideas (culturally conditioned) of what makes a good story;
- material is added to fill in supposed gaps in the story;
- dramatic events are recalled more accurately than other parts and may even be exaggerated and embellished;
- parts of the story which are difficult to understand undergo substantial revision, new material is added in and apparently contradictory material is omitted. In other words a process of rationalisation occurs;
- definite elements disappear quickly e.g., numbers;

- each time an individual attempts a reproduction the general form of his or her account is remarkably persistent once the first version has been given. In other words, the account becomes stereotyped and 'fixed' at an early stage;
- names, phrases and events are changed so that they appear in forms that fit with the social group to which the listener belongs.

As Sheldon points out, similar processes intervene in the party game 'Chinese whispers' (Sheldon 1987). Similarly, in experiments, children call raspberry flavoured jelly dyed green, 'lime'.

What accounts for these patterned tendencies to reorganise material, particularly material that is 'foreign' to us, or 'unusual'? One answer seems to be that in order to 'process' information we draw on pre-existing schemas or frameworks which are composed of past reactions or experiences (Bartlett 1932). In other words, previous experience acts as a filter or organising principle when we 'encode' new information. Thus, if we live in a culture or society where canoes are rare but other kinds of boats are more common, then we are likely to encode 'boats' (a general category) rather than 'canoes' (a specific and extra-ordinary sub-category). Further, given that we tend to encode things in abstract terms e.g., 'requires a boat' or 'done to get food' or 'done on a lake' then it is highly likely that we will make secondary errors. Thus, the English student will join up these particular dots and conclude that the activity is 'fishing' (rather than hunting seals) (Best 1995).

So what? Well, we don't have to look far to see why we should be taking these studies seriously in child protection. We don't have to look far for worrying examples of our tendency to encode new information in the light of previous experiences (memories of a previous case with the same features). Earlier Chapters have discussed the impact of formal theories on the way we perceive behaviour. Child abuse inquiries testify to the impact of case-specific experience on future information processing. Thus, following what the social worker had decided was an unsubstantiated allegation of abuse, Leanne White's social worker decided that two further allegations received from two other neighbours were unfounded and malevolent. Leanne later died. (Nottinghamshire Area Child Protection Committee 1994). More generally, in terms of assessment, our tendency to screen out information that does not easily fit with our schematic representations of people or events, and our ability to over-attend to those aspects which reinforce our views, are never-endingly influential. One such schema that contributed to the tragic death of one infant, can be attributed, in part, to the legacy of John Bowlby in particular and that of the pyscho-analytic conceptualisation of attachment in general—still widely taught on training courses for helping professions.

'He may be ill-fed and ill-sheltered, he may be very dirty and suffering from disease, he may be ill-treated, but, unless his parents have wholly rejected him, he is secure in the knowledge that there is someone to whom he is of value . . . Efforts made to 'save' [such a] child . . . are commonly of no avail since it is his own parents who, for good or ill, he values and with whom he is identified (this is a fact of critical importance when considering how best to help children who are living in intolerable conditions.' (Bowlby and Salter-Ainsworth 1965, pp. 68–70)

This view of child welfare pervaded the case of Paul, the young infant who was horribly neglected by his parents (along with his many siblings) and eventually starved to death. The dominant schema in this case was that the children were 'dirty, smelly but happy' (Bridge Child Care Development Service 1995). No-one ever paused to consider the basis of this judgement, or to challenge others who adhered to it. Probably more than anything else, this 'perception', which appears very early on in the history of professional involvement, served to blind professional staff from seeing what was there to be seen, and asking questions that—with hindsight—so clearly needed to be asked. Hindsight is a dangerous principle for judging professional account-ability, but there is no doubt that in this case, and many others, professional staff failed to attend to important signals *that with a more structured approach to assessment* would have been more likely to be 'seen' and correctly appraised. Professionals in this case 'reinterpreted' a host of warning signals with ref-erence to this particular schema and others. These 'filters' effectively 'closed down' their receptivity to factors which should have triggered a more sceptical and investigative response.

Vagueness

One of the problems which has blinded people to the apparently obvious is a failure to attend to detail, to be specific, and to quantify—provide examples of, or otherwise measure—the extent and nature of particular problems and/or causes for concern. This results in two core difficulties which undermine effective child protection work. First, it leads to assessments that are not particularly helpful and may well be misleading. Secondly it means that workers are not in a position to monitor progress and/or change either for better or worse. It can only serve to exacerbate the influence of the cognitive processes discussed above.

A number of studies have been conducted in which groups of professional staff, such as social workers, magistrates and judges, have been asked to put a percentage rating against a series of quantifying (but vague) adjectives which frequently appear in assessments and in court reports. The range of replies is always salutory, with words like 'probably' producing 'interpretations' ranging from 50–95% and words like 'usually' ranging from 49–99% (see Cutler 1979 and Gibbs 1991). If we accept these 'evaluations' on face value when given to us by parents, or other workers, we can form very distorted views of a child's behaviour or a family's mode of interaction. Given the scope for misinterpretation, the use of such terms can prejudice the view taken of a case by others (for example, at a case conference). Most importantly, perhaps, if we do not go beyond the use of vague terms (which can frequently carry value judgements) we are unlikely to be able to know whether what we have done to improve a child's situation is in fact having the intended effect, and to a degree which is making a meaningful difference. Specificity is also a safeguard against the dangers of opinion, belief and/or thinking which is less than evidence-based.

Three other important sources of bias and error can impact on assessment and decision-making. These influences are particularly relevant to the assessment of *risk*, and are therefore considered in Chapter 14.

Implications for Assessment

Left to make decisions purely on the basis of our experience is itself a highly risky business, even if (some might argue particularly if) we are very experienced. As decision-making agents we are susceptible to a series of misleading influences and errors. How we go about gathering and evaluating information, how we piece together a picture of what has happened in a particular family and what conclusions we draw about the implications for the future, all have an important bearing on our ability to protect children and to optimise their development and well-being. We need to develop individual and organisational strategies to minimise the risk of such threats to good quality assessment—and indeed, to good quality practice. Using a framework within which to organise assessment can help, but only so long as (i) the proform doing the organising is sound and of high quality, and any associated instruments are valid and reliable and (ii) it is not seen as a guarantee of objectivity. The next chapter considers how one approaches the task of assessment, which draws on the strengths of a framework approach, but which stresses strategies and processes aimed at minimising the problems which can conspire to undermine the quality of assessments.

13

STRATEGIES TO SUPPORT EVIDENCE-BASED ASSESSMENT

Information is gathered over time irrespective of the form of an assessment or its duration. This fact should drive home the significance of decisions made at one point for the quality of information and decision-making at subsequent stages. Within each stage the worker (or multi-disciplinary group) will need to make decisions which will impact on the emerging picture. Who one decides to talk to (first), where interviews take place, what questions are asked, what assumptions are made about what is important, are all 'micro-decisions' which can impact on later stages of assessment activity. It is therefore important to be aware of the rationale behind what we do and how we do it, at each stage of an assessment.

Evidence-based decision-making (and therefore assessment) requires not only a sound knowledge base relating to abuse and neglect, but also an understanding of how the process of assessment can be undermined, and the steps than can be taken to protect against this. The last Chapter focused particularly on individual sources of bias and error, but the decisions we make about how to approach the task of assessment themselves influence the process. Figure 13.1 provides an example of the kinds of decisions that face the worker undertaking an assessment. Although the figure appears to present a 'menu' from which to choose, an evidence-based approach requires that each decision can be justified on the grounds of sound evidence, both from research and from the information available on the family as appropriate.

A thought experiment in which one considers the potential impact of focusing down too narrowly to begin with, coupled with the evidence from child abuse inquiries about our tendency to continue with early views, will also underline the need for an approach to assessment that is broad-based at the beginning, covering a range of factors across the ecological landscape,

Decision   **Choices (examples)**

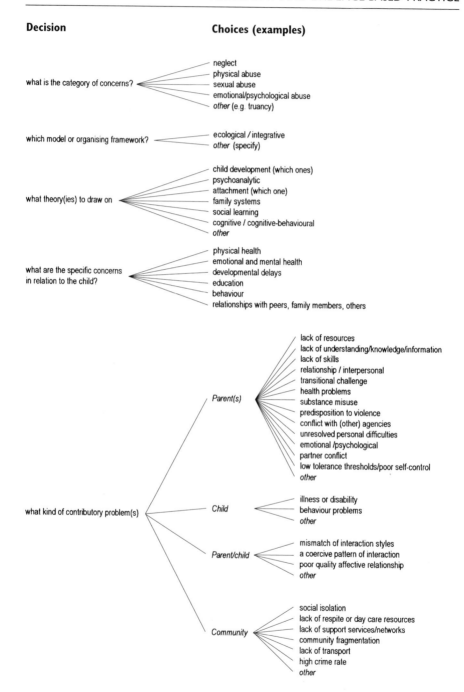

what is the category of concerns?
- neglect
- physical abuse
- sexual abuse
- emotional/psychological abuse
- *other* (e.g. truancy)

which model or organising framework?
- ecological / integrative
- *other* (specify)

what theory(ies) to draw on
- child development (which ones)
- psychoanalytic
- attachment (which one)
- family systems
- social learning
- cognitive / cognitive-behavioural
- *other*

what are the specific concerns in relation to the child?
- physical health
- emotional and mental health
- developmental delays
- education
- behaviour
- relationships with peers, family members, others

what kind of contributory problem(s)

Parent(s)
- lack of resources
- lack of understanding/knowledge/information
- lack of skills
- relationship / interpersonal
- transitional challenge
- health problems
- substance misuse
- predisposition to violence
- conflict with (other) agencies
- unresolved personal difficulties
- emotional /psychological
- partner conflict
- low tolerance thresholds/poor self-control
- *other*

Child
- illness or disability
- behaviour problems
- *other*

Parent/child
- mismatch of interaction styles
- a coercive pattern of interaction
- poor quality affective relationship
- *other*

Community
- social isolation
- lack of respite or day care resources
- lack of support services/networks
- community fragmentation
- lack of transport
- high crime rate
- *other*

Figure 13.1

Decision

Choices (examples)

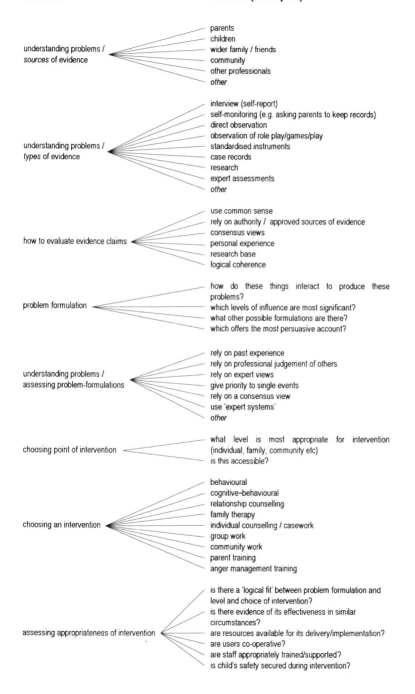

understanding problems /
sources of evidence
- parents
- children
- wider family / friends
- community
- other professionals
- *other*

understanding problems /
types of evidence
- interview (self-report)
- self-monitoring (e.g. asking parents to keep records)
- direct observation
- observation of role play/games/play
- standardised instruments
- case records
- research
- expert assessments
- *other*

how to evaluate evidence claims
- use common sense
- rely on authority / approved sources of evidence
- consensus views
- personal experience
- research base
- logical coherence

problem formulation
- how do these things interact to produce these problems?
- which levels of influence are most significant?
- what other possible formulations are there?
- which offers the most persuasive account?

understanding problems /
assessing problem-formulations
- rely on past experience
- rely on professional judgement of others
- rely on expert views
- give priority to single events
- rely on a consensus view
- use 'expert systems'
- *other*

choosing point of intervention
- what level is most appropriate for intervention (individual, family, community etc)
- is this accessible?

choosing an intervention
- behavioural
- cognitive-behavioural
- relationship counselling
- family therapy
- individual counselling / casework
- group work
- community work
- parent training
- anger management training

assessing appropriateness of intervention
- is there a 'logical fit' between problem formulation and level and choice of intervention?
- is there evidence of its effectiveness in similar circumstances?
- are resources available for its delivery/implementation?
- are users co-operative?
- are staff appropriately trained/supported?
- is child's safety secured during intervention?

and which narrows down in focus as the weight of evidence begins to point in particular directions. Indeed, a good assessment can be thought of as funnel-shaped.

STAGES IN THE ASSESSMENT PROCESS

It is no accident that a substantial section of this book is devoted to providing an overview of the evidence concerning factors associated with, or implicated in, the development of patterns of child maltreatment. Understanding how and why families develop particular patterns of relating and behaving is a pre-requisite of making an evidence-based assessment of how a given family has come to behave toward and to relate to each other. Part B focused on those factors which appear to play a particular role in maltreatment of various kinds. For assessment purposes, this knowledge needs to be set in the broader context of an understanding of:

(i)   child development. What it is that all children need to develop physically, emotionally, and intellectually and if they are to realise their potential?
(ii) the parenting task and how this is impacted upon by social, cultural, and economic factors;
(iii) how the histories and characteristics of individual family members influence their relationships, their expectations of each other and their behaviour towards each other;
(iv) how other particular sets of circumstances effect parenting capacity e.g., mental illness, substance misuse.

In other words, child maltreatment is, in many respects, one endpoint of a number of ways in which parents, and society more widely, fail adequately to meet the needs of children. Parenting is one of a number of roles that many take on in the course of development. For some it is a relatively easy transition into which they grow, with help from friends and family. For others it is not so easy, it comes too soon, it comes in difficult circumstances, it reawakens unresolved problems which interfere with their willingness and ability to nurture their children, it brings unwanted constraints and challenges, and so on. Help for many parents is not always available or sufficient in kind or quantity. Some parents cannot make use of the help that is available.

As indicated in Chapter 5, the multiplicity of factors which impact upon parents' ability adequately to care for their children operate at a number of levels from the personal (e.g., skills, emotional maturity) through to the social (social policy, shared assumptions) and economic (poverty, poor housing). A good assessment is, in the first instance, a review of factors, trends and experience which locates a child and his/her family in this broader context.

Besides increasing the chances of producing accurate assessments of the origins of difficulties and those factors maintaining them and/or preventing change, such an approach to assessment affords the best opportunity to identify potential sources of leverage or influence. For example, if parenting problems and over-use of physical punishment are primarily due to frustrations created by socio-economic pressures rather than lack of skills or impulsivity and lack of control, then the sort of intervention most likely to be effective and to be most ethically appropriate will be that which tried to remove these pressures or contain them. It may well be here that our only option will be to focus on enhancing parenting strategies, but it is important that we recognise that this is a 'second best option' if, again, we are to make best use of it. Parents who appreciate that helpers understand the wider picture and are, perhaps, endeavouring to address that, but who meanwhile are trying to help them to better manage their problems, are less likely to feel blamed, more likely to co-operate and more likely to succeed. A focus on the broader context also means that we can identify strategies which are most likely to be experienced as empowering and which build on strengths.

Inevitably, an approach to assessment which focuses solely, or prematurely, on the 'microsystem' (those situations in which the child has face-to-face contact with influential others) will carry with it maximum risk of premature labelling (because of its focus on person and inter-personal factors), stigmatisation (such a focus maximises the apparent allocation of blame on individuals) and error (the problems and their solution may well lay elsewhere). Similar problems arise when practitioners insist on honing in on any one level to the near exclusion of all others. A tendency predominantly to address factors at one level, perhaps paying lip service to others, can arise because of an enthusiasm for a particular theoretical or conceptual understanding, sometimes favoured for ideological reasons, or because this represents the main repository of knowledge or understanding. The challenge for practitioners wishing to develop an evidence-based approach to assessment in child protection is:

(i) to take a structured approach to assessment so that it attends to the range of influences which may be impacting on a particular situation;
(ii) to be able to identify those factors of most importance in a particular situation and how they interact, with regard to strengths and assets as well as weaknesses and problems;
(iii) to be familiar with the sources of bias and error which can undermine a good quality assessment and/or lead to erroneous conclusions;
(iv) to be able to determine risk and the feasibility of bringing about the changes deemed necessary to secure a child's safety and well-being.

There is a growing number of helpful texts providing accounts of ways in which assessments of children's needs, family functioning and parenting might be organised (Reder and Lucy 1998; DoH 2000), but many of these are geared towards particular theoretical or conceptual models, or types of problems. None take a purposefully evidence-based approach, except insofar as some draw attention to the variety of factors that can influence children's development, the behaviour of adults towards children, and indeed of people more generally. Most do not discriminate between factors which enjoy substantial empirical support and those which are more speculative, even when the importance of an ecological approach is acknowledged. Indeed, one risk inherent in an ecological approach to assessment and intervention is that some will see this as yet one other form of eclecticism, in which all theories and all sources of evidence are seen to be of equal value. The reasons for rejecting such an approach were discussed in Chapter 3. As with intervention, what is important in developing an evidence-based approach to assessment and case planning are: transparency, explicitness and judiciousness. In other words, making transparent the process, making explicit the assumptions upon which decisions and judgements are made, and making judgements based on the best available evidence, or the most sound interpretation of data that is available.

This still leaves the task of conducting assessments in such a way that all relevant information is obtained and its significance appreciated, irrelevant information is set aside, and sense is made of what is happening in any given family or situation. Figure 13.2 presents one approach to the process of assessment which stresses its sequential and 'iterative' nature. To some extent it represents an ideal sequence of information gathering and decision-making (see previous section) and it will certainly not always be achievable— in this sequence—given the rather unpredictable and sometimes chaotic nature of child protection work. Nonetheless, it is achievable in many cases, particularly in those settings or teams where earlier, preventive work is possible, and where a broader approach is taken to working with children in need. It is also important to have a sound understanding of what is needed in order to make sound decisions, so that when, for any reason, one cannot proceed in a more ordered fashion (perhaps because of an emergency, or a crisis) then one at least knows what pieces of the jigsaw are missing. It is often possible, and sometimes essential, to fill in gaps at the earliest possible opportunity. Finally, having a 'ground-plan' of a good assessment should facilitate the compilation of multi-disciplinary assessments. Too often families are referred for 'expert assessment' in the absence of a clear rationale, or in order to answer a question that is indeed most appropriately answered from a particular disciplinary perspective. Also, unless there is a strategic approach to 'making sense' of a range of information from different professionals it is highly likely that erroneous conclusions will be drawn, or important patterns missed. In this regard, the utility of undertaking a chronology of events in a family's life, merits particular attention (see below).

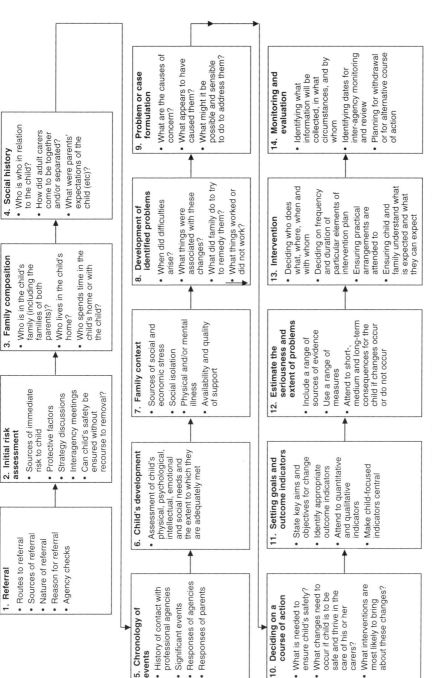

1. Referral
- Routes to referral
- Sources of referral
- Nature of referral
- Reason for referral
- Agency checks

2. Initial risk assessment
- Sources of immediate risk to child
- Protective factors
- Strategy discussions
- Interagency meetings
- Can child's safety be ensured without recourse to removal?

3. Family composition
- Who is in the child's family (including the families of both parents)?
- Who lives in the child's home?
- Who spends time in the child's home or with the child?

4. Social history
- Who is who in relation to the child?
- How did adult carers come to be together and/or separated?
- What were parents' expectations of the child (etc)?

5. Chronology of events
- History of contact with professional agencies
- Significant events
- Responses of agencies
- Responses of parents

6. Child's development
- Assessment of child's physical, psychological, intellectual, emotional and social needs and the extent to which they are adequately met

7. Family context
- Sources of social and economic stress
- Social isolation
- Physical and/or mental illness
- Availability and quality of support

8. Development of identified problems
- When did difficulties arise?
- What things were associated with these changes?
- What did family do to try to remedy them?
- What things worked or did not work?

9. Problem or case formulation
- What are the causes of concern?
- What appears to have caused them?
- What might it be possible and sensible to do to address them?

10. Deciding on a course of action
- What is needed to ensure child's safety?
- What changes need to occur if child is to be safe and thrive in the care of his or her carers?
- What interventions are most likely to bring about these changes?

11. Setting goals and outcome indicators
- State key aims and objectives for change
- Identify appropriate outcome indicators
- Attend to quantitative and qualitative indicators
- Make child-focused indicators central

12. Estimate the seriousness and extent of problems
- Include a range of sources of evidence
- Use a range of measures
- Attend to short-, medium and long-term consequences for the child if changes occur or do not occur

13. Intervention
- Deciding who does what, where, when and with whom
- Deciding on frequency and duration of particular elements of intervention plan
- Ensuring practical arrangements are attended to
- Ensuring child and family understand what is expected and what they can expect

14. Monitoring and evaluation
- Identifying what information will be collected, in what circumstances, and by whom
- Identifying dates for inter-agency monitoring and review
- Planning for withdrawal or for alternative course of action

Figure 13.2 Stages in initial assessment and decision-making

The main thrust of the following discussion relates to what are now frequently referred to as 'core' or 'comprehensive' assessments. Ironically, this usage has come about in recognition of the frequent absence of assessments, rather than denoting a particular kind of assessment. Assessments, if properly conducted, should by their nature be comprehensive ('fit for purpose'), otherwise one must question their utility. Of course, this is not to say that in some circumstances one might well commission assessments about particular areas of functioning, for very particular purposes (e.g., determining whether or not a child is reaching developmental milestones). At best, the terminology of comprehensive or core assessment differentiates a more detailed approach to assessment than that typically used when a family is initially referred to a social services agency. An initial assessment is usual undertaken to determine (i) whether or not the child and his or her family are eligible for assistance from an agency (determined by law in the case of U.K. social services departments), and (ii) whether or not the child(ren) who comprise the basis of the referral are at risk of significant harm and in need of protection. To some extent, an initial assessment is really a screening mechanism for risk (to the child) and eligibility (ascertaining whether a child is 'in need' and therefore eligible for services). Beyond establishing these threshold criteria, such an assessment—conducted as it is in a short period of time and on the basis of incomplete information—is, at best, tentative. That is why, for those children thought to be at risk of significant harm, or who are deemed to be in need, a more detailed assessment is a matter of priority in subsequent case management.

That said, the *kinds* of information required, and the *kinds* of decisions made in an initial assessment are not qualitatively different from those required of a fuller assessment. It is therefore the case that the stages involved in both kinds of assessment overlap (e.g., nature of the problems, causes, family history), and also that at any time in the process, information may transpire that requires a reassessment of the perceived risk to a child. This being so, Figure 13.2 presents the stages in assessment and decision-making within one flow-chart, indicating those which are relevant to each kind of assessment. The level of detail will be determined by what kind of assessment is being undertaken and by constraints that might be operating. The template should help to remind workers what is required of good assessment and case management and what might remain to be done. Each stage is discussed in the following section.

1. *Referral.* There are many routes to referral: self-referrals, referrals by other professionals or referrals by family, friends and neighbours. The latter may be anonymous, and may be more or less detailed or substantiated. There is a chance element in whether or not a family is referred, who refers them, when and with what accompanying message.

Families may well feel ill-used by such referrals, especially when they are not informed. Such ill-feeling will need to be acknowledged and dealt with. The route to referral can have an undue influence on the response of professional staff, e.g., a GP might be taken more seriously than an anonymous phone call from a neighbour, and the process of responding to referrals requires active management if the source of referral is not to be a determining factor in whether or not it is taken seriously. Child protection procedures, such as agency checks, provide an appropriate scaffolding to ensure this, but the *content* of the enquiries remain a matter of professional judgement. The nature of the referral (i.e., its substantive focus), how typical the concern, how long-standing, together with the nature of any threat to the child's welfare need to be ascertained. Familiarity with what is known about such problems should shape the questions to which answers are sought and is important in determining the meaning of the information obtained.

Understanding why a referral has been made is an important starting point for deciding *how* to approach a family, and to establishing appropriate rapport with children and families. As well as speaking with the referrer, it is important to obtain relevant information from all professionals who know the child(ren) concerned, as well as significant others such as extended family, neighbours and so on. Interviewing or otherwise communicating with the child(ren) involved should be assumed unless there is a strong case otherwise. The absence of the child's voice in assessment and decision-making is a common theme in child abuse enquiries, and analysis of social service records suggests this is not a feature unique to these tragic cases.

2. *Initial assessment of risk.* On one level it is misleading to identify risk assessment as a discrete phase, since new information can, at any time, signal the need to re-assess a child's safety. In this sense, the assessment of risk should be seen as a thread running throughout child protection case management. Some referrals will unequivocally indicate high levels of risk and in these circumstances action will be necessary to protect a child pending any other kind of investigation, however 'initial'. However, there is merit in scheduling a planned consideration of risk, as in the absence of this, professional staff have shown themselves to be easily distracted from important warnings in the information available to them. Strategy discussions and requirements for inter-agency action provide two procedural mechanisms within the U.K. child protection system aimed at ensuring that risk is assessed in the process of an initial investigation and assessment. Case conferences provide another opportunity to consider risk in light of more detailed information about a child and his or her circumstances. The assessment of risk is considered in the concluding chapter. Suffice it to say here that a reliance on risk assessment

checklists is unlikely to be of much use, and may well mislead. Some factors should act as warning signs, e.g., a history of violence, including domestic violence. However, an ecological approach to child maltreatment stresses the interactional nature of risks, rather than a 'summative' approach (i.e., the more risk factors the more risk). Care must be taken to ascertain the *meaning* of events and circumstances for adults caring for a child, and how they—and the child(ren)—are perceived (see Reder and Duncan 1999). This is one reason why, as soon as circumstances permit, establishing a genogram or completing a social history and a chronology of events are so important (see below).

3. *Family composition.* It is important to take care in ascertaining who is who in a child's life. Who is in the family, not only in the family unit to which the child belongs, but also in the extended family, and across generations? Who else is significant in a child's life? Not all parents live with their children, and threats can come from parents, partners or other adults living outside the home. Inquiries have highlighted the tendency of professionals to ignore or underestimate the significance (indeed, sometimes the threat) of adults who live outside the family home, or of other adults living in the family home, whether family or otherwise. Parents may have reason to mislead, and children may be inhibited from talking, so information from other agencies is particularly crucial. It is helpful to order this information in ways that make it readily available, and which can serve to draw attention to patterns of behaviour which may extend across relationships (with partners or children) or across generations. Minimally, it is useful to tabulate 'who's who', indicating the relationships between family members. However, given the complex compositions and histories of many of the families referred for child protection concerns, a genogram is preferable (Reder *et al.* 1992, DoH 1999).

4. *Social history.* Understanding who is who in a child's life is central to forming a sound view of his or her circumstances. Information such as how a child's carers came to be together, what their own previous histories were, what their own experience of parenting was, whether or not the child was planned or wanted, who he or she reminds them of, what role is played by other family members, can shed important light on how a child is seen, what expectations parents or other carers have of children and of parents, and how well-equipped they are (aside, perhaps, from other sources of stress) to provide adequate care.

5. *Chronicling the family history.* The Bridge Child Care Development Service has undertaken a number of Part 8 Case Reviews, some of which are well known e.g., the Paul report. A core feature of their approach to this difficult task has been to compile a chronology of events from all available data sources e.g., files from different agencies, interviews etc.

The headings they have used include those identified above, and in preparing these chronologies they have colour coded information according to whether or not it was in the public domain i.e., known to other agencies or professionals. Invariably two things emerge, with depressing regularity. First, there is enough information available amongst agencies to have signalled a course of action other than that in fact taken. Secondly, much of the information was known only to one professional or agency, and not 'pooled' or shared with others. The net result of this failure to compile all available data for careful scrutiny meant that no-one was in a position to appreciate the significance of the information they had access to. Raising the sensible question 'why wait until a child has died' before undertaking such an exercise, the Bridge has since persuaded some local authorities to experiment with the use of such an approach to ongoing cases which give cause for concern. Their approach is to issue a computerised proforma (compatible with most systems) to all agencies, and to ask participating professionals to complete it on the basis of their records and then submit it to the social services agency. The latter combines the individual records of all agencies (done automatically by the program) to produce a complete chronology. This then provides the basis of a case conference discussion, which can take stock of all available facts of a case and make an informed estimate of risk to the child, the nature of the problems, what needs to change and so on. In pilot testing the results have been dramatic, both in terms of clarifying risk and in terms of setting aside worries which, though understandable, can be seen to be no cause for concern when set in the context of all available information (Fitzgerald 1998). This is a very simple and inexpensive way of dramatically improving the quality of assessment information and decision-making. The fact that in the year 2000 it is not commonly in use within child protection procedures must constitute a source of puzzlement. The computerised nature of the approach is not, however, an inextricable feature (although eminently desirable for a host of reasons, not least of all feasibility). Speaking as a social work educator, it is a salutary experience for students to be set the task of compiling such a chronology—and never yet a waste of time.

6. *The child's development.* An adequate assessment must address the extent to which a child's physical, psychological, intellectual, emotional and social needs are being addressed. There are times when expert assessments will be necessary, but information is usually available for most children from the range of agencies who have responsibility for child welfare: health visitors, doctors, teachers, social workers and so on. This should be collated and its significance assessed. Standardised checklists can be useful tools in determining whether or not a child is reaching his or her developmental milestones, and can be useful correctives to

professional optimism ('she's doing better than she was') and to low professional expectations ('all the children in this family have speech problems'). However, as with other sources of information, their usefulness depends partly on the way in which professionals interpret the information they provide, and on their ability to determine whether or not inadequate parenting (or abuse or neglect) might be responsible or contributory factors.

7. *Family context.* In addition to the information detailed above under 'Social history' and 'chronology of events' there are other aspects of a child's family circumstances which may be important. These include: the extent to which the family is experiencing social or economic stress (e.g., poor housing, unemployment); the extent to which it is socially isolated (and the reasons for this); the availability and quality of support from family, friends and neighbours; and the existence of physical or mental ill health, psychological disturbance on the part of significant adults, and so on. Again, what matters is less the existence of any one or more of these factors, than the significance they have for the family, the resilience the family may have, and the possible sources of support that might be available to them via formal or informal services.

8. *Development of identified problems.* There is overlap across many of these assessment stages or tasks, and in the course of compiling a social history or a chronology of events a picture will most certainly begin to emerge of the nature and extent of problems, and how these developed. However, the development of particular problems which have been identified should form a discrete part of an assessment. It entails not only the origins of problems (when things began to go wrong, in what circumstances, what were things like before etc.), but what factors have eased or exacerbated them, what attempts family members have made to resolve them, and with what consequences. It is at this point that one can begin to order the influences on present problems in terms of distal influences, i.e., what long-standing factors may have predisposed parents to care less than adequately for their children (e.g., poor parenting, abuse and neglect, poor education), and more proximal influences i.e., factors in the 'here and now' such as social stressors, relationship problems, difficult child behaviour.

9. *Problem or case formulation.* Assessments are not truth finding exercises. Rather, as indicated earlier, they are attempts to make sense of what is going on in a particular family, what the risks are to a particular child or children, what factors have brought the situation about, and therefore what it might be possible to do to address identified concerns, or expedient to do to protect a child. A problem formulation is simply a summary statement of our understanding, formulated in such a way as to be open to refutation should it be wrong. A good problem formulation

therefore begins with a statement of the nature of the concerns or problems, then says how it appears these have arisen and what factors are responsible for maintaining them. It leads—logically—to a proposal for action which, if the formulation is correct (which it may not be) should bring about changes in the desired direction. A problem formulation is one way of preventing foreclosure on other possible accounts or scenarios because, although it appears to commit the worker or case conference to a particular view, it does so in such a way that there are clear criteria for assessing its validity, based on whether or not the proposed course of action does, in fact, bring about the intended results. Whilst there may be a variety of reasons why an intervention plan fails to succeed, one clear possibility is that the view of the problems on which it was based (the assessment) was inaccurate. This can then be reviewed along with other possible explanations. Finally, formulating one's understanding of a case in this way also makes explicit the assumptions underpinning a proposed course of action and these are therefore open to challenge and discussion, both by professionals and by the family.

10. *Deciding on a course of action.* Decisions will need to be taken as to whether or not a child's safety and well-being are compromised by being left in the care of his or her carers. Whether or not the child is removed, or the family placed in a safer environment, decisions will need to be taken about (i) how the child's safety can be ensured; (ii) what changes need to occur if he or she is to be safe in the care of his or her carers, and his or her needs adequately met; (iii) what interventions are most likely to bring about these changes, and (iv) how will we know if these changes are occurring, or if they are not? Decisions regarding which interventions to select should be made first on the basis of what is known about their effectiveness—essentially what this volume is about. In the absence of persuasive evidence then consider what is most likely to succeed in securing improvements given what we know about the problems, family circumstances, motivation to change and so on. The key point here is that there should be a 'logical fit' between what is known both about the nature of the problems and/or risks and what is done in response to them. If a child is at risk from his or her parents, then no amount of home visiting by professional staff will afford adequate protection, however intensive. There will always be more hours in a day when no professional is in the home, than hours when they are. Similarly, if a child's development is being seriously impaired and neglect is considered to be a major cause, then play-groups and speech therapy may be important adjuncts to an adequate care plan, but this would not be appropriate unless an intervention can be designed and implemented that will, at the same time, bring about a significant shift in the quality of parenting on offer. Similarly, if a major problem inheres in the way a parent perceives a

child, then mainstream (and skill- or knowledge-oriented) parent-training is unlikely to be appropriate. Too often in case records, there appears to be an absence of fit between what can be gleaned about the nature of problems and what is provided by social services and other agencies. It is not unusual for a decision to be taken to refer a family to a family centre, as an intervention *per se*. Many families may need what family centres have to offer, but none needs a 'centre' itself. Usually, such 'cookie-cutter' plans arise because a careful assessment of the kind being discussed here has not been undertaken.

Whether or not decisions are taken on the basis of best available evidence of what works, or on the basis of what makes most sense given other kinds of information available, great care should be taken to monitor the results and to ensure both that desired changes are taking place and that no adverse consequences are ensuing. A major plank in this endeavour it that of setting clear goals and establishing indicators of progress and success. These are therefore dealt with next.

11. *Setting goals and outcome indicators.* It is not uncommon to find goals being expressed in terms of global improvements, whether in 'relationships', or the 'quality of parenting', or of 'coming to terms with' a major change. There is nothing wrong with this as a starting point, but much can go wrong if we do not go beyond this and specify what—for any particular individual, relationship or family—the realisation of such goals would look like. Partly, this is because broad category terms such as 'happy', or 'adequate' mean very different things to different people, but it is also the case that the estimators commonly found in case records (i.e., 'frequently', 'often', 'always', 'never') are equally susceptible to differential interpretation, making the task of monitoring change hopelessly imprecise. Goals need to be phrased in ways which are as precise as possible. If this cannot be done in the first instance, then care must be taken to specify how we will know if and when goals are achieved, and—equally importantly—if they are not. One strategy available is to identify specific outcome indicators which can be agreed, and will provide evidence that goals are being achieved. The advantage of outcome indicators is that they can be tailored to individual circumstances, and are therefore potentially more accurate markers of change than goals themselves. Outcome indicators should be observable. That is to say, wherever possible they should be things we can draw people's attention to, such as behaviour, rather than things that require to be inferred, such as internal states or intentions. They should also be reliable. In other words, two observers would agree on the evidence. The fact that outcome indicators should be established prior to intervention should also mean that disagreements about their meaning or significance should be minimised. These underlying principles are applicable both to goals

which embrace quantitative changes e.g., changes in parenting practices, and those which are more commonly regarded as qualitative e.g., regard for a child's well-being, emotional connectedness, rapport. This is because we can only assess the latter via their behavioural correlates and consequences. This is not to say, however, that the two are synonymous. This is why it is especially important to monitor consequences for the child(ren) in questions, as well as behavioural changes in their carers. The latter do not necessarily lead to improvements in the former.

So, for example, for some families, an improvement in parenting would require parental outcome indicators such as parents doing or not doing things (for example, giving children an adequate diet, or using non-physical methods of discipline), but would also require child-oriented indicators (for example, children making progress in their milestones, attending school, appearing happier and less tired). The selection of outcome indicators is best made on the basis of what it is that needs to change and on what basis we would know that changes had occurred.

One way of identifying appropriate goals and outcome indicators is to ask questions such as, 'If all our worries for this child were removed, how would things be different?'. Parents and children rarely have trouble answering such questions in respect of their own concerns. Professionals should be able to do so, and to reach agreement amongst involved agencies. If they cannot, then it seriously begs the question as to whether they are in a position to adequately monitor the safety and well-being of children they have a responsibility towards, or whether they are in a position to give families clear messages about what is required of them.

Typically, we talk of outcome goals and methods goals (Pincus and Minahan 1973). Outcome goals are end-point changes one is aiming to bring about, the achievement of which might lead us to decide that formal intervention is no longer necessary or can be reduced. Method goals are those changes which need to be brought about in order to achieve outcome goals. Thus, establishing adequate parental care might be our outcome goal, steps to which might include: improving housing, enhancing knowledge of child development, increasing parenting skills, teaching play skills and so on. For each of these it is possible to identify outcome indicators appropriate to a particular child and his or her carers.

12. *Estimating the seriousness and extent of problems.* If one is to securely monitor a child's safety and well-being, and make a secure assessment of improvement or change, then minimally one needs a clear picture of the nature, extent and seriousness of the concerns and problems in question. In order to undertake this part of an assessment, workers need to draw on multiple sources of information. This is, in part, to counter the bias

inherent in the perceptions of particular factors, but it is also important in bringing together as complete and reliable picture as possible. For these reasons too, it is advisable to draw on a number of kinds of information, such as standardised instruments, play, direct observation etc., rather than relying solely on interview data or verbal reports from third parties, even when these are professionally qualified.

Having established an overall picture, this needs to be evaluated in terms of the likely consequences for a child if changes are not secured. In other words, the seriousness of a situation for a child cannot be assessed simply in terms of contemporaneous consequences, but needs to be seen in a developmental context. As a basis for monitoring change, it is important to know what one is seeking to avoid (or achieve) for a particular child by the time he or she is five months older, two years older or whatever. These judgements are important when selecting outcome indicators which will provide meaningful information about progress from the child's perspective, which should be the central focus and benchmark.

13. *Monitoring and evaluation.* Clear goals and identifiable outcome indicators are the end-product of a good assessment, and provide the basis for monitoring and evaluation of progress. Systems need to be in place to estimate the extent and seriousness of problems prior to intervention, and following intervention. Given the importance of qualitative aspects of parenting, it is not appropriate to reduce the business of monitoring and evaluation to quantitative estimates of how much of something is occurring, how often and so on. That said, such information is relevant, and what needs to be avoided is a false either/or approach to the kinds of information that constitute evidence of change, of improvement and of deterioration. Children's developmental needs require quantitative and qualitative inputs. An adequate diet provided with no love or affection does not amount to good enough parenting, but neither does affection unaccompanied by adequate physical care. Deciding what is adequate should not be left to chance or the benefit of hindsight, any more than deciding what evidence one will accept of an emotionally warm environment. In order to safeguard a child's welfare, processes must be established to ensure the collection of relevant and reliable information. Having established outcome indicators this usually becomes a relatively straightforward affair, with clear messages regarding what information needs to be collected by whom, over what period and in what circumstances. It does not remove the need for professional judgement about the overall significance of the information to hand, but it should make the exercise of the judgement more valid and reliable.

Finally, a case plan should contain an explicit timeframe for formal monitoring and review, a timeframe within which it is expected that goals will be reached, and a clear understanding that if this is not achieved, then alternative plans might need to be made e.g., substitute care if appropriate. This is because time is very much of the essence for children, particularly young children, and because decision-drift has long been established as a problem for professionals who are doing their best to work with parents to achieve change.

Summary

Sound assessment and case management are multi-dimensional and multi-professional activities. Having assessment frameworks which indicate what areas of information are likely to be important are useful (i.e., assessment frameworks for 'content'), as are route maps of how to approach assessment tasks, in what order, and how they relate to other key activities such as goal setting and evaluation (i.e., stages in the assessment, monitoring and evaluation). However, an understanding of the range of decisions that are available at each stage, and how those that are made might determine subsequent practice, is also important, and should prompt us to try and build in some personal and organisational checks on what we are doing, and why, and how we will know if an earlier decision turns out to be less than optimal.

This chapter has explored the factors which can undermine the quality of assessments, and has examined the strengths and weaknesses of a framework approach. It has argued that a good assessment is one which is tailored to address the needs of a particular set of circumstances, and which sees assessment as a sequential, iterative process which requires knowledge, skill, and the exercise of professional judgement. A staged approach to assessment, in which the satisfactory completion of each stage provides the basis for decisions taken at the next, is not unattainable in child protection, but may well be difficult to achieve. It should, however, provide the template for the completed assessment. Whilst assessment needs to be constantly adjusted as new information comes to light (including the failure of plans to bring about change) a case has been made for assessment being viewed as a fundamental pre-requisite of sound case planning and case management, and as the basis for the secure monitoring of children's welfare. In child protection, it also requires a multi-professional or interagency approach (Department of Health 1999).

The final section of this Chapter provides a checklist for assessing the quality of those assessments that form the basis of care planning, case management and therapeutic intervention in cases of child protection. It is equally relevant to work with children and families with needs which do not fall into the category of child protection.

ASSESSING THE QUALITY OF ASSESSMENTS

Although assessments will be differently organised according to the nature of the circumstances in which a child is situated, the qualities of a good assessment are, to a large extent, generic. The following checklist is therefore provided as a tool for practitioners and managers to use in evaluating the quality of their assessments and in developing this area of practice. It encapsulates the issues discussed previously and also takes up some issues of good practice which have not been specifically explored, particularly around the process of assessment. If the answer to any of these questions is 'No' then it probably indicates a gap or at least a potential source of error.

Table 13.1:   Checklist for an evidence-based assessment

Q: Does the assessment:

1.	begin with a clear statement of the purpose of, or reasons for, the assessment?	Yes	No
2.	say what was done in order to complete the assessment (and some indication of why)?	Yes	No
3.	confirm that the purpose of the assessment was explained to all family members concerned, and record their responses?	Yes	No
4.	confirm that the nature of the assessment and the expectations it placed on family members was made clear at the outset and records the responses of family members?	Yes	No
5.	contain a summary of who is who in the family, possibly in the form of a genogram?	Yes	No
6.	contain a social history?	Yes	No
7.	provide evidence that the reasons why a certain kind of information is being sought is understood by family members, possibly as a statement to that effect?	Yes	No
8.	contain the express views of all key parties, including children?	Yes	No
9.	provide evidence that the views of children have been sought/obtained in ways that are age-appropriate?	Yes	No
10.	provide evidence that when indirect methods are used to obtain children's views (e.g., play) the theoretical or empirical basis used to organise the session(s) is made clear and appropriate caution is used in interpreting the findings?	Yes	No
11.	use a number of sources of evidence (from different people, and including other professionals)?	Yes	No
12.	use a number of different types of evidence (including standardised measures, direct observation, official records/growth charts, as well as interview data)?	Yes	No
13.	take a critical approach to the evaluation of evidence e.g., consider alternative explanations, include attempts to measure problems i.e., frequency, duration, intensity?	Yes	No
14.	provide evidence of a broad-based approach to data collection, covering all levels of influence relevant to child development and well-being?	Yes	No

Table 13.1:   (*continued*)

15.	provide evidence that the questions asked and topics covered reflect an up-to-date and sound knowledge base relevant to the main presenting problem(s)?	Yes	No
16.	make it transparent to the reader why certain areas have been probed, and others left?	Yes	No
17.	make explicit any theoretical assumptions made when recording and interpreting information e.g., regarding the nature of attachment and its implications for development; the reasons for neglect etc. and—if known—the empirical support for such an assumption/theory? (NB This is important even if assessments are being conducted within a team with a shared understanding of key issues—assessments follow families.)	Yes	No
18.	consider alternative explanations or interpretations when drawing conclusions about the significance of particular aspects of a family's history or present circumstances?	Yes	No
19.	include a problem formulation? That is, a summary statement of the assessor's understanding of how a set of affairs has come about, what is maintaining the problem or problems and what is preventing their resolution.	Yes	No
20.	provide a rationale for the choice of problem formulation, when alternative explanations or conclusions are possible?	Yes	No
21.	phrase the problem formulation in a way that it can easily be shown to be wrong?	Yes	No
22.	provide evidence that information has been shared with family members and differences of opinion have been either resolved or noted if irresolvable?	Yes	No
23.	make suggestions for interventions which are logically related to the problem formulation?	Yes	No
24.	say what level of help is necessary?	Yes	No
25.	say from whom this assistance should be sought?	Yes	No
26.	indicate likely frequency, duration and intensity of assistance required?	Yes	No
27.	state clearly how progress/improvement will be monitored, including both qualitative and quantitative indicators?	Yes	No
28.	state clearly how one will be able to tell if the intervention were to prove successful?	Yes	No
29.	make suggestions for an appropriate system of recording?	Yes	No
30.	identify a maximum period for review?	Yes	No

14

RISK ASSESSMENT AND DECISION-MAKING

Those working in the field of child protection are inextricably in the business of assessing risk and making predictions about the safety and likely well-being of vulnerable children. This Chapter seeks to draw attention to those factors which can impede the quality of these activities. It draws on evidence of sources of bias, such as those described earlier, and more basic 'cognitive errors' or errors of thinking, to which we are prone. It begins by considering something already touched on under sources of observational bias — 'heuristics'.

HEURISTICS

This is the term given to the rules of thumb that, as lay people, we use when making judgements. It is the process whereby we reduce complex inferential tasks (if . . . then . . .) to simple judgmental operations (Nisbett and Ross 1980). In fact, 'judgement' is a rather misleading phrase in this context. Here is a description of the functioning of these 'rules of thumb' by two major contributors in the field;

> 'the utilisation of the heuristics is generally automatic and nonreflective and notably free of any conscious consideration of appropriateness.' (Nisbett and Ross 1980, p. 18)

They are used because they are generally helpful in everyday situations. Nisbett and Ross again:

> 'They are not irrational or even nonrational. They probably produce vastly more correct or partially correct inferences than erroneous ones, and they do so with great speed and little effort. . . . [however] . . . the misapplication of each heuristic does lead people astray in some important inferential tasks.' (Nisbett and Ross 1980, p. 18)

Examples of two heuristics have already been explored. First, the *'availability heuristic'*—the tendency to form a judgement in line with evidence, information, experience that is readily available to us. An easily grasped example is that of asking a group of people what percentage of the workforce is unemployed. Typically, those in employment underestimate this, whilst those who are unemployed over-estimate it. The reasons are not difficult to disinter. Unemployed people probably have more contact with other unemployed people than do those in employment. They spend more time going to job centres, to social security agencies where they meet other unemployed people, and so on. The reality of unemployment may mean this information is 'writ large' in their experience, it is more 'available' to them and so exerts an influence. Of course, members of both groups *could* obtain more accurate information, or could rely on other 'rules of thumb' which were less susceptible (in this case) to availability such as 'when there's a recession there is more unemployment' (see Nisbett and Ross 1980). But experimental evidence suggests that more often than not we do not actively engage in such self-challenges. Similarly with the other heuristic discussed earlier, the *'representativeness heuristic'*, or the tendency to approach problems of categorisation on the basis of simple resemblance of 'goodness of fit'. It can affect the explanations we use (or seek for) as well as our estimates of what is likely to happen. We know that the birth of boys (B) and girls (G) is randomly sequenced, but when asked to choose which of the following three sequences is most likely, most people in Kahneman and Tversky's study chose option three;

1. BBBBBB
2. GGGBBB
3. GBBGGB

This is because it most nearly resembles what people regard as a random pattern, even though on the basis of random probability, it is no more random than the first two (Kahneman and Tversky 1972). Similarly, if we have in our heads a notion of a typical child abuser (perhaps based on a previous case), we are more likely to predict continued abuse in a family which appears similar in key respects (key to us, that is) and to underestimate its likelihood in families which seem not to share those characteristics. Indeed, 'vivid' information, that is to say, information which is emotionally arousing, information which is concrete or detailed, and information which comes via first hand experience, are all examples of information sources likely to extend their influence over us by being more likely to be retained in memory and more easily recalled. All of these factors combine to endow practice experience, and the 'individual case' with unmerited power to inform (and distort) our decisions.

Although these heuristics are biased, it is of course not accidental that they form part of the human animal's repertoire of problem-solving strategies. In recent years work in the field of 'evolutionary psychology' has generated interesting narratives as to why we, in everyday life, have tendencies to concentrate upon the vivid, to be more alert to social illogicalities connected to cheating than to pure illogicality, and so forth. For a social animal operating in small groups these may be useful survival strategies, which may account for the positive component in Nisbett and Ross's observations. Indeed Gigerenzer *et al.* (1999) argue that what are called 'fast and frugal' heuristics may yield viable outcomes in a wider range of everyday situations than we might expect.

Although useful in day-to-day life then, heuristics can be misapplied and misleading in circumstances where decision-making requires a more considered and formal approach. Decision-making and risk assessment in complex circumstances such as child protection are good examples of circumstances which require a more 'tutored' approach. In these areas we are endeavouring to formulate a 'best guess' understanding of what has caused a particular state of affairs and what the likely outcome will be if (i) we do not intervene at all; (ii) if we intervene in *this* way, or (iii) we intervene in *that* way. There is a large body of evidence which demonstrates that in these circumstances, our untutored (spontaneous or intuitive) responses produce wildly inaccurate answers (Dawes and Corrigan 1974). Further, it is generally the case that programmed approaches to decision-making and prediction (such as those used by insurance companies to assess risk) are generally better than the best human decision-maker, even when both have precisely the same information. This pattern of findings is the more worrying since generally it has focused on those who have had some professional training, such as clinicians, lawyers, social workers, psychologists and so on. One response to such ingrained problems is to make use of more formal or 'tutored' approaches to risk assessment and decision-making and examples of these are discussed at the end of this Chapter.

TUTORED APPROACHES TO RISK ASSESSMENT

The distortions of judgement that are brought about by misapplied heuristics are in part attributable to a general absence of formal approach to decision-making and risk assessment, or the failure to make use of tools which are potentially 'corrective'. Fundamentally, intuitive approaches to decision-making ignore the essentially statistical nature of 'probability'. This final Chapter therefore explores some of the more formal tools practitioners could use to improve decision-making. However, it is also the case that such approaches are rarely taught to practitioners and are presently under-utilised. Their statistical nature may well deter practitioners from considering them and their use in day-to-day practice may be circumscribed. However, they are important, and the principles underlying them ought to be understood by anyone undertaking risk assessments. One such tool, Bayes theorem, has been successfully taught to qualifying social workers, the majority of whom had no background in mathematics or science. These students were as intimidated at the prospect as most readers unfamiliar with Bayes will be when they reach page 275. It may well be that such readers will want only to scan these pages and perhaps seek to register the key points. It is always easier to learn such skills by practising them with others, and practitioners and managers are urged to develop their appreciation of the concepts and skills involved, as and when such opportunities present themselves (and perhaps to create them). Meanwhile, this section concludes with a number of more general strategies for improving the quality of assessments and decision-making without recourse to such techniques.

Whether we are considering the likelihood that a particular series of events has led to a present state of affairs, trying to work out what is going to happen in the future, or whether we are endeavouring to assess the effectiveness of a particular course of action then we are essentially weighing up probabilities. This is because we rarely have all the information that 'certainty' would require, and typically we have limited control over the range of contingencies with which we are dealing or upon which we are pondering. As indicated in the previous Chapter, professionals and lay people often refer to probabilities in vague terms which are open to a variety of widely different interpretations ('likely' 'mostly' 'highly probable', 'almost never'). Clear communication and improved decision-making therefore minimally depend on improved understanding and use of probability. Risk assessment is one category of probability estimation or assessment. In order better to understand the task of risk assessment, it is important to familiarise oneself with some key concepts and terms.

Some Common Terms in Assessments of Probability

What often throws practitioners coming to this literature (after all few of us come into social work, psychology or medicine because we adore numbers), is that statisticians typically refer to probability as ranging from 0 (no probability) to 1 (certainty). Most people find it easier to think in percentage terms, but remember that 40% is the same as 0.4. Whatever approach one uses, one related term which is important in both is that of *prior probability*. Prior probability is our estimated probability of something occurring based solely on pre-existing information. So, if we already know that 40% of children sent to a residential home have absconded, then (in the absence of additional information) our best guess is that there is a 40% (0.4) chance that the next young person sent there will also abscond. Similarly, if 20% of parents with learning difficulties of a certain level neglect their children's language development needs, then in the absence of further information our best guess is that there is a 20% (0.2) chance that this will occur for a child born to parents with similar problems.

Other related concepts are *base rate* or *prevalence*. These terms both refer to the relative frequency with which something occurs in particular groups or situations. In some circumstances the prevalence may be our best estimate of the prior probability. Knowing the probability of something occurring can, and should, inform decision-making. It can provide an important corrective to more biased sources of information such as availability or representativeness. Determining probability can be approached in two ways: (i) using actuarial methods and (ii) using Bayes theorem iteratively to modify our estimates. This following section discusses the relevance of these two approaches to decision-making and risk assessment in child protection.

Actuarial Methods (Risk Assessment Instruments)

One of the steps now being taken in an endeavour to improve risk assessment is that of risk assessment instruments. These are instruments which have tried to identify the characteristics that appear to have predictive value (typically by working retrospectively from clinical samples) and then developed ways of measuring these characteristics. These are then tested in a high risk group and statistical techniques are then applied to determine which of the range of characteristics measured have the best predictive value. The instrument is then revised to enable workers to identify high- and low-risk clients and then tested prospectively with a group of new clients (see Gibbs 1991). In medical and life insurance, this approach works very well, and indeed, in most clinical settings (such as psychology and social work) we know that these tools, once developed, produce more accurate predictions than professional judgement (see Dawes *et al.* 1989), and as Gibbs points out, this is one of the reasons for a growing interest in their use, even in a profession such as social work which has hitherto spoken disparagingly of such 'blunt' instruments (see DoH 1999). However, their usefulness depends on the relationship between a number of test characteristics; the two normally taken as central are:

> *Sensitivity* — among those who do, in fact, have a problem, the proportion whom a test or measure identifies as such.
> *Specificity* — among those who do *not*, in fact, have the problem, the proportion whom the test or measure also says do *not* have the problem.

So *sensitivity* focuses on the accuracy of locating those who have the problem; *specificity* focuses on the accuracy of locating those who do not have the problem. For any given test, specificity and sensitivity can have different values. As an extreme example, the pantomime magistrate who shouts 'guilty' as each accused enters the dock, scores well on *sensitivity* (all the truly guilty accused will be labelled 'guilty') and very poorly on *specificity* (none of the innocent accused will be labelled innocent—a *specificity* of zero). And that counter-intuitive ascription of 'sensitivity' to the boorish pantomime magistrate helps to remind us that we are here dealing with 'technical' usages, with specific defined meanings, and our ordinary-language associations are irrelevant. Next, some further interconnected terms:

'*True positives*' refers to positive cases labelled as positive by the test. So *sensitivity* is the proportion of '*true positives*' (thus defined) amongst those who did in fact have a problem (or were guilty).

'*False positives*' refers to non-positive cases labelled as positive by the test (all those innocent people mislabelled as 'guilty'). The proportion of '*false positives*' (thus defined) amongst those who did in fact not have the problem is calculated by the formula: one minus the *specificity*. To understand why this is, remember that people were labelled either as having or not having the problem, so the two proportions sum to one (see above). In the pantomime example, all the innocent were labelled 'guilty', so that proportion was one, and the *specificity* was zero. This last interconnection will be useful later on in this Chapter. For the present we will concentrate on specificity and sensitivity.

The problem we have in child protection is that few instruments have been properly validated (Millner *et al.* 1998) and many have high rates of false positives (so low specificity). When trying to predict very low frequency events (such as child death) the abundance of false positives can so overwhelm the much smaller number of true positives that prediction becomes counterproductive. The distress caused by false positives and the damage to children's welfare that can ensue when these are acted upon (consider the Cleveland and Orkney cases) can outweigh the benefits of test sensitivity. Unfortunately the former is often the price one has to pay for the latter, and the less frequent an event is, the more problematic. Here is one illustration of what can happen in circumstances where a hypothetical test of good sensitivity and specificity is applied to the prediction of fatal child abuse:

Testing for about-to-be infant murderers

'Suppose we could develop a test instrument that determines with apparent accuracy whether or not someone is an about-to-be infant-murderer. By accurate we mean that when presented with an about-to-be infant-murderer the test correctly identifies status 90% of the time (if we have ten potential child-murderers in our class we locate nine of them)—as social science instruments go, impressive. To match this 10% 'false negative' rating, let us assume the test has an equivalent 10% 'false positive' score.

Now suppose we apply the test to you, and you score positive. What, given the above, is the likelihood that you are an about-to-be infant-murderer? (There may be some merit in forming your answer before proceeding.)

Let us conservatively concentrate on those with ready access to the infants—say two 'suspects' per birth. There were . . . in England and Wales, some 10 infant murders per 200 000 live births. The test would correctly identify, on average, nine of these. But, and this is where the trouble arises, it would also identify as about-to-be child-murderers those 10% false-positives. On an 'at risk' population of 400 000 (and remember that this was a conservative estimate) we have some 40 000 'positives'.

Whence, if identified as positive, your probability of being an about-to-be child-murderer is 0.0002 (the chance of being one of the nine 'true' out of the total 40 009 returned positive). This low probability is worth emphasising, since misperception of the predictive power of such tests is common, even amongst the well trained and educated. Such a low probability can only legitimate benign interventions; and benign interventions—by definition—do not need such legitimation.' (Macdonald 1995)

The discrepancy between tutored and untutored understanding is sharpest when, as here, we consider low probability events (because intuition appears to disattend to the number of false-positives). But even in less dramatic examples, the weight of the experimental psychological evidence is that humans are not well 'wired' when it comes to the intuitive evaluation of complex patterns of probability and evidence.

Bayes Theorem

The discussion in the preceding section has, in fact, involved a particular application of Bayes theorem, but Bayes theorem offers a way of generalising these approaches to other areas of risk assessment and decision-making. Bayes theorem differs from actuarial approaches in its inclusion of people's intuitive or 'untutored' theories about what has happened (explanations), or will happen (predictions or 'best-guesses' about the future), and in pro-viding rules as to how these should be modified in the light of the evidence. It is therefore, more closely akin to the approach used in 'real life' situations, such as risk assessment in child protection. However, its use also requires the application of a mathematical formula which, at first sight, may make prac-titioners apprehensive. It is also the case that Bayes is unlikely to be used as a standard tool in decision-making, but it is an important approach which practitioners should be aware of and have a basic understanding of, for the following reasons:

(i)   if used it could undoubtedly improve decision-making in a number of key areas, particularly risk assessment;
(ii) as in the example above, knowing about Bayes can make practitioners appropriately cautious of their subjective judgements and of some of the errors that frequently occur in assessment, problem formulation and decision-making;
(iii) risk assessment and decision-making in circumstances of uncertainty (nearly, if not all, of social work) requires intellectual rigour. Even if we do not formally deploy Bayes, it reminds us that risk assessment should be approached systematically, explicitly and judiciously. The development of such an approach is essential if we are to protect ourselves against ill-founded criticism based on hindsight, such as the assumption that an adverse outcome is itself evidence of a wrong decision. As Carson puts it:

> 'If you have reason to believe that an event is possible, but unlikely, then you should declare and record that likelihood in an explicit form. Unless it can be shown that your estimate was inappropriate it will prove powerful in discouraging any court, or other form of inquiry, from utilising hindsight in order to conclude that the harm, which has now occurred, was more likely than it then seemed. The court has to try to avoid hindsight; why not help it?' (Carson 1996, p. 10)

(iv) Bayes theorem (and the principles underpinning it), as a means of placing decisions on a more secure footing, is therefore an important component of evidence-based practice;
(v)   it is possible to teach this approach to social work students—as has been demonstrated, for example, by courses teaching Bayes as part of a broader course on critical thinking skills (Macdonald and Sheldon 1998; Gibbs and Gambrill 1996 and 1999).

So, take a deep breath and read on. On no account assume that because it is not crystal clear first time that it is incomprehensible, or that you are not able to grasp the key issues. The latter possibilities are both examples of faulty reasoning! It may well be that you need to encounter these principles or explanations in a different context, or with case examples and the possibility of 'hands-on' practice. If that is the case, then aim for a sense of the issues, to be followed up at a later date.

Essential Bayes

A Bayesian approach to risk assessment is essentially one which looks at the way our probabilistic *beliefs* about the world (i.e., about risk) should be modified in the light of *information* about the world. It is a mathematical tool and it does help to know and understand its derivation (see Macdonald and Macdonald 1999). However, these details are omitted here in favour of persuading readers of its usefulness and its accessibility to anyone with basic numeracy skills. The Bayes strategy runs like this:

1. Estimating the likelihood of some outcome based on the information currently available to us (for example, the information on file about a parent or family). This is known as the *prior probability*.
2. Obtaining relevant (and new) data—for example administering some risk-assessment instrument, or identifying a particular cause for concern.
3. Modifying our original beliefs in the light of that data, producing a revised estimate of risk. This is known as the *posterior probability* or the *conditional probability* (the probability after, or conditional upon, the introduction of new information).

Bayes can be used to work out the probability of a particular client having a condition X (having a disease, being an abuser) *given* a positive result from a risk assessment tool such as those discussed earlier.

The mathematics of Bayes theorem can be expressed in a number of different ways. These different formulations arrange the terms in the equation in different groupings, and these groupings map to different verbal expressions of the relationship. But the underlying theorem is unchanged. We begin first with a version of the theorem particularly targeted at the evaluation of a psychological test or predictive instrument. This is the version most frequently encountered in the social work literature. We will later present a version of the theorem better adapted to talk of hypotheses and data in general; this second formulation is arguably more transparent.

Considering first a version of Bayes organised to assess the contribution of some test to determining whether or not a client has 'condition X'. What we need in order to assess this is the following information:

(i)   Some initial estimate of the *prior probability*, attached to the hypothesis that the client has a particular 'condition', X (e.g., is violent). In the absence of further information our best estimate of the prior probability may be simply the *prevalence* of X in the group under consideration (where the group might be husbands, young men, step-parents etc.). On this basis we can arrive at a baseline probability that someone is violent. To take a more neutral example: if a quarter of all trains run late, my best guess that of the probability that the next train will run late—in the absence of any further information—would be 0.25.
(ii) Information on the *sensitivity* of the instrument (its ability correctly to identify positive cases).
(iii) Information on the *specificity* of the instrument (its ability to screen out those cases which are negative).

One formula which can then be applied (although not necessarily the most intelligible, but the one most frequently encountered in the social work literature) is:

$$\frac{conditional}{probability} = \frac{(prevalence) \times (sensitivity)}{[(prevalence) \times (sensitivity)] + [(1 - prevalence) \times (1 - specificity)]}$$

Now, for those of you who have done no mathematics for many years, the following points are worth re-learning:

• First, formulae such as this are not difficult, but they require a step-wise approach. In other words there are numbers of 'mini calculations' to be done before the answer is obtained (see next point).
• Each set of numbers within round brackets has to be worked out first. Some of these will be a single number and need no calculation e.g., prevalence. Others will require a simple calculation e.g., (1−*prevalence*) as in the bottom line-right).
• When numbers in the round brackets have been obtained, then you need to calculate the values within the square brackets. So, for example, along the bottom line again, after working out what (1−*prevalence*) is and having done the same for (1−*specificity*), you then multiply the one by the other.
• When all the calculations within brackets have been done, then a final calculation needs to be made for each line. The first line simply requires that you multiply *prevalence* by *sensitivity*. The second requires that you multiply prevalence by sensitivity and then *add that to* the results of the calculation you have done of the second expression in squared brackets.
• The final step is to divide the numbers on the top line by those on the bottom.

Now let us consider an example.

Case Example

Let us assume we are trying to predict the likelihood of a particular family who have physically injured their children, doing so again in the future. Further, let us assume that 35% of those who have seriously injured their children go on to do so again—that is the *prevalence* of repeat injury in the group who have already injured is 0.35. Assume that the test we are using correctly identifies up 95% of those will injure again (i.e., it has a *sensitivity* of 95%) and correctly identifies 93% of those who will not injure again (i.e., it has a *specificity* of 93%). On this basis we can calculate the conditional probability of (conditional on a 'will injure' test result) any particular family being likely to injure again, based on this information, as follows:

$$conditional\ probability = \frac{(0.35) \times (0.95)}{[(0.35) \times (0.95)] + [(1 - 0.35) \times (1 - 0.93)]} = 0.88$$

In other words, a test like this one would enable us to make a much better job of identifying those most likely to injure their children again, and improving our decision making with regard to these children.

Casework Decisions

It is not only in assessing the predictive value of tests that Bayes is useful. Bayes provides a decision-making aid for any set of circumstances in which we have a pre-existing belief or hypothesis about the probability of something occurring. As we piece together information we inevitably begin to formulate a view of, for example, the safety of a child or the impact of a particular set of circumstances on his or her development and well-being. Two questions present themselves. First, how do we judge the appropriateness of our initial opinion? Secondly, how should that opinion be revised in the light of additional information? Clearly, one hopes that in child protection assessments these prior beliefs will be as soundly based as possible, but one of the strengths of a Bayesian approach is that it provides a basis for articulating what might otherwise remain implicit, and for scrutinising the plausibility and/or consequences of particular views. Bayes theorem is primarily concerned with the second question, hence the terminology used. The steps in this second formulation of Bayes theorem are as follows:

1. *Estimating the prior probability (p).* The *prior probability* refers to our hypothesis or belief about something. This could be how something has happened (i.e., explanatory) or about what is likely to happen (predictive). It could be our opinion about the likelihood of parents being helped to care more adequately for their children if they are referred to a particular parenting programme, or a view of the likely safety of a child if he or she is left in the care of parents who have previously injured them. It requires us to sign a numerical value e.g., 40% likely, rather than relying on adjectival phrases such as 'highly' or 'not very likely'. When considering psychological tests (above) we took prevalence as our best estimate of the prior probability; but the criteria for 'best estimate' will vary with the explanatory task.

2. *Estimating how informative the new data are.* The extent to which a given factor (or set of factors) gives cause for concern depends on two things:

    (i) how frequently they are associated with the occurrence of maltreatment;

(ii) how frequently they occur in the population of non-maltreaters (that is, unassociated with maltreatment).

In more technical terminology, we are interested in comparing (i) the probability of the data if our hypothesis were true (e.g., the probability of finding a step-father in an abusing family) to (ii) the probability of the data if our hypothesis were false (e.g., the probability of finding a step-father in a non-abusing family). Intuitively, if the two probabilities were identical, the occurrence of that data ought not to affect our prior beliefs. It is because the probability of 'having fair hair if you are an abuser' and the probability of 'having fair hair if you are not an abuser' are similar that we do not go around checking for hair-colour. If the likelihood of the data varies between the two groups, then the presence of the data is giving us information—the greater the discrepancy, the more the information. That intuition is captured by dividing the one quantity by the other. So the measure of how informative the data are is given by:

(iii) what the ratio is between the two probabilities, (i) and (ii) above. This is obtained by dividing (i) by (ii). This provides what statisticians refer to as the *diagnostic ratio* (an unfortunate term for application in an essentially social arena, but accurate in a non-medical sense). The diagnostic ratio is the ratio of the *probability of the observed evidence occurring if the hypothesis is true* to *the probability of the observed evidence occurring if the hypothesis were false*.

In other words, something may look highly predictive of abuse because it frequently occurs in maltreating families, but should not be so read if it in fact is also commonly found in families who do not maltreat their children. Professional staff who work predominantly with 'clinical' populations are particularly prone to this kind of error, which arises both from their experience (vivid and available) and an untutored approach to assessing probability. It is easy, for example, for social workers from one social or cultural background, confronted by problem clients from another background, to assume that some common feature displayed by these clients is causally connected to their problem, without checking out the frequency of that feature in the other populations (including their own). It is important to remember that professionals routinely see a biased sample, and that in itself may generate misperceptions. The formalisation of Bayes can provide a useful corrective.

Obviously in the world as it is we may well lack accurate estimates of (i) and (ii). There are then two possible strategies. Firstly, since it is the *diagnostic ratio* that matters (see (iii) above), we may sometimes be able to put a value of this ratio without being able to specify its components (we may have some sense of how much *more* likely something is in one group than the other, without being able to specify frequencies). And secondly, the Bayesian would suggest that even if we are not sure what the exact values are we could explore the implications of our highest and lowest estimates. We can check out the implications of 'worst case' and 'best case' scenarios, to map out the area of uncertainty. This may seem spurious precision, but what it is doing is tightening up the intuitive, unexamined assumptions that we in any case make.

3. The third Bayesian step on this approach is *reviewing (mathematically) that prior belief, in the light of new information*. We review our prior probability in the light of the diagnostic ratio to get to the end result—our revised belief or hypothesis—known as the *posterior probability*. If the diagnostic ratio is one (i.e., the data are equally likely under either assumption: abuser or non-abuser) we obviously don't want to change our prior estimate. If the ratio is greater than one we would wish to increase our estimate of the probability. The mathematical operation of multiplication would capture that intuition (multiplying by one does nothing, multiplying by greater-than-one increases) and is discussed in the next section.

Those who would welcome a rest from the spectre of the maths teachers of their youth (mine was called Miss Fear—honestly), feel free to skip the next section until you feel more robust, or feel more confident in the general principles presented in this chapter. It presents—in user-friendly terms, to the extent that this is possible—the mathematics underpinning this second formulation of Bayes theorem.

Bayes Theorem Revisited

This second form of Bayes theorem follows the intuition that multiplying by one does nothing, and multiplying by greater than one increases some pre-conceived estimate. It can be written:

$$posterior\ odds = prior\ odds \times diagnostic\ ratio$$

For the mathematics to work out, the theorem talks of 'odds' rather than 'probabilities', but as any gambler knows these are simply alternate ways of expressing the same underlying facts about the world. That is, rather than saying something has a 40% (0.4) probability of occurring we say the odds of its occurring are 40/60 or 2 to 3, or 0.66. In symbols, if we use p for 'prior *probability* that the hypothesis or belief is true' then we express the 'prior *odds* of the hypothesis being true' (as opposed to false) as $p/(1-p)$ (remember that probability is typically represented as between 0 and 1 rather than 0 and 100).

This second version of Bayes theorem is more transparent than the jumble of prevalence, sensitivity, specificity in the first equation. Here, the two things (prior odds, diagnostic ratio) which we multiply together each have an intelligible interpretation. And 'multiplication' has an intelligible interpretation. If the diagnostic ratio is one (if the data are as likely to occur if our hypothesis is false as they are if our hypothesis is true) then the data give no information. The result of the multiplication (multiplying by one) which then leaves our prior odds unchanged, captures that intuition. The more information in the data (the bigger the diagnostic ratio) the more we multiply our prior odds to get our posterior odds.

[*An algebraic aside.* You can take it as an *ex cathedra* fact that the versions of Bayes are identical, and skip this paragraph. But simple algebra can show the identity. Our first equation can be written (substituting symbols for words):

$$c = \frac{p \times s}{[p \times s] + [(1 - p) \times (1 - f)]}$$

where we let c stand for conditional probability, p for prior probability (which we were estimating by prevalence), s for sensitivity and f for specificity. Now moving to the second equation. Prior odds we have identified as $p/(1 - p)$. The conditional odds, by exactly similar reasoning, are $c/(1 - c)$. Now consider the diagnostic ratio. The numerator (top line) of the diagnostic ratio is the proportion of true positives returned by the test amongst those who were actually positive—what earlier we called the *sensitivity*. The denominator (bottom line) is the proportion of 'false positives' amongst those who were actually negative—and as was shown above, that is: one minus the *specificity*. So the diagnostic ratio can be written as $s/(1 - f)$. So the second version of Bayes, in the symbols of the first, can be written:

$$\frac{c}{(1-c)} = \frac{p}{(1-p)} \times \frac{s}{(1-f)}$$

conditional	prior	diagnostic
odds	odds	ratio

It is then a matter of simple algebra—which will not be inflicted here—to rearrange the one expression to the other. They are different organisations of the identical relationship.

End of algebraic interlude]

Case Example

So, let us take an example. Suppose a case conference is considering a family referred to social services because of concerns of abuse and neglect. The oldest of three children has been seen in accident and emergency because of a broken arm. The hospital paediatrician made the referral. On the basis of an established injury with no plausible explanation (the stories given by the parents have been inconsistent and there are a number of bruises on the child for which no adequate account is available) the social worker considers that there is a real chance that this child was avoidably, and possibly intentionally, injured by his parents and will be injured again if nothing is done. When asked, she places this risk of further abuse (the prior probability) at 70%. The conference concurs. The case conference then learns that the father is, in fact a step-father who has lived with the mother of the three children for two years. The task is to determine whether this new information should lead to a revision of the original estimate of future abuse, and if so, in what direction. The issue is whether this factor (step-parenthood) is more likely to occur in maltreating families than non-maltreating families. If it is then the original estimate of future abuse will remain the same; if not, it will need to be revised. In order to work this out, we need details of the prevalence of step-parenting in abusive and non-abusive families (or an estimate of the ratio between the two—based on experience, professional judgement or whatever). In fact, one study has suggested that the prevalence of step-fathers in abusing families is 35.5% (Brown and Saqi 1988) compared with 4.8% in non-abusing families. Therefore, we can calculate the posterior odds as follows:

$$\frac{0.7}{(1-0.7)} \times \frac{0.355}{0.048}$$

$$\begin{array}{cc} prior & diagnostic \\ odds & ratio \end{array}$$

That gives the value 17.26. So the prior odds are 2.33; the posterior odds have increased to 17.26. We could keep talking in terms of odds, or convert the result back into the implied posterior probability. The formula to translate from odds to probabilities is simple enough:

If the odds are x, then the probability is $x/(x + 1)$.

In this case:

$$\frac{17.26}{(17.26 + 1)} = 0.95$$

(and you can check that a probability of 0.95 yields, by our earlier formula, an odds of 17.26). So the posterior probability that the application of Bayes suggests, taking into account the evidence (and our assumptions about it) is 0.95. In other words, if Brown and Saqi's study was sound (which, by the way, it is not) the piece of information about step-parenthood substantially increases the risk that abuse will recur in this family. It suggests that the prior probability should be revised upwards to a level almost approaching certainty—or as near to certainty as one might get in social work or child protection. Typically of course, one is working in circumstances where the one's estimates of abuse (prior probability) are much lower. One is also frequently in the business of negotiating different views in which different professionals have different 'priors'. And, as our aside on Brown and Saqi indicates, Bayes provides a rule for revising theories in the light of evidence, but whether we make progress will depend crucially on the quality of our theories and the quality of our evidence.

Summary

In general, developing a more transparent and critical approach to each stage of assessment can go some way to improving their quality and the quality of the decisions which result from them. These principles apply equally to risk assessment, but here there is also scope for improving our decision-making with more formal tools than those usually deployed by child care professionals. In some areas, the dearth of information about the causes and consequences of child abuse means that it is not possible to say precisely how significant a particular feature, characteristic, or circumstance might be. Indeed, the ecological model suggests that it is the interactive nature of risk factors which require recognition and evaluation, rather than a preoccupation with single factors, and that we need to consider factors at all levels, including the individual, the relational, and the circumstantial (see Hagell 1998). Bayes, and actuarial approaches enable us to set about these tasks more soundly than we might otherwise do, given the sources of bias, error and general complexity, and indeed uncertainty, which characterises risk assessment in the field of child protection. Tutored approaches to risk constrain us to make clear and explicit what our prior assumptions are (for example, as held by each participant at the outset of a case conference) and how these are revised (or should be revised) in the light of new information. One of the reasons the Bridge Child Development Services' approach to co-ordinating and recording significant events in a structured way (see Chapter 12) is potentially so useful is that it constrains workers to revise their 'prior probabilities' as new information is added, impacting on the perceived significance of earlier items.

Tutored approaches to probability also require us to be more explicit about the rationale for thinking that a particular case plan will achieve a particular set of outcomes, and a reduction in risk to (or improvement in care of) a particular child. In other words, when devising care plans, or choosing interventions, tutored approaches prompt us to estimate the probability that a particular intervention (say parent training) will achieve a particular outcome (improved child care knowledge and skills), and how that outcome will change the circumstances for a child (improved standards of care), and a related set of more directly child-centred outcomes (e.g., development, attachment, happiness, safety).

Notice, though the bulk of the risk assessment literature concentrates on negative outcomes, that as the preceding example indicates, all of the issues that have been raised concerning the evaluation of risk in the light of evidence apply to positive outcomes as well as to negative ones. Careful professionals have a duty to consider the uncertainty of benefits as well as harms (Macdonald and Macdonald 1999b).

Tutored approaches to risk assessment and risk management also underline the importance of being clear about outcomes, *particularly those related to a child's safety and well-being,* and highlight the importance of careful monitoring and evaluation to assess whether one's predictions (hunches or hopes) are being realised. In no other field is the notion that there is 'many a slip 'twixt cup and lip' more pertinent than in decision-making in complex circumstances of uncertainty. Complexity and uncertainty are among the hallmarks of social intervention in human lives. However secure the evidence-base (in terms of available research) and however good our assessment, it is always possible that something has been overlooked, that our clients differ significantly in some respect from those who participated in outcome research, something untoward happens, or the 'means-to-an-end' changes that we bring about do not deliver the end-point outcomes we are striving for (for example, sex offenders might evidence a range of behavioural changes but still commit further offences; parents may acquire a range of skills, but not deploy them, or might deploy them in a way that perpetuates emotional abuse, even when physical care improves).

Where standardised instruments are available, or good research studies or reviews can provide a basis for any part of that process, then all well and good. But these are not essential, which is fortunate given their dearth. An improved understanding of the nature of probability and the principles underpinning more formal approaches to risk assessment, can themselves go some considerable way to improving practice in this challenging area of work.

REFERENCES

Abel, G. and Rouleau, J. (1990) The nature and extent of sexual assault. In Marshall, W.L., Laws, D. and Barbaree, H. (eds) *Handbook of Sexual Assault*. New York, Plenum.

Abel, G., Becker, J., Cunningham-Rathner, J. and Rouleau, J. (1987) Self-reported sex crimes of 561 non-incarcerated paraphiliacs. *Journal of Interpersonal Violence*, 2(6): 3–25.

Abel, G.G., Becker, J.V., Cunningham-Rathner, J., Mittelman, M.S. and Rouleau, J.L. (1988) Multiple paraphilic diagnoses among sex offenders. *Bulletin of the American Academy of Psychiatry and the Law*, **16**, 153–168.

Aber, J.L. and Allen, J.P (1987) The effects of maltreatment on young children's socioemotional development: An attachment theory perspective. *Developmental Psychology*, **23**: 406–414.

Aber, J.L. and Zigler, E. (1981) Developmental considerations in the development of child maltreatment. In Rizley, R. and Cicchetti, D. (eds) *Developmental Perspectives on Child Maltreatment*. No. 11. San Francisco, Jossey-Bass.

Ainsworth, M.D.S. (1980) Attachment and child abuse. In Gerber, G., Ross, C.J. and Zigler, E. (eds) *Child abuse reconsidered: An agenda for action*. New York, Oxford University Press.

Albee, G.W. (1980) Primary prevention and social problems. In Gerbner, G., Ross, C.J. and Zigler, E. (eds) *Child abuse: an agenda for action*. New York, Oxford University Press.

Alderson, P. (1990) *Listening to Children: Children, Ethics and Social Research*. Barkingside, Essex, Barnardo's.

Alexander, J.F., Barton, C., Schiavo, R.S. and Parsons, B.V. (1976) Systems-behavioral intervention with families of delinquents: Therapist characteristics, family behavior, and outcome. *Journal of Consulting and Clinical Psychology*, **81**: 219–225.

Allam, J., Middleton, D. and Brown, K.D. (1997) Different clients, different ends? Practice issues in community based treatments for sex offenders. *Criminal Behaviour and Mental Health*, **7**: 69–84.

Allen, R.E. and Oliver, H.M. (1982) The effects of child maltreatment on language development. *Child Abuse and Neglect*, **6**: 299–305.

Allessandri, S.M. (1991) Play and social behavior in maltreated preschoolers. *Development and Psychopathology*, **3**: 191–205.

Ammerman, R.T. (1989) Child abuse and neglect. In Hersen, M. (ed.) *Innovations in child behavior therapy*, New York, Springer.

Ammerman, R.T., Van Hasselt, V.B. and Hersen, M. (1988) Maltreatment of handicapped children: A critical review. *Journal of Family Violence*, **3**(1): 53–72.

Andrews, B., Brown, G.W. and Creasey, L. (1990) Intergenerational links between psychiatric disorder in mothers and daughters: the role of parenting experiences. *Journal of Child Psychology and Psychiatry*, **31**: 1115–1129.

Araji, S. and Finkelhor, D. (1986) Abusers: A review of the research. In Finkelhor, D. and Associates (eds) *A Sourcebook on Child Sexual Abuse*, Newbury Park, Sage.

Asdigan, N.L. and Finkelhor, D. (1995) What works for children in resisting assaults? *Journal of Interpersonal Violence*, **10**(4): 402–418.

ATSA (1997) *Position on the Legal Management of Juvenile Offenders*. ATSA, Suite 26, Beaverton, Oregon.

Auden, W.H. (1967) *Collected Shorter Poems (1927–1957)*, New York, Random House.

Augoustinos, M. (1987) Developmental effects of child abuse: recent findings. *Child Abuse and Neglect*, **11**: 15–27.

Ayoub, C. (1991) Physical violence and preschoolers: The use of therapeutic day care in the treatment of physically abused children and children from violent families. *The APSAC Advisor*, **4**(40): 1–16.

Azar, S.T. (1986) A framework for understanding child maltreatment: an integration of cognitive-behavioral and development perspectives. *Canadian Journal of Behavioral Science*, **18**: 340–355.

Azar, S.T. (1989a) Training parents of abused children. In Schaefer, C.E. and Briesmeister, J.M. (eds) *Handbook of parent training*, New York, John Wiley.

Azar, S.T. (1989b) *Unrealistic expectations and attributions of negative intent among teenage mothers at risk for child maltreatment: The validity of a cognitive view of parenting*. Paper presented at the annual meeting of the Association for Advancement of Behavior Therapy, Washington, DC.

Azar, S.T. (1997) A cognitive behavioral approach to understanding and treating parents who physically abuse their children. In Wolfe, D.A., McMahon, R.J. and Peters, R.DeV. (eds) *Child Abuse: New directions in prevention and treatment across the lifespan*, Thousand Oaks, Sage.

Azar, S.T. and Bobar, S.L. (1997) Developmental outcomes in abused children: The result of a breakdown in socialization environment. In Silverman, W. and Ollendick, T. (eds) *Issues in clinical treatment of children*, Needham Heights, MA, Allyn and Bacon.

Azar, S.T. and Rohrbeck, C.A. (1986) Child abuse and unrealistic expectations: Further validation of the Parent Opinion Questionnaire. *Journal of Consulting and Clinical Psychology*, **54**: 867–868.

Azar, S.T., Povilaitis, T.Y., Lauretti, A.F. and Pouquette, C.L. (1998) The current status of etiological theories in intrafamilial child maltreatment. In *Handbook of Child Abuse Research and Treatment: Issues in Clinical Child Psychology*, New York, Plenum Press.

Azar, S.T., Robinson, D.R., Hekimian, E. and Twentyman, C.T. (1984) Unrealistic expectations and problem-solving ability in maltreating and comparison mothers. *Journal of Consulting and Clinical Psychology*, **52**: 687–691.

Baker, A. and Duncan, S. (1985) Child sexual abuse: a study of prevalence in Great Britain. *Child Abuse and Neglect*, **9**: 457–467.

Bandura, A. (1973) *Aggression: A Social Learning Analysis*. Englewood Cliffs NY, Prentice-Hall.

Bandura, A. (1977) *Social Learning Theory*. Englewood Cliffs, NY, Prentice Hall.

Banyard, V.L. (1997) The impact of childhood sexual abuse and family functioning on four dimensions of women's later parenting. *Child Abuse and Neglect*, **21**(11): 1095–1107.

Barbaree, H. E., and Marshall, W. L. (1989) Erectile responses among heterosexual child molesters, father–daughter incest offenders, and matched non-offenders: Five distinct age preference profiles. *Canadian Journal of Behavioural Science*, **21**(1): 70–82.

Barker, W. (1988) *The Child Development Programme: an Evaluation of Process and Outcomes*. Bristol, Early Childhood Development Centre.

Barker, W. (1994) *Child Protection: the impact of the Child Development Programme*. Bristol, Early Childhood Development Unit.

Barlow, D.H. and Hersen, M. (1984) *Single Case Experimental Designs: Strategies for Studying Behaviour Change*. Second Edition, New York, Pergamon Press.

Barlow, J. (1997) *Systematic review of the effectiveness of parent-training programmes in improving behaviour problems in children aged 3–10 years*. Oxford, Health Services Research Unit, University of Oxford.

Baron, R.K. and Kenny, D.A. (1986) The moderator-mediator variable distinction in social psychological research: Conceptual, strategic, and statistical considerations. *Journal of Personality and Social Psychology*, **51**(6): 1173–1182.

Barone, V.J., Greene, B.F. and Lutzker, J.R. (1986) Home safety with families being treated for child abuse and neglect. *Behavior Modification*, **10**: 167–168.

Barth, R.P. (1989) Evaluation of a task-centered child abuse prevention program. *Children and Youth Services Review*, **11**: 117–132.

Barth, R.P. (1991) An experimental evaluation of in-home child abuse prevention services. *Child Abuse and Neglect*, **15**: 363–375.

Barth, R.P., Blythe, B.J. Schinke, S.P. and Schilling. R.F. II. (1983) Self control training with maltreating children. *Child Welfare*, LXII, **4**: 313–324.

Bartlett, F.C. (1932) *Remembering: A Study in Experimental and Social Psychology*, Oxford, Cambridge University Press.

Beal, C.R. (1994) *Boys and girls: The development of gender roles*. New York, McGraw-Hill, Inc.

Becker, J.V., Alpert, J.L., Subia Bigfoot, D., Bonner, B.L., Geddie, L.F., Henggeler, S.W., Kaufmann, K.L. and Walker, C.E. (1995) Empirical Research on Child Abuse Treatment: Report by the Child Abuse and Neglect Treatment Working Group. *Journal of Clinical Child Psychology*, **24** (suppl): 23–46.

Becker, W.C. (1971) *Parents are teachers*. Champaign, Ill, Research Press.

Beckett, R. (1994) Assessment of sex offenders. In Morrison, T., Erooga, M. and Beckett, R.L. (eds) *Sexual Offending Against Children: Assessment and Treatment of Male Abusers*, London, Routledge.

Beckett, R., Beech, A., Fisher, D. and Fordham, A.S. (1998) *Community-based treatment for sex offenders: an evaluation of seven treatment programmes*. London, Home Office Publications.

Beech, A., Fisher, D., Beckett, R. and Scott-Fordham, A. (1998) *An evaluation of the Prison Sex Offender Treatment Programm—STEP 3*. Home Office Research, Development and Statistics Directorate. Research Findings No. 79.

Beeghly, M. and Cicchetti, D. (1994) Child maltreatment, attachment and the self-esteem: Emergence of an internal state lexicon in toddlers at high social risk. *Development and Psychopathology*, **6**: 5–30.

Beitchman, J.H., Zucker, K.J., Hood, J.E., daCosta, G.A. and Akman, D. (1991) A review of the short-term effects of child sexual abuse. *Child Abuse and Neglect*, **15**: 537–556.

Beitchman, J.H., Zucker, K.J., Hood, J.E., daCosta, G.A. and Akman, D. (1992) A review of the long-term effects of child sexual abuse. *Child Abuse and Neglect*, **16**: 101–118.

Belsky, J. (1984) The determinants of parenting: a process model. *Child Development*, **55**: 83–96.

Belsky, J. (1993) Etiology of child maltreatment: A developmental-ecological analysis. *Psychological Bulletin*, **114**: 413–434.

Belsky, J. and Vondra, J. (1989) Lessons from child abuse: the determinants of parenting. In Cichetti, D. and Carlson, V. (eds) *Child Maltreatment: theory and research on the causes and consequences of child abuse and neglect*, New York, Cambridge University Press.

Bentovim, A. (1991) Clinical work with families in which sexual abuse has occurred. In Hollin C.R. and Howells, K. (eds) *Clinical approaches to sex offenders and their families*, Chichester, Wiley.

Beresford, P. and Croft, S. (1993) *Citizen involvement: A practical guide for change*, Basingstoke, Macmillan.

Berliner, L. and Saunders, B. (1995) *Grantee Status Report*. National Center on Child Abuse and Neglect, Washington, DC.

Berliner, L. and Wheeler, R.J. (1987) Treating the effects of sexual abuse on children. *Journal of Interpersonal Violence*, **2**: 415–434.

Berliner, L. (1991) Clinical work within sexually abused children. In G.R. Hollin and K. Howells (eds) *Clinical approaches to sex offenders and their victims*, New York, John Wiley.

Berliner, S. (1997) Trauma-specific therapy for sexually abused children. In Wolfe, D.A., McMahon, R.J. and Peters, R.DeV. (eds) *Child Abuse: New directions in prevention and treatment across the lifespan*, Thousand Oaks, Sage.

Besherov, D.J. (1985) Rights vs. rights: The dilemma of child protection. *Public Welfare*, **43**: 19–27.

Best, J.B. (1995) *Cognitive Psychology*. Minneapolis/St. Paul, West Publishing Company.

Beutler, L.E., Williams, R.E. and Zetzer, H.A. (1994) Efficacy of treatment for victims of child sexual abuse. *Future of Children*, **4**: 156–175.

Bhat, A., Carr-Hill, R. and Ohri, S. (1988) *Britain's Black Population: A New Perspective*. 2nd edition, London, Gower.

Bifulco, A, Brown, G.W. and Adler, Z. (1991) Early sexual abuse and clinical depression in later life. *British Journal of Psychiatry*, **159**: 115–122.

Biringen, Z. and Robinson, J. (1991) Emotional availability in mother-child interactions: a reconceptualisation for research. *American Journal of Orthopsychiatry*, **61**(2): 258–271.

Birmingham City Council (1976) *Joint Inquiry Arising from the Death of Neil Howlett*. Birmingham, Birmingham City Council.

Bishop, S.J. and Leadbeater, B.J. (1999) Maternal social support patterns and child maltreatment. *American Journal of Orthopsychiatry*, **69**(2), 172–181.

Black, M., Dubowitz, H. and Harrington, D. (1994) Sexual abuse: Developmental differences in children's behavior and self-perception. *Child Abuse and Neglect*, **18**: 85–95.

Blaxter, M. (1986) Longitudinal Studies in Britain. In Wilkinson, R.G. (ed.) *Class and Health*, London, Tavistock.

Bloom, M. and Fischer, J. (1982) *Evaluating Practice: Guidelines for the Accountable Professional*. Englewood Cliffs, NY, Prentice-Hall Inc.

Blum, J. (1978) *Pseudoscience and mental ability: the origins and fallacies of the IQ controversy*, New York, Monthly Review Press.

Blumenthal, S., Gudjonsson, G. and Burns, J. (1999) Cognitive distortions and blame attribution in sex offenders against adults and children. *Child Abuse and Neglect*, **23**(2): 129–144.

Boddy, J.M. and Skuse, D. (1994) Annotation: the process of parenting in failure to thrive, *Journal of Child Psychology and Psychiatry and Allied Professions*, **35**: 401–424.

Bowlby, J. and Salter-Ainsworth, M. (1965) *Child Care and Growth of Love*. (2nd edition) London, Penguin.

Bowlby, J. (1951) *Maternal Care and Mental Health*. Bulletin of the World Health Organisation, Geneva (Republished by WHO in 1952).

Bowlby, J. (1969) *Attachment and loss: Vol. 1 Attachment*. New York, Basic Books.

Bowlby, J. (1973) *Attachment and loss: Vol. 2: Separation*. New York, Basic Books.

Bowlby, J. (1980) *Attachment and loss: Vol. 3 Sadness and Depression*. London, Hogarth.

Braddon, F.E.M., Wadsworth, M.E.J., Davies, J.M.C. and Cripps, H.A. (1988) Social and regional differences in food and alcohol consumption and their measurement in a national birth cohort. *Journal of Epidemiology and Community Health*, **42**: 341–349.

Bradley, R.H., Caldwell, B.M., Fitzgerald, J.A., Morgan, A.G., *et al.* (1986) Experiences in day care and social competence among maltreated children. *Child Abuse and Neglect*, **10**(2): 181–189.

Brassard, M., Germain, R. and Hart, S. (1987) *Psychological maltreatment of children and youth*. Elmsford, NY, Pergamon.

Bridge Child Care Development Service (1995) *Paul: Death through Neglect*. Islington Area Child Protection Committee.

Briere, J. and Runtz, M. (1987) Post sexual abuse trauma: Data and implications for clinical practice. *Journal of Interpersonal Violence*, **2**: 367–379.

Briere, J. and Runtz, M. (1989) University males sexual interest in children: Predicting potential indices of 'Paedophilia' in a nonforensic sample. *Child Abuse and Neglect*, **13**: 65–75.

Briere, J. and Runtz, M. (1990) Differential adult symptomatology associated with three types of child abuse histories. *Child Abuse and Neglect*, **14**: 357–364.

Briere, J. and Zaidi, L.Y. (1989) Sexual abuse histories and sequelae in female psychiatric emergency room patients. *American Journal of Psychiatry*, **146**: 1602–1606.

Bronfenbrenner, U. (1979) *The Experimental Ecology of Human Development*. Cambridge, MA, Harvard University Press.

Brown, C. (1984) *Child abuse parents speaking—parents' impressions of social workers and the social work process*. Working Paper 63, Bristol: School of Advanced Urban Studies.

Brown, K. and Saqi, S. (1989) Approaches to Screening for Child Abuse and Neglect. In Browne, K. *et al.* (eds) *Early Prediction and Prevention of Child Abuse*. Chichester, Wiley.

Brunk, M., Henggeler, S.W. and Whelan, J.P. (1987) Comparison of Multisystemic Therapy and Parent Training in the Brief Treatment of Child Abuse and Neglect. *Journal of Consulting and Clinical Psychology*, **55**(2): 171–178.

Bugental, D.B., Mantyla, S.M. and Lewis, J. (1989) Parental attributions as moderators of affective communication to children at risk for physical abuse. In Rizley, R. and Cicchetti, D. (eds) *Developmental Perspectives on Child Maltreatment*. No. 11, San Francisco, Jossey-Bass.

Burke, M.M. (1988) Short-term group therapy for sexually abused girls: A learning theory based treatment for negative effects. *Dissertation Abstracts International*, **49**: 1935.

Bursik, R.J. and Grasmick, H.G. (1993) *Neighbourhoods and crime*. New York, Lexington.

Bushnell, J.A., Wells, J.E. and Oakley-Brown, M.A. (1992) Long term effects of intrafamilial sexual abuse. *Acta Psychiatrica Scandanavica*, **18**: 136–142.

Butler, I. and Williamson, H. (1994) *Children, Trauma and Social Work*. London: NSPCC/Longman.

Caldwell, B., Heider, J. and Kaplan, B. (1966) *The inventory of home situation*. Paper presented at the annual meeting of the American Psychological Association. New York, September.

Camp, B.H. and Thyer, B.A. (1993) Treatment of adolescent sex offenders: a review of empirical research. *The Journal of Applied Social Sciences*, **17**, 2: 191–206.

Campbell, D.T. and Stanley, J.C. (1973) *Experimental and Quasi-Experimental Designs for Research*. Chicago, Rand McNally College Publishing Company.

Campbell, F.A. and Taylor, K. (1996) Early childhood programmes that work for children from economically disadvantaged families. *Young Children*, **51**(4): 74–80.

Campbell, R.V., O'Brien, S., Bickett, A. and Lutzker, J.R. (1983) In home parent training, treatment of migraine headaches, and marital counseling as an ecobehavioral approach to prevent child abuse. *Journal of Behavior Therapy and Experimental Psychiatry*, **14**: 147–154.

Campbell, S.B. (1995) Behavior problems in preschool children: A review of recent research. *Journal of Child Psychology and Psychiatry*, **36**(1): 113–149.

Cannan, C. and Warren, C. (eds) (1997) *Social action with children and families: A community development approach to child and family welfare*. London, Routledge.

Carlile (1987) *A Child in Mind: Protection of Children in a Responsible Society. The Report of Inquiry into the death of Kimberley Carlile*. London: London Borough of Greenwich.

Carlson, V., Cicchetti, D., Barnett, D. and Brunwald, K.D. (1989) Finding order in disorganisation: lessons from research on maltreated infants' attachments to their caregivers. In Cicchetti, D. and Carlson, V. (eds) *Child Maltreatment: Theory and research on the causes and consequences of child abuse and neglect*, New York, Cambridge University Press.

Carr, A. (1991) Milan systemic family therapy: a review of ten empirical investigations. *Journal of Family Therapy*, **13**: 237–263.

Carroll, L.A., Miltenberger, R.G. and O'Neill, H.K. (1992) A review and critique of research evaluating child sexual abuse prevention programs. *Education and Treatment of Children*, **15**: 335–354.

Carson, D. (1996) Risking legal repercussions. In Kemshall, H. and Pritchard, J. (eds) *Good practice in risk assessment and risk management*, London, Jessica Kingsley Publishers.

Casanova, G.M., Domanic, J., McCanne, T.R. and Milner, J.S. (1992) Physiological responses to non-child-related stressors in mothers at risk for child abuse. *Child Abuse and Neglect*, **16**: 33–44.

Cattell, R.B. (1965) *The Scientific Analysis of Personality*. Baltimore, Md, Penguin.

Cautley, P.W. (1980) Treating Dysfunctional Families at Home, *Social Work*, **25**: (5), 380–386.

Cedar, B. and Levant, R.F. (1990) A meta-analysis of the effects of parent effectiveness training. *American Journal of Family Therapy*, **18**: 373–384.

Chess, S. and Thomas, T. (1990) Continuities and discontinuities in temperament. In Robins, L. and Rutter, M. (eds) *Straight and devious pathways from childhood to adulthood*. Cambridge, Cambridge University Press.

Chilamkurti, C. and Milner, J.S. (1993) Perceptions and evaluations of child transgressions and disciplinary techniques in high- and low-risk mothers and their children. *Child Development*, **64**: 1801–1814.

Cicchetti, D. and Rizley, R. (1981) Developmental perspectives on the etiology, intergenerational transmission, and sequelae of child maltreatment. *New directions for Child Development*, **11**: 31–55.

Cicchetti, D. and Toth, S.L. (1995) A developmental psychopathology perspective on child abuse and neglect. *Journal of the American Academy of Child and Adolescent Psychiatry*, **34**: 541–565.

Cicchetti, D. and Toth, S.L. (1997) Transactional ecological systems in developmental psychopathology. In Luthar, S.S., Burack, J.A., Cicchetti, D. and Weisz., J.R. (eds) *Developmental Psychopathology: Perspectives on adjustment, risk, and disorder*, New York, Cambridge University Press.

Cicchetti, D. and Rogosch, M.L. (1997) The role of self-organization in the promotion of resilience in maltreated children: Processes leading to adaptive outcomes. *Development and Psychopathology*, 9: 797–815.

Cicchetti, D., Rogosch, M.L. and Holt, K.D. (1993) Resilience in maltreated children: Processes leading to adaptive outcome. *Development and Psychopathology*, 5: 626–647.

Claussen, A.H. and Crittenden, P.M. (1991) Physical and psychological maltreatment: relations among the types of maltreatment. *Child Abuse and Neglect*, 15(12): 5–18.

Clément, M.-E. and Tourginy, M. (1997) A review of the literature on the prevention of child abuse and neglect: characteristics and effectiveness of home visiting programs. *International Journal of Child and Family Welfare*, 1: 6–20.

The Cochrane Library. Oxford, Update Software, Updated quarterly.

Cohen, J.A. and Mannarino, A.P. (1993) A treatment outcome study for sexually abused preschoolers. *Journal of Interpersonal Violence*, 8: 115–131.

Cohen, J.A. and Mannarino, A.P. (1996) A treatment outcome study for sexually abused preschool children: Initial findings. *Journal of the American Academy of Child and Adolescent Psychiatry*, 35: 42–50.

Cohler, B., Weiss, J. and Greenbaum, H. (1970) Child care attitude and emotional disturbance among mothers of young children. *Genetic Psychology Monographs*, 82, 3–47.

Cohn, A.H. (1986) Preventing adults from becoming sexual molesters. *Child Abuse and Neglect*, 10: 559–562.

Cole, P.M, Woolgar, C., Power, T.G. and Smith, K.D. (1992) Parenting difficulties among adult survivors of father–daughter incest. *Child Abuse and Neglect*, 16: 239–249.

Combs-Orme, T., Reis, J. and Ward, L.D. (1985) Effectiveness of home visits by public health nurses in maternal and child health: An empirical review. *Public Health Reports*, 100: 490–499.

Comprehensive Child Development Program (CCDP) (1988) *http://www.acf.dhhs.gov/programs/rde/ccdp_inf.htm*

Connell, J.P., Kubisch, A.C., Schorr, L.B. and Weiss, C.H. (eds) (1996) *New Approaches to Evaluating Comprehensive Community Initiatives: Concepts, Methods, and Contexts*, Queenstown, The Aspen Institute.

Conte, J.R. (1985) Clinical dimensions of adult sexual abuse of children analysis. *Behavioral Sciences and the Law*, 3: 341–354.

Conte, J.R. (1991) Nature of sex offences against children. In Hollin, C.R. and Howells, K. (eds) *Clinical Approaches to Sex Offenders and their Victims*. Chichester, John Wiley.

Conte, J.R. and Schuerman, J.R. (1987) Factors associated with an increased impact of child sexual abuse. *Child Abuse and Neglect*, 11: 201–212.

Coohey, C. (1996) Child maltreatment: Testing the social isolation hypothesis. *Child Abuse and Neglect*, 20(3): 241–254.

Corder, B.F., Haizlip, D. and Deboer, P (1990) A pilot study for a structured, time limited therapy group for sexually abused pre-adolescent children. *Child Abuse and Neglect*, 14: 243–251.

Coulton, C.J., Korbin, J.E., Su, M and Chow, J. (1995) Community level factors and child maltreatment rates. *Child Development*, 66: 1262–1276.

Cousins, P.S., Fischer, J., Glisson, C. and Kameika, V. (1986) The effects of physical attractiveness and verbal expressiveness on clinical judgements. *Journal of Social Services Research*, **8**(4): 59–74.

Crimmins, D.B., Bradlyn, A.S., St Lawrence, J.S. and Kelly, J.A. (1984) A training technique for improving the parent-child interaction skills of an abusive-neglectful mother. *Child Abuse and Neglect*, **8**: 533–539.

Critical Appraisal Skills Project Report (1999) Available from the Centre for Evidence-Based Social Services, University of Exeter.

Crittenden, P.M. and Ainsworth, M.D.S. (1989) Child maltreatment and attachment theory. In Cicchetti, D. and Carlson, V. (eds) *Child Maltreatment: Theory and research on the causes and consequences of child abuse and neglect*, New York, Cambridge University Press.

Crittenden, P.M. (1981) Abusing, neglecting, problematic, and adequate dyads: Differentiating by patterns of interaction. *Merrill-Palmer Quarterly*, **27**: 201–208.

Crittenden, P.M. (1985) Social networks, quality of parenting, and child development. *Child Development*, **56**: 1299–1313.

Crittenden, P.M. (1988a) Family and Dyadic patterns of functioning in maltreating families. In Browne, K. and Stratton, P. (eds) *Early prediction and prevention of child abuse*, New York, John Wiley.

Crittenden, P.M. (1988b) Relationships at risk. In Belsky, J. and Nezworski, T. (eds) *The clinical implications of attachment*, Hillsdale, MJ, Lawrence Erlbaum.

Crittenden, P.M. (1992) Children's strategies for coping with adverse home environments: An interoperation using attachment theory. *Child Abuse and Neglect*, **16**(3): 329–343.

Crittenden, P.M. (1993) An information processing perspective on the behavior of neglectful parents. *Criminal Justice and Behavior*, **20**(1): 27–48.

Crittenden, P. (1993/4) *Child neglect*. Chicago: National Committee for the Prevention of Child Abuse.

Crittenden, P.M. (1996) Research on maltreating families: Implications for intervention. In Briere, J., Berliner, L., Bulkley, J.A., Jenny, C. and Reid, T. *APSAC Handbook of child maltreatment*, Thousand Oaks, CA, Sage.

Crittenden, P.M. (1998) Dangerous behavior and dangerous contexts: A 35 year perspective on research on the developmental effects of child physical abuse. In Trickett, P.K., Schellenbach, C.J. et al. (eds) *Violence against children in the family and the community*, Washington DC, American Psychological Association.

Crittenden, P.M. (1999) Child Neglect: Causes and Contributions. In Dubowitz, H. (ed) *Neglected Children: Research, Practice and Policy*, Thousand Oaks, Sage.

Crittenden, P.M., Claussen, A.H. and Sugarman, D.B. (1994) Physical and psychological maltreatment in middle childhood and adolescence. *Development and Psychopathology*, **6**: 145–164.

Crouch, J.L. and Milner, J.S. (1993) Effects of child neglect on children. *Criminal Justice and Behavior*, **20**(1): 49–65.

Culp, R.E., Heide, J. and Richardson, M.T. (1987a) Maltreated Children's Developmental Scores: Treatment versus Nontreatment. *Child Abuse and Neglect*, **11**: 29–34.

Culp, R.E., Little, V., Letts, D., Lawrence, H. (1991) Maltreated children's self-concept: Effects of a comprehensive treatment program. *American Journal of Orthopsychiatry*, **61**: 114–121.

Culp, R.E., Richardson, M.P and Heide, J. (1987b) Differential developmental progress of maltreated children in day treatment. *Social Work*, November–December, 497–499.

Cutler, P. (1979) *Problem solving in clinical medicine*, Baltimore, Williams and Wilkins.

Dachman, R.S., Halasz, M.M., Bickett, A.D. and Lutzker, J.R. (1984) A home-based ecobehavioral parent-training and generalization package with a neglectful mother. *Education and Treatment of Children*, **7**: 183–202.

Daro, D. (1988) *Confronting Child Abuse*. New York Free Press, New York.

Daro, D. (1996) Preventing child abuse and neglect. In Briere, J., Berliner, L., Bulkley, J.A., Jenny, C. and Reid, T. (eds) *The APSAC Handbook on Child Maltreatment*, Thousand Oaks, Sage.

Davey-Smith, G. and Egger, M. (1986) Commentary: Understanding it all—health meta-theories and mortality trends. *BMJ*, **313**: 1584–1585.

Davies, M.G. (1995) Parental distress and ability to cope following disclosure of extra-familial sexual abuse. *Child Abuse and Neglect*,**19**: 399–408.

Davis, F.P. and Fantuzzo, J.W. (1989) The effects of adult and peer social initiations on the social behavior of withdrawn and aggressive maltreated pre-school children. *Journal of Family Violence*, **4**: 227–248.

Davis, G.E. and Leitenberg, H. (1987) Adolescent sex offenders. *Psychological Bulletin*, **101**: 417–427.

Dawes, R.M. and Corrigan, G. (1974) Linear models in decision-making. *Psychological Bulletin*, **81**: 95–106.

Deblinger, E., Lippman, J.T. and Steer, R. (1996) Sexually abused children suffering post-traumatic stress symptoms: Initial treatment outcomes findings. *Child Maltreatment*, **4**, 1, 13–20.

Deblinger, E., McCleer, S.V., Atkins, M.S., Ralphe, D. and Foe, E. (1989) Post-traumatic stress in sexually abused, physically abused, and nonabused children. *Child Abuse and Neglect*, **13**: 403–408.

Dempster, H.L., and Roberts, J. (1991) Child sexual abuse research: A methodological quagmire. *Child Abuse and Neglect*, **15**(4): 593–595.

DePanfilis, D. (1996) Social isolation of neglectful families: A review of social support assessment and intervention models. *Child Maltreatment*, **1**: 37–52.

Department of Health (1988) *Protecting Children: A Guide for Social Workers Undertaking a Comprehensive Assessment*. London, HMSO.

Department of Health (1991) *Child Abuse: A study of inquiry reports 1980–1989*. London HMSO.

Department of Health (1995) *Child Protection: Messages from Research*. London, HMSO.

Department of Health, Home Office, Department for Education and Employment (1999) *Working Together to Safeguard Children: A guide to inter-agency working to safeguard and promote the welfare of children*. London, The Stationery Office.

Department of Health, Department for Education and Employment, Home Office (2000) *Framework for the Assessment of Children in Need and their Families*. London, The Stationery Office.

Dickersin, K., Scherer, R. and Lefebvre, C. (1995) Identifying relevant studies for systematic review. In Chalmers, I. and Altman, D.G. (eds) *Systematic Reviews*, Plymouth, BMJ Publishing Group.

Dingwall, R. (1989) Some problems about predicting child abuse and neglect. In Stevenson, O. (ed.) *Child Abuse: Professional practice and public policy*. Harvester Wheatsheaf, London.

Dix, T. (1991) The affective organization of parenting: Adaptive and maladaptive processes. *Psychological Bulletin*, **110**(1): 3–25.

Dix, T.H., Ruble, D.N. and Zambarano, R.J. (1989) Mothers' implicit theories of discipline: Child effects, parent effects, and the attribution process. *Child Development,* **60**: 1373–1391.

Dobash, R.E. and Dobash, R.P. (1992) *Women, violence and social change.* New York, Routledge.

Donohue, B. and Van Hasselt, V.B. (1999) Development and description of an empirically based ecobehavioural treatment program for child maltreatment. *Behavioral Interventions,* **14**: 55–82.

Douglas, J.W.B. (1986) *The home and the school.* London, MacGibbon and Kee.

Dowdney, L., Skuse, D., Rutter, M., Quinton, D. and Mrazek, D. (1985) The nature and qualities of parenting provided by women raised in institutions. *Journal of Child Psychology and Psychiatry,* **28**: 599–625.

Drake, B. and Pandey, S. (1996) Neighbourhood poverty and child maltreatment. *Child Abuse and Neglect* **20**(11): 1003–1018.

Drotar, D., Eckerle, D., Satola, J., Pallotta, J. and Wyatt, B. (1990) Maternal interactional behavior with nonorganic failure-to-thrive infants: a case comparison study. *Child Abuse and Neglect,* **14**: 41–51.

Dubowitz, H., Black, M., Starr, R.J. and Zuravin, S. (1993) *Intra-family and extra-family factors associated with child neglect: Final report.* (NCCAN Grant #90–CA-1431). Morganton, NS, Western Carolina Center.

Duerr-Berrick, J. and Duerr, M. (1997) Preventing Child Neglect: A Study of an In-Home Program for Children and Families. In Berrick, J.D., Barth, R. and Gilbert, N. (eds) *Child Welfare Research Review: Volume Two.* New York, Cambridge University Press.

Dumas, J.E. and Wahler, R.G. (1983) Predictors of treatment outcome in parent training: Mother insularity and socioeconomic disadvantage. *Behavior Assessment,* **5**: 301–313.

Duncan, A., Giles, C. and Webb. S. (1995) *The impact of subsidising childcare.* London, Equal Opportunities Commission.

Dyson, L.L. (1991) Families of young children with handicaps: Parental stress and family functioning. *American Journal on Mental Retardation,* **95**: 623–629.

Eckenrode, J., Laird, M. and Doris, J. (1993) School performance and disciplinary problems among abused and neglected children. *Developmental Psychology,* **29**: 53–62.

Eckman, P. (1992) Facial expressions of emotion: New findings, new questions. *Psychological Science,* **3**: 34–38.

Edgington, A., Hall, M., Rosser, R.S. (1980) Neglectful Families: Measurement of treatment outcome. Paper presented at *Tri-regional Workshop for Social Workers in Maternal and Child Health.* Raleigh, NC, USA.

Edleson, J. (1999) The Overlap Between Child Maltreatment and Women Battering. *Violence Against Women,* **5**(2): 134–154.

Egan, K. (1983) Stress management with abusive parents. *Journal of Clinical Child Psychology,* **12**: 292–299.

Egeland, B. and Brunnquell, D. (1979) An at-risk approach to the study of child abuse: Some preliminary findings. *Journal of the American Academy of Child Psychiatry,* **18**: 219–235.

Egeland, B. and Erickson, M.F. (1987) Psychologically unavailable caregiving. In Brassard, M.R., Germain, R. and Hart, S.N. (eds) *Psychological maltreatment of children and youth,* Elmsford, NY, Pergamon.

Egeland, B. and Sroufe, A. (1981) Developmental sequelae of maltreatment in infancy. In Risley, R. and Cichetti D.R. (eds) *New Directions for Child Development.* San Francisco, Jossey Bass.

Egeland, B., Jacobvitz, D. and Papatola, K. (1984) *Intergenerational continuity of parental abuse.* Proceedings from Conference on Biosocial Perspectives on Child Abuse and Neglect, Social Science Research Council, York, ME, May 20–23.

Egeland, B., Sroufe, L.A. and Erickson, M. (1983) The developmental consequences of different patterns of maltreatment. *Child Abuse and Neglect,* **7**: 459–469.

Elder, G.H. (1974) *Children of the Great Depression,* Chicago, The University of Chicago Press.

Elwood, P. (1997) Cochrane and the benefits of Asprin. In Maynard, A. and Chalmers, I. (eds) Non random reflections on health services research. On the 25th Anniversary of Archie Cochrane's *Effectiveness and Efficiency,* Plymouth, BMJ Publishing Group.

Emery, R.E. (1989) Family violence. *American Psychologist,* **44**: 321–328.

English, D. (1995) Risk Assessment: What do we know? Findings from three research studies on children reported to child protective services. In E. Wattenberg (ed) *Children in the shadows: the fact of children neglecting families.* Minneapolis, University of Minnesota Press.

Epps, K. (1999) Looking after young sexual abusers: child protection, risk management and risk reduction. In Erooga, M. and Masson, H. (eds) *Children and Young People Who Sexually Abuse Others,* London, Routledge.

Erickson, M.F. and Egeland, B. (1987) A developmental view of the psychological consequences of maltreatment. *School Psychology Review,* **16**: 156–168.

Erickson, M.F. and Egeland, B. (1996) Child Neglect. In Briere, J., Berliner, L., Bulkley, J.A., Jenny, C. and Reid, T. (eds) *The APSAC Handbook on Child Maltreatment,* Thousand Oaks, Sage.

Erickson, M.F., Egeland, B. and Pianta, R. (1989) The effects of maltreatment on the development of young children. In Cicchetti, D. and Carlson, V. (eds) *Child Maltreatment: Theory and research on the causes and consequences of child abuse and neglect.* New York, Cambridge University Press.

Erooga, M. and Masson, H. (1999) (eds) *Children and Young People who Sexually Abuse Others,* London, Routledge.

Everson, M.D., Hunter, W.M., Runyan, D.K., Edelsohn, G.A. and Coulter, M.L. (1989) Maternal support following disclosure of incest. *American Journal of Orthopsychiatry,* **59**: 197–207.

Fahlberg, V. I. (1991) *A Child's Journey through Placement,* UK Edition, London, British Agencies for Adoption and Fostering.

Famularo, R., Kinscherff, R. and Fenton, T. (1992) Psychiatric diagnoses of maltreated children: Preliminary findings. *Journal of the American Academy of Child and Adolescent Psychiatry,* **31**: 863–867.

Fantuzzo, J., Sutton-Smith, B., Meyers, R., Atkins, M., Stevenson, H., Coolahan, K., Weiss, A. and Manz, P. (1996) Community based resilient peer treatment of withdrawn maltreated preschool children. *Journal of Consulting and Clinical Psychology,* **64**(6): 1377–1386.

Fantuzzo, J., Weiss, D.A. and Coolahan, K.C. (1997) Community-based partnership directed research: Actualising community strengths to treat child victims of physical abuse and neglect. In Lutzker, J.R. (ed.) *Handbook of Child Abuse Research and Treatment,* New York, Plenum Press.

Fantuzzo, J.W. (1990) Behavioral treatment of the victims of child abuse and neglect. *Behavior Modification* **14**: 316–339.

Fantuzzo, J.W. and Twentyman, C.T. (1986) Child abuse and psychotherapy research: merging social concerns and empirical investigation. *Professional Psychology: Research and Practice,* **17**: 375–380.

Fantuzzo, J.W., DePaola, L.M., Lambert, L., Martino, T., Anderson, G. and Sutton. S.

(1991) Effects of Interparental violence on the psychological adjustment and competencies of young children. *Journal of Consulting and Clinical Psychology*, **59**: 258–265.

Fantuzzo, J.W., Jurecic, L., Stovall, A., Hightower, A.D., Goins, C. and Schachtel, D. (1988) Effects of adult and peer social initiations on the social behavior of withdrawn, maltreated preschool children. *Journal of Consulting and Clinical Psychology*, **56**: 34–39.

Fantuzzo, J.W., Stovall, A., Schachtel, D., Coins, C. and Hall, R. (1987) The effects of peer social initiations on the social behavior of withdrawn maltreated preschool children. *Journal of Behavior Therapy and Experimental Psychology*, **18**: 357–363.

Farrington, D.P. (1996) Criminological Psychology: Individual and Family Factors in the Explanation and Prevention of Offending. In Hollin, C.R. (ed.) *Working with Offenders; Psychological practice in offender rehabilitation*, Chichester, John Wiley.

Faust, J., Runyon, M.K. and Kenny, M.C. (1995) Family variables associated with the onset and impact of intrafamilial childhood sexual abuse. *Clinical Psychology Review*, **15**: 443–456.

Feiring, C. (1995) Concept of romance in 15 year old adolescents. *Journal of Research on Adolescence*, **6**(2): 181–200.

Feldman, M. and Walton-Allen, N. (1997) Effects of maternal mental retardation and poverty on intellectual, academic, and behavioral status of school-age children. *American Journal on Mental Retardation*, **101**: 352–364.

Feldman, M.A. (1998) Parents with Intellectual Disabilities: Implications and interventions. In Lutzker, J.R. (ed.) *Handbook of Child Abuse Research and Treatment* New York, Plenum Press.

Feldman, M.A. Case, L., Rincover, A., Towns, F. and Betel, J. (1989a) Parent education project 111. Increasing affection and responsivity in developmentally handicapped mothers: Component analysis, generalisation, and effects on child language. *Journal of Applied Behavior Analysis*, **22**: 211–222.

Feldman, M.A. Case, L., Towns, F. and Betel, J. (1989b) Parent education project 1: Development and nurturance of children of mentally retarded parents. *American Journal of Mental Deficiency*, **90**: 253–258.

Feldman, M.A. Leger, M. and Walton-Allen, N. (1997) Stress in mothers with intellectual disabilities. *Journal of Child and Family Studies*, **6**(4): 471–485.

Feldman, M.A., Case, L. and Sparks, B. (1992a) Effectiveness of a child-care training program for parents at-risk for child neglect. *Canadian Journal of Behavioral Science*, **24**: 14–28.

Feldman, M.A., Case, L., Garrick, M., MacIntyre-Grande, W., Carnwell, J. and Sparks, B. (1992b) Teaching child care skills to parents with developmental disabilities. *Journal of Applied Behavior Analysis*, **25**: 205–215.

Feldman, M.A., Sparks, B. and Case, L. (1993) Effectiveness of home-based early intervention on the language development of children of mothers with mental retardation. *Research in Developmental Disabilities*, **14**: 387–408.

Fergusson, D.M. and Mullen, P.E. (1999) *Childhood Sexual Abuse: An evidence based perspective*, Thousand Oaks, Sage.

Fergusson, D.M., Horwood, L.J. and Lyunskey, M.T. (1996) The role of adolescent peer affiliations in the continuity between childhood behavioral adjustment and juvenile offending. *Journal of Abnormal Child Psychology*, **24**: 205–221.

Ferri, E. (1993) *Life at 33: The Fifth Follow-up of the National Child Development Survey*, London, National Children's Bureau and City University.

Feshbach, N.D. and Feschbach, S. (1982) Empathy training and the regulation of aggression: Potentialities and limitations. *Academic Psychology Bulletin*, **4**: 399–413.

Fink, A. and McCloskey, L. (1990) Moving Child Abuse and Neglect Prevention Programs Forward: Improving Program Evaluations. *Child Abuse and Neglect*, **14**: 187–206.

Finkelhor, D. (1980) Risk factors in the sexual victimisation of children. *Child Abuse and Neglect*, **4**: 265–273.

Finkelhor, D. (1984) *Child Sexual Abuse: New Theory and Research*. New York, Free Press.

Finkelhor, D. (1990) Early and long-term effects of child sexual abuse: An update. *Professional Psychology: Research and Practice*, **21**: 325–330.

Finkelhor, D. (1995) The victimization of children: A developmental perspective. *American Journal of Orthopsychiatry*, **65**: 177–193.

Finkelhor, D. and Berliner, L. (1995) Research on the treatment of sexually abused children: A review and recommendations. *Journal of the American Academy of Child and Adolescent Psychiatry*, **34**: 1408–1423.

Finkelhor, D. and Dziuba-Leatherman, J. (1995) Victimization prevention programs: A national survey of children's exposure and reactions. *Child Abuse and Neglect*, **19**: 129–139.

Finkelhor, D. and Strapko, N. (1992) Sexual abuse prevention education: A review of evaluation studies. In Willis, D.J., Holden, E.W. and Rosenberg, M. (eds) *Prevention of child maltreatment*, New York, Wiley.

Finkelhor, D., Hotaling, G., Lewis, I. and Smith, C. (1990) Sexual abuse in a national study of adult men and women: Prevalence, characteristics and risk factors. *Child Abuse and Neglect*, **14**: 19–28.

Fisher, D. (1994) Adult sex offenders: who are they? Why and how do they do it? In Morrison, T., Erooga, M. and Beckett, R.L. (eds) *Sexual Offending Against Children: Assessment and Treatment of Male Abusers*, London, Routledge.

Fisher, D. (1998) *The treatment of sex offenders who target children*. PhD Thesis, University of Birmingham.

Fisher, D. and Beech, A. (1998) Reconstituting Families after Sexual Abuse: The Offender's Perspective. *Child Abuse Review*, **7**: 420–434.

Fisher, D. and Maier, G. (1998) A review of classification systems for sex offenders. *Home Office Research and Statistics Directorate Research Findings*, **78**: 1–4.

Fisher, D. and Thornton, D. (1993) Assessing risk of re-offending in sexual offenders. *Journal of Mental Health* **2**: 105–117.

Fitzgerald, J. (1998) Policy and Practice in Child Protection: Its Relationship to Dangerousness. In R.J. Dent (ed.) *Dangerous Care: Working to Protect Children*. London, The Bridge Child Care Development Service.

Fleming, J., Mullen, P.E. and Bammer, G. (1997) A study of potential risk factors for sexual abuse in childhood. *Child Abuse and Neglect*, **21**: 49–58.

Fleming, J., Mullen, P.E., Sibthorpe, B. and Bammer, G. (1999) The Long-Term Impact of Childhood Sexual Abuse in Australian Women. *Child Abuse and Neglect*, **23**(2): 145–160.

Flor-Henry, P., Lang, R.A., Koles, Z.J. and Frenzel, R.R. (1991) Quantitative EEG studies of paedophilia. *International Journal of Psychophysiology*, **10**: 253–258.

Fonagy, P., Steele, M., Steele, H., Higgit, A. and Target, M. (1994) The Emanuel Miller Memorial Lecture 1992: The theory and practice of resilience. *Journal of Child Psychology and Psychiatry*, **35**(2): 231–257.

Fox, L., Long, S. and Langlois, A. (1988) Patterns of language comprehension deficit in abused and neglected children. *Journal of Speech and Hearing Disorders*, **53**: 239–244.

Fraenkel, P., Schoen, S., Perko, K., Mendelson, T., Kusher, S., Islam, S., Coxon, L.

and Baird Taylor, D. (1998) The Family Speaks: Family Members' Descriptions of Therapy for Sexual Abuse. *Journal of Systemic Therapies*.

Franklin, D.L. (1986) Does client social class affect clinical judgement? *Social Casework*, **67**: 424–432.

Freund, K., Watson, R.J. and Diceky, R. (1990) Does sexual abuse in childhood cause pedophilia: An exploratory study. *Archives of Sexual Behavior*, **19**: 557–568.

Friedrich, W.N. (ed.) (1990) *Psychotherapy of sexually abused children and their families*. New York, Norton.

Friedrich, W.N. (1991) *Casebook of sexual abuse treatment*. New York, Norton.

Friedrich, W.N. (1993) Sexual victimization and sexual behavior in children: A review of the recent literature. *Child Abuse and Neglect*, **17**: 59–66.

Friedrich, W.N., Beilke, R.L. and Urquiza, A. (1987) Children from sexually abusive families: A behavioral comparison. *Journal of Interpersonal Violence*, **2**: 391–402.

Friedrich, W.N., Luecke, W.J., Belke, R.L. and Place, V. (1992) Psychotherapy outcomes of sexually abused boys: An agency study. *Journal of Interpersonal Violence*, **7**: 396–409.

Fromuth, M. and Burkhart, B. (1987) Childhood Sexual Victimisation Among College Men: Definitional and Methodological Issues. *Violence and Victims*, **2**(4): 241–253.

Fryer, Jr. G.E., Kraizer, S.K. and Miyoshi, T. (1987a) Measuring actual reduction of risk to child abuse: a new approach. *Child Abuse and Neglect*, **11**: 173–179.

Fryer, Jr. G.E., Kraizer, S.K. and Miyoshi, T. (1987b) Measuring children's retention of skills to resist stranger abduction: use of the simulation technique. *Child Abuse and Neglect*, **11**: 181–185.

Furby, L., Weinrott, M.R. and Blackshaw, L. (1989) Sex offender recidivism: A review. *Psychological Bulletin*, **105**: 3–30.

Gabel, S., Swanson, A.J. and Schindledecker, R. (1990) Aggressive children in a day treatment program: Changed outcome and possible explanations. *Child Abuse and Neglect*, **14**: 515–523.

Gabel, S., Finn, M. and Ahmad, A. (1988) Day treatment outcome with severely disturbed children. *American Academy of Child and Adolescent Psychiatry*, **27**: 479–482.

Gaensbauer, T.J. and Hiatt, S. (1984) Facial communication of emotion in early infancy. In Fox, N. and Davidson, R. (eds) *The psychobiology of affective development*. Hillsdale, NJ, Erlbaum.

Gambrill, E. (1989) Behavioral family therapy with child abuse and neglect. In Thyer, B.A. (ed.) *Behavioral Family Therapy*. Springfield, Ill., Charles C. Thomas.

Gambrill, E. (1997) *Social Work Practice A Critical Thinker's Guide*. New York, Oxford University Press.

Garbarino, J. (1986) Can we measure success in preventing child abuse? Issues in policy, programming and research. *Child Abuse and Neglect*, **14**: 187–206.

Garbarino, J. (1991) Not all developmental outcomes are the result of child abuse. *Developmental Psychopathology*, **3**: 45–50.

Garbarino, J. (ed) (1992) *Children and Families in the Social Environment*, Second edition. New York, Aldine de Gruyter.

Garbarino, J. and Kostelny, K. (1992) Child maltreatment as a community problem. *International Journal of Child Abuse and Neglect*, **16**(4): 455–464.

Garbarino, J. and Kostelny, K. (1993) Neighbourhood and community influences on parenting. In Luster, T. and Okagaki, L. (eds) *Parenting: An Ecological Perspective*. Hillsdale NJ.: Lawrence Erlbaum Associates, Inc.

Garbarino, J. and Long, F.N. (1992) Developmental Issues in the Human Services. In

Garbarino, J. (ed.) *Children and Families in the Social Environment.* Second edition. New York, Aldine de Gruyter.

Garbarino, J. and Sherman, D. (1980) High risk neighbourhoods and high-risk families: The human ecology of child maltreatment. *Child Development,* **51**: 188–198.

Garbarino, J. and Vondra, J. (1987) Psychological maltreatment: Issues and perspectives. In Brassard, M.R., Germain, R. and Hart, S.N. (eds) *Psychological maltreatment of children and youth,* New York, Pergamon Press.

Garbarino, J., Guttman, E. and Seeley, J.A. (1996) *The psychologically battered child.* San Francisco, Jossey Bass.

Garbarino, K. and Stott, F.M. (1992) *What children can tell us: Eliciting, interpreting and evaluating critical information from children,* San Francisco, Jossey Bass.

Garrison, E.G. (1987) Psychological maltreatment of children: An emerging focus for inquiry and concern. *American Psychologist,* **42**(2): 157–159.

Gaudin, J. (1993) Effective interventions with neglectful families. *Criminal Justice and Behavior,* **20**: 66–89.

Gaudin, J.M., Polansky, N.A., Kilpatrick, A.C. and Shilton, P. (1996) Family functioning in neglectful families. *Child Abuse and Neglect,* **20**(4): 363–377.

Gaudin, J., Wodarski, J.S., Arkinson, M.K. and Avery, L.S. (1990–1991) Remedying child neglect: effectiveness of social network interventions. *Journal of Applied Social Sciences,* **15**: 97–123.

Gaudin, J.M. and Dubowitz, H. (1997) Family functioning in neglectful families. In Berrick, J.D., Barth, R. and Gilbert, N. (eds) *Child Welfare Research Review: Volume Two,* New York, Cambridge University Press.

Gelles, R.J. (1987) *Family Violence,* Newbury Park, Sage.

Gelles, R.J. (1991) Physical violence, child abuse, and child homicide: A continuum of violence or distinct behaviors? *Human Nature,* **2**: 59–72.

Gelles, R.J. (1992) Poverty and violence toward children. *American Behavioural Scientists,* **35**: 258–264.

Gelles, R.J. (1997) *Intimate Violence in Families.* (3rd edition) Thousand Oaks, CA, Sage.

Gelles, R.J. and Cornell, C.P. (1985, 1990) *Intimate Violence in Families,* Newbury Park, CA, Sage.

Gelles, R.J. and Straus, M.A. (1990) The medical and psychological costs of family violence. In Straus, M.A. and Gelles, R.J. (eds) *Physical violence in American families: Risk factors and adaptations to violence in 8,145 families,* New Brunswick, NJ, Transaction Books.

Gendreau, P. (1996) Offender rehabilitation: What we know and what needs to be done. *Criminal Justice and Behaviour,* **23**: 144–161.

George, C. (1997) A representational perspective of child abuse and prevention: internal working models of attachment and caregiving. *Child Abuse and Neglect,* **20**(5): 411–424.

Gibbons, J., Conroy, S. and Bell, C. (1995) *Operating the Child Protection System: A Study of Child Protection Practices in English Local Authorities,* London, HMSO.

Gibbs, L. (1991) *Scientific Reasoning for Social Workers: Bridging the Gap Between Research and Practice,* New York, Macmillan.

Gibbs, L. and Gambrill, E. (1996; 1999) *Critical Thinking for Social Workers: Exercises for the helping professions,* Thousand Oaks, Ca. Pine Forge Press.

Gigerenzer, G., Todd, P.M. and the ABC Research Group (1999) *Simple Heuristics That Make Us Smart,* New York, Oxford University Press.

Giovannoni, J.M. (1989) Definitional issues in child maltreatment. In Cicchetti, D. and Carlson, V. (eds) *Child Maltreatment: Theory and research on the causes and consequences of child abuse and neglect,* New York, Cambridge University Press.

Giovannoni, J.M. and Beccera, R.M. (1979) *Defining child abuse.* New York, Free Press.

Girshick, L.B. (1993) Teen dating violence. *Violence Update,* **3**: 1–2, 4, 6.

Glaser, D. (1993) Emotional Abuse. In Hobbs, C.J. and Wynne, J.M. (eds) *Clinical Paediatrics: Child Abuse,* London, Balliere Tindall.

Glaser, D. (2000) Child Abuse and Neglect and the Brain – A Review. *Journal of Child Psychology and Psychiatry and Allied Professions,* **41,1**: 97–116.

Glaser, D. and Prior, V. (1997) Is the term child protection applicable to emotional abuse? *Child Abuse Review,* **6**(5): 315–329.

Goldfried, M.R. and Robins, C. (1982) On the facilitation of self-efficacy. *Counselling Therapy and Research ,* **6**(4): 361–379.

Goldfried, M.R. and Robins, C. (1983) Self-schema, cognitive bias, and the processing of therapeutic experiences. In P.C. Kendall (ed.) *Advances in cognitive-behavioral research and therapy,* Vol. 2 (35–50) New York, Academic Press.

Golding, J. (1990) Children of the Nineties: A Longitudinal Study of Pregnancy and Childhood Based on the Population of Avon (ALSPAC). *West of England Medical Journal,* **105** (iii) September, 80–82.

Goodman, G.S., Taub, E.P., Jones, D.P.H., England, P., Port, L.K., Ruby, L. and Prado, L. (1992) Testifying in criminal courts: Emotional effects of criminal court in child sexual assault. *Monograph of the Society for Research in Child Development,* **57**: Chicago, University of Chicago Press.

Gordon, D. and Loughran, F. (1997) Child poverty and needs-based budget allocation. *Research, Policy and Planning,* **15**(3): 28–38.

Gorey, K.M. and Leslie, D.R. (1997) The prevalence of child sexual abuse: integrative review adjustment of potential response and measurement bias. *Child Abuse and Neglect,* **21**(4): 391–398.

Gough, R. (1993). *Child Abuse Interventions.* Public Health Research Unit, University of Glasgow, HMSO.

Gowan, J. (1993) *Effects of neglect on the early development of children: Final report.* Washington, DC, National Clearinghouse on Child Abuse and Neglect, National Center on Child Abuse and Neglect, Administration for Children and Families.

Gracia, E. (1995) Visible but unreported: A case for the 'not serious enough' cases of child maltreatment. *Child Abuse and Neglect,* **19**(9): 1083–1093.

Gray, J.D., Cutler, C.A., Dean, J.G. and Kempe, C.H. (1979a) Prediction and prevention of child abuse. *Seminars in Perinatology,* **3**: 85–90.

Gray, J.D., Cutler, C.A., Dean, J.G. and Kempe, C.H. (1979b) Prediction and prevention of child abuse and neglect. *Journal of Social Issues,* **35**: 127–139.

Green, A.H. (1981) Core affective disturbance in abused children. *Journal of the American Academy of Psychoanalysis,* **9**: 435–446.

Green, A.H. (1983) Dimension of psychological trauma in abused children. *Journal of the American Academy of Child Psychiatry,* **22**: 231–237.

Green, A.H. (1993) Child sexual abuse: Immediate and long-term effects and intervention. *Journal of the American Academy of Child and Adolescent Psychiatry,* **32**: 890–902.

Greenwald, E., Leitenberg, H., Cado, S. and Tarran, M.J. (1990). Childhood sexual abuse: Long-term effects on psychological and sexual functioning in a nonclinical nonstudent sample of adult women. *Child Abuse and Neglect,* **14**: 503–513.

Gregory, R.L. (1966) *Eye and Brain,* New York, McGraw-Hill.

Gregory, R.L. (1970) *The Intelligent Eye,* London, Weidenfeld and Nicolson.

Gribbens, M. (1992) *What the Mums Say,* Belfast, Barnardo's.

Griest, D.L. and Forehand, R. (1982) How can I get any parent training done with all these other problems going on?: The role of family variables in child behavior therapy. *Child and Family Behavior Therapy*, **4**(1): 73–80.

Griest, D.L. and Wells, K.C. (1983) Behavioral family therapy with conduct disorders in children. *Behavior Therapy*, **14**: 38–43.

Griest, D.L, Forehand, R., Wells, K.C. and McMahon, R.J. (1980) An examination of differences between non-clinic and behavior-problem clinic-referred children and their mothers. *Journal of Abnormal Psychology*, **89**: 497–500.

Groth, A.N. (1982) The incest offender. In Sgroi, S.M. (ed.) *Handbook of clinical intervention in child sexual abuse*, Lexington, MA, Health and Company.

Guterman, N.B. (1997) Early prevention of physical child abuse and neglect: Existing evidence and future directions. *Child Maltreatment*, **2**: 12–34.

Guterman, N.B. (1999) Enrolment strategies in early home visitation to prevent physical child abuse and neglect and the 'Universal verus Targeted' debate: A meta-analysis of population-based and screening-based programs. *Child Abuse and Neglect*, **23**(9): 863–883.

Hagell, A. (1998) *Dangerous Care: reviewing the risks to children from their carers*. London, Policy Studies Institute and the Bridge Child Care Development service.

Hall, G.C.N. (1995) Sexual offender recidivism revisited: A meta-analysis of recent treatment studies. *Journal of Consulting and Clinical Psychology*, **63**: 802–809.

Halper, G. and Jones, M.A. (1981) *Serving families at risk of dissolution: Public preventive services in New York*, Human Resources Administration.

Hamburg, D. (1992) *Today's Children–Creating a future for a generation in crisis*. Random House.

Hansen, D.J., Pallotta, G.M., Tishelman, A.C. and Conaway, L.P. (1989) Parental problem-solving skills and child behavior problems: A comparison of physically abusive, neglectful, clinic, and community families. *Journal of Family Violence*, **4**: 353–368.

Hanson, R.K. (1990) Characteristics of sex offenders who were sexually abused as children. In Langevin, R. (ed.) *Sex offenders and their victims*. Oakville, Ontario, Juniper.

Hanson, R.K. and Brussiere, M.T. (1998) *Predictors of sexual offender recidivism: A meta-analysis*, Ministry of the Solicitor General of Canada.

Hanson, R.K. and Harris, A. (1998) *Dynamic predictors of sexual recidivism*. Report of the Research Department of the Solicitor General Canada.

Hanson, R.K. and Lambert, M. (1996) Clinical significance. An overview of methods. *Journal of Mental Health*, **5**: 17–24.

Hanson, R.K., Steffy, R.A. and Gauthier, R. (1993) Long-Term Recidivism of Child Molesters. *Journal of Consulting and Clinical Psychology*, **61**(4): 646–652.

Hardy, J.B. and Streett, R. (1989) Family support and parenting education in the home: an effective extension of clinic-based preventive health care services for poor children. *Journal of Pediatrics*, **115**: 927–931.

Hare, R.D. (1980) A scale for the assessment of psychopathy in criminal populations. *Personality and Individual Differences*, **1**: 111–119.

Hare, R.D. (1991) *The Hare Psychopathy Checklist – Revised*. Toronto, Ontario, Multi Heath Systems.

Harrold, M., Lutzker, J.R., Campbell, R.V. and Touchette, P.E. (1992) Project Ecosystems: An ecobehavioral approach to families with children with developmental disabilities. *Journal of Developmental and Physical Disabilities*, **4**: 1–14.

Hart, S.N. (1987) Mental health neglect–proposed definitions, standards, and procedures for legal and social services intervention. In Brassard, M., Germain, B. and

Hart, S. (eds) *Psychological maltreatment of children and youth* Elmsford, NY, Perga-
   mon.
Hart, S.N. and Brassard, M.R. (1991) Psychological maltreatment: Progress achieved.
   Developmental Psychopathology, **3**: 61–70.
Hart, S.N., Brassard, M.R. and Karlson, H.S. (1996) Psychological Maltreatment. In
   Briere, J., Berliner, L., Bulkley, J.A., Jenny, C. and Reid, T. (eds) *The APSAC Hand-
   book on Child Maltreatment,* Thousand Oaks, Sage.
Haskett, M. and Kistner, J.A. (1991) Social interactions and peer perceptions of young
   physically abusive, neglectful, clinic and community families. *Journal of Family Violence,* **4**: 353–368.
Hayashino, D.S., Wurtele, S.K. and Klebe, K.J. (1995) Child Molesters: An Examination of Cognitive Factors. *Journal of Interpersonal Violence,* **10**(1): 106–
   116.
Haywood, T.W., Grossman, L.S., Kravitz., H.M. and Wasyliw, O.E. (1994) Profiling
   psychological distortion in alleged child molesters. *Psychological reports,* **75**:
   915–927.
Hazelrigg, M.D., Cooper, H.M. and Bourduin, C.M. (1987) Evaluating the Effectiveness of Family Therapies: An Integrative Review and Analysis. *Psychological
   Bulletin,* **101**(3): 428–442.
Hazzard, A., Webb, C., Kleemeier, C., Angert, L. and Pohl, J. (1991) Child sexual
   abuse prevention: evaluation and one year follow-up. *Child Abuse and Neglect,* **15**:
   133–138.
Heffer, S. (1998) *Like The Roman: The Life of Enoch Powell,* London, Weidenfeld & Nicol-
   son.
Heller, S.S., Larrieu, J.A., D'Imperio, R. and Boris, N.W. (1999) Research on resilience
   to child maltreatment: Empirical considerations. *Child Abuse and Neglect,* **23**(4): 321–
   338.
Hempel, C. (1966) Recent probems of induction. In Colodney, R. (ed.) *Mind and
   Cosmos,* Pittsburgh, University of Pittsburgh.
Hendrick, H. (1997) Constructions and Reconstructions of British Childhood: An
   Interpretive Survey 1800 to the Present. In James, A. and Prout, A. (eds) (2nd
   edition) *Constructing and Reconstructing Childhood,* London, Falmer Press.
Heptinstall, E., Puckering, C., Skuse, D., Start, K., Zur-Spiro, S. and Dowdney, L.
   (1987) Nutrition and mealtime behaviour in families of growth retarded children.
   Human nutrition: applied nutrition. **41**: 390–402.
Herrenkohl, R.C., Herrenkohl, E.C. and Egolf, B.P. (1983) Circumstances surrounding
   the occurrence of child maltreatment. *Journal of Consulting and Clinical Psychology,*
   51: 424–431.
Herronkohl, E.C. Herrenkohl, R.C., Rupert, L.J. and Egolf, B.P. (1994) Resilient early
   school age children from maltreatment homes: Outcomes in late adolescence.
   American Journal of Orthopsychiatry **64**: 301–309.
Herronkohl, E.C., Herrenkohl, R.C., Rupert, L.J., Egolf, B.P. and Lutz, J.G. (1995) Risk
   factors for behavioral dysfunction: The relative impact of maltreatment, SES, phys-
   ical health problems, cognitive ability, and quality of parent-child interaction. *Child
   Abuse and Neglect,* **19**: 191–213.
Hess, P.M., Folaron, G. and Jefferson, A.B. (1992) Effectiveness of Family reunifica-
   tion Services: An Innovative Evaluative Model. *Social Work,* **37**(4): 304–311.
Higgins, D.J. and McCabe, M.P. (1994) The relationships of child sexual abuse and
   family violence to adult adjustment: Towards an integrated risk-sequelae model.
   Journal of Sex Research, **34**: 4: 255–266.
Hildebran, D. and Pithers, W.D. (1989) Enhancing offender empathy for sexual abuse

victims. In Laws, D.R. (ed.) *Relapse Prevention with Sex Offenders*, New York, Guilford.

Hill, S.D., Bleichfield, B., Brunstetter, R.D., Hebert, J.E. and Steckler, S. (1989) Cognitive and physiological responsiveness of abused children. *Journal of the American Academy of Child and Adolescent Psychiatry*, **28**: 219–224.

Himelein, M.J. and McElrath, J.A.V. (1996) Resilient child sexual abuse survivors: cognitive coping and illusion. *Child Abuse and Neglect*, **20**(8): 747–758.

Hindman, J. (1988) New insight into adult and juvenile sex offenders. *Community Safety Quarterly*, **1**: 3.

HMSO (1992) *Report of the Inquiry into the Removal of Children from Orkney in February 1991*. Edinburgh, HMSO.

Holmes, W.C. and Slap, G.B. (1998) Sexual Abuse of Boys: Definition, Prevalence, Correlates, Sequelae, and Management. *JAMA*, **280**(21): 1855–1862.

Holtermann S. (1992) *Investing in young children: costing an education and day care service*, London, National Children's Bureau.

Holtermann S. (1997) *Weighing it up: Applying economic evaluations to Social Welfare Programmes*. York, Joseph Rowntree Foundation.

Howe, D. (1989) *The Consumer's View of Family Therapy*. Aldershot, Gower.

Howells, K. (1979) Some meanings of children for pedophiles. In Cook, M. and Wilson, G. (eds) *Love and Attraction*, Oxford, Pergamon.

Howing, P.T., Wodarski, J.S., Kurtz, P.D. and Guadin, J.M. (1993) *Maltreatment and the school-age child: developmental outcomes and system issues*, New York, Haworth Press.

Hucker, S.J., Langevin, R., Wortzman, G., Bain, J., Handy, L., Chambers, J. and Wright, S. (1986) Neuropsychological impairment in pedophiles. *Canadian Journal of Behavioural Science*, **18**: 440–448.

Hudson, S.M. and Ward, T. (1998) Intimacy, Loneliness and Attachment Style in Sexual Offenders. *Journal of Interpersonal Violence*, **12**(3): 323–339.

Hudson, W.W. and Harrison, D.F. (1986) Conceptual issues in measuring and assessing family problems. *Family Therapy*, **13**: 85–94.

Hughes, G.V., Hogue, T.E. and Hollin, C.R. (1999) First stage evaluation of a treatment programme for personality disordered offenders. *Journal of Forensic Psychiatry*, **8**(3): 515–527.

Illsely, R. (1967) The Sociological Study of Reproduction and its Outcome. In Richardson, S.A. and Guttmacher, A.F. (eds) *Childbearing—its Social and Psychological Aspects*, Baltimore, Md, Williams and Wilkins.

Imrie, J. and Coombs, Y. (1995) *No time to waste: the scale and dimensions of the problem of children affected by HIV/AIDS*. Barkingside, Essex, Barnardo's.

Iwaniec, D. (1997) Evaluating parent-training for emotionally abusive and neglectful parents: comparing individual versus individual and group intervention. *Research on Social Work Practice*, **7**(3): 329–349.

Jaffe, P., Wolfe, D.A. and Wilson, S. (1990) *Children of battered women*, Newbury Park, CA, Sage.

Jaffe, P.G., Suderman, M. and Reitzel, D. (1992) Working with Children and Adolescents to End the Cycle of Violence: A social learning approach to intervention and prevention programs. In R. DeV. Peters, R., McMahon, R.J. and Quinsey, V.L. (1992) *Aggression and Violence Throughout the Life Span*, Newbury Park, Sage.

Janoff-Bulman, R. (1989) Assumptive worlds and the stress of traumatic events: Applications of the schema construct. *Social Cognition*, **7**: 113–136.

Jehu, D. (1988) *Beyond sexual abuse: therapy with women who were childhood victims*. Chichester, Wiley.

Jehu, D., Gazan, M. and Klassen, C. (1984) Common therapeutic targets among women who were sexually abused. *Journal of Social Work and Human Sexuality*, **3**: 25–45.

Jinich, S. and Litrownik, A.J. (1999) Coping with sexual abuse: Development and evaluation of a videotape intervention for non-offending parents. *Child Abuse and Neglect*, **23**, 2: 175–190.

Johnson, S.M., Kurtz., M.E., Tomlinson, T. And Howe, K.R. (1986) Students' stereotypes of patients as barriers to clinical decision-making. *Journal of Medical Education*, **61**: 727–735.

Johnson, Z., Howell, F. and Molloy, B. (1993) Community mothers' programme: randomised controlled trial of non-professional intervention in parenting. *British Medical Journal*, **306**: 1449–1452.

Johnston, C. (1996) Addressing parent cognitions in interventions with families of disruptive children. In Dobson, K. S. and Craig, K.D. (eds) *Advances in cognitive behavioural therapy*, Thousand Oaks, CA, Sage.

Jumper, S. (1995) A meta-analysis of the relationship of child sexual abuse to adult psychological adjustment. *Child Abuse and Neglect*, **19**(6): 715–728.

Kadushin, S. (1988) *Child welfare services*, New York, Macmillan.

Kahneman, D. and Tversky, A. (1972) Subjective probability: A judgement of representativeness. *Cognitive Psychology*, **3**: 237–251.

Kaufman, J. and Zigler, E. (1989) The intergenerational transmission of child abuse. In Cicchetti, D. and Carlson, V. (eds) *Child Maltreatment: Theory and research on the causes and consequences of child abuse and neglect*, New York, Cambridge University Press.

Kaufman, J., Cook, A., Amy, L., Jones, B.A. and Pittinsky, T. (1994) Problems defining resiliency: Illustrations from the study of maltreated children. *Developmental Psychopathology*, **6**: 215–229.

Kazdin, A.E. (1987) Treatment of antisocial behavior in children: current status and future directions. *Psychological Bulletin*, **102**: 187–203.

Kazdin, A.E. (1990) Premature Termination from Treatment among Children Referred for Antisocial Behavior. *Journal of Child Psychology and Psychiatry*, **31**(3): 415–425.

Kazi, M.A.F. and Wilson, (1996) Applying Single-Case Evaluation in Social Work. *Research on Social Work Practice* **6**: 5–26.

Kelly, R.J. (1982) Behavioral reorientation of pedophiliacs: can it be done? *Clinical Psychology Review*, **2**: 387–408.

Kempe, R.S. and Kempe, C. (1978) *Child Abuse*. Cambridge, Massachusetts, Harvard University Press.

Kendall-Tackett, K.A., Williams, L.M. and Finkelhor, D. (1993) Impact of sexual abuse on children: A review and synthesis of recent empirical studies. *Psychological Bulletin*, **113**: 164–180.

Ketring, S.A. and Feinauer, L.L. (1999) Perpetrator–Victim Relationship: Long-term effects of sexual abuse for men and women. *The American Journal of Family Therapy*, **27**: 109–120.

Kleemeier, C., Webb, C., Hazzard, A. and Pohl, J. (1988) Child sexual abuse prevention: evaluation of a teacher training model. *Child Abuse and Neglect*, **12**: 555–561.

Klein, M. and Stern, L. (1971) Low birth weight and the battered child syndrome. *American Journal of the Disabled Child*, **122**: 15–18.

Knight, R.A. and Prentky, R.A. (1990) Classifying sexual offenders: The development and corroboration of taxonomic models. In Marshall, W.L., Laws, D.R. and Barbaree, H.E. (eds) *Handbook of Sexual Assault: Issues, theories, and treatment of the offender*, New York, Plenum.

Knopp, F.M., Freeman-Longo, R.E. and Stevenson, W. (1992) *Nationwide Survey of Juvenile and Adult Sex Offender Treatment Programs*. Orwell, Vermont, Safer Society Press.

Kolko, D.J. (1986) Social cognitive skills training with a sexually abused and abusive child psychiatric inpatient: Training, generalization and follow-up. *Journal of Family Violence*, 1: 149–165.

Kolko, D.J. (1987) Treatment of child sexual abuse: Programs, progress and prospects. *Journal of Family Violence*, 2: 303–318.

Kolko, D. (1992) Characteristics of child victims of physical violence: Research findings and clinical implications. *Journal of Interpersonal Violence*, 7: 244–276.

Kolko, D.J., Moser, J.T. and Weldy, S.R. (1990) Medical/health histories and physical evaluation of physically and sexually abused child psychiatric patients: A controlled study. *Journal of Family Violence*, 5: 249–267.

Kolko, D.J., Moser, J.T. and Huges, J. (1989) Classroom training in sexual victimization awareness and prevention skills: an extension of the red flag/green flag program. *Journal of Family Violence*, 4: 25–45.

Kolko, D.J., Moser, J.T., Litz, J. and Huges, J. (1987) Promoting awareness and prevention of child sexual victimization using the red flag/green flag program: an evaluation with follow-up. *Journal of Family Violence*, 2: 11–35.

Kolvin, I., Miller, F.J., Garside, R.F., Wolstenholme, F. and Gatzanis, S.R.M. (1983) A Longitudinal Study of Deprivation: Lifecycle changes in one generation—Implications for the next Generation. In Schmidt, M.H. and Remschmidt, H. (eds) *Epidemiology Approaches in Child Psychiatry 11*, Stuttgart and New York, G. Thieme.

Kotch, J.B., Browne, D.C., Dufort, V., Winsor, J. and Catellier, D. (1999) Predicting child maltreatment in the first 4 years of life from characteristics assess in the neonatal period. *Child Abuse and Neglect*, 23(4): 305–319.

Kruk, S. and Wolkind, S.N. (1983) A longitudinal study of single mothers and their children. In Madge, N. (ed.) *Families at Risk*. London, Heinemann Educational.

Kuh, D.J.L. and Cooper, C. (1992) Physical activity at 36 years: patterns and childhood predictors in a longitudinal study. *Journal of Epidemiology and Community Health*, 46(2): 114–119.

Kuh, D.J.L. and Wadsworth, M.E.J. (1991) Childhood influences on Adult Male Earnings in a Longitudinal Study. *British Journal of Sociology*, 42: 533–555.

Kuh, D.J.L. and Wadsworth, M.E.J. (1993) Physical health status at 36 years in a British national birth cohort. *Social Science and Medicine*, 37(7): 905–916.

Kurtz, M.E, Johnson, S.M. and Rice, S. (1989) Students' clinical assessments: Are they affected by stereotyping? *Journal of Social Work Education*, 25(1): 3–12.

Lachenmeyer, J.R. and Davidovicz, H. (1987) Failure to thrive: a critical review. In Lahey, B. and Kazdin, L. (eds) *Advances in clinical child psychology*, New York, Plenum Press.

Lamb, M.E., Gaensbauer, T.J., Malkin, C.M. and Schultz, L.A. (1985) The effects of child maltreatment on security of infant-adult attachment, *Infant Behavior and Development*, 8: 35–45.

Lane, S.L. and Lobanov-Rostovsky, C. (1997) Special populations: children, females, the developmentally disabled, and violent youth. In Ryan, G. and Lane, S. (eds) *Juvenile Sexual Offending. Causes, Consequences and corrections*. Lexington MA, Lexington Books.

Lange, A., De Beurs, E., Dolan, C., Lachnit, T., Sjollema, S. and Hanewald, G. (1999) Long-term Effects of Childhood Sexual Abuse: Objective and Subjective Characteristics of the Abuse and Psychopathology in Later Life. *The Journal of Nervous and Mental Diseases,* **187**(3): 150–158.

Langevin, R., Handy, L., Day, D. and Russon, A. (1985) Are incestuous fathers pedophilic, aggressive and alcoholic? In Langevin, R. (ed.) *Erotic Preference, Gender Identity and Aggression,* Hillsdale, NJ, Erlbaum.

Lanktree, C.B. and Briere, J. (1995) Outcome of therapy for sexually abused chidren: A repeated measures study. *Child Abuse and Neglect,* **19**: 1145–1155.

Larner, M. (1990) A 'fair start' for parents and infants. *High Scope Review.* 9(1): 5–6, 8–10.

Larrance, D.T. and Twentyman, C.T. (1983) Maternal attributions in child abuse. *Journal of Abnormal Psychology;* **92**: 449–457.

Lealman, G.T., Haigh, D., Phillips, J.M., Stone, J. and Ord-Smith, C. (1983) Prediction and prevention of child abuse—An empty hope? *The Lancet,* June 25. 1: 8339, 1423–1424.

Lesnik-Oberstein, M., Koers, A.J. and Cohen, L. (1995) Parental hostility and its sources in psychologically abusive mothers: A test of the three factor theory. *Child Abuse and Neglect,* **19**(1): 33–49.

Lewis, D.O., Mallouh, C. and Webb, V. (1989) Child abuse, delinquency and criminality. In D. Chiccheti and Carlson, V. (eds) *Child Maltreatment: Theory and research on the causes and consequences of child abuse and neglect.* Cambridge, Cambridge University Press.

Little, M. and Kelly, S. (1995) *A life without problems?,* Aldershot, Arena.

Lobitz, G. and Johnson, S. (1975) Normal versus deviant children. *Journal of Abnormal Child Psychology,* **3**: 353–374.

Luthar, R.S. and Zigler, E. (1991) Vulnerability and competence: A review of research on resilience in childhood. *American Journal of Orthopsychiatry,* **61**: 6–22.

Luthar, S.S., Cushing, G. and McMahon, T.J. (1997) Interdisciplinary interface: Developmental principles brought to substance abuse research. In Luthar, S.S., Burack, J.A., Cicchetti, D. and Weisz, J.R. (eds) *Developmental Psychopathology: Perspectives on Adjustment, Risk and Disorder,* New York, Cambridge University Press.

Lutzker, J.R. and Campbell, R.V. (1994) *Ecobehavioral family interventions in developmental disabilities,* Pacific Groves, CA, Brooks Cole.

Lutzker, J.R. and Rice, J.M. (1984) Project 12-Ways: Measuring outcome of a large-scale in-home service for the treatment and prevention of child abuse and neglect. *Child Abuse and Neglect,* **8**: 519–524.

Lutzker, J.R. and Rice, J.M. (1987) Using recidivism data to evaluate Project 12-Ways: An ecobehavioral approach to the prevention and treatment of child abuse and neglect. *Journal of Family Violence,* **2**: 283–290.

Lutzker, J.R., Bigelow, K.M., Doctor, R.M., Gershater, R.M. and Greene, B.F. (1998) An ecobehavioral model for the precention and treatment of child abuse and neglect. In Lutzker, J.R. (ed.) *Handbook of Child Abuse Research and Treatment,* New York, Plenum Press.

Lutzker, J.R., Huynen, K.B. and Bigelow, K.M. (1988) Parent training. In Van Hasselt, V.B. and Hersen, M. (eds) *Handbook of psychological treatment protocols for children and adolescents,* Hillside, NH, Erlbaum.

Lutzker, J.R., Megson, D.A., Webb, M.E. and Dachman, R.S. (1985) Validating and training parent–child interaction skills to professionals and to parents indicated for child abuse and neglect. *Journal of Child and Adolescent Psychotherapy,* **2**: 91–104.

Lynch, M.A. and Browne, K.D. (1997) Editorial: The Growing Awareness of Emotional Maltreatment. *Child Abuse Review,* **6**(5): 313–314.

Lynch, M.A. and Roberts, J. (1982) *Consequences of Child Abuse*. London, Academic Press.

Lynskey, M.T. and Fergusson, D.M. (1997) Factors protecting against the development of adjustment difficulties in young adults exposed to childhood sexual abuse. *Child Abuse and Neglect*, **21**(12): 1177–1190.

Lyons, P., Doueck, H.J. and Wodarski, J.S. (1996) Risk assessment for child protective services: A review of the empirical literature on instrument performance. *Social Work Research* **20**: 143–155.

Maccoby, E.E. and Martin, J.A. (1983) Socialization in the context of the family: Parent–child interaction. In Mussen, P.H. (series ed.) and Hetherington, E.M. (vol. ed.) *Handbook of child psychology, Vol 4: Socialization, personality, and social development*, New York, Wiley.

Macdonald, G. (1990) Allocating blame in Social Work. *British Journal of Social Work*, **20**, 1, 525–546.

Macdonald, G. and Roberts, H. (1996). *What works in the early years?* Barkingside: Barnardo's.

Macdonald, G.M. (1997a) Social Work Research: The State We're In. *Journal of Interprofessional Care*, **11**(1): 57–65.

Macdonald, G.M. (1997b) Social Work: Beyond Control? In Maynard, A. and Chalmers, I. (eds) *Non-random Reflections on Health Services Research. On the 25th anniversary of Archie Cochrane's Effectiveness and Efficiency*, Plymouth, BMJ Publishing Group.

Macdonald, G.M. (1998) Promoting Evidence-Based Practice in Child Protection. *Clinical Child Psychology and Psychiatry*, **3**(1): 71–85.

Macdonald, G. M. and Sheldon, B. (1998) Changing One's Mind: The Final Frontier? *Issues In Social Work Education*, **18**: 1.

Macdonald, G.M. and Sheldon, B. with Gillespie, J. (1992) Contemporary Studies of the Effectiveness of Social Work. *British Journal of Social Work*, **22**: 615–643.

Macdonald, G.M. and Macdonald, K.I. (1995) Ethical issues in social work research. In Hugman, R. and Smith, D. (eds) *Ethical Issues in Social Work*. London, Routledge.

Macdonald, K.I. (1995) Comparative homicide and the proper aims of social work: a sceptical note. *British Journal of Social Work*, **25**: 489–497.

Macdonald, K.I. and Macdonald, G. (1999a) Empowerment: a critical view. In Shera, W. and Wells, L.M. (eds) *Empowerment Practice in Social Work: Developing Richer Conceptual Foundations*, Toronto, Canadian Scholars' Press.

Macdonald, K.I. and Macdonald, G.M. (1999b) Perceptions of risk. In Parsloe, P. (ed.) *Risk Assessment in Social Care and Social Work*, Aberdeen, Research Highlights.

MacMillan, H.L., Fleming, J.E., Troome, N., Boyles, M.H., Wong, M., Racine, Y.A., Beardslee, W.R. and Offord, D.R. (1997) Prevalence of child physical and sexual abuse in the community: Results from the Ontario Health Supplement. *Journal of the American Medical Association*, **278**: 131–135.

MacMillan, H.L., MacMillan, J.H., Offord, D.R., Griffith, L. and MacMillan, A. (1994a) Primary Prevention of Child Physical Abuse and Neglect: A Critical Review. Part 1. *Journal of Child Psychology and Psychiatry and Allied Professions*, **35**(5): 835–856.

MacMillan, H.L., MacMillan, J.H., Offord, D.R., Griffith, L. and MacMillan, A. (1994b) Primary Prevention of Child Sexual Abuse: A Critical Review. Part 2. *Journal of Child Psychology and Psychiatry and Allied Professions*, **35**: 5: 857–876.

Magura, S. and Moses, B.S. (1984) *Outcome measures for child welfare services: Theory and Applications*, Washington DC, Child Welfare League of America.

Main, M. and George, C. (1985) Responses of abused and disadvantaged toddlers to distress in agemates: A study in the day care setting, *Developmental Psychology*, **21**: 407–412.

Main, M. and Goldwyn, R. (1984) Predicting rejection of her infant from mother's representation of her own experience: Implications for the abused-abusing intergenerational cycle. *Child Abuse and Neglect*, **8**: 203–217.

Maker, A.H., Kemmelmeier, M. and Peterson, C. (1999) Parental Sociopathy as a Predictor of Childhood Sexual Abuse. *Journal of Family Violence*, **14**(1): 47–59.

Maletsky, B.M. (1993) Factors associated with success and failure in behavioural and cognitive treatment of sexual offenders. *Annals of Sex Research*, **6**: 241–258.

Malinosky-Rummell, R. and Hansen, D. (1993) Long-term consequences of child physical abuse. *Psychological Bulletin*, **114**: 68–79.

Mann, S.L., Wadsworth, M.E.J. and Colley, J.R.T. (1992) Accumulation of factors influencing respiratory illness in members of a national birth cohort and their offspring. *Journal of Epidemiology and Community Health*, **46**: 286–292.

Mannarino, A.P. and Cohen, J.A. (1996) Abuse related attributions and perceptions, general attributions, and locus of control in sexually abused girls. *Journal of Interpersonal Violence*, **11**: 162–180.

Manocha, K.F. and Mezey, G. (1998) British adolescents who sexually abuse: a descriptive study. *Journal of Forensic Psychiatry*, **9**(3): 588–608.

Markus, E., Lange, A. and Pettigre, T.F. (1990) Effectiveness of family therapy: a meta-analysis. *Journal of Family Therapy* **12**: 205–221.

Marques, J., Nelson, C., West, M.A. and Day, D.M. (1994) The relationships between treatment goals and recidivism among child molesters. *Behaviour Research and Therapy*, **32**: 577–588.

Marques, J.K. (1998) The sex offender treatment and evaluation project: California's new outcome study. *Annals of the New York Academy of Science*, **528**: 235–242.

Marsh, P. and Triseliotis, J. (1996) *Ready to Practise? Social Workers and Probation Officers: Their Training and Their First Year of Work*, Aldershot, Avebury.

Marshall, P. (1997) The prevalence of convictions for sexual offending. *Home Office Research and Statistics Directorate Research Findings* Number **55**, London, Home Office.

Marshall, W.L. (1994) Treatment effects of denial and minimisation in incarcerated sex offenders. *Behaviour Research and Therapy*, **32**, 559–564.

Marshall, W.L. (1996) Assessment, treatment and theorising about sex offenders: Developments during the past twenty years and future directions. *Criminal Justice and Behaviour*, **23**: 162–199.

Marshall, W.L., Barbaree, H.E. and Christophe, D. (1986) Sexual offenders against female children: Sexual preferences for age of victim and type of behaviour. *Canadian Journal of Behavioural Science*, **18**: 424–439.

Marshall, W.L., Ward, T., Jones, R., Johnstone, P and Barbaree, H.E. (1991) An Optimistic Evaluation of Treatment Outcome with Sex Offenders. *Violence Update*, **1**: 8–11.

Mash, E.J., Johnston, C. and Kovitz, K.R. (1983) A comparison of the mother-child interaction of physically abused and nonabused children during play and task situations. *Journal of Clinical Child Psychology*, **12**: 337–346.

Masten, A.S., Best, K.M. and Garmezy, N. (1991) Resilience and development: Contributions from the study of children who overcome adversity. *Development and Psychopathology*, **2**: 425–444.

Mathiesen, B., Skuse, D., Wilke, D. and Reilly, S. (1989) Oral motor dysfunction and failure to thrive among inner city infants. *Developmental Medicine and Child Neurology*, **31**: 15–35.

Mayer, J.E. and Timms, N. (1970) *The Client Speaks*. London, Routledge & Kegan Paul.

Mayes, L.C. and Volkmar, F.R. (1993) Nosology of eating and growth disorders in early childhood. *Child and Adolescent Psychiatry Clinics of North America*, **2**: 15–35.

McAuley, R. and McAuley, P. (1977) *Child behavior problems*. Basingstoke, Macmillan.

McAuley, R. and McAuley, P. (1980) The effectiveness of behaviour modification with families. *British Journal of Social Work*, **10**(1): 43–54.

McCann, I.J., Sakheim, D.K. and Abrahamson, D.J. (1988) Trauma and victimization: A model of psychological adaptation. *Counseling Psychologist*, **16**: 531–594.

McCleer, S.V., Deblinger, E., Henry, D. and Orvaschel, H. (1992) Sexually abused children at high risk for post-traumatic stress disorder. *Journal of the American Academy of Child and Adolescent Psychiatry* **31**: 875–879.

McCord, J. (1978) A thirty-year follow-up of treatment effects. *American Psychologist*, **33**: 284–289.

McConaghy, N., Blaszczynski, A. and Kidson, W. (1988) Treatment of sex offenders with imaginal desensitization and/or medroxyprogesterone. *Acta Psychiatria Scandinavia*, **77**: 199–206.

McGee, R.A. and Wolfe, D.A. (1991) Psychological maltreatment: towards an operational definition. *Development and Psychopathology*, **3**: 3–18.

McGrath, R.J. (1991) Sex offender risk assessment and disposition planning: A review of empirical and clinical findings. *International Journal of Offender Therapy and Comparative Criminology*, **35**: 4, 328–350.

McMahon, R.J. and Wells, R.C. (1989) Conduct disorders. In Mash, E.J. and Barkley, R.A. (eds) *Treatment of childhood disorders*, New York, Guilford.

McMahon, R.J., Forehand, R. and Griest, D.L. (1981) An assessment of who drops out of therapy during parent behavioral training? *Behavior Counselling Quarterly*, **1**: 79–85.

McWhirter, J.J., McWhirter, B.T., McWhirter, A.M. and McWhirter, E.H. (1993) *At risk youth: A comprehensive approach*. Pacific Grove, CA, Brooks/Cole.

Meadows, S. (1996) *Parenting Behaviour and Children's Cognitive Development*, Hove, Psychology Press.

Medawar, P. (1982) *Pluto's Republic*, London, Methuen.

Meehl, P.E. (1979) Why I do not attend case conferences. *Psychodiagnostic Papers*, 225–302, Minneapolis, MN, University of Minnesota Press.

Melton, G.B. (1992) The improbability of prevention of sexual abuse. In Willis, D., Holden, E.W. and Rosenberg, M. (eds) *Prevention of child maltreatment: developmental perspectives*. New York, John Wiley.

Mennen, F.E. and Meadow, D. (1994) A preliminary study of the factors related to trauma in childhood sexual abuse. *Journal of Family Violence*, **9**: 125–142.

Milner, J.S. and Dopke, C. (1997) Child physical abuse: Review of offender characteristics. In Wolfe, D.A., McMahon, R.J. and Peters, R.DeV. (eds) *Child Abuse: New directions in prevention and treatment across the lifespan*, Thousand Oaks, Sage.

Millner, J.S., Murphy, W.D., Valle, L.A., Tolliver, R.M. (1998) Assessment issues in child abuse evaluations. In J.R. Lutzker (ed) *Handbook of Child Abuse Research and Treatment*. Plenum Press, New York.

Moeller, T.O., Bachmann, G.A. and Moeller, J.R. (1993) The combined effects of physical, sexual, and emotional abuse during childhood: Long-term health consequences for women. *Child Abuse and Neglect*, **17**: 623–640.

Monck, E. (1997) Evaluating Therapeutic Intervention With Sexually Abused Children. *Child Abuse Review*, **6**: 163–177.

Morrison, T., Erroga, M. and Beckett, R.C. (1994) (eds) *Sexual Offending Against Children: Assessment and Treatment of Male Abusers*, London, Routledge.

Morrow, K.B. and Sorell, G.T. (1989) Factors affecting self-esteem, depression and negative behaviours in sexually abused adolescents. *Journal of Marriage and the Family*, 51: 677–686.

Mullen, P.E., Martin, J.L., Anderson, J.C., Romans, S.E. and Herbison, G.P. (1993) Childhood sexual abuse and mental health in adult life. *British Journal of Psychiatry* 163: 721–732.

Munro, E. (1998) *Understanding Social Work: An Empirical Approach*, London, The Athlone Press.

Munro, E. (1999) Common errors of reasoning in child protection work. *Child Abuse & Neglect*, 23(8): 745–758.

Murphy, W.D. and Peters, J.M. (1992) Profiling child sexual abusers: Psychological considerations. *Criminal Justice and Behavior*, 19: 24–37.

Murphy, W.D. and Smith, T.A. (1996) Sex offenders against children: empirical and clinical issues. In Briere, J., Berliner, L., Bulkley, J.A., Jenny, C. and Reid T. (eds) *The APSAC Handbook on Child Maltreatment*, Thousand Oaks, Sage.

Murphy, W.D., Haynes, M.R., Stalgaitis, S.J. and Flanagan, B. (1986) Differential sexual responding amongst four groups of sexual offenders against children. *Journal of Psychopathology and Behavioural Assessment*, 8: 339–353.

Nash, M.R., Zivney, O.A. and Hulsey, T. (1993a) Long-term sequelae of childhood sexual abuse: Perceived family environment, psychopathology, and dissociation. *Journal of Consulting and Clinical Psychology*, 61: 276–283.

Nash, M.R., Zivney, O.A. And Hulsey, T. (1993b) Characteristics of sexual abuse associated with greater psychological impairment among children. *Child Abuse and Neglect*, 17: 401–408.

National Research Council (1993) *Understanding child abuse and neglect*, Washington DC, National Academy Press.

Needell, B., Webster, D., Barth, R.P., Monks, J. and Armijo, M. (1995) Performance indicators for child welfare services in California: 1994. Unpublished report, Berkley, University of California School of Social Welfare, Family Welfare Research Group.

Nelki, J.S. and Waters, J. (1988) A group for sexually abused young children: Unravelling the web. *Child Abuse and Neglect*, 13: 369–377.

Newberger, C.M. and Cook, S.J. (1983) Parental awareness and child abuse: A cognitive-developmental analysis of urban and rural samples. *American Journal of Orthopsychiatry*, 53: 512–524.

Newberger, C.M., Gremy, I.M. Waternaux, C.M. and Newberger, E.H. (1993) Mothers of sexually abused children: Trauma and repair in longitudinal perspective. *American Journal of Orthopsychiatry*, 33: 92–102.

Ney, P.G., Fung, T. and Wickett, A.R. (1993) Child Neglect: The Precursor to Child Abuse. *Pre- and Perinatal Psychology Journal* 8(2): 95–112.

Ney, P.G., Fung, T. and Wickett, A.R. (1994) The worst combinations of child abuse and neglect. *Child Abuse and Neglect*, 18: 705–714.

Nibert: D., Cooper, S., Ford, J., Fitch, I.K. and Robinson, J. (1989) The ability of young children to learn abuse prevention. *Response*, 12: 14–20.

Nicol, A.R., Smith, J., Kay, B., Hall, D., Barlow, J. and Williams, B. (1988) A Focused Casework Approach to the Treatment of Child Abuse: A Controlled Comparison. *Journal of Child Psychology and Psychiatry*, 29(5): 703–711.

Nisbett, R. and Ross, L. (1980) *Human Inferences: Strategies and Shortcomings of Social Judgement*. Englefield Ciffs, NJ, Prentice Hall Inc.

Nomellini, S. and Katz, R.C. (1983) Effects of anger control training on abusive parents. *Cognitive Therapy and Research*, 7(1): 57–68

Nottinghamshire Area Child Protection Committee (1994) *Report of Overview Group into the Circumstances Surrounding the Death of Leanne White*. Nottingham: Nottinghamshire County Council.

Nugent, O. (1996) Issues of bonding and attachment. *Child Care in Practice* 2(4): 24–28.

O'Callaghan, D. (1998) Practice Issues in Working with Young Abusers who have Learning Disabilities. *Child Abuse Review*, 7: 435–448.

O'Connor, S., Vietze, P.M., Sherrod, K.B., Sandler, H.M. and Altemeier III, W.A. (1980) Reduced incidence of parenting inadequacy following rooming-in. *Pediatrics*, 66: 176–182.

O'Donohue, W.T. and Elliott, A.N. (1992) Treatment of the sexually abused child: A review. *Journal of Clinical Child Psychology*, 21: 218–228.

O'Hagan, K. (1995) Emotional and Psychological Abuse: Problems of Definition. *Child Abuse and Neglect*, 19(4): 449–461.

O'Leary, K.D. and Emery, R.E. (1983) Marital discord and child behavior problems. In Levine, M.D. and Satz, P. (eds) *Developmental variation and dysfunction*. New York, Academic Press.

Oakley, A. (2000) *Experiments in Knowing: gender and method and the social sciences*. Cambridge, Polity Press.

Oakley, A. (1989) Who's Afraid of the Randomised Controlled Trial? Some Dilemmas of the Scientific Method and 'Good' Research Practice. *Women and Health*, 15: 25–59.

Oates, R.K. and Bross, D.C. (1995) What have we learned from treating physical abuse? *Child Abuse and Neglect*, 19(4): 463–473.

Oates, R.K., Gray, J., Schweitzer, L., Kempe, R.S. and Harmon, R.J. (1995) A therapeutic preschool for abused children: The Keepsafe Project. *Child Abuse and Neglect* 19(11): 1379–1386.

Oates, R.K., O'Toole, N.I., Lynch, D.L., Stern, A. and Cooney, G. (1994) Stability and change in outcomes for sexually abused children. *Journal of the American Academy of Child and Adolescent Psychiatry*, 33(7): 945–953.

Oldershaw, I., Walters, G.C. and Hall, D.J. (1986) Control strategies and non-compliance in abusive mother-child dyads: An observational study. *Child Development*, 57: 722–732.

Oldfield, D., Hays, B.J. and Megel, M.E. (1996) Evaluation of the effectiveness of project Trust; An elementary school-based victimization prevention strategy, *Child Abuse and Neglect*, 20(9): 821–832.

Olds, D. (1997) The Prenatal Early Infancy Project: Preventing Child Abuse and Neglect in the Context of Promoting Child and Maternal Health. In Wolfe, D.A., McMahon, R.J. and Peters, R.DeV. (eds) *Child Abuse: New directions in prevention and treatment across the lifespan*, Thousand Oaks, CA, Sage.

Olds, D., Henderson, C., Chamberlain, R. and Tatelbaum, R. (1986) Preventing child abuse and neglect: a randomised trial of nurse home visitation. *Pediatrics*, 78: 65–78.

Olds, D., Henderson, C.R. and Kitzman, H. (1994) Does prenatal and infancy nurse home visitation have enduring effects on qualities of parental caregiving and child health and 25 to 50 months of life? *Pediatrics*, 93: 89–98.

Olds, D., Henderson, C.R. Kitzman, H and Cole, R. (1995) Effects of prenatal and infancy nurse home visitation on surveillance of child maltreatment. *Pediatrics*, 95: 365–372.

Olds, D.L. and Kitzman, H. (1990) Can home visiting improve the health of women and children at environmental risk? *Pediatrics*, 86: 108–116.

Olds, D.L. and Kitzman, H. (1993) Review of research on home visiting. *The Future of Children*, 3(4): 51–92.

Olds, D.L. Pettit, L.M., Robinson, J., Eckenrode, J., Kitzman, H., Cole, R.C. and Powers, J. (1997) Reducing risks for antisocial behavior with a program of prenatal and early childhood home visitation. *Journal of Community Psychology*, 26(1): 65–83.

Olds, D.L., Henderson, Jr., C.R., Chamberlain, R., Kitzman, H., Eckenrode, J., Cole, R.C. and Tatelmaum, R. (1999) Prenatal and Infancy Home Visitation by Nurses: Recent Findings. *The Future of Children*, 9(1): 44–65.

Onyskiw, J.E. and Harrison, M.J. (1999) Formative evaluation of a collaborative community-based child abuse prevention project. *Child Abuse and Neglect*, 23(11): 1069–1081.

Osborn, A.F. and Milbank, J.E., (1985) *The Association of Preschool Educational Experience with Subsequent Ability, Attainment and Behaviour*, Report to the Department of Education and Sciences, Bristol, Department of Child Health, University of Bristol.

Overholser, J.C. and Beck, S. (1986) Multimethod assessment of rapists, child molesters, and three control groups on behavioral and psychological measures. *Journal of Consulting and Clinical Psychology*, 54: 683–687.

Paley, J. (ed.) (1990) *Child Protection Adviser's Resource Pack: A Compendium for Child Protection Advisers in Health and Local Authorities*, London, NSPCC.

Patterson, G.R. (1976) The aggressive child: victim and architect of a coercive system. In Hamerlynck, L.A., Handy, L.C. and Marsh, E.H. (eds) *Behavior Modification and Families*, New York, Castalia.

Patterson, G.R. (1982) *A social learning approach to family intervention: 111 Coercive family process.* Eugene, Oregon, Castalia Publishing.

Patterson, G.R., Chamberlain, P. and Reid, J.B. (1982) A comparative evaluation of a parent training program. *Behavior Therapy*, 13: 638–650.

Patterson, G.R. and Reid, J.B. (1970) Reciprocity and Coercion: Two facets of social systems. In C. Neuniger and J.L. Michael (eds) *Behavior Modification in Clinical Psychology*, New York, Appleton-Century-Crofts. ACPC.

Pediatrics (1996) 98(2):4.

Peled, E. and Edleson, J.L. (1995) Process and outcome in small groups for children of battered women. In Peled, E., Jaffe, P.G. and Edelson, J.L. (eds) *Ending the cycle of violence: Community Responses to Children of Battered Women*, Thousand Oaks, CA, Sage.

Pelton, L. (1981) *The social context of child abuse and neglect*, New York, Human Services Press.

Peluso, E. and Putnam, N. (1996) Case study: Sexual abuse of boys by females. *Journal of the American Academy of Child and Adolescent Psychiatry*, 35: 51–54.

Peraino, J.M. (1990) Evaluation of a preschool antivictimization prevention program. *Journal of Interpersonal Violence*, 5: 520–528.

Perez, C.L. (1988) A comparison of group play therapy and individual therapy for sexually abused children. *Dissertation Abstracts International*, 48: 3079.

Perkins, D., Hammond, S., Coles, D. and Bishopp, D. (1998) *Review of Sex Offender Treatment Programmes*, Department of Psychology, Broadmoor Hospital.

Perry, B., and Pollard, R. (1998) Homeostasis, stress, trauma and adaptation. *Child and Adolescent Clinics of North America*, 7: 33–51.

Peters, D.K. and Range, L.M. (1995) Childhood sexual abuse and current suicidality in college women and men. *Child Abuse and Neglect*, 19: 335–341.

Petersik, J.T. (1982) Perception of eye-scans with the Müller-Lyer stumuli: Evidence for filter theory. *Perceptual and Motor Skills*, 54: 683–692.

Phoenix, A. (1990) *Young Mothers.* Cambridge: Polity.

Pianta, R., Egeland, B. and Erikson, M.F. (1989) The antecedents of maltreatment: results of the Mother–Child Interaction Project. In Cicchetti, D. and Carlson, V. (eds) *Child Maltreatment: Theory and research on the causes and consequences of child abuse and neglect,* New York, Cambridge University Press.

Pilkington, B. and Kremer, J. (1995a) A review of the epidemiological research on child sexual abuse: Clinical samples. *Child Abuse Review,* **4**(3): 191–207.

Pilkington, B. and Kremer, J. (1995b) A review of the epidemiological research on child sexual abuse: Community and college samples. *Child Abuse Review,* **4**(2): 84–98.

Pincus, A. and Minahan, A. (1973) *Social Work Practice: Model and Method* 16, IL, Peacock.

Pittmann, A., Wolfe, D.A. and Wekerle, C. (1998) Prevention during adolescence: the Youth Relationship Project. In Lutzker, J.R. (ed.) *Handbook of Child Abuse Research and Treatment,* New York, Plenum Press.

Poche, C., Roder, P. and Miltenberger, R. (1988) Teaching self protection to children using television techniques. *Journal of Applied Behavior Analysis,* **21**: 253–261.

Polan, H.J., Leon, A., Kaplan, M.D., Kessler, D.B., Stern, D.N. and Ward, M.J. (1991) Disturbances of affect expression in failure-to-thrive. *Journal of the American Academy of Child and Adolescent Psychiatry,* **30**(6): 897–903.

Polansky, N.A., Chalmers, M.A., Buttenweiser, E. and Williams, D.P. (1981) *Damaged parents: An anatomy of neglect,* Chicago Il, University of Chicago.

Polansky, N.A., Gaudin, F.M., Ammons, P.W. and Davis, K.B. (1985) The psychological ecology of the neglectful mother. *Child Abuse and Neglect,* **9**: 265–275.

Pollack, N.L. and Hashmall, J.M. (1990) The excuses of child molesters. *Behavioral Sciences and the Law,* **9**: 53–59.

Pollak, S.D., Cicchetti, D., Klorman, R. and Brumaghim, J.T. (1997) Cognitive Brain Event-Related Potentials and Emotion Processing in Maltreated Children. *Child Development,* **68**(5): 773–787.

Pollitt, E. and Eichler, A.W. (1976) Behavioral disturbances among failure-to-thrive children. *American Journal of Orthopsychiatry,* **45**: 525–537.

Pollitt, E., Eichler, A.W. and Chan, C.K. (1975) Psychosocial development and behavior of mothers of failure-to-thrive children. *American Journal of Orthopsychiatry,* **45**: 525–537.

Pollitt, E., Gilmore, M. and Valcarcel, M. (1978) Early mother-infant interaction and somatic growth. *Early Human Development,* **1**: 325–336.

Polster, R.A., Dangel, R.F. and Rasp, R. (1987) Research in behavioral parent training in social work: a review. *Behavior Modification,* **1**: 323–350.

Poppen, R. (1988) *Behavioral relaxation training and assessment.* New York, Pergamon.

Pransky, J (1991) *Prevention: the critical need.* Springfield, MO, Burrell Foundation.

Prentky, R.A. (1996) A rationale for the treatment of sex offenders: Pro Bono Publico. In McGuire, J. (ed.) *What works: Reducing reoffending. Guidelines from research and practice,* Chichester, John Wiley.

Prentky, R.A., Knight, R.A., Sims-Knight, J.E., Straus, H., Rokous, F. and Cerce, D. (1989) Developmental antecedents of sexual aggression. *Development and Psychopathology,* **1**: 153–169.

Prior, M. (1992) Childhood Temperament, *Journal of Child Psychology and Psychiatry,* **33**: 249–279.

Pugh, G. and McQuail, S. (1995) *Effective organisation of early childhood services.* London, National Children's Bureau.

Puri, B.K., Lambert, M.L. and Cordess, C.C. (1996) Characteristics of Young Offenders detained under Section 53(2) at a Young Offenders' Institution. *Medicine, Science and the Law,* **36**(1): 69–76.

Quinsey, V.L. and Earls, C.M. (1990) The modification of sexual preferences. In Marshall, W.L., Laws, D.R. and Barbaree, H.E. (eds) *Handbook of Sexual Assault: Issues, Theories and Treatment of the Offender,* New York, Plenum Press.

Quinton, D.L. (1996) Outcome measurement in work with children: A response to Huxley. *Child Abuse Review,* **5**: 83–89.

Quinton, D.L. and Rutter, M. (1984a) Parents with children in care: 1. Intergenerational continuities. *Journal of Child Psychology and Psychiatry,* **25**: 158–201.

Quinton, D.L. and Rutter, M. (1984b) Parents with children in care: 11. Intergenerational continuities. *Journal of Child Psychology and Psychiatry,* **25**: 231–250.

Rachman, S.J. and Wilson, G.T. (1980) *The effects of psychological therapy,* Oxford, Pergamon.

Radke-Yarrow, M. and Klimes-Dougan, B. (1997) Children of depressed mothers: A developmental and interactional perspective. In Luthar, S.S., Burack, J.A., Cicchetti, D. and Weisz, J.R. (eds) *Developmental Psychopathology: Perspectives on Adjustment, Risk and Disorder,* New York, Cambridge University Press.

Raynor, P. and Rudolph, M.C.J. (1996) What do we know about children who fail to thrive? *Child Care, Health and Development,* **22**: 241–150.

Reder, P. and Duncan, S. (1999) *Lost Innocents: A follow-up study of fatal child abuse,* London, Routledge.

Reder, P. and Lucey, C. (1998) *Assessment of parenting: psychiatric and psychological contributions,* London, Routledge.

Reder, P., Duncan, S. and Gray, M. (1992) *Beyond Blame: Child Abuse Tragedies Revisited,* London, Routledge.

Reed, R. and Reed, S. (1965) *Mental retardation: A family study.* New York, Saunders.

Reid, J.B., Kavanagh, K., Baldwin, D.V. (1987) Abusive parents' perceptions of child behavior problems: an example of parental bias. *Journal of Abnormal Child Psychology,* **15**: 457–466.

Reid, J.B., Taplin, P.S. and Lorber, R. (1981) A social interactional approach to the treatment of abusive families. In Stuart, R. (ed.) *Violent behavior: Social learning approaches to prediction, management and treatment,* New York, Brunner/Mazel.

Reid, W. (1994) The Empirical Practice Movement. *Social Services Review,* June, 165–184.

Resnick, G. (1985) Enhancing parental competencies for high risk mothers: an evaluation of prevention effects. *Child Abuse and Neglect,* **9**: 479–489.

Rice, M.E., Quinsey, V.I. and Harris, G.T. (1991) Sexual recidivism among child molesters released from a maximum security psychiatric institution. *Journal of Consulting and Clinical Psychology,* **59**: 381–386.

Richardson, G., Graham, F., Bhate, S.R. and Kelly, T.P. (1995) A British Sample of Sexually Abusive Adolescents: Abuser and Abuse Characteristics. *Criminal Behaviour and Mental Health,* **5**: 187–208.

Rickard, K.M., Forehand, R., Wells, K.C., Griest, D.L. and McMahon, R.J. (1980) Factors in the referral of children for behavioral treatment: A comparison of mothers of clinic-referred deviant, clinic-referred non-deviant and non-clinic-referred children. *Behavioral Research and Therapy,* **19**: 201–205.

Ricks, M. (1985) The social transmission of parental behavior: Attachment across generation. In Bretherton, L. and Waters, E. (eds) *Growing points of attachment theory and research. Monographs for the Society for Research in Child Development,* **50** (1–2, Serial No. 209): 211–227.

Rind, B. and Tromovitch, P. (1997) A meta-analytic review of findings from national samples on psychological correlates of child sexual abuse. *Journal of Sex Research,* **34**: 237–255.

Rind, B., Tromovitch, P. and Bauserman, R. (1998) A meta-analytic examination of assumed properties of child sexual abuse using college samples. *Psychological Bulletin,* **12**: 22–52.

Rispens, J., Aleman, A. and Goudena, P.P. (1997) Prevention of child sexual abuse victimization: A meta-analysis of school programs. *Child Abuse and Neglect,* **21**(10): 975–987.

Rivera, B. and Widom, C.S. (1990) Childhood victimization and violent offending. *Violence and Victims,* **5**: 19–35.

Roberts, H. (1997) Children, inequalities and health. *British Medical Journal,* **314**: 1122–1125.

Roberts, H. (1999) *What works in reducing child health inequalities?* Barkingside, Essex, Barnardo's.

Robins, C.J. and Hayes, A.M. (1993) An appraisal of cognitive therapy. *Journal of Consulting and Clinical Psychology,* **61**(2): 205–214.

Rogosch, F.A., Cicchetti, D. and Aber, J.L. (1995) The role of child maltreatment in early deviations in cognitive and affective processing abilities and later peer relationship problems. *Development and Psychopathology,* **7**: 591–609.

Rohrbeck, C.A. and Twentyman, C.T. (1986) Multimodal assessment of impulsiveness in abusing, neglecting and non maltreating mothers and their preschool children. *Journal of Consulting and Clinical Psychology,* **54**(2): 231–236.

Romans, S.E., Martin, J.L., Anderson, J.C., O'Shea, M.L. and Mullen, P.E. (1995) Factors that mediate between child sexual abuse and adult psychological outcome. *Psychological Medicine,* **25**: 127–142.

Roosa, M.W., Reinholtz, C. and Angelini, P.J. (1999) The Relation of Child Sexual Abuse and Depression in Young Women: Comparisons Across Four Ethnic Groups. *Journal of Abnormal Child Psychology,* **27**(1): 65–76.

Rose, S. and Meezan, W. (1997) Defining Child Neglect: Evolution, influences, and issues. In Berrick, J.D., Barth, R. and Gilbert, N. (eds) *Child Welfare Research Review: Volume Two,* New York, Cambridge University Press.

Rose, S.D. (1986) Group methods. In Kanfer, F.G. and Goldstein, A.P. (ed.) *Helping People Change* (3rd Edition) Oxford, Pergamon.

Rowe, J. and Lambert, L. (1973) *Children who wait,* London, Association of British Adoption Agencies.

Rubin, K.H. and Mills, R.S.L. (1990) Maternal beliefs about adaptive and maladaptive social behaviors in normal, aggressive, and withdrawn preschoolers. *Journal of Abnormal Child Psychology,* **18**: 419–435.

Russell, D. (1984) *The Secret Trauma: Incest in the lives of girls and women.* New York, Basic Books.

Rutter, M. (1972) Maternal deprivation reconsidered. *Journal of Psychosomatic Research,* **16**(4): 241–250.

Rutter, M. (1985) Relience in the face of adversity: Protective factors and resistance in psychiatric disorder. *British Journal of Psychiatry,* **147**: 598–611.

Rutter, M. (1989) Intergenerational continuities and discontinuities in serious parenting difficulties. In Cicchetti, D. and Carlson, V. (eds) *Child Maltreatment: Theory and research on the causes and consequences of child abuse and neglect.* New York, Cambridge University Press.

Rutter, M. (1990) Psychosocial resilience and protective mechanisms. In Rolf, J., Masten, A.S., Cicchetti, D., Neucherlein, K. and Weintraub, S. (eds) *Risk and protective factors in the development of psychopathology*, New York, Cambridge University Press.

Rutter, M. and Quinton, D.L. (1984) Parental psychiatric disorder: Effects on children. *Psychological Medicine*, **14**: 853–880.

Ryan, G., Miyoshi, T.J., Metzner, J.L., Krugman, R.D., Gryer, G.E. (1996) Trends in a national sample of sexually abusive youths. *Journal of American Child and Adolescent Psychiatry*, **35**: 17–25.

Sack, W.J., Mason, R. and Collins, R. (1987) A long-term follow-up study of a children's psychiatric day treatment center. *Child Psychiatry and Human Development*, **18**: 58–68.

Sameroff, A. (1998) Management of clinical problems and emotional care: Environmental risk factors in infancy. *Pediatrics*, **102**(5) (suppl): 1287–1292.

Sameroff, A.J. and Chandler, M.J. (1975) Reproductive risk and the continuum of caretaking casualty. In F.D. Horowitz (ed.) *Review of child development research*, **4**: 187–244, Chicago, University of Chicago Press.

Sameroff, A.J. and Feil, L.A. (1985) Parental concepts of development. In Sigel, I. (ed.) *Parental belief systems: The psychological consequences for children*. Hillsdale, NJ, Erlbaum.

Sanders, R., Colton, M. and Roberts, S. (1999) Child abuse fatalities and cases of extreme concern: lessons from reviews. *Child Abuse and Neglect*, **23**(3): 257–268.

Sarber, R.E., Halasz, M.M., Messmer, M.C., Bickett, A.D. and Lutzker, J.R. (1983) Teaching planning and grocery shopping skills to a mentally retarded mother. *Mental Retardation*, **21**: 101–106.

Scally, B.G. (1957) Marriage and mental handicap: Some observations in Northern Ireland. In de la Cruz, F.F. and La Veck, G.D. (eds) *Human sexuality and the mentally retarded*, New York, Brunner/Mazel.

Schaeffer, S. and Lewis, M. (1988–1989) Social behavior of maltreated children: A naturalistic study of day care. *Annual report No. 12: Research and Clinical Center for Child Development*, Sapporo, Japan, Hokkaido University, Faculty of Education.

Schechter, M.D. and Roberge, L. (1976) Sexual exploitation. In R.E. Helfer and C.H. Kempe (eds) *Child Abuse and Neglect: The Family and the Community*, Cambridge, Mass.

Schneider-Rosen, K. and Cicchetti, D. (1984) The relationship between affect and cognition in maltreated children: Quality of attachment and the development of visual self-recognition. *Developmental Psychology*, **27**: 481–488.

Schneider-Rosen, K. and Cicchetti, D. (1991) Early self-knowledge and emotional development: Visual self-recognition and affective reactions to mirror self-image in maltreated and nonmaltreated toddlers. *Developmental Psychology*, **27**: 481–488.

Schweinhart, L.J., Barnes, H.V. and Weikart, D.P. (1993) *The High/Scope Perry Preschool Study through age 27*. Ypsilanti, MI, The High/Scope Press.

Scott, R.L. and Stone, D. (1986) MMPI profile constellation in incest families. *Journal of Consulting and Clinical Psychology*, **54**: 364–368.

Seagull, E.A.W. (1987) Social support and child maltreatment: A review of the evidence. *Child Abuse and Neglect*, **11**: 41–52.

Sedlak, A.J. and Broadhurst, D.D. (1996) *Third annual incidence study of child abuse and neglect. Final Report*. Washington DC, US Department of Health and Human Services.

Selvini, M. (1991) Comment. *Journal of Family Therapy*, **13**: 265–266.

Serketich, W.J. and Dumas, J.E. (1996) The effectiveness of behavioural parent training to modify anti-social behaviour in children: a meta-analysis. *Behavior Therapy* **27**: 171–186.

Sheldon, B. (1978) Theory and Practice in Social Work: A ReExamination of a Tenuous Relationship. *British Journal of Social Work*, **8**(1): 1–18.

Sheldon, B. (1988) Single case evaluation methods. In Lishman, J. (ed.) 2nd edition. *Evaluation*, London, Jessica Kingsley.

Sheldon, B. (1987) The Psychology of Incompetence. *After Beckford: essays on themes related to child abuse.* Egham, Royal Holloway and Bedford New College.

Siegal, E., Bauman, K.E., Schaefer, E.S., Saunders, M.M. and Ingram, D.D. (1980) Hospital and home support during infancy: impact on maternal attachment, child abuse and neglect, and health care utilisation. *Pediatrics*, **66**: 183–190.

Silverman, A., Reinherz, H.Z. and Giaconia, R.M. (1996) The long-term sequelae of child and adolescent abuse: a longitudinal study. *Child Abuse and Neglect*, **20**(8): 709–723.

Silverman, W.A. (1980) *Retrolental fibroplasia: A modern parable.* New York, Grune and Stratton.

Simons, R.L., Lorenz, F.O., Conger, R.D. and Wu, C.-I. (1992) Support from spouse as mediator and moderator of the disruptive influence of economic stress on parenting. *Child Development*, **63**: 1282–1301.

Simpson, L. (1994) *Evaluation of treatment methods in child sexual abuse: a literature review.* SSRADU, University of Bath and Dorset Area Child Protection Review.

Skuse, D. (1985) Non-organic failure to thrive: a reappraisal. *Archives of Disease in Childhood*, **60**(17): 173–178.

Skuse, D., Bentovim, A., Hodges, J., Stevenson, J., Andreou, C., Lanyado, M., New, M., Williams, B. and McMillan, D. (1998) Risk factors for development of sexually abusive behaviour in sexually victimised adolescent boys: cross sectional study. *British Medical Journal*, **317**: 175–179.

Smith, A.N. and Lopez, M. (1994) *A comprehensive child development program: A national family support program.* Interim report to Congress, Washington DC, US. Department of Health and Human Services.

Smith, C. (1996) *Developing Parenting Programmes.* London, National Children's Bureau.

Smith, J.E. and Rachman, S.J. (1984) Non-accidental injury to children–11: A controlled evaluation of a behavioural management programme. *Behaviour Research and Therapy*, **22**(4): 349–366.

Snyder, M. and White, P. (1981) Testing hypotheses about other people: strategies of verification and falsification. *Personality and Social Psychology Bulletin* 7, 1, 39–43.

Spaccarelli, S. (1994) Stress, appraisal and coping in child sexual abuse. *Psychological Bulletin,* **116**: 340–362.

Spaccarelli, S. (1995) Measuring abuse stress and negative cognitive appraisals in child sexual abuse: Validity data on two new scales. *Journal of Abnormal Psychology,* **23**: 703–727.

Spaccarelli, S. and Kim, S. (1995) Resilience criteria and factors associated with resilience in sexually abused girls. *Child Abuse and Neglect,* **19**: 1171–1182.

Spoth, R. and Redmond, C. (1995) Parent motivation to enrol in parenting skills programs: A model of family context and health belief predictors. *Journal of Family Psychology,* **9**: 294–310.

Sroufe, L.A. and Fleeson, J. (1986) Attachment and construction of relationships. In Hartup, W. W. and Rubin, Z. (eds) *Relationships and development*, New York, Cambridge University Press.

Sroufe, L.A. (1979) Socioemotional development. In Osofsky, J. (ed.) *Handbook of infant development.* (1st edition) New York, John Wiley.

Sroufe, L.A. and Rutter, M. (1984) The domain of developmental psychopathology. *Child Development*, **55**: 17–29.

Stauffer, L.B. and Deblinger, E. (1996) Cognitive behavioral groups for nonoffending mothers and their young sexually abused children: A preliminary treatment outcome study. *Child Maltreatment*, **1**: 65–76.

Stein, T.J. and Gambrill, E.D. (1976) Behavioural Techniques in Foster Care. *Social Work*, **21**(1): 34–39.

Steinmitz, S. and Strauss, M.A. (1974) *Violence in the Family*, New York, Dodd Mead.

Stermac, L.E., Segal, Z.V. and Gillis, R. (1990) Social and cultural factors in sexual assault. In Marshall, W.L., Laws, D.R. and Barbaree, H.E. (eds) *Handbook of sexual assault: Issues, theories and treatment of the offender*, New York, Plenum.

Stevenson, J., Bailey, V. and Simpson, J. (1988) Feasible intervention in families with parenting difficulties: a primary preventive perspective on child abuse. In Browne, K.D., Davies, C. and Stratton, P. (eds) *Early prediction and prevention of child abuse*, Chichester, John Wiley.

Strauss, M.A. (1983) Ordinary violence, child abuse, and wife beating: What do they have in common? In Finkelhor, D., Gelles, R.J., Hotaling, G.T. and Strauss, M.A. (eds) *The dark side of families: Current family violence research*, Beverley Hills, CA, Sage.

Striefel, S., Robinson, M.A. and Truhn, P. (1998) Dealing with child abuse and neglect within a comprehensive family-support program. In Lutzker, J.R. (ed.) *Handbook of Child Abuse Research and Treatment*, New York, Plenum Press.

Sudermann, M., Jaffe, P.G. and Hastings, E. (1995) Violence prevention programs in secondary (high) schools. In Peled, E., Jaffe, P.G. and Edleson, J.L. (eds) *Ending the cycle of violence: Community responses to children of battered women*, Thousand Oaks, CA, Sage.

Suomi, S.J., Collins, M.L., Harlow, H.F. and Ruppenthal, G.C. (1976) Effects of maternal and peer separations on young monkeys. *Journal of Child Psychology and Psychiatry and Allied Disciplines*, **17**(2): 101–112.

Sutcliffe, P., Lovell, J. and Walters, M. (1985) New Directions for family therapy: rubbish removal as a task of choice. *Journal of Family Therapy*, **7**: 175–182.

Swenson, C.C. and Hanson, R.F. (1997) Sexual abuse of children: assessment, research, and treatment. In Lutzker, J. (ed.) *Handbook of Child Abuse Research and Treatment: Issues in clinical child psychology*, New York, Plenum Press.

Sylva, K. (1994) School Influences on Children's Development. *Journal of Child Psychology and Psychiatry and Allied Professions*, **35**(1): 135–170.

Teasdale, J.D. (1993) Emotion and two kinds of meaning: Cognitive therapy and applied cognitive science. *Behaviour Research and Therapy*, **31**(4): 339–354.

Tertinger, D.A., Greene, B.F. and Lutzker, J.R. (1984) Home safety: Development and validation of one component of an ecobehavioral treatment program for abused and neglected children. *Journal of Applied Behavior Analysis*, **17**: 159–174.

The Bridge Child Care Development Service (1999) *Neglect and Developmental Delay: Part 8 Case Overview*. Caerphilly, November.

Thoburn, J., Lewis, A. and Shemmings, D. (1995) *Paternalism or Partnership? Family Involvement in the Child Protection Process*. London, HMSO.

Thomas, A., Chess, S. and Birch, H.G. (1968) *Temperament and Behaviour Disorder in Children*. New York, New York University Press.

Thomas, E.J. and Santa, C.A. (1992) Unilateral family therapy for alcohol abuse: A working conception. *American Journal of Family Therapy*, **10**: 49–60.

Thomas, J.N. (1981) personal communication cited in Groth, A.N. and Loredo, C.M. Juvenile sex offenders: guidelines for assessment. *International Journal of Offender Therapy and Comparative Criminology*, **25**: 31–39.

Thompson, A.E. and Kaplan, C.A. (1993) Childhood Emotional Abuse. *British Journal of Psychiatry*, **168**: 143–148.

Thompson, D. and Brown, J. (1997) Men with intellectual disabilities who abuse: a review of the literature. *Journal of Applied Research in Intellectual Disabilities*, **10**: 140–158.

Thompson, R.A. (1994) Social support and the prevention of child maltreatment. In Melton, G.B. and Barry, F.D. (eds) *Protecting children from abuse and neglect*, New York, Guilford.

Thompson, R.A. (1995) *Preventing child maltreatment through social support: A critical analysis*, Thousand Oaks, CA, Sage.

Thyer, B.A. (1989) *Behavioral Family Therapy*. Springfield, Ill. Charles C. Thomas.

Todres, R. and Bunston, T. (1993) Parent-education programme evaluation: a review of the literature. *Canadian Journal of Community Mental Health* **12**: 225–257.

Tong, L., Oates, K. and McDowell, M. (1987) Personality development following sexual abuse. *Child Abuse and Neglect*, **11**: 371–383.

Towl, G.J. and Crighton, D.A. (1996) *The Handbook of Psychology for Forensic Practitioners*, London, Routledge.

Trickett, P.K. (1993) Maladaptive development of school-aged, physically abused children: relations with the child rearing context. *Journal of Family Psychology*, **7**: 134–147.

Trickett, P.K. (1997) Sexual and physical abuse and the development of social competence. In Luthar, S.S., Burack, J.A., Cicchetti, D. and Weisz, J.R. (eds) *Developmental Psychopathology: Perspectives on adjustment, risk, and disorder*, New York, Cambridge University Press.

Trickett, P.K. and McBride-Chang, C. (1995) The developmental impact of different forms of child abuse and neglect. *Developmental Review*, **15**: 311–337.

Trickett, P.K., McBride-Chang, C. and Putnam, F.W. (1994) The classroom performance and behavior of sexually abused females. *Development and Psychopathology*, **6**, 183–194.

Tulkin, S.R. (1972) An analysis of the concept of cultural deprivation. *Developmental Psychology*, **6**: 326–339.

Tyen, J., Levanthal, J.M., Yazdgerdi, S.R. and Perrin, J.M. (1997) Concerns about child maltreatment in hospitalised children. *Child Abuse and Neglect*, **21**: 187–198.

Tymchuk, A. and Feldman, M. (1991) Parents with mental retardation and their children: Review of research relevant to professional practice. *Canadian Psychology*, **32**: 486–496.

Verleur, D., Hughes, R.E. and Dobkin de Rios, M. (1986) Enhancement of self-esteem among female adolescent incest victims: A controlled comparison. *Adolescence*, **XII**(84): 843–854.

Vizard, E., Monck, E. and Misch, P. (1995) Child and Adolescent Sex Abuse Perpetrators: A review of the research literature. *Journal Of Child Psychology And Psychiatry and Allied Disciplines*, **36**(5): 731–756.

Volgeltanz, N.D., Wilsnack, S.C., Harris, T.R., Wilsnack, R.W., Wonderlich, S.A. and Kristjanson, A.F. (1999) Prevalence and Risk Factors for Childhood Sexual Abuse in Women: National Survey Findings. *Child Abuse and Neglect*, **23**(6): 579–592.

Vondra, J.I., Barnett, D. and Cicchetti, D. (1989) Perceived and actual competence among maltreated and comparison schoolchildren. *Development and Pathology*, **1**: 237–255.

Vondra, J.I., Barnett, D. and Cicchetti, D. (1990) Self-concept, motivation and competence among preschoolers from maltreating and comparison families. *Child Abuse and Neglect*, **14**: 525–540.

Wadsworth, M.E.J. (1985) Parenting skills and their transmission through generations. *Adoption and Fostering*, **9**: 28–32.

Wadsworth, M.E.J. (1991) *The Imprint of Time: Childhood, History and Adult Life*, Oxford University Press.

Wadsworth, M.E.J. and Maclean, M. (1986) Parents' Divorce and Children's Life Chances. *Children and Youth Services Review*, **8**: 145–159.

Wahler, R.G. (1980) The insular mother: her problems in parent-child treatment. *Journal of Applied Behavior Analysis*, **13**: 207–219.

Wahler, R.G. and Afton, A.D. (1980) Attentional processes in insular and noninsular mothers: some differences in their summary reports about child problem behavior. *Child Behavior Therapy*, **2**: 25–41.

Wahler, R.G. and Dumas, J.E. (1989) Attentional problems in dysfunctional mother–child interactions: An interbehavioral model. *Psychological Bulletin*, **105**: 116–130.

Walker, L.E.A. (1989) Psychology and violence against women. *American Psychologist*, **2044**: 695–702.

Ward, T. and Hudson, S.M. (1997) Future directions in the assessment and treatment of sexual offenders. *Behaviour Change*, **14**(4): 215–225.

Ward, T., Hudson, S.M., Johnson, L. and Marshall, W.L. (1997) Cognitive distortions in sex offenders: an integrative review. *Clinical Psychology Review*, **17**: 479–507.

Weaver, T.I. and Clum, G.A. (1995) Psychological distress associated with interpersonal violence: A meta-analysis. *Clinical Psychology Review*, **15**(2): 115–140.

Webster-Stratton, C. (1991) Annotation: Strategies for Helping Families with Conduct Disordered Children. *Journal of Child Psychology and Psychiatry and Allied Professions*, **32**(7): 1047–1062.

Webster-Stratton, C. (1998) Parent-training with low-income families: promoting parental engagement through a collaborative approach. In Lutzker, J.R. (ed.) *Handbook of Child Abuse Research and Treatment*, New York, Plenum Press.

Webster-Stratton, C. and Herbert, M. (1993) What really happens in parent-training? *Behavior Modification*, **17**: 407–456.

Webster-Stratton, C. and Herbert, M. (1994) *Troubled Families–Problem Children. Working with parents: A collaborative process.* Chichester, John Wiley.

Weinber, K. and Tronick, E. (1998) Emotional care of the at-risk infant: Emotional characteristics of infants associated with maternal depression and anxiety, *Pediatrics*, **102**(5) (supp): 1298–1304.

Weiss, B., Dodge, K.A., Bates, J.E. and Pettit, G.S. (1992) Some Consequences of Early Harsh Discipline: Child Aggression and a Maladaptive Social Information Processing Style. *Child Development*, **63**: 1321–1335.

Weissberg, R., Caplan, M. and Harwood, R. (1991) Promoting competent young people in competence-enhancing environments: a systems-based perspective on primary prevention. *Journal of Consulting and Clinical Psychology*, **59**(6): 830–841.

Weisz, J.R. (1997) Effects of interventions for child and adolescent psychological dysfunction: Relevance of context, developmental factors, and individual difference. In Luthar, S.S., Burack, J.A., Cicchetti, D. and Weisz, J.R. (eds) *Developmental Psychopathology: Perspectives on adjustment, risk, and disorder*, New York, Cambridge University Press.

Werner, E.E. (1989) High Risk Children in Young Adulthood: A longitudinal study from birth to 32 years. *American Journal of Orthopsychiatry*, **59**: 72–81.

Wesch, D. and Lutzker, J.R. (1991) A comprehensive 5-year evaluation of Project 12-Ways: an ecobehavioral program for treating and preventing child abuse and neglect. *Journal of Family Violence*, **6**: 17–35.

White, S., Halpin, M.M., Strom, G.A. and Santilli, G. (1988) Behavioral comparisons of young sexually abused, neglected, and non-referred children. *Journal of Clinical Child Psychology*, **17**: 53–61.

Whiteman, M., Fanshel, D. and Grundy, J.F. (1987) Cognitive-behavioral interventions aimed at anger of parents at risk of child abuse. *Social Work*, Nov–Dec, 469–474.

Whittaker, J. K. (1983) Social support networks in child welfare, in Whittaker, J.K. and Garbarino, J. (eds) *Social support networks*, New York, Aldine.

Widom, C.S. (1989) The cycle of violence. *Science*, **244**: 160–166.

Widom, C.S. (1988) Sampling biases and implications for child abuser research. *American Journal of Orthopsychiatry*, **58**: 260–270.

Widom, C.S. (1991) Avoidance of criminality in abused and neglected children. *Psychiatry*, **54**: May, 162–174.

Widom, C.S. (1991b) Childhood victimization: Risk factor for delinquency. In M.E. Colton and S. Gore (eds) *Adolescent Stress: Causes and Consequences*. New York, Aldine de Gruyter.

Wilding, J. and Thoburn, J. (1997) Family support plans for neglected and emotionally maltreated children. *Child Abuse Review*, 6, 5, 343–356.

Williams, L.M. and Finkelhor, D. (1990) The characteristics of incestuous fathers: A review of recent studies. In Marshall, W.L., Laws, D.R. and Barbaree, H.E. (eds) *Handbook of sexual assault: Issues, theories and treatment of the offender*, New York, Plenum.

Wilson, J.P. and Keane, T.M. (1997) (eds) *Assessing Psychological Trauma and PTSD*, New York, Guilford Press.

Wodarski, J.S. and Thyer, B.A. (1989) Behavioral Perspectives on the Family: An Overview. In Thyer, B.A. (ed.) *Behavioral Family Therapy*. Springfield Ill., Charles C. Thomas.

Wodarski, J.S., Howing, P.T., Kurthz, P.D. and Gaudin, J.M. (1990) Maltreatment and the school-age child: Major academic, socio-emotional and adaptive outcomes. *Social Work*, **35**: 506–513.

Wolf, S.C. (1985) A multi-factorial model of deviant sexuality. *Victimitology: An International Journal*, **10**: 359–374.

Wolfe, D.A. and Sandler, J. (1981) Training abusive parents in effective child management. *Behavior Modification*, **5**: 320–335.

Wolfe, D., Kaufman, K., Aragona, J. and Sandler, J. (1981) *The child management program for abusive parents: Procedures for developing a child abuse intervention program*, Winter Park, FL, Anna Publishing.

Wolfe, D.A. (1985) Child-abusive parents: An empirical review and analysis. *Psychological Bulletin*, **97**: 462–482.

Wolfe, D.A., Edwards, B., Manion, I. and Koverola, C. (1988) Early Intervention for Parents at Risk of Child Abuse and Neglect: A Preliminary Investigation. *Journal of Consulting and Clinical Psychology*, **56**(1): 40–47.

Wolfe, D.A. and McGee, R. (1994) Dimensions of child maltreatment and their relationship to adolescent adjustment. *Developmental Psychopathology*, **6**: 165–181.

Wolfe, D.A. and Wekerle, C. (1993) Treatment strategies for child physical abuse and neglect: A critical progress report. *Clinical Psychology Review*, **13**: 473–500.

Wolfe, D.A. Wekerle, C. and Scott, K. (1997) *Alternatives to violence: Empowering youth to develop healthy relationships*, Thousand Oaks, CA, Sage.

Wolfe, D.A., Edwards, B., Manion, I. and Koverola, C. (1988) Early intervention for parents at risk for child abuse and neglect: A preliminary report. *Journal of Consulting and Clinical Psychology*, **56**: 40–47.

Wolfe, D.A., McPherson, T., Blount, R. and Wolfe, V.V. (1986) Evaluation of a brief intervention: educating school children in awareness of physical and sexual abuse. *Child Abuse and Neglect*, **10**: 83–91.

Wolfe, D.A., Sandler, J. and Kaufman, K. (1981) A competency based parent training program for abusive parents. *Journal of Consulting and Clinical Psychology*, **49**, 633–640.

Wolfe, D.A., St. Lawrence, J.S., Graves, K., Brehony, K., Bradlyn, A.S. and Kelly, J.A. (1982) Intensive behavioral parent training for a child abusive mother. *Behavior Therapy*, **13**: 438–451.

Wolfe, D.A., Wekerle, C., Reitzel-Jaffe, D., Grasley, C., Pittman, A. and MacEachran, A. (1997) Interrupting the cycle of violence: Empowering Youth to Promote Healthy Relationships. In Wolfe, D.A., McMahon, R.J. and Peters, R.DeV. (eds) *Child Abuse: New directions in prevention and treatment across the lifespan*, Thousand Oaks, CA, Sage.

Wolfe, V.V. and Gentile, C. (1992) Psychological assessment of sexually abused children. In O'Donohue, W.T. and Geer, J.H. (eds) *The Sexual Abuse of Children. Volume 1: Theory and Research*, Hillsdale, NJ, Lawrence Erlbaum.

Wolfe, V.V., Gentile, C. and Wolfe, D.A. (1989) The impact of sexual abuse on children: A PTSD formulation. *Behavior Therapy*, **20**: 215–228.

Wolfkind, G.D. and Gelles, R.J. (1993) A profile of violence toward children: A national study. *Child Abuse and Neglect*, **17**: 197–212.

Wolock, I. and Horowitz, B. (1984) Child maltreatment as a social problem: the neglect of neglect. *American Journal of Orthopsychiatry*, **54**(4): 530–543.

Wolock, I. and Horowitz, G. (1979) Child maltreatment and material deprivation among AFDC-recipient families. *Social Services Review* **53**: 179–194.

Wootton, B. (1959) *Social Science and Social Pathology*, London, Allen Unwin.

Wurtele, S.K., Kast, L.C., Miller-Perin, C.L. and Kondrick, P.A. (1989) Comparison of programs for teaching personal safety to preschoolers. *Journal of Consulting and Clinical Psychology*, **57**: 505–511.

Young, L. (1964) *Wednesday's children: A study of child neglect and abuse*, New York, McGraw Hill.

Youngblade, L.M. and Belsky, J. (1992) Social and emotional consequences of child maltreatment. In Ammerman, R.T. and Hersen, M. (eds) *Children at risk: An evaluation of factors contributing to child abuse and neglect*, New York, Plenum.

Zeahnah, C. and Larrieu, J. (1998) Intensive intervention for maltreated infants and toddlers in foster care. *Child and Adolescent Psychiatric Clinics of North America*, **7**: 357–371.

Zeahnah, C.H. and Zeanah, P.A. (1989) Intergenerational transmission of maltreatment: Insights from attachment theory and research. *Psychiatry*, **52**(2): 177–196.

Zigler, H. (1980) Controlling child abuse: Do we have the knowledge and / or the will? In Gerbner, G., Ross, C.J. and Zigler, E. (eds) *Child Abuse: An agenda for action*, New York, Oxford University Press.

Zimmerman, M.A. and Arunkumar, R. (1994) Resilience research: Implications for schools and policy. *Social Policy Report: Society for Research in Child Development*, **8**: 1–17.

Zoritch, B., Roberts, I. and Oakley, A. (1997) The health and welfare effects of day care for pre-school children: a systematic review of randomised controlled trials. *The Cochrane Library, Issue 4*.

Zubrich, S. (1997) *Western Australian Child Health Survey: Education, Health and Competence*, Institute for Child Health Research.

Zuravin, S.J. (1989) The ecology of child abuse and neglect: Review of the literature and presentation of data. *Violence and Victims*, **4**: 102–120.
Zuravin, S.J., and DiBlasio, F.A. (1996) The correlates of child physical abuse and neglect by adolescent mothers. *Journal of Family Violence*, **2**: 149–166.

INDEX